The Future of Energy Consumption, Security and Natural Gas

"This book about natural gas and LNG especially in Baltic Sea region, edited by Professor Kari Liuhto, should be the basic material for politicians, civil servants, businesspeople and academia to better understand the sector and the transition. Its logic is sound, statistics collected are impressive."

—Seppo Remes, *Professor in Practice, Lappeenranta University of Technology, former member of the Board of Russian plastics and petrochemical giant Sibur Holding*

"This study is a topical and very useful presentation that opens up new perspectives for security research as well. The book deals extensively with the ongoing development and the future of natural gas—especially LNG—in the Baltic Sea region. Because energy is the foundation of our modern lives, it's role and development also affect regional and international security. The study provides an excellent demonstration of how economic interdependence is forcing the countries of the Baltic Sea region to tighten their partnerships. The most important message of the book is to show that energy issues are both political and economic from the point of view of comprehensive security."

—Military Professor, *LTC Marko Palokangas, Finland's National Defence University*

Kari Liuhto
Editor

The Future of Energy Consumption, Security and Natural Gas

LNG in the Baltic Sea region

palgrave
macmillan

Editor
Kari Liuhto
University of Turku
Turku, Finland

ISBN 978-3-030-80366-7 ISBN 978-3-030-80367-4 (eBook)
https://doi.org/10.1007/978-3-030-80367-4

Cover credit: Marina Lohrbach_shutterstock.com

This Palgrave Macmillan imprint is published by the registered company Springer Nature Switzerland AG
The registered company address is: Gewerbestrasse 11, 6330 Cham, Switzerland

Preface

Although liquefied natural gas (LNG) was already manufactured in the nineteenth century and the regular LNG exports started already 60 years ago, in international gas trade the LNG boom only started in the beginning of this millennium. As a consequence of this boom, the volume of international LNG trade has tripled in the past two decades. In fact, the LNG supply has grown faster than its consumption, which has led to the LNG oversupply and a fall in prices. Despite the current oversupply, international LNG trade is forecasted to double its current level by 2040.

The roots of this book are in the year 2015, when the Centrum Balticum Foundation (www.centrumbalticum.org/en) operating in Turku, Finland compiled a research brief 'Natural Gas Revolution and the Baltic Sea Region'. This book returns to that revolution to analyse how the revolution has progressed in the Baltic Sea region. The main purpose of this book is to describe the development of natural gas—particularly LNG—in the Baltic Sea region and to assess the security of energy supply linked with LNG.

This book is a collection of articles. This book begins with Mariusz Ruszel's article examining the global LNG development. This Polish professor discusses in his article the way the geoeconomic factors impact the LNG exports, the way the competition between LNG exporters is turning out and the way the corona pandemic will change the global LNG market. Ruszel observes that many long-term gas contracts will expire within the next ten years. What these contracts will be replaced with has an impact on the entire European gas market. After the global perspective, the book deals with the European Union. Kari Liuhto analyses the development of natural gas—particularly LNG—in the energy consumption of the European Union in this millennium. Following a detailed review, this Finnish professor addresses the energy supply risk caused by the fact that few LNG tankers are owned by EU countries. After these two introductory chapters, the analysis turns to the Baltic Sea region, the geographic focus of the book.

Leonid Grigoryev and Dzhanneta Medzhidova approach a role of LNG in the Baltic Sea countries through climate change and the EU's Green Deal. This Russian duo seeks to find out what kind of role will liquefied natural gas have in the transition from fossil fuels to renewable energy in the Baltic Sea region. The third Russian expert of the book Andrey Shadurskiy describes in detail the current state of Russian LNG export terminals and outlines the future development of the Russian LNG exports. Shadurskiy writes that Russia aims at being at least the world's second largest LNG exporter within the next 15 years.

Mykhailo Gonchar and Igor Stukalenko examine Russian natural gas exports through pipelines. These Ukrainian experts analyse the position of the Nord Stream gas pipes, Belarus and Ukraine in the Russian gas exports to the European Union. They reveal startling historic evidence of the way the former Soviet Union strove to use natural gas and gas pipelines for its geopolitical purposes and the way the natural gas pipelines have returned to Russian foreign policy during President Vladimir Putin's terms in office. Gonchar and Stukalenko also introduce a novel idea that the EU could utilise Ukraine's large underground gas storages when aiming at enhancing the EU's security of supply of natural gas.

In his article, Jakub M. Godzimirski deals with the hydrocarbon reserves of Europe's second largest energy exporter Norway, as well as the development of their production and exports to the European Union and Great Britain. Godzimirski's article reveals the decrease in Norway's gas production in the 2030's and Norway's significant role as gas supplier to Poland through Baltic Pipe. The article also points out that Norwegian natural gas may have an essential role in the production of green hydrogen. Norway's relatively voluminous gas reserves, well-developed energy infrastructure and access to renewable hydropower can make Norway a dream partner for the EU in a new era of green hydrogen.

In his article, Professor Dariusz Zarzecki examines the progress of the LNG revolution in Poland, i.e. how Poland built the Baltic Sea region's largest LNG import terminal in Świnoujście in north-western Poland. Poland intends to expand this LNG terminal and is planning to build a second LNG receiving port in Gdańsk in north-eastern Poland. Once Świnoujście has been expanded, the Gdańsk LNG import terminal and Baltic Pipe have been constructed, the import capacity of these units exceed Poland's annual natural gas consumption. From Poland, we move to the Baltic States. Our first point of interest is the LNG import terminal opened in Lithuania in 2014. Thanks to this LNG receiving unit, the Baltic States are no longer solely dependent on Russian natural gas. The article by Tadas Jakštas studies the energy security of the Baltic States and the significance of Lithuania's LNG import terminal to security of energy supply in the Baltic States. Both the articles of Zarzecki and Jakštas indisputably demonstrate that the LNG receiving facilities in these countries have decreased the dependence on Russian natural gas and lowered the price of gas deliveries from Russia by breaking Gazprom's unnatural natural gas monopoly.

Reinis Āboltiņš analyses the energy production and energy consumption in the Baltic States, as well as Latvia's plans to build LNG import infrastructure on its soil. In addition to describing Latvia's plans for an LNG receiving port, Āboltiņš presents an extremely significant factor in the security of energy supply of all the Baltic States, i.e. the underground gas storage in Inčukalns, Latvia, which is the largest in the Baltic States. This gas storage allows all the three Baltic States and Finland to meet their natural gas needs during the whole winter season.

After the Baltic States, we turn to Finland. Laura Klemetti and Hanna Mäkinen study the development of natural gas—particularly LNG—in Finland and the role of the Balticconnector gas pipeline between Estonia and Finland in Finland's energy supply. These Finnish researchers point out that Balticconnector alone does not bring true gas diversification for Finland, and therefore the security and diversification of gas supply in Finland and the Baltic States necessitates the completion of the gas interconnection between Poland and Lithuania (GIPL).

At the end of the book, Anna Mikulska assesses the significance of the diversification of gas imports in the Baltic Sea region countries and the integration of gas transport infrastructures to the security of energy supply in the region. Using a calculation model, this Polish-born energy expert, who currently lives in the USA, shows how much the Baltic Sea region countries still now are over-dependent on Russian natural gas.

In the epilogue, Kari Liuhto, the editor of the book, gathers the main observations of the chapters and attempts to outline the future development of natural gas in the European Union and the Baltic Sea region.

Turku, Finland Kari Liuhto

Contents

Notes on Contributors

Reinis Āboltiņš is energy and climate policy researcher at the Riga Technical University. Previously, he was involved in developing smart energy services with Lattelecom and energy trading company as energy market expert. He has been a consultant on energy, climate and environment at the Latvian Parliament and energy policy researcher at the Centre for Public Policy PROVIDUS. He has been a member of the State President's Energy Security Commission and has also served as an invited expert at the Energy and Transport Working Groups of the Foreign Investors' Council in Latvia. His areas of specialisation include national, regional and EU energy and climate policy, energy security, energy market liberalisation, renewable energy resources and energy efficiency. He is currently working on his Ph.D. in environmental engineering at the Riga Technical University. He holds European Master's degree in Human Rights and Democratisation from the University of Padova in Italy and Raul Wallenberg Institute of Human Rights at the Lund University in Sweden.

Jakub M. Godzimirski holds a Ph.D. in Social Anthropology. Godzimirski is a Research Professor at the Norwegian Institute of International Affairs NUPI. Since 1995, he has been a senior research fellow and later research professor at the Department of Russian and Eurasian Studies. In 2009–2010, he headed the NUPI Energy Programme, and in 2012–2013, he headed the Research Group on European Affairs. His research interests include Russian and European foreign and security policy, with a focus on the role of energy and Russia's relations with the West. He has authored, co-authored, edited and co-edited several volumes on these issues and published many peer-reviewed articles and book chapters with leading academic publishers, such as Palgrave Macmillan, Routledge and Ashgate. His most recent major publications include Russian Energy in a Changing World. What Is the Outlook for the Hydrocarbons Superpower? (Ashgate, 2013), EU Leadership in Energy and Environmental Governance: Global and Local Challenges and Responses (Palgrave Macmillan, 2016), The Political Economy of Russian Aluminium. Between the Dual State and Global Markets (Palgrave Macmillan, 2018) as well as New Political Economy of Energy in Europe. Power to Project, Power to Adapt (Palgrave Macmillan, 2019).

Mykhailo Gonchar is an expert with 35 years of experience in fields of national and international security, energy, and energy security. Gonchar has a unique employment history in governmental agencies, energy companies and think tanks. He founded the Centre for Global Studies 'Strategy XXI' and has been holding the position of President of the Centre since 2008. He held the top management positions in private and state-owned energy companies, including Naftogaz of Ukraine, from 2000 to 2006. He was an advisor to the Secretary of the National Security and Defense Council of Ukraine from 1996 to 2000.

Leonid Grigoryev is Professor, Head of Department of Global Economy, Higher School of Economics (HSE), Moscow. In addition, he is Chief Adviser of the Head of Analytical Center under the Government of the Russian Federation and the member of the Board of Trustees—WWF-Russia. He has published more than three hundred research works, edited a dozen books and produced numerous scientific media works. His key interests lay with Russian Transition as he served as a Deputy Minister of Finance in the Transition Government in 1991–1992. In the last two decades, he has worked extensively on global growth, energy, and on elites, middle class and inequality, and the BRICS.

Tadas Jakštas, Dr., is an independent energy security expert with the main expertise on the protection of critical infrastructure and cyber resilience. Previously, he worked at the NATO Energy Security Centre of Excellence (NATO ENSEC COE) where he led analytical projects in the area of critical energy infrastructure protection, cyber security and maritime security issues. Before joining NATO ENSEC COE, Dr. Jakštas worked at NATO Allied Command Transformation in Norfolk (the USA), the Ministry of National Defence of Lithuania and the Council of the European Union where he focused on cyber security and defence policy issues. Dr. Jakštas was appointed as a civil expert for NATO's Civil Emergency Planning Committee to serve as an adviser on all aspects of regional energy resilience, including in response to hybrid threats. He also serves as an active member of the European Centre of Excellence for Countering Hybrid Threats experts' pool. He holds a Ph.D. in Government from the University of Essex and he has two postgraduate degrees in International Relations and Security Studies—one from the Leiden University and another one from the University of Southampton.

Laura Klemetti, M.Soc.Sc. (Political Science), works as Project Researcher at the Pan-European Institute, University of Turku, Finland. Klemetti examines the interplay between energy infrastructure and policy development in general, and the oil and gas sector's cumulative effects on society in particular. She specialises in Russian affairs and follows the long-term trends of economic and societal development in the regions and federal cities.

Kari Liuhto received his Ph.D. from the University of Glasgow, the United Kingdom, in 1997, and the degree of Doctor of Science from the Turku School of Economics, Finland, in 2000. Liuhto was nominated as a tenure professor in International Business at the Lappeenranta University of Technology in the year 2000, and he has been Director of the Pan-European Institute at the University of Turku since 2003 and Director of Centrum Balticum Foundation since 2011. Professor Liuhto has been involved in several projects funded by the European Commission and various Finnish ministries. Liuhto is the founder and the editor-in-chief of one of the world's leading discussion platforms dealing with the Baltic Sea region, namely the Baltic Rim Economies (BRE) review, which has been published quarterly since the year 2004 (https://sites.utu.fi/bre/).

Dzhanneta Medzhidova holds a position of a lecturer at the Department of World Economy at the Higher School of Economics (HSE) Moscow (since 2019) and a junior researcher at the Institute of World Economy and International Relations (IMEMO RAS) (since 2016). In 2014, she graduated from the Faculty of International Relations, St. Petersburg State University. In 2015–2017, she studied the world economy at the master's programme of HSE. In 2020, she graduated from Doctoral School of Economics, HSE. Medzhidova works currently on her Ph.D. thesis on asset specificity on gas markets.

Anna Mikulska is Nonresident Fellow in energy studies at the Rice University's Baker Institute for Public Policy and Senior Fellow at the Foreign Policy Research Institute. Mikulska's research focuses on the geopolitics of energy in the EU, the former Soviet bloc and Russia. Her current interests include the potential use of natural gas as a geoeconomic tool and ways in which US LNG exports could bolster European energy security. Mikulska received a law degree from the Adam Mickiewicz University, a master's degree in international relations from the University of Windsor in Canada, and a Ph.D. in political science from the University of Houston, the USA.

Hanna Mäkinen, M.A. (General History), works as Project Researcher at the Pan-European Institute, University of Turku, Finland. Her research interests include contemporary Russian politics, society and economic development, with a particular emphasis on regional development trends. Mäkinen has also studied the role of foreign companies in the development of Russian energy and maritime industries, both in the Eastern Baltic Sea region and the Russian Arctic. She has published various articles on her research topics and has several years of experience in research projects related to, for instance, energy and maritime sectors.

Mariusz Ruszel, Ph.D., D.Sc. is Associate Professor in the Department of Economy of the Faculty of Management at the Ignacy Łukasiewicz Rzeszów University of Technology. Ruszel is a graduate of the Faculty of International and Political Science Studies at the University of Łódź. He has conducted research at the University of Venice (2014), the University of Geneva (2014), the Deutsches Institute Wirtschaftsforschung (2015) and the Freie Universität Berlin (2016 and 2018). He is an expert in the Presidential Expert Programme 'Laboratory of Ideas'—Chancellery of the President of the Republic of Poland (2012–2013). He was qualified in 2017 to the group of experts: The National Centre for Research and Development under the Intelligent Development Operational Programme 2014–2020, and in 2018 he was placed in the expert database of the National Academic Exchange Agency (NAWA) and the Foundation for Polish Science under the Intelligent Development Operational Programme 2014–2020 for Measure 4. 4. 'Increasing the human resources potential of the R&D sector'. Ruszel is also expert at Research Executive Agency (REA) of the European Commission. He is the founder and editor-in-chief of the international scientific journal Energy Policy Studies. Scholarship of the Minister of Science and Higher Education for outstanding young scientists, Minister of Science and Higher Education (2017). He is also Chairman of the Ignacy Łukasiewicz Energy Policy Institute. His scientific interests revolve around geopolitics, geoeconomics, energy policy, energy security and natural gas market.

Andrey Shadurskiy is an independent researcher focusing on energy security, LNG markets and environmental responsibility of oil and gas companies. Holding a doctorate from the St. Petersburg University, Russia, he previously also worked for the WU Vienna, the HEC Lausanne and the University of St. Gallen.

Igor Stukalenko has more than 25 years of experience in energy and gas sector. Igor Stukalenko currently works in the team of the Centre for Global Studies 'Strategy XXI'. Earlier, he worked for the Naftogaz of Ukraine for 14 years and held different positions, including the position of Deputy Head of the Natural Gas Transit and Supply Department. He has extensively been involved in the natural gas transit and storage issues. He also participated in the negotiation process on the Ukraine-EU Association Agreement.

Dariusz Zarzecki, professor dr hab, is an expert in the field of finance and business valuation. Zarzecki has over 30 years of experience in business and intellectual property valuation. He is Ordinary Professor at the University of Szczecin. Professor Zarzecki is an author of numerous publications. Moreover, he is a member of the editorial board of Financial Internet Quarterly and a manager and the principal investigator in several research projects, such as Multifactor model for estimating the cost of equity—operational approach, Financial performance versus market valuation of banks in Poland, Control premium in the Polish capital market, Business Valuation Standards and Lack of Marketability Discounts in Business Valuation. Zarzecki is a team leader responsible for developing business valuation standards for the Polish Federation of Appraisers' Associations. He has been a lecturer at numerous courses and conferences, including M.B.A. studies and dedicated courses for company boards, business and property appraisers, financial analysts and accountants. Zarzecki is a co-founder and a chairman of the Association of Business Appraisers in Poland (SBWPwP). In addition, he is Chief of the M.B.A. Programme at the University of Szczecin. Professor Zarzecki has acted as a court expert in the field of business valuation and lost benefits estimation.

Abbreviations

°C	Degree Celsius
°F	Degree Fahrenheit
ACER	Agency for the Cooperation of Energy Regulators
AFID	Alternative Fuel Infrastructure Directive
ATR	Auto Thermal Reforming
bcm	Billion Cubic Metres
bcma	Billion Cubic Metres Annually
BEMIP	Baltic Energy Market Interconnection Plan
BP	British Petroleum
BRE	Baltic Rim Economies (A review dealing with the Baltic Sea region)
BRICS	Brazil, Russia, India, China and South Africa
ca	Circa (Around)
CCGT	Combined Cycle Gas Turbines
CCS	Carbon Capture and Storage
CCUS	Carbon Capture, Utilisation and Storage
CEE	Central and Eastern Europe
CEF	Connecting Europe Facility
CEO	Chief Executive Officer
CHPP	Combined Heat and Power Plant
CMEA	Council for Mutual Economic Assistance (a.k.a. SEV and COMECON)
CNG	Compressed Natural Gas
CO_2	Carbon Dioxide
COVID-19	Coronavirus Disease 2019 (A disease caused by SARS-CoV-2 virus)

CPSU	Communist Party of the Soviet Union
DSME	Daewoo Shipbuilding & Marine Engineering Co.
EC	European Commission
EEA	European Economic Area
e.g.	Exempli Gratia (For example)
EGF	European Guarantee Fund
EIB	European Investment Bank
ENTSO-G	European Network of Transmission System Operators for Gas
ETS	Emissions Trading System
EU	European Union
EUR	Euro, € (A currency of the European Union)
FOB	Free on Board
FRG	Federal Republic of Germany (a.k.a. West Germany)
FRU	Floating Regasification Unit
FSRU	Floating Storage Regasification Unit
GCU	Gas Compressor Unit
GDP	Gross Domestic Product
GHG	Greenhouse Gas
GIE	Gas Infrastructures Europe
GIPL	Gas Interconnection Poland-Lithuania
GTS	Gas Transmission System
GUS	Główny Urząd Statystyczny (Central Statistical Office of Poland)
GW	Gigawatt
HPP	Hydroelectric Power Plant
i.e.	Id Est (That is)
IEA	International Energy Agency
IGU	International Gas Union
IP	Interconnection Point
ISO	International Organization for Standardization
ITC	Inter-TSO Compensation for Transit
JKM	Japan Korea Marker
kWh	Kilowatt Hour
LBG	Liquefied Biogas
LLSU	Latvian-Lithuanian Interconnection Improvement project
LNG	Liquefied Natural Gas
m^3	Cubic Meter
MBtu	Million British Thermal Units
mcm	Million Cubic Metres
mt	Million Tonnes
mtoe	Million Tonnes of Oil Equivalent
mtpa	Million Tonnes Per Annum
MW	Megawatt
MWh	Megawatt Hour

NATO	North Atlantic Treaty Organization
NAWA	National Academic Exchange Agency (of Poland)
NBP	National Balancing Point (A spot-traded natural gas market in the UK)
NCG	NetConnect Germany (A gas trading hub in Germany)
NDAA	National Defense Authorization Act (of the USA)
NECP	National Energy and Climate Plan (of Latvia)
NGO	Non-Governmental Organisation
Nm^3	Normal Cubic Meter
NOK	Norwegian Krone (A currency of Norway)
NPD	Norwegian Petroleum Directorate
NPP	Nuclear Power Plant
OECD	Organisation for Economic Co-operation and Development
OMV	Österreichische Mineralölverwaltung (Austrian Mineral Oil Administration)
PBG	Earlier Piecobiogaz (A Polish energy-related engineering company)
PCI	Project of Common Interest
PGE	Polska Grupa Energetyczna (A Polish state-owned public power company)
PGNiG	Polskie Górnictwo Naftowe i Gazownictwo (A Polish state-owned energy company)
PLN	Polish Zloty (A currency of Poland)
PLUA	Poland-Ukraine Interconnector
PSA	Production Sharing Agreement
PSE	Polskie Sieci Elektroenergetyczne (A Polish state-owned transmission system operator)
R&D	Research and Development
REA	Research Executive Agency (of the European Commission)
RES	Renewable Energy Source
RSI	Residual Supply Index
RZD	Russian Railways
SCV	Submerged Combustion Vaporiser
Sm^3 o.e.	Standard Cubic Meter of Oil Equivalent (1,000 $m^3$of natural gas)
SMR	Steam Methane Reforming
SoS	Security of Supply
SSB	Statistisk Sentralbyrå (Statistics Norway)
SVA	Security Vulnerability Assessment
tcm	Thousand Cubic Metres
TEEC	Treaty Establishing Energy Community
TEN-T	Trans-European Transport Network
TES	Total Energy Supply
TEU	Twenty-Foot Equivalent Unit

TJ	Terajoule
toe	Tonne of Oil Equivalent
TPA	Third Party Access
TSO	Transmission System Operator
TTF	Title Transfer Facility (A virtual trading point for natural gas in the Netherlands)
TWh	Terawatt Hour
UAH	Ukrainian Hryvnia (A currency of Ukraine)
UAVTP	Ukrainian Virtual Trading Point
UGS	Underground Gas Storage
UGSF	Underground Gas Storage Facility
UK	United Kingdom
UN	United Nations
USA	United States of America
USD	US Dollar, $ (A currency of the USA)
USSR	Union of Soviet Socialist Republics (a.k.a. the Soviet Union)
V4	Visegrád Four (Czechia, Hungary, Poland and Slovakia)
VEB	Vnesheconombank
WTO	World Trade Organization

List of Figures

List of Tables

List of Maps

CHAPTER 1

The Development of Global LNG Exports

Mariusz Ruszel

Introduction

Global consumption of natural gas has been steadily increasing over recent decades. In the period 2000–2019 alone, consumption increased by nearly 60% from 2,400 billion cubic metres (bcm) to over 3,900bcm (BP, 2020). Despite increased global consumption, documented natural gas reserves are also growing as a result of new technology developments and discoveries of new gas fields. During the period 2000–2019, the volume of documented natural gas reserves increased from 138,900 bcm to 198,800 bcm, of which nearly 50% are located in the Russian Federation, Iran and Qatar. At the same time, the share of natural gas in global primary energy consumption is increasing. Analysing the process of consumption growth, we observe that natural gas consumption is growing fastest in the Middle East, Asia–Pacific and Africa. The fastest growth in the last two decades has occurred in global exports of liquefied natural gas. Between 2000 and 2019, international trade in liquefied natural gas increased from 140 to 485 bcm, i.e. more than threefold, with particularly rapid growth over the past five years (Liuhto, 2020).

M. Ruszel (✉)
Ignacy Łukasiewicz Rzeszów University of Technology, Rzeszów, Poland
e-mail: mruszel@prz.edu.pl

K. Liuhto (ed.), *The Future of Energy Consumption, Security and Natural Gas*, https://doi.org/10.1007/978-3-030-80367-4_1

Although the SARS CoV-19 pandemic, i.e. COVID-19, has contributed to a decline in gas consumption globally in 2020, the annual global LNG trade is expected to increase to 585 bcm by 2025. The pandemic contributed to a correction of the IEA's forecasts reducing the assumed average annual growth rate from 1.8% to 1.5% by 2025, which means a loss of 75 bcm of natural gas growth in this period (International Energy Agency, 2020a). This underlines the strategic importance of LNG in enhancing the security of supply to end users, and contributes to a competitive natural gas market in an environmentally sustainable manner. Discovery of further sources of natural gas in places remote from the existing and planned routes of transmission pipelines, as well as the development of maritime transport have contributed to the dynamic development of the global liquefied natural gas market (Gałczyński et al., 2017).

The development of global trade in liquefied natural gas is determined by the number of countries with energy infrastructure capable of exporting and importing it. The availability of liquefied natural gas on the global market, which is being increasingly liberalised, is steadily increasing (Shabaneh & Schenckery, 2020). LNG supply contracts are increasingly flexible, they are concluded for a short period of time, and the raw material price is indexed to the price of gas hubs. This means that the process of development of the global LNG market is similar to the way the global oil trade has developed (Wang et al., 2020).

The objective of this article is to analyse the development perspectives of the global LNG exports. Thus, the following research questions have been formulated:

- What geoeconomic factors influence the development of LNG exports?
- How is the competition between liquefied natural gas exporters developing?
- How is the development of LNG infrastructure for liquefied natural gas exports developing?
- What is the impact of the SARS CoV-2 pandemic on the liquefied natural gas market?

The following research hypothesis was developed: the oversupply of liquefied natural gas combined with the economic impact of the SARS

CoV-2 pandemic will contribute to the acceleration of the liquefied natural gas trade until 2030.

The article uses the theory of geoeconomics. A neo-realistic approach (structural realism) is also visible, as strategic interests in the area of energy security have been identified, and the rivalry between countries in a defined system, i.e. the global liquefied natural gas supply market, has been analysed (Waltz, 1990).

This chapter includes firstly the identification of the factors that shape the development of global LNG exports. Thereafter, the chapter analyses the competition between the current and new exporters in a time of natural gas oversupply. Thirdly, the projection of the development of LNG export terminals is given. The article ends with conclusions and policy implications related to the development of LNG exports.

The Geoeconomy Shaping Global LNG Exports

The supply of liquefied natural gas is of strategic importance in the context of strengthening the energy security of importing countries and improving the competitiveness of their economies. The global LNG market is characterised by a high rate of competition between suppliers for end customers. The article assumes that countries use their economic potential as a tool to achieve strategic geopolitical goals. The research limitation is the intention that the issue of energy security is analysed from the perspective of the state as the most important actor in international relations, which is part of the theory of realism. However, the approach has been narrowed down to liquefied natural gas. The classical geopolitical approach is characterised by reasoning based on the perception of space as an area of competition for the territory and authorities over it (Kjellén, 1899; Ratzel, 1897; Spykman, 1944). Geopolitics determines how countries compete for natural resources in a given area (Flint, 2012).

The territorial area is important from the perspective of its use for extraction, transmission, storage or distribution activities in the context of energy resources. If there are deposits in the area, they are regarded as strategic resources. On the other hand, the territory is used for transit, that is to say, for transmission by land or sea. Simultaneously, the country's territorial location is of a great importance in terms of shaping its foreign policy objectives and energy strategy (Correlj'e & van der Linde, 2006). Geopolitics is increasingly seen through geoeconomics as a result of developing economic interdependencies, new technologies and international law (Luttwak, 1990). Moreover, modern competition between countries takes place in the economic and technological spheres (Waltz, 1993). However, economic policy, including instruments stemming from energy policy, is subordinated to strategic objectives. In this article, the research assumption was that states can use their economic potential to achieve geoeconomic and even geopolitical goals (Luttwak, 1990). Globally, natural gas supplies have already been used on many occasions as an instrument of political pressure to achieve specific geopolitical objectives (Bettzüge & Lochner, 2009; De Jong et al., 2010; Yergin, 2012; Goldthau & Boersma, 2014; Ruszel, 2015a; Stulberg, 2017). When analysing the issue of global development of liquefied natural gas exports in view of the geoeconomic approach, the following premises are seen (Waltz, 1990).

Firstly, it is strategically important for a country to have a proven natural gas resource that is sufficient to produce enough natural gas to be exported. With the development of new technologies to drill deeper wells and the use of unconventional forms of natural gas production, the global reserves of natural gas are increasing, exceeding global consumption. The discovery of new deposits or the commencement of exploitation of existing natural gas deposits on a larger scale provides the basis for the construction of energy infrastructure enabling the exports of natural gas in a liquefied form. At the same time, liquefied natural gas transport technology has improved, and the fleet of modern methane carriers on the global market has grown. These factors are contributing to a steady increase in the number of countries able to export and import LNG. At the end of 2020, liquefied natural gas was being exported by 21 countries and imported by 42 countries (International Energy Agency, 2020a).

Secondly, individual natural gas exporting countries aim to create their own geoeconomic space, which is an international system, i.e. an area of co-operation or competition between individual countries. Simultaneously, a system defined in this way becomes an essential condition for achieving its strategic objectives. It is based on the creation of appropriate natural gas transmission corridors via pipelines through transit countries or shipping routes transporting liquefied natural gas from an LNG export terminal to an LNG import terminal. In addition to building the appropriate energy infrastructure, it is necessary to guarantee the security of continuity of raw material transport by land or sea.

Thirdly, the areas of geoeconomic activity created by individual countries in the supply of liquefied natural gas infringe other areas defined by other exporters. In this way, there is direct competition between individual LNG exporters for end users. This process puts pressure on the structure of natural gas contracts, their flexibility, and the prices of the liquefied natural gas supplied. This is all the more the case since maintaining the exporter's position of dependence on its LNG supply is strategic as it constitutes an instrument to support geopolitical objectives (Jean, 2003; Ruszel, 2015b, 2019). As the amount of natural gas available on the global market increases, competition between producers and exporters will increase. The strongest states will be able to defend their geoeconomic spaces, as this will be an indication of their state power. At the same time, it will be strategically important to maintain the position of supply to the customer in question, especially in a situation of increasing market competition and the effects of the SARS-CoV-2 pandemic.

In this context, the shaping of the global LNG market is influenced by geoeconomic factors, of which the following are the key factors. First of all, already in 2018 there was a global oversupply of natural gas, which contributed to a decrease in gas prices on global trading platforms and hubs. In 2019, LNG spot prices in the Asian market fell by 44% compared to 2018 (International Energy Agency, 2020a). In 2019, the price of natural gas in the largest European gas hub, TTF in the Netherlands, fell by 45% compared to 2018, and in the American Henry Hub by 19% at the same time (International Energy Agency, 2020a).[1] In 2020, the decline in the European TTF hub deepened to a record low. The price of natural gas fell threefold from EUR 25.0/1 MWh to around EUR 8.5/1 MWh in the 2018–2020 period. At a record low point, it reached EUR 7.5/1 MWh, which was the lowest TTF gas price since 2006. Increased natural gas production has contributed to the accumulation of record-breaking natural gas reserves in global terms, which has increased pressure on the price of natural gas in global markets.

Secondly, the SARS CoV-2 pandemic has contributed to the global economic slowdown, with the fuel sector in particular being hit by a sharp drop in consumption. The IEA estimates that the global fall in natural gas consumption will be three percent in 2020, or nearly 120 bcm (International Energy Agency, 2020c). Under these circumstances, the high

[1] TTF, the Title Transfer Facility, is a virtual marketplace where it offers gas to other parties. TTF was set up in 2003.

flexibility of natural gas markets in adapting to sudden falls in demand has been ensured by the global LNG trade. While the natural gas market has changed significantly in the wake of the pandemic, the role of LNG trade with its supply flexibility may make this type of transaction more dynamic than traditional pipeline supplies.

The IEA estimates that despite a decrease in natural gas consumption due to the SARS CoV-2 pandemic, the annual world LNG trade is expected to increase to 585 bcm by 2025. However, market uncertainty and the economic downturn due to the pandemic may have their effects in the coming years. In 2020, there was a reduction in demand for natural gas in European countries, which in turn reduced the maritime supply. This situation is being effectively exploited by the People's Republic of China, which is rapidly trying to return to the GDP growth of 2019, and this contributes to increasing demand for natural gas, including globally cheap LNG. On the other hand, the natural gas supplied to Europe, mainly by the Russian company Gazprom, is partly based on indexing the price to oil, and this is proving to be beneficial for consumers under the current circumstances, as oil has noted record declines. However, this will cause further financial problems for this Russian company, which will reduce the budget revenues of the Russian State. Simultaneously, the drop in gas prices, including liquefied natural gas prices, has also negatively affected US exporters, for whom the current market conditions make their gas no longer competitive. This means that the SARS CoV-2 pandemic is having a huge impact on the price of liquefied natural gas on the world market (International Energy Agency, 2020a).

Thirdly, gas contracts are an important element influencing the development of the liquefied natural gas market. At present, many natural gas consumers depend on a long-term onshore supply contract which discourages a policy of diversification of natural gas supply sources and development of alternative energy infrastructure allowing them to benefit from the global LNG market. Many liquefied natural gas importers have also signed long-term gas contracts. It is estimated that between 2021 and 2025 nearly 30% of long-term LNG contracts will expire, and by 2030 as much as 40% (International Energy Agency, 2020b). This will increase competition between exporters for end users. It will be important whether the contracts include a destination clause,[2] which most LNG

[2] The 'destination clause' in long-term contracts restricts the possibility of further distribution of natural gas.

supply contracts in 2020 were signed with. The current market situation may reduce contracts with the possibility of a flexible delivery point. In the period 2019–2020, the number of contracts with the possibility of a flexible delivery location decreased by more than 50%, the number of new long-term contracts (over 10 years) decreased almost five times, and the number of short-term (under 5 years) contracts increased. In the first nine months of 2020, however, a small number of flexible-destination contracts have been signed (less than 10 bcm). For comparison, in 2019 an average of 60 bcm of the flexible delivery location volumes were signed (International Energy Agency, 2020b).

In addition, the SARS CoV-2 pandemic caused the number of contracts above two billion cubic metres per year to decrease significantly and the number of contracts below two billion cubic metres per year to increase. This means that current conditions have accelerated the transformation of the structure of contracts on the natural gas market to a model similar to that of the oil market, where short-term contracts for smaller quantities rather than a larger number of suppliers predominate.

Fourthly, the economic situation of many entities on the natural gas market has, as a result of the SARS CoV-2 pandemic, contributed to a decrease in energy company profits, and a decrease in share prices of the largest energy companies, i.e. BP, Chevron, Eni, ExxonMobil, Shell and Total. By mid-2020, nearly 150 upstream, midstream and downstream investment projects have been cancelled or postponed. The implications of this situation are the loss of shares by some companies, acquisitions of energy companies, consolidation processes and thus changes of owners. This will contribute to changes in the strategies of some energy companies in the natural gas industry, as well as adjustments to investment plans for liquefied natural gas.

Moreover, there is an increase in the use of LNG as a transport fuel. According to the International Energy Agency (2020a), nearly ten billion cubic metres will be used annually as fuel for heavy transport and maritime transport in the years to 2025. In late 2020, it was predicted that LNG as a transport fuel will grow at an average rate of 2.6%. New regulations on greenhouse gas emissions and environmental standards for fuels in maritime transport are contributing to the increased importance of liquefied natural gas in maritime transport. This process will be reinforced by developments on the Asian market, particularly in the People's Republic of China. The development of this new application for liquefied natural gas will contribute to the growing demand for LNG on the world market.

Current and New LNG Exporters—Competition in the Time of Natural Gas Glut

In 2019, the world's largest exporters of liquefied natural gas were Qatar (22% of world exports), followed by Australia (21%), the USA (10%) and the Russian Federation (8%) and Malaysia (7%). The greatest growth in the volume of LNG exports was recorded by the USA and the Russian Federation. Both of these countries have increased their export volume by over 60% compared to 2018. In 2019, Argentina became a new exporter of LNG and Gibraltar became a new importer (International Gas Union, 2020a).

In 2020, Australia took the lead in global LNG exports, which despite the COVID-19 pandemic, reduced its exports by only 0.8% compared to 2019. The three largest countries, namely Australia, Qatar and the USA, accounted for over 50% of global LNG exports in 2020. When assessing energy security from the perspective of an LNG exporter, it is important to have various gas importers. In this respect, the USA is best represented, supplying LNG to 32 countries and Qatar to 24 countries in 2019. Australia sells its liquefied natural gas to 10 countries, primarily to the People's Republic of China and Japan, which together purchased nearly 75% of Australian LNG. This means that the USA among all LNG exporters has the most strategic policy, because the USA exports gas to the greatest number of countries. A similar strategy was followed by the Russian Federation, which supplied liquefied natural gas to 24 countries in 2019 (International Gas Union, 2020b). The Russian Federation is an important supplier of natural gas transmitted via pipelines to many countries in Europe and Asia.

When analysing the rivalry on the global LNG market, the following aspects should be observed. First of all, the current situation shows that competition for geopolitical influence between the USA and the Russian Federation is intensifying, with energy markets being its geoeconomic space. The construction of the Nord Stream 2 gas pipeline may contribute to reducing the role of Ukraine as a transit country for Russian gas supplies to the EU. In the third quarter of 2020, the share of the natural gas transit through Ukraine to Europe reached only 25% compared to 47% in the same time in 2019 (European Commission, 2020). The key question is whether Nord Stream 2 would be covered by all regulations under the Third Energy Package. If all the regulations relating to competition law were applied to it, then the gas transported could prove less profitable for end customers. On the other hand, if derogations from EU law were applied to the Nord Stream 2 pipeline, the gas transported through it could be cheaper than US LNG. However, there is no doubt that an oversupply of LNG on the world market would put downward pressure on the price of pipeline gas. The key question is how gas contracts would be concluded for gas transported by Nord Stream 2 and the liquefied natural gas delivered by sea. Certainly, the construction of the gas pipeline would increase the geopolitical rivalry between the Russian Federation and the USA in CEE. So far, the USA has focused on blocking Russian strategic investments, such as Nord Stream and Nord Stream 2, but with the development of shale gas production and the start of LNG exports, the USA has gained a real instrument of direct competition with the Russian Federation in areas it considers to be within its zone of political influence. 'The Three Seas Initiative' promoted by American diplomacy is a strategic concept, the component of which is to increase American natural gas supplies to European countries that have so far been dependent on Russian supplies.[3] The projection of events coincides with the expiring long-term natural gas contracts in many European countries. A parallel area of direct competition between the USA and Russia is construction of nuclear power and oil supplies. Bearing these circumstances in mind, it seems that 2021 and the following years will be a time of increasingly intense geoeconomic competition between the USA and the Russian Federation. Given the effectiveness of US diplomacy, which is able to contract the largest number of importers worldwide for its LNG supplies (32 countries in 2019), these countries are seen as 'American bridgeheads'. If the volume of American LNG supplies to each of these 32 countries increases, the position of the Russian Federation as a natural gas supplier will be limited. At the same time, this process is dynamising the growing exports of LNG from pro-American countries, i.e. Qatar, Australia and Canada, which are preparing to start their LNG exports.

Secondly, the current international competition on the LNG market has resulted in a reduction in LNG re-exports. The analysis of the period 2018–2019 indicates a decrease of nearly 60%. The largest volume of

[3] 'The Three Seas Initiative' gets its name from three seas, namely the Baltic Sea, the Black Sea and the Adriatic Sea. The main goal of this initiative is to develop the infrastructure in Europe for economic growth. Twelve states take part in this initiative: Austria, Bulgaria, Croatia, the Czech Republic, Estonia, Hungary, Latvia, Lithuania, Poland, Romania, Slovakia and Slovenia.

re-exported liquefied natural gas came from Europe (58% of global re-exports), with Asia being the main destination. The largest re-exporters of liquefied natural gas in 2019 were France (39% of the global re-exports), Singapore (26%), the Netherlands (9%) and Belgium (8%) (International Gas Union, 2020b). In turn, the largest recipient of re-exported LNG was the People's Republic of China (32%). These aspects indicate that the current conditions of the global LNG market are reducing the number of commercial transactions involving intermediaries registered in Europe. This has increased the number of direct transactions between the seller and the recipient.

Thirdly, the countries with a strategy of diversifying their liquefied natural gas customers will dominate the market vis-à-vis countries basing their strategy on regional supplies. This argument is supported by the analysis of the current situation with the structure of suppliers 15 years ago. In 2006, the main LNG producers were successively as follows: Qatar, Malaysia, Indonesia, Algeria, Nigeria, Trinidad and Tobago, Egypt and Oman. With the exception of Qatar, these countries exported liquefied natural gas to regional markets and the high price of ocean freight was a factor which led to this regionalisation (Gałczyński et al., 2017). After several years, Qatar has maintained its position while the other countries have been overtaken by new exporters. The reduction of maritime transport costs and the expansion of LNG terminals have changed the main suppliers. The IEA estimates that the USA will be the world's largest exporter of liquefied natural gas and the People's Republic of China the largest importer in 2025 (International Energy Agency, 2020a). Then, China will account for 22% (128 bcm) of total LNG demand (585 bcm) and contribute about 40% of growth in total imports in 2025. Simultaneously, the estimated volume of the USA in global LNG exports will reach about 130 bcm annually.

Fourthly, an important role will be played by policy decisions on the part of importers, which will influence the shape of the market and competition between exporters. At present, the largest LNG consumers on a global scale are countries located in the Asia Pacific and Asia, i.e. Japan (22% of the global imports), the People's Republic of China (17%) and South Korea (11%). Three largest importers are responsible for purchasing 50% of liquefied natural gas supplies. Simultaneously, Japan, the People's Republic of China and South Korea have the most extensive energy infrastructure globally to receive liquefied natural gas. The leading countries with the largest LNG storage capacities are the same. Among

European countries, Spain is the leader in liquefied natural gas imports (4% of world LNG imports) (International Gas Union, 2020a).

The Projection of the Development of LNG Export Terminals

Globally, new exporters of liquefied natural gas are expected to emerge. In 2019, there were record investments (USD 65 billion) in new LNG export terminals with a confirmed new annual supply capacity of 95 bcm (Canada, Mauritania, Mozambique, Nigeria, the Russian Federation, Senegal and the USA) increasing global export capacity by 16% (International Energy Agency, 2020a). Canada may soon play a particularly important role in the global export market. Currently, Canada has only one LNG import terminal, namely Canaport in New Brunswick on the East Coast. However, as unconventional natural gas production in the USA has increased, the amount of natural gas exported through pipelines from Canada to the USA has decreased. This has had a negative impact on Canada's economic situation and has led to plans to build LNG export infrastructure (Table 1.1).

Canada forecasts that investment in LNG export infrastructure will increase natural gas production, and as a result of the development of investment, create new jobs for the Canadian economy. The planned investments would result in an export capacity of 318.63 bcm LNG for Canada. Most of Canada's LNG export terminals are planned on the West Coast in the province of British Columbia. Canadian LNG exports could contribute to an overall increase in the oversupply of LNG on the global market, which would put more pressure on gas prices in Europe as well. However, it seems that nearly a third of the projects will be cancelled (more than 115 bcm). The author estimates that Canada will finally build less than 100 bcm LNG export capacity by 2026.

The production and exports of LNG from African countries is also estimated to increase. Further investments are being made in Algeria. New investments in liquefied natural gas export infrastructure in Nigeria are also seen. Huge deposits of natural gas are located in Mozambique (close to the potential of Norway) as well as Tanzania.[4] Both these countries

[4] BP (2020) does not recognise the substantial natural gas reserves of Mozambique or Tanzania in its annual report of 2020.

Table 1.1 Planned LNG export terminals in Canada

Project	*Location*	*Export licence*	*Annual export volume (bcm)*	*Planned start of operation*
A C LNG (Nova Scotia)	East Coast	25 years	20.40	2023
Bear Head LNG (Nova Scotia)	East Coast	25 years	16.32	2025
Energie Saguenay (Quebec)	East Coast	25 years	14.96	2026
Goldboro LNG (Nova Scotia)	East Coast	20 years	13.60	2026
StoltLNGaz (Quebec)	East Coast	25 years	0.68	No data available
Total East Coast	–	–	65.96	–
Cedar LNG Project	West Coast	25 years	8.70	2025
Discovery LNG	West Coast	25 years	27.20	No data available
Kitimat LNG	West Coast	20 years	13.60	2025
Kitsault Energy Project	West Coast	20 years	27.20	No data available
LNG Canada	West Coast	40 years	35.36	2025
New Times Energy	West Coast	25 years	16.32	No data available
Orca LNG	West Coast	25 years	32.64	2026
Steelhead LNG: Kwispaa LNG	West Coast	25 years	40.80	2026
Stewart LNG Export Project	West Coast	25 years	40.80	No data available
Triton LNG (On Hold)	West Coast	25 years	3.12	No data available
Watson Island	West Coast	–	–	No data available
WesPac LNG Marine Terminal	West Coast	25 years	4.08	No data available
Woodfibre LNG	West Coast	25 years	2.85	2025
Total West Coast	–	–	252.67	–
Grand total			318.63	

Source The Author, based on Government of Canada (2020)

are planning to build LNG export facilities. In addition to Mozambique and Tanzania, Mauritania and Senegal will join the group of exporters in 2023. Both countries are implementing projects in co-operation with BP, which could lead to a total annual export capacity of 30 bcm in 2030 (Ouki, 2020).

It is also important to bear in mind the investments of the Russian Federation, which it plans to execute by 2035. The Russian Federation assumes the completion of the following LNG terminals in the near future: Arctic LNG 2 (Novatek and Total), Baltic LNG (Gazprom), Shtokman LNG (Gazprom, Total and StatoilHydro) and Sakhalin I LNG (Rosneft, Exxon Mobile, SODECO and ONGC Videsh). Given the negative impact of the SARS CoV-2 pandemic on investments in the energy generation sector, it will be difficult for Russia to realise all these projects. In fact, the Russian Federation has missed the period of the LNG revolution, and therefore it is now trying to make up for lost time. One of the future directions of Russian LNG exports will be India, which is investing in liquefied natural gas projects in Russia, i.e. Sakhalin-1 (NDTV, 2019).[5] The possible exports of Russian natural gas from the Arctic to Europe or Asia will be cheaper by sea than by pipeline (Koz'menko et al., 2018).

Parallel to the expansion of the export infrastructure of LNG terminals, investments will be conducted in countries importing natural gas. The People's Republic of China, India and even Bangladesh are particularly active in Asia. In 2019, supplies of liquefied natural gas to these countries increased while they fell to Japan and South Korea. In the first half of 2020, gas imports to Japan were further reduced by five percent compared to 2019 and to South Korea by 14% as a result of a warm winter and the SARS CoV-2 pandemic. As a whole, the Asian gas market reduced its gas consumption by seven percent in the first half of 2020 compared to the same period in 2019 (International Energy Agency, 2020a).

When analysing the 2018–2019 growth of liquefied natural gas imports globally, it can be seen that the highest growth took place in Europe (International Energy Agency, 2020a). In Europe, liquefied natural gas import capacity at the end of 2019 was 241 bcm, while in the EU28 alone it was 212 bcm. On the 31st of January 2020, the UK, with 48 bcm of LNG regasification capacity, left the EU, so the LNG import capacity of the EU27 has fallen to 164 bcm. If the planned LNG import

[5] The shareholders of the project are US Exxon Mobile (30%), Japanese SODECO (30%), Russian Rosneft (20%) and Indian ONGC Videsh (20%).

terminals are built in Europe, the regasification capacity will increase to 304 bcm in Europe and 228 bcm in the EU27 by 2026 (LNG Investment Database, 2020).

Currently, 24 import LNG terminals are planned, nine of which are floating storage regasification units (FSRUs), including one floating regasification unit. At present, the Federal Republic of Germany plans to build the most regasification terminals in Europe. The most advanced is the Brunsbüttel LNG terminal with a capacity of eight billion cubic metres (2022), the others are the FSRU Wilhelmshaven with a regasification capacity of ten billion cubic metres (2022), the Stade GmBh LNG in Lower Saxony with a capacity of 12 bcm with the possibility of expansion to 15 bcm, and a small LNG reloading terminal in Rostock. Other LNG terminals are planned in the following European countries: Albania, Cyprus, Estonia, Finland, Greece, Ireland, Italy, Latvia, Poland, Spain, Sweden, Turkey, Ukraine and the United Kingdom. In addition, existing LNG terminals in France (FosCavaou LNG Terminal, Montoir-de-Bretagne LNG Terminal), Spain (Mugardos LNG Terminal), the Netherlands (Gate Terminal Rotterdam), Turkey (Aliaga Izmir LNG Terminal, Marmara Ereglisi LNG Terminal), Ukraine (Yuzhnyi LNG Terminal) and the United Kingdom (Isle of Grain LNG Terminal) will be expanded (LNG Investment Database, 2020).

Conclusions and Policy Implications Related to the Development of LNG Exports

The global LNG market has developed dynamically in recent years and the growth will continue over subsequent decades. The development of liquefied natural gas exports is influenced by geoeconomic factors. Proven natural gas reserves, which provide the basis for increasing production and building energy infrastructure to export gas in a liquefied form, are strategically important. Access to the sea and the ability to ensure the safety of maritime transport routes to end customers are essential as well. As the market becomes even more oversupplied with natural gas, competition between exporters of liquefied natural gas and exporters of gas through pipelines increases. The more liquefied natural gas displaces pipeline gas, the more it will affect the development of maritime exports. Particularly in the context of new market conditions shaped by the corona pandemic, it is recognised that LNG has provided a high degree of flexibility for gas markets to adapt to sudden falls in demand. The key point in this context is that a significant proportion of long-term gas supply contracts will expire in the coming years, and this allows for a change in the source and direction of supply.

The oversupply of natural gas in the global market will intensify competition among LNG exporters. It is possible that local or regional armed conflicts will contribute to the cessation of production or paralyse exports. It will be critical to identify areas of reduction in gas supply or production costs, as this will translate into competitiveness of LNG for end users.

Canada plans the largest investments in the expansion of its LNG export infrastructure. Their implementation would allow Canada to export over 300 bcm per year. In addition to Canada, significant investments are planned in Africa in countries, such as Algeria, Nigeria, Mozambique, Tanzania, as well as Mauritania and Senegal. In addition, strategic investments are currently being undertaken by the Russian Federation, which plans to be one of the leading exporters of liquefied natural gas by 2035. Further investments in LNG import terminals are planned and constructed in Europe, and their implementation by 2026 would contribute to an increase in regasification capacity at 304 bcm, and 228 bcm in the EU27.

The LNG market is significantly affected by its oversupply globally, combined with the effects of the SARS CoV-2 pandemic, overlapping with the expiration of natural gas contracts, as well as the growing use of LNG in transport and industry. In the short run, the SARS CoV-2 pandemic will have a major impact on global natural gas demand. The demand is estimated to grow by nearly three percent in 2021 compared to 2020, but the protracted pandemic will differentiate markets and also lead to the cancellation of further investment plans. In Africa, Asia and the Middle East, economic recovery will accelerate and stimulate growing demand for natural gas, while some mature markets may only experience a return to the 2019 economic level in 2022 or 2023. Weather conditions also play an important role in the global demand for natural gas. For several years now, warmer winters have followed each other (the average temperature between December and February above 0 °C), which until now have been characterised by lower temperatures (the average temperature below −5 °C). Naturally, warmer winters decrease energy consumption, including a decrease in natural gas consumption.

As a result of the SARS CoV-2 pandemic, many planned investments in new LNG terminals for exports or imports will be delayed and some of them cancelled due to the worsening financial situation of several energy companies. The largest companies in the energy sector have noted record reductions in share prices on the stock exchange, and as a result of financial difficulties these companies have launched savings programmes, and in extreme case these firms will be taken over by other companies or they will go bankrupt. This will result in significant consolidation processes in the energy sector and the process may be accompanied by a revision of investment plans in accordance with the goals of new shareholders. For this reason, economic policy instruments will contribute even more strongly to the global geopolitical picture following the SARS CoV-2 pandemic.

The research hypothesis that the oversupply of liquefied natural gas combined with the effects of the pandemic will contribute to the acceleration of LNG trade has thus been proven. This is significantly influenced by the changing trend of natural gas contracts and the appearance of an increasing number of suppliers on the market. Simultaneously, it also exacerbates international competition between liquefied natural gas market players for geopolitical influence. Further investments are being made and are dynamising this process. If at least some of the planned projects are completed, the global LNG market will be characterised by increasing oversupply and increasing competition for end users. The geoeconomic areas of individual exporters will increasingly overlap, and importers will play a key role in the market. A particularly important role may be played by geoeconomic relations allowing importers of liquefied natural gas to carry out investments in the export infrastructure of a country possessing gas resources, to take over shares in deposits or to establish companies with a majority share of the importing country.

The projection of trends in the global liquefied natural gas market indicates that it will develop in a similar way to the oil market, as the basis for increasing competition and the growing liberalisation of this market are the opportunities related to LNG transportation by sea. At the same time, increasing pressure and competition will lead to regional political conflicts between exporters as well as importers, during which global powers will play out their geopolitical interests.

These findings assist in the verification of the research hypothesis and answer the research questions. Given the methodological assumption that the interests of the state are prioritised, the following policy recommendations are to be made (Table 1.2). It should be noted that they take into account the perspective of LNG exporting countries.

Table 1.2 Policy recommendations

1. It is in the interest of countries with natural gas resources to invest in the development of infrastructure to enable liquefied natural gas exports. Political relations and appropriate economic diplomacy contributing to the conclusion of gas contracts with gas importers are of key importance in this context
2. From the perspective of an LNG exporting country, it is of strategic importance to maintain its position as an exporter in the context of growing competition for end users, as this is how countries will pursue their geoeconomic as well as geopolitical interests. For this reason, exporting countries should seek to reduce the costs of producing or transporting liquefied natural gas to end customers, also by dispensing with liquefied natural gas brokers
3. The SARS CoV-2 pandemic is causing financial losses to many energy companies and a decline in their share prices on the stock market. Therefore, it will be crucial to adapt the strategies of energy companies associated with the LNG market to the current conditions shaped by the coronavirus pandemic. From the perspective of countries seeking economic expansion, the key will be to take advantage of opportunities for asset consolidation and share acquisitions, while from the perspective of energy companies experiencing a loss of liquidity, the key will be to maintain ownership control during a difficult period for the company
4. It is in the interest of LNG exporters to take advantage of a situation where more than 40% of long-term LNG contracts are due to expire by 2030, as well as contracts for the supply of gas through pipelines. Exporters with the best economic diplomacy, as well as the most competitive price for liquefied natural gas supplied, can increase their market of customers and consequently geopolitical influence

Source The Author

These policy recommendations have been narrowed down to the most important aspects of strategic importance from the perspective of LNG exporting countries. However, the perspective of the LNG importing countries is also important, as including both sides illustrates the diversity of interests. Therefore, the main findings of the article have been formulated to refer to both exporters and importers (Table 1.3).

The impact of the coronavirus pandemic on the energy sector will contribute to a decline in the share prices of energy companies, consolidation of their assets, and will also lead to the abandonment of many investment projects. On the one hand, a rebound in the global gas market is expected, but on the other hand, the key factor will be the price of oil. If it remains low in the long term, it will also affect the profitability of shale gas extraction. Moreover, the global energy transition process is an important factor supporting coal-to-gas switching mainly in the USA and

Table 1.3 A summary of the main findings

1.	The availability of proven natural gas reserves provides a basis for the development of energy infrastructure to enable the exports of liquefied natural gas
2.	With expanding natural gas production and growing oversupply in the gas market, competition between exporters of liquefied natural gas and gas transported by pipeline is intensifying, putting downward pressure on the price of gas for end customers and increasing the flexibility of gas contracts
3.	The SARS CoV-2 pandemic has contributed to the cancellation of many investment projects in the gas sector, as well as reducing the profitability of energy companies and their share prices on the stock market
4.	It is estimated that between 2021 and 2030 nearly 40% of long-term LNG contracts will expire, and this will increase competition between exporters for end users
5.	Three leading countries, Australia, Qatar and the USA, accounted for over 50% of global LNG exports in 2020
6.	Of all the LNG exporters, the USA has the most strategic policy as it supplies gas to 32 countries worldwide
7.	The coronavirus pandemic has contributed to a reduction in the amount of LNG re-exported, thus increasing direct transactions between exporters and importers
8.	In 2025, the USA will be the largest exporter of LNG and the People's Republic of China the largest LNG importer
9.	Given the planned investments in LNG export infrastructure globally, Canada will join the ranks of major exporters in forthcoming years

Source The Author

China. Liquefied natural gas is an energy raw material that provides flexibility and support for volatile renewable energy sources. The natural gas market has changed significantly as a result of the coronavirus pandemic, increasing the importance of flexible forms of liquefied gas supply.

References

Bettzüge, M. O., & Lochner, S. (2009). Der russisch-ukrainische Gaskonflikt im Januar 2009 – Eine modell-gestützte Analyse. *EnergiewirtschaftlicheTages-fragen, 59*(7), 26–30.

BP. (2020). *Statistical Review of World Energy 2020.* https://www.bp.com/en/global/corporate/energy-economics/statistical-review-of-world-energy.html. Accessed 14 January 2021.

Correlj'e, A., & van der Linde, C. (2006). *Energy supply security and geopolitics: A European perspective* (Energy Policy No. 34) (pp. 532–543). https://doi.org/10.1016/j.enpol.2005.11.008. Accessed 2 April 2021.

De Jong, S., Wouters, J., & Sterkx, S. (2010). The 2009 Russian-Ukrainian gas dispute: Lessons for European energy crisis management after Lisbon. *European Foreign Affairs Review* (15), 511–538.

European Commission. (2020). Quarterly Report on European Gas Markets with focus on the impact of Covid-19 on the global LNG market. *DG Energy, 13*(3).

Flint, C. (2012). *Introduction to geopolitics*. Routledge.

Gałczyński, M., Ruszel, M., Turowski, P., Zajdler, R., & Zawisza, A. (2017). *Global LNG Market*. Ignacy Lukasiewicz Energy Policy Institute. Rzeszów-Warszawa.

Goldthau, A., & Boersma, T. (2014). The 2014 Ukraine-Russia crisis: Implications for energy markets and scholarship. *Energy Research & Social Science* (3), 13–15. https://doi.org/10.1016/j.erss.2014.05.001. Accessed 27 January 2021.

Government of Canada. (2020). *Canadian LNG projects*. https://www.nrcan.gc.ca/our-natural-resources/energy-sources-distribution/clean-fossil-fuels/natural-gas/canadian-lng-projects/5683. Accessed 3 February 2021.

International Energy Agency. (2020a). *Gas 2020*. https://www.iea.org/reports/gas-2020. Accessed 14 January 2021.

International Energy Agency. (2020b). *Global Gas Security Review 2020*. https://www.iea.org/reports/global-gas-security-review-2020. Accessed 21 January 2021.

International Energy Agency. (2020c). *The Covid-19 crisis highlights LNG's key role in global natural gas security*. https://www.iea.org/news/the-covid-19-crisis-highlights-lng-s-key-role-in-global-natural-gas-security. Accessed 20 January 2021.

International Gas Union. (2020a). *World LNG Report 2020*. https://www.igu.org/resources/2020-world-lng-report/. Accessed 1 February 2021.

International Gas Union. (2020b). *Global Voice of Gas 2020, 1*(1). https://www.igu.org/news/global-voice-of-gas-issue-1-vol-1-2/. Accessed 21 January 2021.

Jean, C. (2003). *Geopolityka*. ZakladNarodowyimieniaOssolinskich – Wydawnictwo. Wrocław.

Kjellén, R. (1899). Studier öfver Sveriges politiska gränser. *Ymer H, 3*, 283–331.

Koz'menko, S. Y., Masloboev, V. A., & Matviishin, D. A. (2018). Justification of economic benefits of Arctic LNG transportation by sea. *Journal of Mining Institute* (233), 554–560.

Liuhto K. (2020, August 1). *Natural gas in the Baltic Sea region: A special emphasis on liquefied natural gas (LNG)*. Slide package. https://www.researchgate.net/publication/343350581_Natural_gas_in_the_Baltic_Sea_region_A_special_emphasis_on_liquefied_natural_gas_LNG. Accessed 6 March 2021.

LNG Investment Database. (2020). https://www.gie.eu/index.php/gie-publications/databases/lng-investment-database. Accessed 1 February 2021.

Luttwak, E. (1990). From geopolitics to geo-economics: Logic of conflict. Grammar of Commerce. *The National Interest* (20), pp. 17–24.

NDTV. (2019). *Russia's Gazprom starts supplying LNG to India as first shipment arrives in Gujarat*. https://www.ndtv.com/india-news/russias-gazprom-starts-supplying-lng-to-india-as-first-shipment-arrives-in-gujarat-1862619. Accessed 17 February 2021.

Ouki, M. (2020). *Mauretania – Senegal: An emerging New African Gas Province—Is it still possible?* (The Oxford Institute for Energy Studies. No. 163).

Ratzel, F. (1897). *Politische Geographie*. R. Oldenbourg.

Ruszel, M. (2015a). *Analysis of selected informal way of influencing the EU's energy policy on the example of the Russian Federation* (National Security No. 3).

Ruszel, M. (2015b). The influence of the Russian-Ukrainian gas crises on the EU energy policy—Theoretical approach. *Przegląd Politologiczny* (2), 49–58.

Ruszel, M. (2019). Natural gas supplies as an instrument of geopolitical conflict between the Russian Federation and Ukraine. *Politykaenergetyczna – Energy Policy Journal, 22*(2), 33–46.

Shabaneh, R., & Schenckery, M. (2020). *Assessing energy policy instruments: LNG imports into Saudi Arabia* (Energy Policy No. 137). https://doi.org/10.1016/j.enpol.2019.111101. Accessed 2 April 2021.

Spykman, N. J. (1944). *The geography of the peace*. Harcourt Brace & Co.

Stulberg, N. A. (2017). Natural gas and the Russia-Ukraine crisis: Strategic restraint and the emerging Europe-Eurasia gas network. *Energy Research & Social Science* (24), 71–85. https://doi.org/10.1016/j.erss.2016.12.017. Accessed 1 March 2021.

Waltz, K. N. (1990). Realist thought and neorealist theory. *Journal of International Affairs, 44*(1), 21–37.

Waltz, K. N. (1993). The emerging structure of international politics. *International Security* (2), 52–67.

Wang, T., Zhang, D., Ji, Q., & Shi, X. (2020). Market reforms and determinants of import natural gas prices in China. *Energy, 196*, 117105. https://doi.org/10.1016/j.energy.2020.117105. Accessed 1 March 2021.

Yergin, D. (2012). *The Quest: Energy, security and the remaking of the modern world*. Penguin Books.

CHAPTER 2

Natural Gas in the EU in the Twenty-First Century: A Special Emphasis on LNG

Kari Liuhto

Introduction

LNG is not a miracle fuel. It is ordinary natural gas consisting mostly of methane and cooled down to liquid form. The extreme cooling process—in temperatures below minus 162 °C (−260 °F)—liquefies gas and compresses it down to 1/600 of its original volume (Jensen, 2004). The cooling process enables natural gas to be transported by means other than pipelines. LNG is not a fuel type of its own—rather, it is a rationalised transport solution for natural gas. LNG could be compared to cellular phones, which have liberated mobile phone users from the old-fashioned fixed telephone line network.

LNG is not a new fuel either. Cryogenic industry has its early start already in the nineteenth century, when air and gas separation technologies were developed and methane was liquefied (Chiu, 2008). The first LNG liquefaction plant was opened in 1917–1918 and the first commercial liquefaction plant was built in the USA in 1940–1941. The

K. Liuhto (✉)
University of Turku, Turku, Finland
e-mail: Kari.Liuhto@utu.fi

K. Liuhto (ed.), *The Future of Energy Consumption, Security and Natural Gas*, https://doi.org/10.1007/978-3-030-80367-4_2

first international LNG transportation took place in 1959, when a ship called MetánPioneer sailed from the Charles Lake in the USA with cargo containing LNG to the Canvey Island in the United Kingdom. The first regular LNG exports took place between Algeria and the UK in the 1960s (Hrastar, 2014; Proprietary, 2021).

Although regular LNG trade started six decades ago, the boom did not begin in earnest until the turn of the millennium. The boom has led to the tripling of LNG exports in the last 20 years. Export growth was strongest in 2010, when exports rose by 20% year on year (BP, 2020; IGU, 2018).

As a result of the corona pandemic, the world economy shrank in 2020 by 3.5%, which led to a decrease of 4–7% in global natural gas consumption (Bresciani et al., 2020; IMF, 2021; Sampson, 2020). The global march of LNG has also slowed down due to the pandemic. However, a survey of the world's largest LNG consumers indicates that the slump in international LNG trade is likely to be temporary (Agosta et al., 2020).

The impetus for this article comes from the LNG boom of this millennium and the EU's quarter-share of global LNG trade. The main objective of the article is to describe how the role of natural gas—and of LNG in particular—has developed in the European Union since the start of the millennium.

This chapter consists of two parts. The first part discusses the role of natural gas in the EU's energy supply. The second part delves into the (r)evolution of LNG.

Natural Gas in the EU

Global natural gas consumption was nearly 4,000 bcm in 2019, which is over 60% more than at the start of the millennium. The EU's share of global natural gas consumption was 12% in 2019.[1] In other words, the EU28 consumed some 480 bcm of natural gas. The three largest gas consumers of the EU28 were Germany, the UK and Italy. Their combined consumption—approximately 240 bcm—amounted to half of the EU's total consumption. The UK alone consumed nearly 80 bcm of natural gas in the last year of the past decade (BP, 2020). Although the

[1] Europe, excluding Russia, accounted for less than two percent of the globe's total proved natural gas reserves in 2019 (BP, 2020).

EU's total gas consumption fell by three percent in 2020, most probably it will increase again as the Union recovers from the pandemic and member states embark on the carbon-neutral energy policy (European Commission, 2020c).[2]

In 2020, the EU member states managed to supply less than 15% of their gas consumption with their own production, i.e. member states had to buy in over 85% of their natural gas consumption from outside of the Union. Gas import dependence will increase in the future as a result of the exit of the UK, which was the largest gas producer within the EU28. In addition to Brexit, it should also be noted that gas production by current member states is nosediving. The EU's gas production fell by nearly a quarter in 2020, and continues to fall (European Commission, 2020c).[3]

This apparent trend is supported by the fact that in 2020, the contemporary EU's largest gas producer, the Netherlands, only produced less than 25 bcm, which is a third its production volume ten years earlier (BP, 2020; European Commission, 2020c). The Dutch gas production will continue to decrease, as the Dutch Government has announced that, due to tremors, it will close down regular production at Groningen, the EU's largest natural gas field, in 2022. The final decision on the shutdown of regular production is expected in autumn 2021 (Meijer, 2019, 2021). In recent years, Groningen has supplied three quarters of the Dutch natural gas production (DW, 2018; BP, 2020).

The rapid weakening of the EU's gas independence is aptly illustrated by the fact that at the start of the millennium, member states were still able to produce a third of the EU's gas consumption. Today, the figure has fallen to less than a half of that. Gas production by the EU member states could fall to five percent of the EU's total consumption by the end of the current decade, which would bring the EU's gas import dependence to the same level as its oil import dependence (European Commission, 2020a; Eurostat, 2020b).

Even though the EU's gas production has decreased sharply, the share of gas in its energy consumption has increased. In 2018, the share of natural gas was 22% of the gross inland consumption of the EU27, which is 1.5 percentage points higher than at the start of the millennium

[2] In 2020, natural gas consumption of the EU27 was 394 bcm (European Commission, 2020c).

[3] In 2020, the EU27 produced 54 bcm of natural gas (European Commission, 2020c).

(European Commission, 2020a).[4] Although the percentage growth may appear modest, it is worth noting that in terms of volume, the EU's gas consumption increased by some 50 bcm between 2014 and 2020 (European Commission, 2020c). It is likely that natural gas and renewables will increase their share of the EU's energy consumption in conjunction with the Union's efforts to reduce its carbon dioxide emissions over the next three decades, as '*the EU aims to be climate-neutral by 2050—an economy with net-zero greenhouse gas emissions*' (European Commission, 2021a).

As a result of the carbon-neutrality goal, the share of renewables in the EU's energy consumption will increase significantly. The EU's target is to have renewables covering 32% of energy consumption by 2030 (European Commission, 2021b). In 2018, the share of renewables in the EU was 15%. The goal is highly ambitious but not entirely unrealistic. The possibility of a successful green revolution is supported by the fact that at the beginning of the millennium, renewables amounted to only six percent of the current member states' energy consumption. This means that the share of renewables has grown 2.5-fold in just two decades (European Commission, 2020a). An increased share of renewables in the EU's energy supply does not mean just a more environmentally friendly energy policy, but also reduced dependence on imported energy.

Map 2.1 shows the share of natural gas in primary energy consumption in 2019. The map illustrates the great variance of gas dependence between member states. For example, Cyprus does not use any natural gas, whereas in Malta, which has the highest gas dependence in the EU, the share of natural gas was half of the country's energy supply (BP, 2020; IEA, 2020).

In Belarus, one of the EU's eastern neighbours, natural gas dependence is even higher than in Malta. The share of natural gas in Belarus is two thirds of the country's primary energy consumption. Because Belarus imports all of its natural gas from Russia, its energy supply is to a great extent dependent on Moscow (BP, 2020). The geopolitical status of Belarus was weakened by the completion of the LNG terminal in the Kaliningrad region in January 2019. The Kaliningrad region is no longer dependent on gas transit through Belarus and Lithuania, since the LNG

[4] The share of natural gas of the EU's primary energy consumption is around two percentage points lower than the global average. In other words, the EU is less orientated towards natural gas than the world on average (BP, 2020).

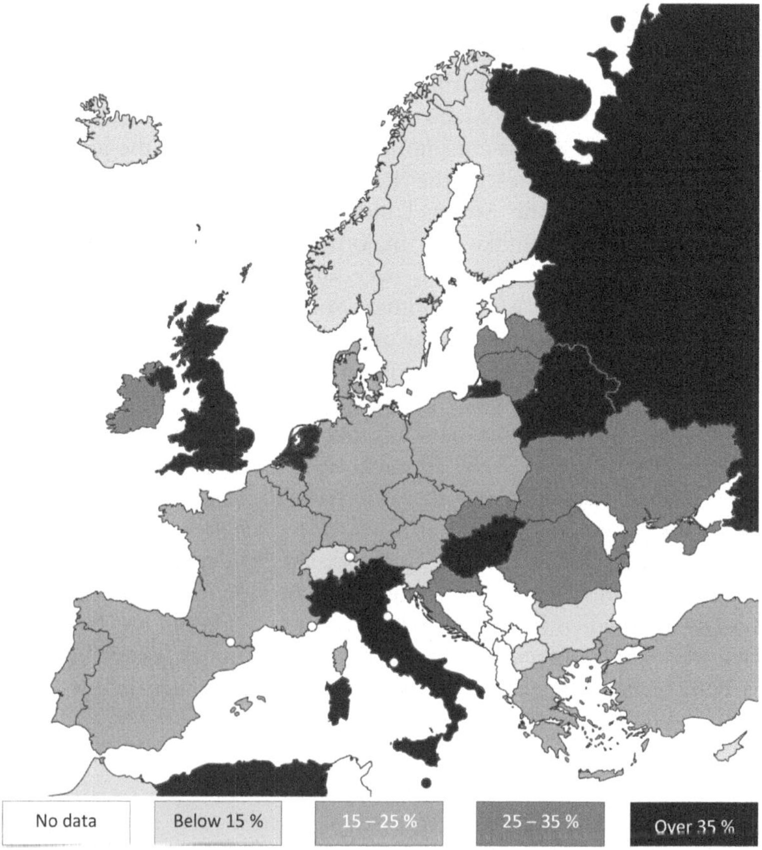

Map 2.1 A share of natural gas in primary energy consumption in Europe in 2019 (%) (*Source* The Author, based on BP, 2020; IEA, 2021a; mapchart.net, 2021)

unit in Kaliningrad enables the Kremlin to deliver gas to its exclave—situated between Lithuania and Poland—by shipping LNG via the Baltic Sea

(GIE, 2019).[5] Therefore, LNG has also improved the energy security of Russia, the world's largest energy exporter.

In 2019, the share of natural gas exceeded 35% of energy consumption in Hungary, Italy, Malta and the Netherlands (BP, 2020; IEA, 2021a). In Hungary, gas consumption has its origins in the joint projects of the CMEA countries in the 1960s, which saw the construction of gas pipelines from the Soviet Union to Central and Eastern Europe and further west.[6] Unlike the majority of the former socialist countries, Hungary has not found it necessary to reduce its dependence on gas imports from Russia, the primary successor of the Soviet Union. In Italy, the share of natural gas has grown gradually over the last 50 years. At the beginning on the 1970s, natural gas amounted to less than ten percent of Italy's primary energy consumption. Today, its share is as high as 40% (BP, 2020). Malta has only been using natural gas since 2017, when its first and only LNG terminal was opened (GIE, 2019). Due to Malta's small economy, the share of natural gas in the country's total energy supply reached nearly 50% just one year after the opening of the terminal (IEA, 2021a). In the Netherlands, gas dependence rose rapidly when the country increased its own gas production in the late 1960s. Gas has retained its importance despite the steep fall in the Netherlands' own production in recent years. In 2010, the country was still producing 75 bcm of natural gas. Today, its production has fallen below 25 bcm,

[5] The FSRU in the Kaliningrad region has an annual capacity of nearly four billion cubic metres (GIE, 2019), while the region's gas consumption is around two billion cubic metres (Usanov & Kharin, 2014). At the 50% capacity utilisation rate, the FSRU could cover the entire gas consumption of the region, i.e. without gas transit via Belarus and Lithuania. However, the FSRU has not been used to supply energy to the region, except during test runs. In fact, at the start of 2021, the Kaliningrad FSRU unit was leased out for LNG transit between Africa and China (Pipeline & Gas Journal, 2021), which suggests that, despite the cold relations between the EU and Russia, the geopolitical situation in Europe has not reached a point where Russia would deem it necessary to return the FSRU to Kaliningrad.

[6] The Bratsvo (Brotherhood) pipeline was completed in the late 1960s, and Soyuz (Union) in the latter half of the 1970s. Both pipelines travel across Ukraine to the European Union (UA Transmission System Operator, 2021). Further pipelines have been built from Russia to the west, including Yamal-Europe across Belarus (1996), Blue Stream beneath the Black Sea to Turkey (2003), the sub-Baltic Sea pipeline Nord Stream to Germany (2011) and a second sub-Black Sea pipeline to Turkey, TurkStream (2020) (EIA, 2021; Gazprom, 2021a).

and will continue to fall as the Netherlands is set to close down the EU's largest gas field in Groningen in 2022 (BP, 2020).

If the four aforementioned countries are the most gas addicted, the other extreme is represented by Cyprus, Sweden, Bulgaria, Estonia, Finland and Slovenia. In these six countries, the share of gas in primary energy consumption is fairly low, less than 15%. At the time of writing, Cyprus does not consume gas at all, but its first LNG import terminal is set to open in 2022 (NS Energy, 2020). In Sweden, the share of gas is only a couple of percent. In fact, natural gas has never been a strategic energy source in Sweden. The situation is different in Bulgaria, Estonia and Finland. In these countries, the share of gas has decreased since the dissolution of the Soviet Union. Bulgaria and Estonia appear to have consciously sought to reduce their dependence on Russian energy supplies. In Finland, the main reason for the reduction in gas consumption is the preference towards domestic fuels—such as biogas—instead of gas imported from Russia. This preference is enforced by stricter taxation of natural gas. In Slovenia, natural gas has held its position despite the dissolution of the Soviet Union. Its share of Slovenia's primary energy consumption has remained around ten percent for the past three decades (BP, 2020).

In the remaining 17 member states, the share of natural gas in primary energy consumption ranges between 15 and 35%. The role of natural gas has evolved in these countries in different ways. In Denmark, Latvia, Luxembourg, Romania and Slovakia, the share of natural gas has decreased since the turn of the millennium, whereas in Croatia, Germany, Greece, Ireland, Poland, Portugal and Spain it has increased. The share of natural gas has increased particularly rapidly in Greece, Portugal and Spain. It has more than doubled since the turn of the millennium in these three Mediterranean countries (BP, 2020).

There are several reasons for the different trajectories. In some countries, their own gas production has decreased, which has then led to a smaller gas share of total energy consumption. These countries have compensated for the decrease in gas production with domestically produces renewables instead of importing gas. Similarly, certain eastern member states of the EU have sought to curb Russia's economic leverage by buying less gas from Russia, which has decreased the share of natural gas in primary energy consumption.[7] Conversely, in some member states, nuclear power plant closures and reduced coal consumption have increased the share of natural gas and led to more gas imports, especially from Russia. In addition, increased LNG supply and its highly affordable price due to global oversupply have led some EU member states to increase the share of natural gas in their energy mix. This has been evident in the Mediterranean region in particular.

Although the role of natural gas has changed in the 12 member states mentioned above, there has been little change in its strategic importance in Austria, Belgium, Czechia, France and Lithuania between 2000 and 2019. The change between the two years is unremarkable, but it does not mean that there have been no changes in the interim period. Lithuania is a good example.

In 2009, Lithuania closed down the Ignalina nuclear power plant. In the following year, the share of natural gas in the country's primary energy consumption leapt from 30% to almost 45%. After the sudden spike, the situation began to stabilise, and currently the share of natural gas is 'only' a third of the country's primary energy consumption. Another significant change in Lithuania was the opening of the LNG terminal in Klaipeda in December 2014 and the resultant geographical diversification of Lithuania's gas imports. That said, the Klaipeda terminal has not freed Lithuania entirely from Russian natural gas. It should be noted that Lithuania continues to import pipe gas from Russia, and a fifth of its LNG also originates from Russia.

In 2020, 48% of natural gas imported by the EU originated from Russia. Norway's share was 24%. The remainder originated mainly from Qatar, North Africa and the USA. The US share was six percent. Three quarters of the EU's natural gas imports was pipe gas. The remaining quarter was delivered by LNG tankers (European Commission, 2020c).

Pipe gas also dominates in Russian gas imports into the EU. In 2020, the share of pipe gas was 90% versus ten percent for LNG in the EU's gas imports from Russia. In 2020, the first Nord Stream twin pipeline

[7] The Russo-Georgian War (2008) and the Ukraine War (since 2014) have not had a notable impact on the EU's energy purchases from Russia. Although the volume of crude oil imports from Russia fell by approximately 15% between 2010 and 2018, the volumes of gas imports and hard coal imports increased by 25 and 60%, respectively (European Commission, 2020a). It should be noted that in 2019, member states purchased mineral fuels from Russia at a value of nearly EUR 100,000 million, which corresponds to two thirds of the EU's total imports of goods from Russia (European Commission, 2020d).

took over as the main transit route of gas imports from Russia to the EU. The share of Nord Stream was 40%, while the Ukraine transit route delivered 30% of Russia's pipe gas supplies to the EU (European Commission, 2020c). The change is significant from the point of view of the geopolitical balance in Eastern Europe. Before the 2011 completion of the first Nord Stream pipeline, roughly 80% of the EU's gas imports from Russia came via the Ukraine transit route (Henley, 2014). In the 1990s, Ukraine's share was even higher, i.e. approximately 95%. Map 2.2 shows the share of Russian natural gas in EU member states' gas imports in the first half of 2020.

The media, in particular, often draws far-reaching conclusions about the EU's dependence on Russian natural gas solely on the basis of Russia's share in gas imports. Such conclusions are inadequate, as they do not take into account the role of natural gas in individual countries' energy consumption. By combining the two indicators, a somewhat more accurate tool can be provided for the analysis of member states' strategic dependence on Russian gas. The two indicators are examined in Table 2.1.

Table 2.1 shows that Hungary has the highest addiction to Russian natural gas among member states, because natural gas represents a very high proportion of Hungary's energy supply, the country does not produce significant volumes of natural gas, and it imports practically all of its gas supply from Russia. When analysing Hungary's dependence on Russian natural gas, it should be noted that its gas imports have nearly doubled in the past decade, i.e. during Viktor Orbán's premierships (Eurostat, 2021b). On the other hand, the fact that Hungary has a large gas storage capacity is often overlooked in dependence analyses. Hungary's operational storage capacity covers over 60% of its annual gas consumption (GIE, 2018).

Other high-risk consumers of natural gas include Romania, Latvia, Slovakia and Italy. However, closer examination reveals that Romania's dependence on gas imports is very low thanks to its own production, which also means that it has low dependence on natural gas imports from Russia. In fact, Romania's gas import dependence is the second lowest in the EU after Denmark, which continues to be a net exporter of natural gas (Eurostat, 2020b).

Whereas Romania is able to satisfy a large part of its natural gas needs with its own production, the situation is not that good in Latvia and Slovakia. They have to import all of their gas supply from other countries,

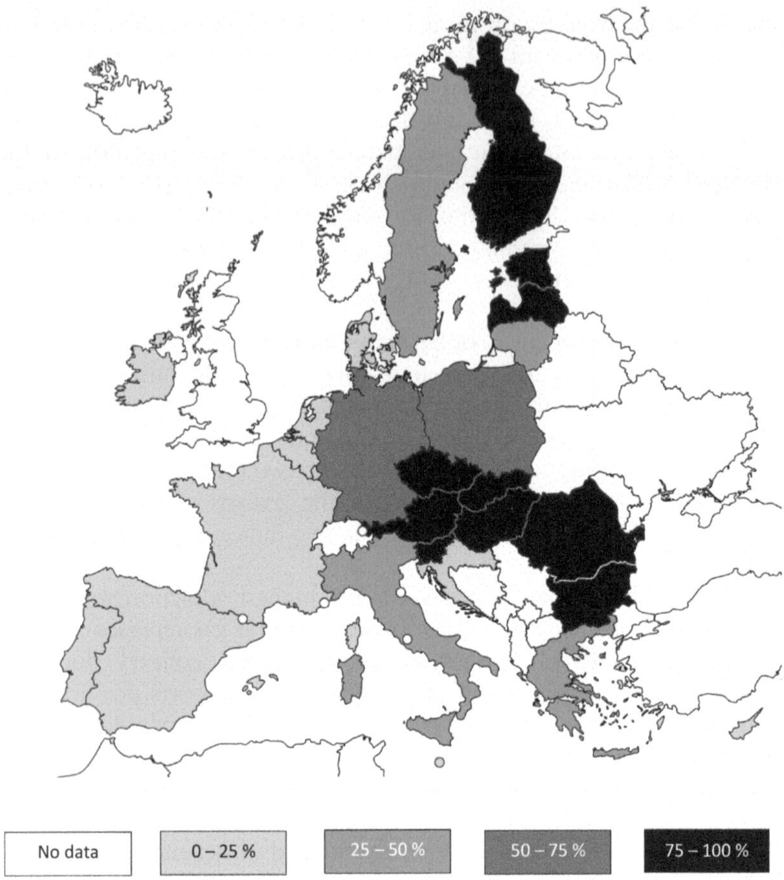

Map 2.2 A share of Russia in the natural gas imports from outside the EU in January–June 2020 (*Source* The Author, based on Eurostat 2020a; mapchart.net, 2021)

which in their case is Russia. Latvia's strategic position is strengthened by the Inčukalns underground gas storage, which could meet the country's natural gas needs for nearly two years.[8] Alternatively, the Inčukalns

[8] It is technically possible to increase the capacity of Inčukalns to 3.2 bcm (Conexus Baltic Grid, 2021).

Table 2.1 The Russia gas dependence matrix of the EU27 in 2019–2020

	Not dependent on Russian gas (0–25% of gas imports)	*Moderately dependent on Russian gas (25–50% of gas imports)*	*Highly dependent on Russian gas (50–75% of gas imports)*	*Extremely dependent on Russian gas (75–100% of gas imports)*
Extremely dependent on gas (over 35% of primary energy consumption)	Malta, **Netherlands**	Italy		Hungary
Highly dependent on gas (25–35% of primary energy consumption)	Croatia,[8] Ireland	Lithuania		Latvia, **Romania**, Slovakia
Moderately dependent on gas (15–25% of primary energy consumption)	Belgium, **Denmark**, France, Luxembourg, Portugal, Spain	Greece	Germany, Poland	Austria, Czechia
Not dependent on gas (below 15% of primary energy consumption)	Cyprus	Sweden		Bulgaria, Estonia, Finland, Slovenia

Note The countries with natural gas import dependence (gas imports/gas consumption) less than 25% have been marked in bold. Denmark is an exception among the exceptions, as it was the EU's only net gas exporter, i.e. its gas exports exceeded its gas imports in 2019
Source The Author, based on BP (2020), Eurostat (2020a), and IEA (2021a)

storage could provide enough gas through even the coldest winter for all three Baltic States and Finland, provided that the storage is full before winter. The Baltic States and Finland could also acquire additional natural gas via Lithuania's LNG terminal in the event of a sudden disruption in Russian gas supply. Slovakia also has significant gas storage that can cover nearly two thirds of its annual gas needs (BP, 2020; GIE, 2018).

[8] Three quarters of Croatia's natural gas came from Hungary in 2019. Because Hungary imports virtually all of its natural gas supply from Russia, it would be appropriate to place an equal sign between deliveries from Hungary and Russia (Eurostat, 2021a). In other words, Croatia should be placed alongside Latvia, Romania and Slovakia in Table 2.1.

Whereas Latvia and Slovakia have to import all gas they consume, Italy's situation is slightly better, as it produces around five percent of its gas consumption. To put it differently, Italy has to import some 95% of its gas. Although nearly half of Italy's gas imports came from Russia in 2019, the country's strategic dependence on Russian gas is alleviated by the pipelines from Algeria, Azerbaijan and Libya, Italy's LNG terminals and the gas storage facilities which can hold a quarter of Italy's annual gas needs (GIE, 2018; Eurostat, 2021a).[10]

The total capacity of operational gas storage facilities in the EU was approximately 100 bcm in 2018. It would last the EU for two very cold winter months, provided that the storage facilities are full before the winter season (Table 2.2).[11]

The above analysis shows that when assessing strategic dependence on Russian gas, at least the following five factors should be taken into account: (1) the share of natural gas in total energy consumption, (2) the share of imported natural gas in gas consumption or, conversely, the share of the country's own production, (3) the share of Russian gas in imports, (4) the capacity and fill rate of gas storages, and (5) how extensively and rapidly alternative energy sources can be accessed in the event of a sudden disruption in the supply of gas from Russia.

Whichever method is used to assess the EU's dependence on Russian natural gas, it is clear that the Union's energy supply would face great difficulty if Russia were to completely stop delivering energy to the Union. As things stand, the EU would be unable to compensate for a complete energy supply stoppage from Russia with its own production or by importing energy from other countries.

[10] The Trans-Mediterranean natural gas (Transmed) pipeline is nearly a 2,500-kilometre pipe from Algeria via Tunisia to Italy. The construction of the pipe was completed in 1983. The annual capacity of the pipe is more than 30 bcm (Hydrocarbons Technology, 2021). In turn, the 500-kilometre Greenstream underwater pipeline connects Libya and Italy. The annual capacity of this pipe is over ten billion cubic metres per year (GEM, 2020). Due to the social turbulence in North African countries after the Arab Spring in 2011, supply cuts and supply irregularities have occurred in the pipe between Libya and Italy. In addition to the North African pipes, Trans Adriatic Pipeline (TAP), connecting Azerbaijan via Turkey, Greece and Albania to Italy was put into operation in December 2020 (IGU, 2021). The current operational capacity of the pipe is ten billion cubic metres but the pipe can be expanded to deliver 20 bcm per annum (TAP, 2021). TAP began its operation in December 2020 (European Commission, 2020c).

[11] In January 2020, the EU consumed 50 bcm of natural gas (European Commission, 2020c).

Table 2.2 Natural gas storages in the EU27 in 2018 (bcm)

	Operational capacity	*Capacity under construction*	*Planned capacity*	*Total capacity*	*Operational capacity/consumption 2019 (%)*
Austria	8.4			8.4	94
Belgium	0.8			0.8	5
Bulgaria	0.6		1.0	1.6	21
Croatia	0.5		0.1	0.6	17
Cyprus				0.0	0
Czechia	3.7	0.2		3.9	45
Denmark	0.9			0.9	31
Estonia				0.0	0
Finland				0.0	0
France	12.1		0.4	12.5	28
Germany	23.7	0.0	0.9	24.6	27
Greece			0.4	0.4	0
Hungary	6.2			6.2	63
Ireland				0.0	0
Italy	17.8	3.0	3.7	24.5	25
Latvia	2.2			2.2	169
Lithuania				0.0	0
Luxembourg				0.0	0
Malta				0.0	0
Netherlands	11.8		0.1	11.9	32
Poland	3.3	0.2	0.8	4.2	16
Portugal	0.3	0.0		0.3	5
Romania	3.1		1.1	4.2	28
Slovakia	3.2		0.3	3.6	65
Slovenia				0.0	0
Spain	2.9			2.9	8
Sweden	0.0			0.0	1
Total	101.6	3.3	8.8	113.8	28

Source The Author, based on GIE, 2018; BP, 2020

It should be noted that the EU also imports other energy supplies from Russia, and not just natural gas. Russia contributes approximately 20% of the EU's uranium imports, 30% of crude oil imports and 40% of coal imports (Euratom Supply Agency, 2020; European Commission, 2020a,

2020b).[12] Overall, Russian energy covers a quarter of the EU's primary energy consumption, which means that over 100 million EU citizens are entirely dependent on Russian energy. Russia's share in the EU's energy supply has grown far too high due to the drop in the EU's own energy production and its eastern enlargements.[13] The EU's excessive energy dependence on Russia limits the Union's freedom in foreign policy and even weakens its cohesion.

Although Russia depends on income from its energy exports, it should be noted that the dependencies of the EU and Russia are asymmetrical in terms of time. In winter, energy supply in the EU would descend into chaos in a matter of weeks if Russia decided to stop energy deliveries. Russia's reserve funds would delay the impact of loss of revenue from energy exports further into the future, because, as the following analysis shows, Russia is not immediately dependent on its gas export revenues.

In 2019, oil and natural gas contributed together 40% of Russia's budget revenues (Ministry of Finance, 2021). When assessing specifically the role of natural gas in the federal budget, it should first of all be noted that Russia's revenue from natural gas does not come exclusively from exports, as the federal budget also gets domestic tax revenues from natural gas. Secondly, it should be noted that natural gas exports

[12] China, Russia's eastern neighbour, is considerably less dependent on Russian fossil fuels compared to the EU. Russia contributes only 15% of China's crude oil imports and two percent of its oil product imports. In 2019, Russia contributed just three percent of China's natural gas imports, including LNG. Although Russia's share in China's natural gas imports is set to increase in the coming years, China's dependence on Russian energy will still be nowhere near as high as the European Union's dependence (BP, 2020; Liuhto, 2019). On the other hand, China is dependent on natural gas imports, although currently not specifically on imports from Russia. In 2019, China's gas import dependence was already 45%. Ten years earlier, it was only 15% (O'Sullivan, 2021).

[13] The EU as a whole is not particularly dependent on electricity imports from third countries (European Commission, 2019b; Eurostat, 2020c). Finland and Lithuania are the only member states currently importing electricity from Russia (INTERRAO, 2021). The share of Russian electricity in Finland's electricity consumption was only around three percent in 2020 (Finnish Energy, 2020). In Lithuania, the share of electricity imported from Russia is significantly higher. In 2018, it was approximately a third of Lithuania's electricity consumption (IAEA, 2020; INTERRAO, 2021). On the other hand, although Lithuania imported six terawatt hours of electricity from Russia, it exported four terawatt hours to other countries according to 2019 figures (INTERRAO, 2021; KNOEMA, 2021). Since electricity is perhaps the most sensitive energy to react to geopolitical changes, reducing its import dependence should be among the European Commission's top priorities.

contribute significantly less budget revenue than oil exports. Taking the year 2020 as an example, Russia's oil export revenues rose to approximately USD 120 billion, whereas natural gas exports contributed only a quarter of that (Liuhto, 2020c; Bank of Russia, 2021). Thirdly, it should be noted that one fifth of Russia's natural gas exports are destined outside of Europe, and the volume of these exports—especially to Asia—is increasing (BP, 2020). Although the author did not have access to detailed budget accounts of the Russian Federation, the available information indicates that natural gas exports to the EU contribute less than five percent of Russia's federal budget revenue. In addition, it should be noted that Russia has considerable reserve funds. At the beginning of 2021, the value of the funds was USD 180 billion (BOFIT, 2021). Since Russia's budget revenue was around USD 250 billion in 2020 (Ministry of Finance, 2021; TASS, 2021), the reserve funds would cover nearly two years of complete loss of budget revenue from oil and natural gas. To put it differently, the value of Russia's reserve funds at the beginning of 2021 was over five times the value of Russia's total revenues from natural gas exports in 2020 (Bank of Russia, 2021; BOFIT, 2021).

This simple calculation of energy dependence shows that the EU is more dependent on Russia than vice versa. In addition, the EU's dependence on Russia has an immediate effect, whereas Russia is dependent on the EU in the long term or until it is able to cut the EU's share in its exports. The analysis of the EU's role in Russia's exports shows that in 2020, the share of the EU27 in Russia's exports was only 34%, which is 17 percentage points lower than in 2013 before the start of the Ukraine War (Customs Russia, 2021a, 2021b). And further, when analysing Russia's dependence on the EU, it should be noted that since the turn of the millennium Russia has systematically reduced its dependence on exports to the EU by constructing oil and gas pipelines to China (Liuhto, 2019, 2020a, 2020b).

If Russia's aggressive foreign policy and slip away from democratic principles have led to a new low in EU-Russia relations, on the other hand the EU has a stable and close relationship with Europe's other energy superpower, Norway. In 2020, Norway was the EU's second largest natural gas supplier, with a 24% share (European Commission, 2020c). Although Norway is the world's fourth largest natural gas exporter after Russia, Qatar and the USA, it primarily exports to Europe rather than globally (BP, 2020). In other words, the majority of Norway's exports are destined to the EU or the UK. Another distinct feature of Norway's energy exports is that the share of LNG in its total natural gas exports was only six percent in 2019 (BP, 2020). Since Norway exports its gas mostly by pipelines, it is clear that its share of the EU's LNG imports cannot increase significantly. According to IGU (2020a), Norway's share of the LNG imports of all European countries was only five percent in 2019.[14]

Although Norway is a major supplier of natural gas to the EU, forecasts indicate that its natural gas production will fall to just over 90 bcm by the start of the 2030s—a significant drop from the peak of 2017, when Norway produced over 120 bcm of natural gas (BP, 2020; Hall, 2018). Chapter 6 contains detailed discussion of Norway's natural gas production and exports, and therefore no further discussion of the current state and future of Norwegian natural gas is provided here.

In addition to Russia and Norway, LNG was another important 'source' of natural gas. LNG's share of the EU's natural gas imports was a quarter in 2020 (European Commission, 2020c). A role of LNG in the EU is examined more closely in the following section.

Liquefied Natural Gas in the EU

In 2019, the global volume of natural gas trade was nearly 1,300 bcm, which means that a third of all natural gas produced in the world was exported to another country. The share of LNG in international gas exports has increased. In 2000, the volume of international LNG trade was 140 bcm. By 2019, it had risen to 485 bcm, which represents 40% of the total global trade of natural gas. Ten years earlier, LNG's share had been ten percentage points lower (BP, 2011, 2020). Some 20 years from now the share of LNG in natural gas trade will be close to 60% (IGU, 2020b). RD Shell expects global LNG demand to reach 950 bcm by 2040 (OGJ, 2021b).

The bulk of natural gas trade across EU borders still takes place via pipelines. However, the situation is evolving rapidly. At the turn of the millennium, the share of LNG was just over ten percent of the EU28's natural gas imports from outside the Union. By 2020, it had risen to a quarter (European Commission, 2019a, 2020c).

[14] In the 4th quarter of 2020, Norway's share in the EU's LNG imports was just 0.1% due to a fire incident in the Hammerfest LNG plant. The plant is estimate to work normally in October 2021 (European Commission, 2020c).

To compare, it should be noted that LNG contributed only two percent of the US natural gas imports. In China, the share of LNG in natural gas imports was over 60% in 2019 (BP, 2020). On the other hand, the share of pipeline gas is set to increase, as Russia opened a gas pipeline with a capacity of nearly 40 bcm towards China in December 2019, and there are plans to increase pipeline capacity in the coming years (Afanasiev, 2020; Gazprom, 2021b).[15] In the light of current export volumes, the pipeline capacity expansion may seem odd at first glance, as Russia exported less than five billion cubic metres of pipeline gas to China in 2020 (Argus Media, 2020). Russia is expanding its export capacity to China despite the low export volumes, because the Russian leadership believes that China's gas consumption will increase as the country aims for carbon neutrality by 2060 (McGrath, 2020). In addition to economic motives, the Russian leadership also seeks to reinforce Russia's geopolitical status in the eyes of its eastern neighbour through energy exports.

Spain, France, Italy, the Netherlands and Belgium were the EU's largest LNG importers in 2020. These countries' combined share of the Union's LNG imports was over 80%. The three largest suppliers of LNG to the EU were the USA, Qatar and Russia.[16] These three countries supplied almost two thirds of LNG in the EU. In 2020, the EU's LNG imports declined by five percent. In terms of volume, the EU27's LNG imports totalled to 84 bcm (European Commission, 2020c).

Although LNG represents a quarter of the EU's natural gas imports, it should be noted that half of the current 27 EU member states did not import any LNG in 2019 (Table 2.3). LNG's absence from the energy mix of these 14 member states is explained by the fact that five of them—Austria, Czechia, Hungary, Luxembourg and Slovakia—do not have any coastline and are therefore unable to build LNG import ports. Austria,

[15] '*China is aiming to grow its transmission pipeline network by 60% by 2025. ... China is also aiming to raise storage capacity to 10% of its demand*' (IGU, 2020b, 5). "*China is aiming to grow its transmission pipeline network by 60% by 2025. ...China is also aiming to raise storage capacity to 10% of its demand*" (IGU, 2020b, 5). China imported over 130 bcm of natural gas in 2019 (BP, 2020).

[16] The value of the US LNG supply to the EU in 2019 was EUR 2.6 billion (European Commission, 2019a), which corresponds to only one percent of the total value of goods exports from the USA to the EU (European Commission, 2020e). Even if the US LNG exports to the EU may grow, the USA would still see the LNG exports more as a way to protect NATO partners from Russia's leverage, rather than as a money-making opportunity.

Table 2.3 LNG in the natural gas imports of the 27 EU member states in 2019

	Natural gas imports (bcm)	*LNG share in gas imports (%)*	*Three main countries supplying LNG and their share in the LNG imports*
Austria	14.2	0	
Belgium	23.2	29	Qatar (65%), Russia (28%), USA (5%)
Bulgaria	2.9	0	
Croatia	2.0	0	
Cyprus	0.0	0	
Czechia	9.5	0	
Denmark	1.1	0	
Estonia	0.5	5	No data
Finland	2.6	7	Russia (64%), Norway (21%), re-exports received (14%)
France	55.0	37	Russia (32%), Nigeria (19%), Algeria (17%)
Germany	94.8	0	
Greece	5.2	54	Algeria (19%), Qatar (19%), Norway (19%)
Hungary	18.6	0	
Ireland	2.9	0	
Italy	71.1	19	Qatar (48%), Algeria (22%), USA (12%)
Latvia	1.4	0	
Lithuania	2.7	57	Norway (71%), Russia (22%), USA (5%)
Luxembourg	0.8	0	
Malta	0.4	100	Trinidad and Tobago (68%), Norway (16%), Egypt (14%)
Netherlands	59.3	18	Russia (53%), USA (25%), Peru (6%)
Poland	17.7	20	Qatar (68%), USA (27%), Norway (5%)
Portugal	6.1	92	Nigeria (58%), USA (23%), Qatar (12%)
Romania	2.7	0	

(continued)

Table 2.3 (continued)

	Natural gas imports (bcm)	*LNG share in gas imports (%)*	*Three main countries supplying LNG and their share in the LNG imports*
Slovakia	6.7	0	
Slovenia	0.9	0	
Spain	37.2	58	Qatar (20%), Nigeria (20%), USA (20%)
Sweden	1.1	28	Norway (38%), Russia (31%), re-exports received (31%)

Note The natural gas imports include the imports from another EU country as well
Source The Author, based on GIIGNL, 2020; Eurostat, 2021b

Czechia, Hungary and Slovakia import all or most of their natural gas via pipelines from Russia (Eurostat, 2020a; Gazprom, 2020). In addition to these four central member states, Luxembourg—which is nestled among Belgium, France and Germany—also did not import any LNG. In 2019, Luxembourg imported only pipe gas via Belgium or Germany. Luxembourg's natural gas imports consist of three rather similarly sized components. One third was imported from other member states, one third from Norway and one third from Russia (Eurostat, 2021a, 2021b).

History as well as geography explains why some member states do not consume LNG. Of the fourteen member states that consume only pipe gas, eight are former CMEA countries, over which the Soviet Union exerted control by way of pipelines. Three of the eight countries are landlocked: Czechia, Hungary and Slovakia. In other words, five ex-socialist countries that consume only pipe gas have a coastline: Bulgaria, Romania, Latvia, Slovenia and Croatia.

The two member states that have coastline on the Black Sea—Bulgaria and Romania—have no plans, at least not officially, to build LNG port terminals. Latvia has plans for an FSRU, but currently it looks like its large-scale LNG port initiative will be replaced by gas collaboration between the Baltic States and Finland (GLE, 2019). Latvia's LNG plans are discussed in more detail in Chapter 9. Slovenia has also continued with pipe gas due to the country's low consumption of natural gas. For Croatia, the data in Table 2.3 is out of date, as its first LNG terminal received the first LNG delivery on the 1st of January 2021. Croatia's LNG terminal will reduce the country's dependence on pipe gas, which in its case means reduced dependence on Russia. The capacity of Croatia's LNG terminal is 2.6 bcm, which exceeds the country's annual gas consumption (BP, 2020; LNG Croatia, 2021).

Of the ex-socialist countries with coastline, Lithuania and Poland opened LNG terminals in the mid-2010s. Lithuania opened an FSRU unit in Klaipeda in 2014 (Jakštas, 2019; Liuhto, 2015). The unit's capacity is four billion cubic metres, which means that the terminal is able to cover Lithuania's annual gas needs at the 50% capacity utilisation rate.[17] Poland opened a five-billion-cubic-metre natural gas terminal in Świnoujście in the northwest of the country in 2016. Poland intends to increase the unit's capacity to at least 7.5 bcm—possibly even to ten billion cubic metres. In addition to expanding the Świnoujście unit, Poland plans to open an FSRU with a capacity of over four billion cubic metres in Gdańskin the near future. The combined capacity of the two units would in theory cover over half of Poland's natural gas consumption (BP, 2020; GIE, 2019). The LNG units of Poland and Lithuania are discussed in more detail in Chapters 7 and 8, and therefore the terminals and their strategic importance are not covered in further detail here.

Currently, Cyprus does not consume any natural gas, and therefore understandably does not have an LNG terminal (IEA, 2021b). The situation will change in 2022 with the completion of the first LNG import terminal in Cyprus (NS Energy, 2020). The terminal's annual capacity will be 2.4 bcm, which will give natural gas an important role in the energy supply of the island state and its million citizens (GLE, 2019). Confusingly, Cyprus appears to have no plans for an LNG export terminal, even though it is planning to start natural gas production in its territorial waters. It is possible that Cyprus is refraining from relying too much on natural gas production because Turkey, a NATO member, has sought to obstruct the start of Cypriot offshore production (Cyprus Profile, 2020; Pitel & Sheppard, 2020; GEM, 2021a).[18] Co-operation between Cyprus

[17] The capacity utilisation rate of Lithuania's terminal was just under 50% in 2019 (IGU, 2020a).

[18] Several significant offshore gas fields have been found in the vicinity of Cyprus, with estimated combined reserves in excess of 500 bcm (Henderson, 2019). For comparison, Norway's proved gas reserves are 1,500 bcm (BP, 2020).

and Israel increases the possibility of natural gas production around Cyprus becoming a reality (Geropoulos, 2021).

In addition to Cyprus, the northern maritime country Denmark also does not have its own LNG terminal or any apparent plans to acquire one (GLE, 2019). There are many reasons for Denmark's reluctance to build an LNG import terminal. First of all, Denmark is expected to remain a net exporter of natural gas until at least 2035 (DEA, 2018; Elliott & Hunter, 2020). Secondly, the country's location adjacent to another gas producer, Norway, supports pipe gas as a solution. And thirdly, it appears that instead of compensating for the reduction in its natural gas production with imported gas, Denmark intends to take a leap from fossil fuels to renewables as it winds down its oil and gas production (Greenpeace, 2020; Hall, 2020).

In terms of natural gas, Germany is a peculiarity. It is the largest consumer of natural gas in the EU and the second largest in the world after China (Liuhto, 2020c). In spite of its gigantic gas import volumes, Germany has not built a single LNG terminal on its soil. Germany's natural gas supply currently consists of the country's own production, which covers five percent of its gas consumption, and imports—95%—by pipelines from other countries. In 2019, approximately half of Germany's gas imports came from Russia, one quarter came from Norway, and the remaining quarter arrived from the Netherlands. Germany's gas imports from the Netherlands are about to change in the coming years, as the Dutch gas production plummets. In 2019, Germany imported nearly 25 bcm of natural gas from the Netherlands (BP, 2020).[19]

In addition to the production decline in the Netherlands, another headache for Germany is the fact that Germany's gas consumption is likely to increase after the planned closure of its nuclear power plants by the end of 2022 (World Nuclear Association, 2019). In order to cover for the loss of nuclear energy exclusively with natural gas, Germany would have to import nearly 20 bcm more than today (BP, 2020; Liuhto, 2020c). That said, even an increase of 45 bcm would not necessarily require the

[19] When analysing Germany's gas imports from the Netherlands, it is important to remember that in 2019, the Netherlands was already importing around a quarter of its natural gas from Russia, and the share of Russian gas is likely to grow significantly in the coming years (Eurostat, 2021a).

construction of Nord Stream 2, as the Ukraine pipeline network has sufficient unused capacity.[20] The pipeline network of Ukraine and its capacity are discussed in Chapter 5.

In recent years, Germany has been planning four LNG terminals. The proposed locations are Brunsbüttel, Rostock, Stade and Wilhelmshaven (GIE, 2019). In the plans, the size of the Brunsbüttel terminal is eight billion cubic metres, but the final decision on the investment is not expected until mid-2021, and therefore the terminal would not be completed in 2022 as originally scheduled (German LNG Terminal, 2021; GLE, 2019). Russian Novatek has announced that it will build a medium-scale LNG import terminal in Rostock by 2023. Set to be the only German terminal on the Baltic Sea coast, the unit has a planned capacity of 0.4 bcm (PortNews, 2020). The Stade facility is the largest of the planned LNG import terminals. The port's planned capacity is 12 bcm. The terminal is expected to open in 2025 (Elliott, 2020, 2021).[21] There are also plans for a ten-billion-cubic-metre LNG import terminal for Wilhelmshaven. Finnish-owned Uniper has announced that it will build an FSRU unit there. However, in late 2020 the future of this LNG terminal seemed quite uncertain, as German city authorities and businesses that use gas had not placed binding LNG orders in sufficient numbers (Bajic, 2020; LNG Wilhelmshaven, 2021). In addition to the corona pandemic, the possible completion by the end of 2021 of the Nord Stream 2 gas pipeline also adds to the uncertainty (Assenova, 2021).

On the other hand, even if Nord Stream 2 were not to open, the majority of Germany's natural gas imports would still rely on pipelines, as the combined capacity of the four LNG terminals would only cover a third of the volume of Germany's current gas imports (BP, 2020). Since it is certain that not all four terminals will be built, and the ones that are built would not run at 100% capacity, the share of LNG would remain well under ten percent of Germany's natural gas imports by the end of this decade.

Whereas Germany has an unusually reserved stance on LNG, Ireland's relationship with LNG is quite peculiar as well. Natural gas plays an important role in Ireland's energy supply, and yet the island nation

[20] There is some scepticism about the capacity of the Ukraine network to transmit Russian natural gas (Bochkarev, 2021).

[21] The owner of Stade LNG is Hanseatic Energy Hub (GEM, 2021e; HEH, 2021).

consumes no LNG. The reason for the peculiar situation is that Ireland covers over a third of its gas needs with its own production, and the rest comes from the UK via pipelines (GIE, 2019; SEAI, 2021).

For a long time, Ireland had plans for two major LNG terminals, Cork LNG and Shannon LNG. Their combined capacity would have been 12 bcm, and at the 50% capacity utilisation rate they could have supplied all of Ireland's natural gas consumption (BP, 2020). Resistance to the projects from the Green Party was surprisingly strong, and in the end both projects had been shelved by the start of 2021 due to the political opposition (Chapa & Shiryaevskaya, 2021; Crosson, 2020, 2021; Elliott & Weber, 2021; GEM, 2021c, 2021d). Abandoning the LNG terminal projects is not entirely rational in light of Ireland's future energy plans and the decreasing gas production in Great Britain, as the British ability to export its natural gas becomes weaker year by year. However, it appears that, in preventing the construction of the LNG terminals, Ireland wanted to both protect its domestic gas production from foreign competition and make room for renewable sources of energy (DCENR, 2020).

While LNG has no role in the gas imports of Germany and Ireland, the EU member state with the highest share of LNG in its gas imports is Malta. The island nation imports all of its natural gas in a liquefied form, because it has no pipeline connection to gas-producing North African countries and no interconnection to Sicily, which is Italy's gas logistics hub for gas transported from North Africa. Malta's natural gas consumption is very low (less than 0.5 bcm), and therefore the construction of pipelines would not be economically feasible, which means that LNG will hold its monopoly in Malta's natural gas market (Eurostat, 2021a).

Alongside Malta, Portugal also uses primarily the liquefied form of natural gas. In 2019, LNG contributed over 90% of Portugal's gas imports, and its share was growing (Eurostat, 2021b). By 2020, LNG covered 100% of Portuguese gas consumption. In fact, Portugal even exported natural gas to Spain. The strong position of LNG in Portugal shows that LNG can be competitively priced compared with pipe gas, since Portugal's alternative would have been to import more of its gas via pipelines from Algeria via Morocco and Spain (BP, 2020; Gallarati, 2020).[22]

[22] There are two natural gas pipes between Algeria and Spain, namely Medgaz (a 200-kilometre subsea pipe with a capacity of some 8 bcm) and Maghreb-Europe Gas Pipeline

Although Greece, Lithuania and Spain are not as addicted to LNG as Portugal, LNG still covered over half of their natural gas imports. Greece and Spain have a much longer history of using LNG terminals than Lithuania, which opened its FSRU unit in December 2014. Another notable difference is the share of Russia in the LNG imports of these three countries. Russia has no share in the LNG imports of Greece and Spain, whereas in Lithuania, Russian LNG contributed a fifth of the country's LNG imports in 2019 (GIIGNL, 2020).

In Belgium, France and Sweden, LNG covered roughly 30–40% of natural gas imports. Whereas Belgium and France have long traditions of using LNG and it plays a strategic role in their energy supplies, the situation is completely different in Sweden, which has built two small-scale LNG terminals in the past decade. The two small-scale LNG terminals do not have a strategic role in Swedish energy supply, as the share of natural gas in the country's primary energy consumption is only a couple of percent (BP, 2020). What the three countries have in common, however, is the considerable share of Russia in their LNG imports. In 2019, Russian LNG contributed approximately 30% of their LNG imports (GIIGNL, 2020).

In Italy, the Netherlands and Poland, LNG accounts for around one fifth of natural gas imports. Although the percentage is relatively small, the imported volumes are very high: total natural gas imports are around 60–70 bcm in Italy and the Netherlands, and nearly 20 bcm in Poland (Eurostat, 2020a). In Poland and Italy, Russian LNG does not have a significant role, even though Russia dominates the pipeline gas market.[23] In the Netherlands, Russia already contributes half of LNG imports, and its share could well increase as the Dutch gas production plummets (GIIGNL, 2020).

LNG does not have a particularly significant role in the gas imports of Estonia and Finland. In both countries, LNG contributed less than ten percent of total imports of natural gas in 2019. The strategic importance of LNG is further diminished by the fact that natural gas does not play a major role in the two countries' energy consumption. Due to the co-effect of these factors, for Estonia and Finland LNG is more of a maritime

(capacity over 10 bcm). Maghreb-Europe Gas Pipeline travels from Algeria via Morocco to Spain and further to Portugal (EMPL, 2021; NS Energy, 2021).

[23] In 2019, Russia's share of gas imports was over 50% in Poland and nearly 50% in Italy (BP, 2020; Eurostat, 2021a).

fuel than a strategic component of their energy mixes. Nevertheless, the Estonian LNG imports are worth noting and somewhat curious due to the fact that the country has no LNG import terminal, not even a small-scale one, even though it imports LNG. The main reason for the imports appears to be LNG's use as fuel in vehicles and ships (LNG EestiGaas, 2021; Industry, 2019). Whereas Estonia does not have its own LNG terminal, Finland had two relatively small LNG terminals at the time of writing, and a third one was set to open in October 2021 (Hamina LNG, 2020; Finnish Gas Association, 2021). Russian LNG forms the lion's share of LNG imported to Finland, and its share is increasing. In 2020, Russian LNG accounted for approximately 80% of Finland's LNG imports. This represented an increase of 20 percentage points from the previous year (GIIGNL, 2020; Finnish Customs, 2021). LNG in Finland and the Finnish LNG terminals are discussed in more detail in Chapter 10.

In 2019, the combined nominal annual capacity of the EU28's operational LNG terminals was over 210 bcm, of which member states were able to utilise around half (GLE, 2019; Eurostat, 2021b).[24] As a result of Brexit, nearly 50 bcm was lost from the capacity of the EU's LNG terminals, and the combined capacity of the EU27's LNG terminals fell to around 165 bcm (GLE, 2019). Although the EU can import natural gas from/via the UK, it is worth remembering that Great Britain was able to produce only half of its natural gas consumption in 2019, and the production has dropped to a third of what it was at the start of the millennium (BP, 2020). In practice, this means that the EU is not able to increase its reliance on the British LNG terminals in its energy security plans. The British LNG terminals can therefore be set aside in the following analysis of the EU's LNG terminals (Table 2.4).[28]

By May 2019, nine of the current EU27 had built themselves a large-scale LNG import terminal. However, since thirteen member states were consumers of LNG, in practice four member states which consumed

[24] The capacity utilisation rate of the EU's LNG import terminals is slightly higher than the global average. The average global utilisation rate of LNG terminals was approximately 45% in 2019 (IGU, 2020a).

[28] '*The UK has always been playing an important role as berthing site of LNG vessels for continental Europe and shipments are transported to Europe* via*gas interconnectors with Belgium and the Netherlands. However, during the winter period LNG shipments rather serve for domestic consumption in the UK, especially regarding the limited storage capacities*' (European Commission, 2020c, 14).

Table 2.4 Operational large-scale LNG importing terminals in the EU as of May 2019[25]

Country	*Name*	*Start-up year*	*Annual capacity (bcm)*	*Capacity / gas consumption 2019*
Belgium[26]	Zeebrugge LNG	1987	9	0.52
France	Fos-Tonkin LNG	1972	3	0.78
	Montoir-de-Bretagne LNG	1980	10	
	Fos Cavaou LNG	2010	8	
	Dunkerque LNG	2016	13	
Greece	Revithoussa LNG	2000	7	1.37
Italy	Panigaglia LNG	1971	3	0.21
	Porto Levante LNG (OS)	2009	8	
	FSRU OLT Offshore LNG Toscana (F)	2013	4	
Lithuania	FSRU Independence (F)	2014	4	1.82
Netherlands	Gate terminal Rotterdam	2011	12	0.33
Poland	Świnoujście LNG	2016	5	0.25
Portugal	Sines LNG	2004	8	1.31
Spain[27]	Barcelona LNG	1968	17	1.75
	Huelva LNG	1988	12	
	Cartagena LNG	1989	12	
	Bilbao LNG	2003	9	
	Sagunto LNG	2006	9	
	Mugardos LNG	2007	4	

Note The abbreviation 'OS' means an offshore unit and the abbreviation 'F' a floating unit. All the other units are onshore LNG terminals. The British LNG terminals have been excluded from the table above

Source The Author, based on GIE, 2019; BP, 2020; IGU, 2020a; Eurostat, 2021a

[25] One may find the following small-scale and medium-scale units in the EU: Tornio Manga and Pori in Finland, Delimara in Malta, and Lysekil and Nynäshamn in Sweden (GIIGNL, 2020). For a more detailed description of Europe's LNG receiving terminals, see King & Spalding (2018).

[26] The capacity of Zeebrugge LNG terminal is to be expanded by eight billion cubic metres by 2026 (OGJ, 2021a).

[27] El Musel LNG terminal in Gijon with an annual capacity of seven billion cubic metres was completed in 2021 but it was mothballed and it has not been put into operation (GEM, 2021b).

LNG did not have their own large-scale LNG terminal. These countries are Estonia, Finland, Malta and Sweden (GIE, 2019). Estonia has no LNG terminal, and Finland, Malta and Sweden each have small-scale or medium-scale LNG import terminal(s). Malta's small-scale LNG terminal has strategic importance in the energy supply of the country and its half a million citizens.[29]

Belgium, France, Italy and Spain are long-standing consumers of LNG. They opened their first large-scale LNG terminals in the late 1960s and early 1970s. With the exception of Italy, these countries are in theory able to satisfy at least half of their annual natural gas consumption with their LNG terminals. Spain has the highest LNG terminal capacity of the four countries relative to its natural gas consumption. The capacity is nearly double Spain's annual gas consumption. Italy trails behind the other three countries, as the maximum capacity of its LNG terminals can only cover one fifth of its annual gas consumption. The situation will not change in the near future, since the planned eight-billion-cubic-metre LNG port in Sicily appears to have been postponed to an unknown date (GLE, 2019; IGU, 2020a).

Whereas Belgium, France, Italy and Spain have decades of experience with LNG, Greece, Lithuania, Portugal, Poland and the Netherlands have opened their first large-scale LNG import terminals in this millennium (GIE, 2019; IGU, 2020a).

Greece, Lithuania and Portugal have taken great strides in incorporating LNG into their energy mix. In these three countries, the capacity of LNG terminals exceeds annual natural gas consumption (BP, 2020; GIE, 2019). 'The overcapacity' is justified, since in practice the utilisation rate of LNG terminals cannot reach 100%—due to weather conditions, for a start. Poland as a close fourth is set to increase the capacity of its existing LNG terminal in Świnoujście, northwest Poland, to at least 7.5 bcm, and the country is about to open a four-billion-cubic-metre FSRU unit in Gdańsk in the northeast. With the Świnoujście expansion and the new LNG terminal in Gdańsk, the combined capacity of Poland's LNG terminals could cover more than half of the country's current consumption of natural gas in the near future (GLE, 2019; Eurostat, 2020a). In the Netherlands, the gas supply situation is challenging. Natural gas

[29] The Maltese LNG unit has a strategic importance to Malta's energy supply, as the country may satisfy all its natural gas needs with this terminal. Natural gas provided nearly a half of Malta's overall energy supply in 2018 (IEA, 2021a).

contributes a large share of the country's primary energy consumption, but its gas production is about to collapse. Despite the impending collapse in production, gas consumption in the Netherlands has decreased very little. The figures are clear: in the 2010s, natural gas production in the Netherlands has fallen by approximately 50 bcm, while its consumption has reduced by only ten billion cubic metres. In 2019, the Netherlands—the EU's largest natural gas producer—was able to cover 'only' three quarters of its consumption with its own production (BP, 2020). The steep drop in natural gas production will force the Netherlands to both grow its renewable energy production and increase its gas imports (IEA, 2020). Since the Netherlands does not intend to increase substantially its LNG import capacity in the coming years (GLE, 2019; IGU, 2020a), its alternatives are more or less limited to increasing the volume of pipe gas imports. It is unlikely that the Netherlands would be able to increase imports from Norway, and therefore it will probably have to import more gas from Russia. In 2019, Russia covered a quarter of the Dutch natural gas imports, but it is within the realms of possibility that Russia's share could rise considerably from the 2019 level (Eurostat, 2021a).

In addition to the large-scale terminals described in Table 2.4, it is worth mentioning the new LNG terminal with a 2.6-bcm annual capacity, which opened on the Krk Island in Croatia in January 2021 (LNG Croatia, 2021). Cyprus is also currently in the process of building a large-scale LNG terminal. The FSRU unit with a capacity of over two billion cubic metres is expected to open in 2022 (GIIGNL, 2020; NS Energy, 2020).

As at February 2020, the IGU list of LNG terminals currently under construction does not include any projects in the member states apart from the Croatian unit, which opened at the start of 2021, and the terminal under construction in Cyprus. The absence of the German units from the list suggests that their construction will probably be delayed or some projects will be cancelled (IGU, 2020a).

When examining the role of LNG in the EU's energy supply, attention should be paid to LNG tankers as well as import terminals. In late 2019, the world's LNG tanker fleet consisted of approximately 600 vessels, whose combined operational capacity was nearly 90 bcm (GIIGNL, 2020). Despite the fact that the world's largest LNG fleet is owned by one of the EU member states, namely Greece (Hellenic Shipping News, 2019), the European Commission's assessments should include critical examination of the ownership of European LNG fleets and the role of the owner's nationality in terms of the EU's energy security. Although the risks relating to the availability of LNG tankers are ultimately borne by individual governments and owners of LNG import terminals in the EU, the European Commission could perhaps act as a catalyst for increasing LNG tanker ownership in the EU. Co-ownership of tankers by LNG terminal owners in the EU could be one way to increase ownership and thus improve LNG supply security in the EU.

Concluding Remarks

Although the EU27 consumes roughly the same amount of energy as it did at the start of the millennium, the structure of energy consumption in the Union has changed. The shares of oil, coal and nuclear power have decreased, and the shares of renewables and natural gas have increased (European Commission, 2020a). And although consumption of natural gas in the EU fell by three percent in 2020 due to the corona pandemic, the drop is likely to be temporary (European Commission, 2020c). The share of gas in the EU's energy consumption will grow as a result of the Union's actions towards carbon neutrality and Germany closing its nuclear power plants in 2022. After the nuclear power plant closures, in order to make up for the drop in its energy production with natural gas alone, Germany would have to source nearly 20 bcm more than it currently does (BP, 2020).

Despite the growing role of natural gas, the EU's gas self-sufficiency has fallen sharply in this millennium, and it will fall further as the largest producer, the Netherlands, is set to close down the EU's largest gas field in 2022 (Eurostat, 2020b). It is worth emphasising that in 2019, the Netherlands supplied nearly 25 bcm of natural gas to the EU's largest consumer, Germany, whose annual natural gas consumption is around 100 bcm (BP, 2020).

The drop in the EU's own production, combined with increasing demand for natural gas, will lead to an increase in gas imports. Even if LNG imports were to grow, it seems likely that Russia's share in the EU's natural gas imports will rise well above 50% by the end of this decade and will continue to grow in the next decade as the decrease in Norway's gas production accelerates.

Pipelines will continue to be the main way of distribution for Russian natural gas despite the fact that Russia is one of the EU's main suppliers of LNG. At the time of writing, it seems possible that Nord Stream 2 could be completed by September 2021. (Gardner, 2021).

Although the EU is able to cover more than a quarter of its annual natural gas consumption with its gas storage capacity, its strategic dependence on Russian natural gas is very high. Bearing in mind that the EU also imports a significant part of its uranium, oil and coal from Russia, the total share of Russian energy is around a quarter of the EU's total primary energy consumption. The eastern member states of the EU have the highest dependence on Russian energy.

In terms of the EU's future, excessive dependence on authoritarian Russia that engages in aggressive foreign policy would be risky, especially in a scenario where Russia's dependence on the EU decreases as Russia seeks to reduce its dependence on exports to the EU by exporting more to China and other Asian countries. In fact, one would have expected the wars in Georgia and Ukraine to prompt European politician and policymakers to reduce member states' dependence on imports from Russia. This has not happened in all EU member states.

The EU's dependence on Russian energy imports could be reduced in a number of ways. Firstly, it could be done by investing in energy savings, which would reduce the need for imported energy. A second noteworthy way to reduce dependence on Russia is to invest in the production of renewable energy. Renewables currently cover around 15% of the EU's energy consumption. With the Green Deal, the EU aims to double the share of renewables in its energy consumption in less than ten years (European Commission, 2021b). Thirdly, the EU could reduce its dependence on Russian energy by diversifying its energy imports. LNG offers great diversification potential, although it should be remembered that Russia was the EU's third-largest LNG supplier in 2020 (European Commission, 2020c).

At the start of the millennium, LNG's share in European natural gas imports was a bit over ten percent. By 2020, it had risen to a quarter (European Commission, 2019a, 2020c). Future growth of LNG's share is hindered not so much by the lack of LNG import infrastructure, but rather by the new pipelines from Russia towards the west. For example, the completion of TurkStream under the Black Sea may suppress interest in the development of LNG import terminals in Bulgaria and Romania

(Gazprom 2021a).[30] And similarly, the completion of Nord Stream 2 will probably delay or even stop some of the plans for LNG terminals in Germany (Bajic, 2020).

Although Poland is in the process of expanding the capacity of its existing LNG terminal in the northwest and constructing another unit in the northeast, it is possible that no new large-scale LNG receiving terminals will follow in the Baltic Sea basin.[31] The LNG revolution is being hindered in the Baltic Sea region by gas pipelines as well as the possible hydrogen revolution.

The total investment in renewable hydrogen production in Europe is expected to reach EUR 200–500 billion over the next three decades (European Commission, 2020f, 2021c). Although hydrogen currently covers less than two percent of the EU's energy consumption, its share is estimated to reach 13–14% by 2050. This means that in 30 years' time, hydrogen is expected to produce energy volumes equivalent to the combined output of the EU's current 120+ nuclear power plants (Euratom, 2020).

Although hydrogen can play a significant role in the EU's energy supply in 30 years, it is important to remember that 'transitional energy' will be needed in the interim period, which probably means that lower-pollution conventional energy sources such as natural gas will retain their place in the EU's energy supply for some decades yet. And as long as natural gas is a part of the EU's energy mix, so will LNG also continue to have a role in the Union's energy scene.

[30] The EU used half of its LNG import terminal capacity in 2020 (GLE 2019; European Commission 2020c).

[31] Of the four LNG terminals being planned in Germany, only the Rostock unit is on the Baltic Sea coast, and it is not a large-scale unit. The Nordic countries currently have no plans to construct any large-scale terminals on their soil. The large-scale LNG terminal plans of Estonia and Latvia may not come to fruition, and Lithuania has no need for a larger LNG terminal. Russia already has an FSRU unit that can service the Kaliningrad region. In summary, it is possible that after the large-scale LNG projects of Poland, only small-scale and medium-scale LNG import terminals will be constructed in the Baltic Sea region.

References

Afanasiev, V. (2020, November 3). *Gazprom kicks off extension of huge gas export pipeline to China*. Upstream. https://www.upstreamonline.com/field-development/gazprom-kicks-off-extension-of-huge-gas-export-pipeline-to-china/2-1-905523. Accessed 20 February 2021.

Agosta, A., Browne, N., Bruni, G., & Tan, N. (2020, August 17). *How COVID-19 and market changes are shaping LNG buyer preferences*. McKinsey. https://www.mckinsey.com/industries/oil-and-gas/our-insights/how-covid-19-and-market-changes-are-shaping-lng-buyer-preferences. Accessed 10 February 2021.

Argus Media. (2020, December 3). *China extends Russian gas import pipeline: Update*. Argus Media. https://www.argusmedia.com/en/news/2165620-china-extends-russian-gas-import-pipeline-update. Accessed 23 February 2021.

Assenova, M. (2021, February 1). Clouds darkening over Nord Stream two pipeline. *Eurasia Daily Monitor*. https://mailchi.mp/jamestown.org/eurasia-daily-monitor-volume-18-issue-17?e=c87b290143. Accessed 9 February 2021.

Bajic, A. (2020, November 9). *Uniper to re-evaluate Wilhelmshaven LNG plans*. Offshore Energy. https://www.offshore-energy.biz/uniper-to-re-evaluate-wilhelmshaven-lng-plans/. Accessed 9 February 2021.

Bank of Russia. (2021). *Energy exports*. http://cbr.ru/eng/statistics/macro_itm/svs/. Accessed 22 January 2021.

Bochkarev, D. (2021, March 1). *Ukraine might not be ready for the energy transition*. CEENERGY NEWS. https://ceenergynews.com/voices/ukraine-might-not-be-ready-for-the-energy-transition/. Accessed 12 March 2021.

BOFIT. (2021). *Russia statistics*. https://www.bofit.fi/en/monitoring/statistics/russia-statistics/. Accessed 2 March 2021.

BP. (2011). *Statistical Review of World Energy: June 2011*. http://large.stanford.edu/courses/2011/ph240/jan2/docs/bp2011.pdf. Accessed 9 February 2021.

BP. (2020). *Statistical Review of World Energy—All data, 1965–2019*. https://www.bp.com/en/global/corporate/energy-economics/statistical-review-of-world-energy.html. Accessed 22 January 2021.

Bresciani, G., Heiligtag, S., Lambert, P., & Rogers, M. (2020, September 21). *The future of liquefied natural gas: Opportunities for growth*. McKinsey & Company. https://www.mckinsey.com/industries/oil-and-gas/our-insights/the-future-of-liquefied-natural-gas-opportunities-for-growth. Accessed 9 March 2021.

Chapa, S., & Shiryaevskaya, A. (2021, January 17). *Europe turns down more U.S. LNG on greenhouse gas concerns*. World Oil. https://www.worldoil.

com/news/2021/1/15/europe-turns-down-more-us-lng-on-greenhouse-gas-concerns. Accessed 12 March 2021.

Chiu, C.-H. (2008, November 18). *History of the development of LNG technology*. AIChE Annual Conference “Hundred Years of Advancements in Fuels and Petrochemicals”. Philadelphia. http://folk.ntnu.no/skoge/prost/proceedings/aiche-2008/data/papers/P139095.pdf. Accessed 10 February 2021.

Conexus Baltic Grid. (2021). *Inčukalns UGS*. https://www.conexus.lv/incukalns-ugs-459. Accessed 22 January 2021.

Crosson, K. (2020, November 9). *Planning permission for Shannon LNG quashed*. Green News. https://greennews.ie/shannon-lng-planning-permission-quashed/. Accessed 14 February 2021.

Crosson, K. (2021, January 14). *Plans to import fracked gas through Port of Cork scrapped*. Green News. https://greennews.ie/port-of-cork-scrapped-lng-imports/. Accessed 12 March 2021.

Customs Russia. (2021a). *Итогивнешнейторговли с осноонымистранами: Январь - декабрь 2020*. https://customs.gov.ru/folder/511. Accessed 13 February 2021.

Customs Russia. (2021b). *Итогивнешнейторговли с основнымистранами: Январь - декабрь 2013*. https://customs.gov.ru/folder/511. Accessed 8 February 2021.

CyprusProfile. (2020, November). *Harnessing the hydrocarbons potential*. https://www.cyprusprofile.com/sectors/energy-and-environment. Accessed 23 January 2021.

DCENR. (2020). *The White Paper: Ireland’s transition to a low carbon energy future 2015–2030*. Department of Communications, Energy and Natural Resources. https://www.gov.ie/ga/foilsiuchan/550df-the-white-paper-irelands-transition-to-a-low-carbon-energy-future-2015-2030/. Accessed 14 February 2021.

DEA. (2018). *Resource assessment and production forecasts*. Danish Energy Agency. https://ens.dk/sites/ens.dk/files/OlieGas/ressourcer_og_prognoser_20180829_rev_en.pdf. Accessed 28 February 2021.

DW. (2018, March 30). *EU’s biggest gas field set for shutdown*. https://www.dw.com/en/eus-biggest-gas-field-set-for-shutdown/av-43198798. Accessed 13 February 2021.

EestiGaas. (2021). *The leading LNG supply and bunkering expertise in the Baltic Sea region*. https://www.gaas.ee/en/for-business/lng-liquefied-natural-gas/lng-bunkering/. Accessed 20 February 2021.

EIA. (2021, October 31). *Russia*. U.S. Energy Information Administration. https://www.eia.gov/international/analysis/country/RUS. Accessed 24 January 2021.

Elliott, S. (2020, December 9). *German Stade LNG developer launches non-binding import capacity open season*. https://www.spglobal.com/platts/

en/market-insights/latest-news/natural-gas/120920-german-stade-lng-developer-launches-non-binding-import-capacity-open-season. Accessed 14 February 2021.

Elliott, S. (2021, February 22). *Interest in Germany's Stade LNG plant supports 'full planned capacity': Developer*. https://www.spglobal.com/platts/en/market-insights/latest-news/coal/022221-interest-in-germanys-stade-lng-plant-supports-full-planned-capacity-developer. Accessed 23 February 2021.

Elliott, S., & Hunter, N. (2020). *Denmark's Tyra gas field restart pushed back to June 2023: Total*. SPGlobal. https://www.spglobal.com/platts/en/market-insights/latest-news/natural-gas/110620-denmarks-tyra-gas-field-restart-pushed-back-to-june-2023-total. Accessed 28 February 2021.

Elliott, S., & Weber, H. (2021). *New blow for Irish LNG as plans shelved for floating terminal at Cork*. https://www.spglobal.com/platts/en/market-insights/latest-news/natural-gas/011421-new-blow-for-irish-lng-as-plans-shelved-for-floating-terminal-at-cork. Accessed 12 March 2021.

EMPL. (2021). *The Maghreb-Europe Gas Pipeline is a system of high-pressure gas pipelines that carry natural gas from the wells in HassiR'Mel (Algeria) to Spain and Portugal*. http://www.emplpipeline.com/en/. Accessed 8 February 2021.

Euratom Supply Agency. (2020). *Annual Report 2019*. https://ec.europa.eu/euratom/ar/last.pdf. Accessed 22 January 2021.

European Commission. (2019a). *Quarterly report on European gas markets*, 12(4). https://ec.europa.eu/energy/data-analysis/market-analysis_en. Accessed 9 February 2021.

European Commission. (2019b). *Quarterly report on European electricity markets*, 12(4). https://ec.europa.eu/energy/data-analysis/market-analysis_en. Accessed 4 March 2021.

European Commission. (2020a). *EU energy in figures*. https://ec.europa.eu/energy/data-analysis/energy-statistical-pocketbook_fi. Accessed 22 January 2021.

European Commission. (2020b). *Quarterly report on European gas markets*, 13(1). https://ec.europa.eu/energy/sites/default/files/quarterly_report_on_european_gas_markets_q1_2020.pdf. Accessed 22 January 2021.

European Commission. (2020c). *Quarterly report on European gas markets*, 13(4). https://ec.europa.eu/energy/sites/default/files/quarterly_report_on_european_gas_markets_q4_2020_final.pdf. Accessed 11April 2021.

European Commission. (2020d). *European Union, trade in goods with Russia*. https://webgate.ec.europa.eu/isdb_results/factsheets/country/details_russia_en.pdf. Accessed 8 February 2021.

European Commission. (2020e). *European Union, trade in goods with USA*. https://webgate.ec.europa.eu/isdb_results/factsheets/country/details_usa_en.pdf. Accessed 23 February 2021.

European Commission. (2020f, July 8). *A hydrogen strategy for a climate-neutral Europe*. Communication from the Commission to the European Parliament, the Council, the European Economic and Social Committee and the Committee of the Regions. COM(2020) 301 final. https://ec.europa.eu/energy/sites/ener/files/hydrogen_strategy.pdf. Accessed 3 March 2021.

European Commission. (2021a). *2050 long-term strategy*. https://ec.europa.eu/clima/policies/strategies/2050_en. Accessed 24 January 2021.

European Commission. (2021b). *2030 climate & energy framework*. https://ec.europa.eu/clima/policies/strategies/2030_en. Accessed 13 February 2021.

European Commission. (2021c). *Hydrogen*. https://ec.europa.eu/energy/topics/energy-system-integration/hydrogen_en#:~:text=EU%20hydrogen%20strategy%20The%20EU%20strategy%20for%20energy,and%20its%20wider%20scope%20warrant%20a%20specific%20approach. Accessed 3 March 2021.

Eurostat. (2020a, October). *EU imports of energy products—Recent developments*. https://ec.europa.eu/eurostat/statistics-explained/pdfscache/46126.pdf. Accessed 23 January 2021.

Eurostat. (2020b, October 29). *Natural gas supply statistics*. https://ec.europa.eu/eurostat/statistics-explained/index.php?oldid=401136. Accessed 8 February 2021.

Eurostat. (2020c, July). *Electricity generation statistics—First results*. https://ec.europa.eu/eurostat/statistics-explained/pdfscache/9990.pdf. Accessed 3 March 2021.

Eurostat. (2021a). *Energy trade*. https://ec.europa.eu/eurostat/cache/infographs/energy_trade/entrade.html. Accessed 24 January 2021.

Eurostat. (2021b, January 21). *Imports of natural gas by partner country*. https://appsso.eurostat.ec.europa.eu/nui/show.do?dataset=nrg_ti_gas&lang=en. Accessed 8 February 2021.

Finnish Customs. (2021). *ULJAS foreign trade statistics database*. https://uljas.tulli.fi/v3rti/. Accessed 20 February 2021.

Finnish Energy. (2021). *Energy year 2020—Electricity*. https://energia.fi/files/4381/Electricity_Year_2020.pdf. Accessed 3 March 2021.

Finnish Gas Association. (2021). *Kaasu Suomessa*. https://www.kaasuyhdistys.fi/kaasu-suomessa. Accessed 20 February 2021.

Gallarati, L. (2020, May 20). *LNG makes up Portugal's entire gas supply in April*. Argus Media. https://www.argusmedia.com/en/news/2107030-lng-makes-up-portugals-entire-gas-supply-in-april. Accessed 9 February 2021.

Gardner, T. (2021, March 6). *Cruz puts hold on Biden's CIA pick Burns over Nord Stream 2 Pipeline*. Reuters. https://www.reuters.com/article/us-usa-nord-stream-2-cruz-idUSKBN2AY0FG. Accessed 14 March 2021.

Gazprom. (2020). *PJSC Gazprom Annual Report 2019*. https://www.gazprom.com/f/posts/72/802627/gazprom-annual-report-2019-en.pdf. Accessed 20 February 2021.

Gazprom. (2021a). *TurkStream*. https://www.gazprom.com/projects/turk-stream/. Accessed 24 January 2021.

Gazprom. (2021b). *Power of Siberia*. https://www.gazprom.com/projects/power-of-siberia/. Accessed 20 February 2021.

GEM. (2020, January 25). *Greenstream Pipeline*. Global Energy Monitor. https://www.gem.wiki/Greenstream_Pipeline. Accessed 8 February 2021.

GEM. (2021a, January 12). *Cyprus LNG Terminal*. https://www.gem.wiki/Cyprus_LNG_Terminal. Accessed 10 February 2021.

GEM. (2021b, January 15). *El Musel LNG Terminal*. https://www.gem.wiki/El_Musel_LNG_Terminal. Accessed 10 February 2021.

GEM. (2021c, January 14). *Cork LNG terminal*. https://www.gem.wiki/Cork_LNG_Terminal. Accessed 14 February 2021.

GEM. (2021d, February 4). *Shannon LNG Terminal*. https://www.gem.wiki/Shannon_LNG_Terminal. Accessed 14 February 2021.

GEM. (2021e, February 22). *Stade LNG Terminal*. https://www.gem.wiki/Stade_LNG_Terminal#cite_note-own-1. Accessed 5 March 2021.

German LNG Terminal. (2021). *German LNG Terminal*. https://germanlng.com/. Accessed 14 February 2021.

Geropoulos, K. (2021, March 12). *Israel, Cyprus plan to share Aphrodite gas field, talk first*. New Europe. https://www.neweurope.eu/article/israel-cyprus-plan-to-share-aphrodite-gas-field-talk-first/. Accessed 15 March 2021.

GIE. (2018, July 1). *Storage map*. https://www.gie.eu/index.php/gie-publications/databases/storage-database. Accessed 24 January 2021.

GIE. (2019). *LNG Map 2019*. https://www.gie.eu/download/maps/2019/GIE_LNG_2019_A0_1189x841_FULL_Final3.pdf. Accessed 23 January 2021.

GIIGNL. (2020). *GIIGNL Annual Report 2020*. https://giignl.org/sites/default/files/PUBLIC_AREA/Publications/giignl_-_2020_annual_report_-_04082020.pdf. Accessed 8 February 2021.

GLE. (2019). *LNG investment database*. https://www.gie.eu/index.php/gie-publications/databases/lng-investment-database. Accessed 10 February 2021.

Greenpeace. (2020, December 4). *Denmark cancels new oil and gas permits and sets date to end existing production*. Greenpeace International. Press releases. https://www.greenpeace.org/international/press-release/45831/denmark-cancels-new-oil-and-gas-permits-and-sets-date-to-end-existing-production/. Accessed 28 February 2021.

Hall, M. (2018). *Norwegian gas exports: Assessment of resources and supply to 2035* (OIES Paper: NG 127). The Oxford Institute for Energy Studies. https://www.oxfordenergy.org/wpcms/wp-content/uploads/2018/03/Norwegian-Gas-Exports-Assessment-of-Resources-and-Supply-to-2035-NG-127.pdf. Accessed 15 February 2021.

Hall, M. (2020, December). *Denmark's phase-out of upstream oil and gas: Effective climate policy or symbolic gesture*. The Oxford Institute for Energy Studies. Oxford Energy Comment. https://www.oxfordenergy.org/wpcms/wp-content/uploads/2020/12/Denmarks-phase-out-of-upstream-oil-gas.pdf. Accessed 3 March 2021.

Hamina LNG. (2020). https://www.haminalng.fi/. Accessed 2 April 2021.

HEH. (2021). *The LNG terminal in Stade, Germany*. Hanseatic Energy Hub. https://www.hanseatic-energy-hub.de/en/. Accessed 5 March 2021.

Hellenic Shipping News. (2019, October 10). *Greek ship owners dominate the LNG market*. https://www.hellenicshippingnews.com/greek-ship-owners-dominate-the-lng-market/. Accessed 21 February 2021.

Henderson, S. (2019, March 1). *Cyprus gas discovery could be an East Mediterranean game-changer*. The Washington Institute for Near East Policy. https://www.washingtoninstitute.org/policy-analysis/cyprus-gas-discovery-could-be-east-mediterranean-game-changer. Accessed 2 March 2021.

Henley, J. (2014, March 3). Is Europe's gas supply threatened by the Ukrainian crisis? *The Guardian*. https://www.theguardian.com/world/2014/mar/03/europes-gas-supply-ukraine-crisis-russsia-pipelines. Accessed 23 February 2021.

Hrastar, J. (2014). *Liquid natural gas in the United States a history*. McFarland & company.

Hydrocarbons Technology. (2021). *Trans-Mediterranean natural gas pipeline*. https://www.hydrocarbons-technology.com/projects/trans-med-pipeline/. Accessed 8 February 2021.

IAEA. (2020). *Country Nuclear Power Profiles 2020: Lithuania*. https://www-pub.iaea.org/MTCD/publications/PDF/cnpp2020/countryprofiles/Lithuania/Lithuania_tables.htm. Accessed 3 March 2021.

IEA. (2020). *The Netherlands 2020: Energy Policy Review*. https://www.iea.org/reports/the-netherlands-2020. Accessed 10 February 2021.

IEA. (2021a). *Malta*. https://www.iea.org/countries/malta. Accessed 23 January 2021.

IEA. (2021b). *Cyprus*. https://www.iea.org/countries/cyprus. Accessed 10 February 2021.

IGU. (2018). *2018 World LNG Report*. https://www.igu.org/resources/2018-world-lng-report-27th-world-gas-conference-edition/. Accessed 10 February 2021.

IGU. (2020a). *2020 World LNG Report*. https://www.igu.org/resources/2020-world-lng-report/. Accessed 21 February 2021.

IGU. (2020b). *Global Gas Report*. https://www.igu.org/resources/global-gas-report-2020/. Accessed 2 March 2021.

IGU. (2021). *Global Voice of Gas*, 1(3). https://www.igu.org/magazines/. Accessed 9 March 2021.

IMF. (2021). *World Economic Outlook Update: January 2021*. https://www.imf.org/en/Publications/WEO/Issues/2021/01/26/2021-world-economic-outlook-update. Accessed 10 February 2021.

INTERRAO. (2021). *Trading*. https://www.interrao.ru/en/activity/traiding/. Accessed 3 March 2021.

Jakštas, T. (2019). *Creation of regional gas market in the Baltic States and Finland: Challenges and opportunities* (BSR Policy Briefing 8/2019). Centrum Balticum Foundation. https://www.centrumbalticum.org/files/4383/BSR_Policy_Briefing_8_2019.pdf. Accessed 20 February 2021.

Jensen, J. T. (2004). *The development of a global LNG market: Is it likely? If so when?* The Oxford Institute for Energy Studies, NG 5. https://www.oxfordenergy.org/wpcms/wp-content/uploads/2010/11/NG5-TheDevelopmentofAGlobalLNGMarketIsItLikelyIfSoWhen-JamesJensen-2004.pdf. Accessed 10 February 2021.

King & Spalding. (2018). *An overview of LNG import terminals in Europe*. https://www.kslaw.com/attachments/000/006/010/original/LNG_in_Europe_2018_-_An_Overview_of_LNG_Import_Terminals_in_Europe.pdf?1530031152. Accessed 2 March 2021.

KNOEMA. (2021). *Lithuania—Total electricity exports*. https://knoema.com/atlas/Lithuania/topics/Energy/Electricity/Electricity-exports. Accessed 13 March 2021.

Liuhto, K. (Ed.). (2015). *Natural gas revolution and the Baltic Sea region* (BSR Policy Briefing 1/2015). Centrum Balticum Foundation. https://www.centrumbalticum.org/files/1910/BSR_policy_briefing_1_2015.pdf. Accessed 20 February 2021.

Liuhto, K. (2019, August 3). *Foreign economic relations of China*. Slide package. https://www.researchgate.net/publication/334947535_Foreign_economic_relations_of_China. Accessed 22 January 2021.

Liuhto, K. (2020a, January 7). *Foreign economic relations of Russia*. Slide package. https://www.researchgate.net/publication/338411749_Foreign_economic_relations_of_Russia. Accessed 22 January 2021.

Liuhto, K. (2020b, March 31). *100 slides on the EU-Russia economic cooperation*. Slide package. https://www.researchgate.net/publication/340297123_100_slides_on_the_EU-Russia_economic_cooperation. Accessed 22 January 2021.

Liuhto, K. (2020c, August 1). *Natural gas in the Baltic Sea region: A special emphasis on liquefied natural gas (LNG)*. Slide package. https://www.researchgate.net/publication/343350581_Natural_gas_in_the_Baltic_Sea_region_A_special_emphasis_on_liquefied_natural_gas_LNG. Accessed 22 January 2021.

LNG Croatia. (2021). *First LNG carrier arrives to the terminal*. https://lng.hr/en/first-LNG-carrier-arrives-to-the-terminal. Accessed 10 February 201.

LNG Industry. (2019, August 16). *Alexela opens LNG fuelling station in Estonia*. LNG Industry. https://www.lngindustry.com/liquid-natural-gas/16082019/alexela-opens-lng-fuelling-station-in-estonia/. Accessed 20 February 2021.

LNG Wilhelmshaven. (2021). https://lng-wilhelmshaven.com/en/. Accessed 23 February 2021.

mapchart.net. (2021). https://mapchart.net/. Accessed 1 September 2020.

McGrath, M. (2020, September 12). *Climate change: China aims for 'climate neutrality by 2060'*. BBC News. https://www.bbc.com/news/science-environment-54256826. Accessed 5 March 2020.

Meijer, B. H. (2019, September 10). *Netherlands to halt Groningen gas production by 2022*. Reuters. https://www.reuters.com/article/us-netherlands-gas-idUSKCN1VV1KE. Accessed 23 January 2021.

Meijer B. H. (2021, February 11). *Groningen gas output can be cut by more than 50%, government says*. Reuters. https://www.reuters.com/article/uk-netherlands-gas-groningen/groningen-gas-output-can-be-cut-by-more-than-50-government-says-idUKKBN2AB0SX. Accessed 13 February 2021.

Ministry of Finance. (2021). *Federal budget of the Russian Federation*. https://minfin.gov.ru/en/statistics/fedbud/. Accessed 22 January 2021.

NS Energy. (2020). *Cyprus breaks ground on €289m LNG import terminal at Vassiliko Port*. https://www.nsenergybusiness.com/news/cyprus-lng-import-terminal-vassiliko-port/. Accessed 10 February 2021.

NS Energy. (2021). *The Medgaz Pipeline*. https://www.nsenergybusiness.com/projects/medgaz-gas-pipeline/. Accessed 8 February 2021.

OGJ. (2021a, March 1). Fluxys takes FID on Zeebruge LNG expansion. *Oil & Gas Journal*.

OGJ. (2021b, March 8). Shell expects global LNG demand to almost double by 2040. *Oil & Gas Journal*.

O'Sullivan, S. (2021). *China's Natural Gas Development Report: A tale of two years* (Energy Insight 85). The Oxford Institute for Energy Studies. https://www.oxfordenergy.org/wpcms/wp-content/uploads/2021/02/Insight-85-Chinas-Natural-Gas-Development-Report.pdf. Accessed 3 March 2021.

Pipeline & Gas Journal. (2021, February 10). *Gazprom resumes gas supply to Russia's Kaliningrad*. https://pgjonline.com/news/2021/february/gazprom-resumes-gas-supply-to-russias-kaliningrad. Accessed 11 February 2021.

Pitel, L., & Sheppard, D. (2020, July 19). *Turkey fuels regional power game over Mediterranean gas reserves*. https://www.ft.com/content/69a222d4-b37c-4e7e-86dc-4f96b226416d. Accessed 22 January 2021.

PortNews. (2020, October 29). *Novatek to launch LNG terminal in Rostock (Germany) in 2023*. https://en.portnews.ru/news/303976/. Accessed 14 February 2021.

Proprietary. (2021). http://proprietary.sk/en/alternative-fuels-lng-cng/history-of-lng/. Accessed 10 February 2021.

Sampson, J. (2020, April 7). *Coronavirus to hit LNG demand at world's largest LNG importers, says ICIS*. Gas World. https://www.gasworld.com/coronavirus-to-hit-lng-demand-/2018816.article. Accessed 10 February 2021.

SEAI. (2021). *Production and imports YTD 2020*. https://www.seai.ie/data-and-insights/seai-statistics/monthly-energy-data/gas/. Accessed 14 February 2021.

TAP. (2021). *How TAP operates*. https://www.tap-ag.com/infrastructure-operation/how-tap-operates. Accessed 9 March 2021.

TASS. (2021, January 21). *Russia's 2020 budget executed with deficit of 3.8% of GDP*. https://tass.com/economy/1247359. Accessed 22 January 2021.

UA Transmission System Operator. (2021). *History*. https://tsoua.com/en/about-us/history/. Accessed 24 January 2021.

Usanov, A., & Kharin, A. (2014). *Energy security of Kaliningrad and geopolitics* (BSR Policy Briefing 2/2014). Centrum Balticum Foundation. https://www.centrumbalticum.org/files/3804/BSR_Policy_Briefing_2_2014.pdf. Accessed 11 February 2021.

World Nuclear Association. (2019, December). *Nuclear power in Germany*. https://www.world-nuclear.org/information-library/country-profiles/countries-g-n/germany.aspx. Accessed 14 February 2021.

CHAPTER 3

Energy Transition in the Baltic Sea Region: A Controversial Role of LNG?

Leonid Grigoryev and Dzhanneta Medzhidova

Introduction

This chapter will provide an analysis of the energy transition in the Baltic Sea region and the role of natural gas, current problems and future development. The authors will focus on the implications of the changes in energy balances, GHG emission and gas market evolution—particularly on the LNG trade in ten Baltic Sea countries. The year 2020—the year of the COVID-19 pandemic and the Great Lockdown (the decline of 3.2% in global GDP)—changes the course of events, demand and prices, investments and financing. An expected recovery in 2021 (6.0%) would require adjustments in the policy of all countries (IMF, 2021b). Dramatic anti-recession policies in 2020, especially in the health care sector and

L. Grigoryev (✉) · D. Medzhidova
Higher School of Economics (HSE), Moscow, Russia
e-mail: lgrigoriev@hse.ru

D. Medzhidova
e-mail: dmedzhidova@hse.ru

K. Liuhto (ed.), *The Future of Energy Consumption, Security and Natural Gas*, https://doi.org/10.1007/978-3-030-80367-4_3

the assistance to the low-income—domestically and internationally—may draw resources from other priorities.

Possible environmental consequences of the imports of the pipeline gas and the LNG are considered in view of the EU policy on climate change mitigation. Natural gas may become shortly 'a missed bridge' and provide environmental safety in the EU strategy by announced policies. Nevertheless, both LNG and pipeline gas should be tested on ecological safety and economic efficiency in the short and long run.

The authors focus on the economic and climate-related rational logic of LNG's role in the Baltic Sea region. We consider the rest of the factors as politically motivated and out of the economic analysis. Moreover, we comment briefly on the countries' strategies for an energy transition.

The recovery from the Great Lockdown of 2020 may take more time, especially for tourism-dependent countries and regions, as the COVID-19 pandemic seriously hit the service sectors. By the autumn of 2020, we observe the resurgence of the COVID-19 pandemic in many countries across Europe. It means that we cannot expect the end of the epidemic restriction globally at any defined time horizon, and we must prepare ourselves for a prolonged recovery. Meanwhile, the energy demand and the emission of GHG are declining. The governments have already added about twelve trillion dollars (as of September 2020) of liquidity to prevent the liquidity crunch (IMF, 2020). For now, these monetary flows have affected stock markets and real estate markets with unusual prices growth, which is not healthy in the long run. The investment crisis is following the general decline. The Maastricht norms are suspended, and state debts are rising. General economic recovery in the world, excluding China, is expected in 2021 (Table 3.1). It is not a comfortable period for energy transition globally, and relatively low prices for oil and coal may not help the ambitious targets of the climate and energy policies globally. However, the EU sees it as an opportunity (IEA, 2020a).

In this article, the Baltic Sea region is represented by ten countries: Denmark, Estonia, Finland, Germany, Latvia, Lithuania, Norway, Poland, Russia and Sweden. These countries have different economic size, population, GDP per capita and energy consumption. However, they are a part of the developed world and the participants of both the Paris Agreement of 2015 and Sustainable Development goals of the UN 2015. The year 2020 could have brought some changes in the implementation

Table 3.1 GDP and primary energy consumption of the Baltic Sea region countries

	GDP (constant prices, %)				*Primary energy consumption (%)*	
	2009	*2019*	*2020*	*2021*	*2009*	*2019*
Denmark	−4.9	2.9	−3.3	2.8	−6.0	−0.5
Estonia	−14.4	5.0	−2.9	3.4	−11.2	−19.6
Finland	−8.1	1.3	−2.9	2.3	−7.2	−4.3
Germany	−5.7	0.6	−4.8	3.6	−6.2	−2.2
Latvia	−14.3	2.0	−3.6	3.9	−5.4	2.0
Lithuania	−14.8	4.3	−0.8	3.2	−8.3	−0.5
Norway	−1.7	0.9	−0.8	3.9	−7.6	−7.2
Poland	2.8	4.5	−2.7	3.5	−3.6	−2.4
Sweden	−4.3	1.4	−2.8	3.1	−8.4	3.5
Russia	−7.8	2.0	−3.0	4.4	−5.0	−0.8
World	−0.1	2.8	−3.2	6.0	-1.5	1.3
EU	−4.2	1.7	−6.1	4.4	−5.8	−1.4

Source The Authors, based on IMF (2021a, 2021b) and BP (2020)

patterns and focus on sustainable development goals (Bobylev & Grigoryev, 2020). Indeed, this decade has long been regarded as a decisive one for reaching Paris Agreement goals (Millar et al., 2017).

Energy Transition: Demand and GHG Emission in the Baltic Sea Region

An energy transition is a topic widely discussed in energy studies for several decades (Fouquet & Pearson, 1998; Smil, 2005). The term 'energy transition' has many different connotations and meanings—in a similar manner, 'market liberalisation of RES' or 'a shift from one fuel to another'. The World Energy Council defines the transition process as a connected policy challenge, and its success involves managing three core dimensions (World Energy Trilemma Index, 2019): (1) energy security, (2) energy equity and (3) the environmental sustainability of energy systems throughout the transition process. This definition is closely connected to climate change issues and brings us to the global agenda.

Our study refers to energy transition as a process of structural changes in energy balance when some fuels are replaced with others. Furthermore, energy transition does not lead to an ultimate replacement of fuel, but a substantial reduction of its share. Based on this definition, we highlight four stages of the energy transition: (1) coal replaced wood and waterpower in the middle of the nineteenth century, (2) oil replaced coal at the beginning of the twentieth century, (3) natural gas replaced oil in the 1970s and (4) renewables are replacing gas, coal and oil at the moment.

Each phase has its particular grounds and consequences. However, there is still much in common. Firstly, the shift happens when supplies are endangered. Similarly, the wide use of coal in the UK was preceded by shortages in wood supply (Solomon & Krishna, 2011). Moreover, importing countries paid attention to natural gas after several oil crises, and oil prices appeared volatile. Besides, fuel prices play a crucial role. Sometimes low prices for certain fuels (for example, coal) may act as obstacles for the transition, as countries with modest GDP per capita cannot afford oil and gas, not to mention renewables.

We support the opinion that price is a crucial variable for industries and households when choosing between several fuels. However, fuel prices are not responsible for the transition alone (Leach, 1992). Furthermore, such a factor as oil energy density was one reason for the second energy transition. Due to new technologies and innovations—diesel engine, for example—global oil demand snowballed. Therefore, oil became more energy-efficient and less costly in certain industries. Sociotechnical issues remain crucial for the success of the transition (Geels & Schot, 2007; Smith et al., 2010). Besides, the energy transition occurred in a period of predictable prices and stable supply. Last but not least comes energy policy, including climate change mitigation. The latter became an influential factor at the end of the twentieth century after the Kyoto protocol and global acknowledgement of the urgent need to address environmental safety. The role of transition politics and of institutions is not even argued (Avelino et al., 2016).

Natural gas is considered the least harmful fossil fuel and mainly regarded in developed countries as a bridge to renewables (Melsted & Pallua, 2018). However, natural gas extraction leads to greenhouse gas emission; while the new century promotes renewable energy sources (RES), such as solar panels, wind power plants, et cetera.

The fourth phase of the energy transition is a non-economically driven process, initialised by policymakers concerned with global problems, such as climate change and energy affordability. This phase probably will not become a ground for rapid economic growth. Nevertheless, the energy transition might provide humanity with safe and clean energy. In any case a global green carbon-free economy is not a matter of the near future, as it takes the global community's consolidating actions, not only individual efforts of certain countries (Grigoryev & Medzhidova, 2020). On the national level countries, that have a limited lock-in around fossil fuels, can carry out energy transition process more quickly (Bridge et al., 2012).

In energy balances globally different fuels coexist: oil, natural gas, coal, renewables, biofuels and waste, nuclear energy and hydropower. Figure 3.1 illustrates the structure of the world energy balance by fuel. As we see, fossil fuels, namely oil, gas and coal, still represent 84% of the world's total primary consumption. Renewables' share is relatively low—5%, although it has grown significantly in recent years. The structure of energy consumption depends on many factors: GDP per capita, geographical and geological characteristics, climate policy and resource availability. Consumption of natural gas is mainly driven by industry and residential sector, totalling almost 70% (BP, 2020).

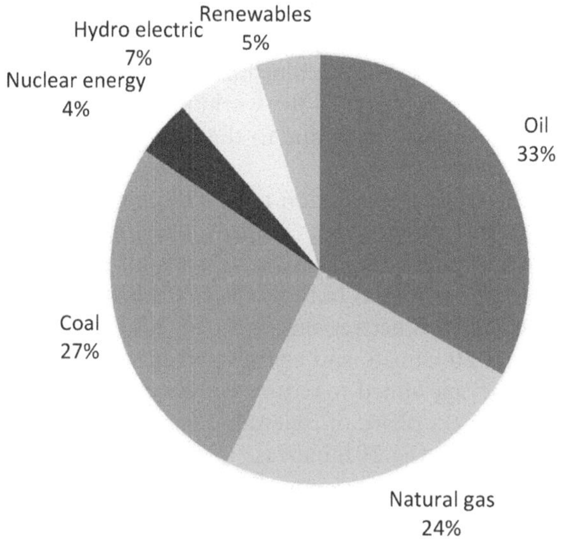

Fig. 3.1 Primary energy consumption in the world by fuel in 2019 (%) (*Source* The Authors, based on BP [2020])

Table 3.2 The emissions of the Baltic Sea region countries and their share in the globe's total emissions (million tonnes of CO_2)

	1990	*Global share (%)*	*2000*	*Global share (%)*	*2010*	*Global share (%)*	*2019*	*Global share (%)*
Denmark	56	0.26	58	0.24	51	0.16	33	0.10
Estonia	38	0.18	17	0.07	23	0.07	20	0.06
Finland	58	0.27	60	0.25	66	0.21	43	0.13
Germany	1,008	4.72	854	3.61	783	2.52	684	2.00
Latvia	18	0.09	7	0.03	9	0.03	8	0.02
Lithuania	36	0.17	11	0.05	13	0.04	12	0.04
Norway	29	0.14	34	0.14	37	0.12	34	0.89
Poland	374	1.75	300	1.27	324	1.04	304	0.89
Russia	2,234	10.47	1,453	6.14	1,492	4.80	1,533	4.49
Sweden	67	0.32	58	0.24	57	0.18	46	0.14

Source The Authors, based on BP (2020)

The world is on its way to the fourth phase of the energy transition. This statement is particularly true for the European countries. The share of the EU emissions in global emissions was reduced from over 17% in 2000 to 10% in 2019. Table 3.2 illustrates the Baltic Sea region countries' emissions and their shares in the world's total emissions. Russia and Germany have the largest shares due to their industrial development and population numbers.

We witness the trend of reduction in overall emissions. Unfortunately, GHG emissions are still growing in many developing countries, especially in Asia. Accordingly, the decrease in shares of the Baltic Sea region countries should be attributed both to their efforts and to the significant growth of emissions in other regions.

In 2009, the 2020 climate and energy package was enacted in legislation. The 2009 package aimed to reduce GHG emissions by 20% from the 1990 level, increase the share of renewable energy sources in the energy mix by 20%, and reach the 20% increase in energy efficiency (Table 3.3). The EU Emissions Trading System (ETS), created in 2005, is used to fulfil ambitious goals.[1] The system covers around 45% of total emissions

[1] ETS operates in the EU, Iceland, Liechtenstein and Norway. This mechanism sets a cap on the total amount of certain greenhouse gases (carbon dioxide, nitrous oxide, perfluorocarbons) emissions. Companies are able to receive or buy emission allowances, which they can trade later on. The cap is reduced over time in order to reduce total GHG

Table 3.3 The EU's climate targets

	2020 (%)	*2030 (%)*
Cut in GHG emissions from the 1990 level	20	55
Share for renewable energy sources	20	32
Improvement in energy efficiency	20	33

Source The Authors, based on European Commission (2020a, 2021)

in the region and includes all the sectors except for housing, agriculture, waste and transport, excluding aviation, included in the system. Grubb and Neuhoff (2006) note that the objective of emissions cap-and-trade is to secure emission reductions at the lowest possible cost. To cover the remaining 55% of emissions, effort-sharing regulation was adopted in 2018, and the targets differ depending on the nation's wealth (European Commission, 2020a). Although the EU seems to achieve its goals, the results vary from a country to another.

According to the European Commission (2020a), all the Baltic Sea region's EU members have accomplished their 20-20-20 national targets, and some of them have already elaborated the new ones for 2030. Some countries have taken decisions on significant non-ETS emissions reduction, such as Denmark, Estonia and Sweden, while the targets of other countries, namely Latvia and Poland, are more modest (Table 3.4).

According to Climate Action Network Europe (2018), however, only Sweden shows promising results in fighting global climate change for 2030. The results of other countries in the region were mentioned as poor (Denmark, Germany, Latvia, Lithuania) and very poor (Estonia, Poland).

In 2019, the EU set a more ambitious goal—to achieve carbon neutrality by 2050 (European Council, 2019).[2] This goal includes achieving GHG emissions reductions by 80–100% compared to 1990 by 2050, providing energy-efficient and promoting renewable energy. According to Ursula von der Leyen and Werner Hoyer (2021), meeting the new 2030 emission-reduction targets will require EUR350 billion annually, which appears to be undervalued. The EIB is ready to invest

emissions. Sectors that are not covered by the ETS are: transport (excluding aviation and shipping), agriculture, waste and industrial emissions.

[2] Carbon neutrality means having a balance between emitting carbon and absorbing carbon from the atmosphere in carbon sinks (European Council, 2019).

Table 3.4 The targets of the Baltic Sea region countries on climate change mitigation for 2030

	Targets on climate change mitigation
Denmark	To reduce GHG by 70% compared to 1990
	Share of RES in gross final energy consumption should reach 55%
Estonia	To reduce GHG by 70% compared to 1990
	Share of RES in gross final energy consumption should reach 42%
	To reduce emissions the non-emissions trading sectors by 13%
Germany	To reduce GHG emissions by 55% compared to 1990 level
Finland	To reduce GHG emissions from the non-emissions trading sectors by 39% compared to 2005
Latvia	To reduce GHG by 5% compared to 2005
	Share of RES in gross final energy consumption should reach 50%
Lithuania	To reduce GHG by 9% compared to 2005
	Share of RES in gross final energy consumption should reach 45%
Norway	To reduce GHG by 40% compared to 1990
Poland	To reduce GHG emissions by 7% compared to 2005
	Share of RES in gross final energy consumption should reach 21%
Russia	To reduce GHG emissions by 25–30% compared to 1990
Sweden	To reduce GHG by 63% compared to 1990
	Share of RES in gross final energy consumption should reach 65%

Note GHG = greenhouse gases; RES = renewable energy sources
Source The Authors, based on European Commission (2020a)

EUR1,000 billion to mitigate climate change and support environmental stability in the next decade. An important implication for this article is even a more urgent necessity for the Baltic Sea region countries to diminish emissions and ensure a climate policy that will contribute to the EU's carbon neutrality as a whole. That new ambitious objective is changing specific targets and instruments of energy policy, investment patterns and character of financing, including private and public funding.

The Finnish Government believes that it is possible to reach carbon neutrality by 2035 (The Finnish Government, 2020). The target to reduce GHG from non-ETS by 16% (by 2020) is already achieved. The next stage is to reduce GHG by 39% (by 2030), compared to the 2005 level. However, if carbon-neutrality is set as a goal for 2035, the latter objective for 2030 will be changed.

As a participant of the Paris Agreement, Russia has set a goal of emissions reduction by 25–30% by 2030 compared to the 1990 level. However, current Russian emissions are less than in 1990, as after the collapse of the Soviet Union the country went through a challenging period of economic transition. In other words, the projections show that the current level of emissions is expected to grow by 2050, although it will not exceed the 1990 level.

Table 3.5 gives a heterogenous picture of the GHG emissions across the region, in time and by type. Germany and Sweden have a common feature: production-based emissions declined much faster than consumption-based ones. On the contrary, Russia is consuming domestically a lot and exports vast amounts of fossil fuels. With a massive share of gas in its energy balance, Russia has limited options to reduce consumption (The Russian Government, 2017). For now the country has the following strategy:

- more efficient energy consumption with the best available technology—transport, housing and others;
- a reduction of domestic personal consumption (probably it will be a good idea for other—more developed countries as well); and
- a reduction of the exports of fossil fuels or energy-intensive goods.

The difference between GHG emissions by production and consumption is widely known in the literature (Kander & Lindmark, 2006; Lenzen, 1998; Peters & Hertwich, 2006).[3] We define consumption-related emission as lifestyle-related consumption. It is a conscious choice of the population on different levels of wellbeing. In turn, reducing domestic production-related emission can be reached by various ways and means—for example, by increasing the industry and transportation effectiveness, reducing dependency on fossil fuel technologies and importing chemicals, fuel, metals paper, fertilisers and others. Interestingly, the option of changing the lifestyle is much less present in the European decarbonisation initiatives.[4]

We understand that the reduction of households' domestic energy consumption may be much less popular among the voters. The latter prefer the reduction of emission by technological means at the expense

[3] The issue has been discussed in the context of the BRICS—OECD energy and climate relations and other aspects of climate policies (Makarov & Sokolova, 2017).

[4] Excluding the high taxes for the gasoline consumption in the EU or the German automobile carbon tax, which targets consumers—not the producers.

Table 3.5 GHG emissions by production and consumption in the Baltic Sea region countries (million tonnes of CO_2)

	1990		*2000*		*2010*		*2017*	
	Production-based	*Consumption-based*	*Production-based*	*Consumption-based*	*Production-based*	*Consumption-based*	*Production-based*	*Consumption-based*
Denmark	53.6	57.5	54.3	62.8	49.2	62.1	34.8	53.0
Estonia	37.1	31.8	15.4	17.4	19.0	17.5	18.7	18.3
Finland	57.0	69.0	57.0	70.8	64.1	83.6	44.7	66.7
Germany	1,050.0	1,160.0	900.4	1,060.0	832.4	977.7	798.0	894.8
Latvia	19.5	22.6	7.1	11.0	8.6	13.0	7.2	12.9
Lithuania	35.8	42.5	11.8	16.7	13.7	20.8	13.4	23.0
Norway	35.3	37.2	42.5	31.6	46.2	51.1	43.7	49.4
Poland	377.0	361.6	318.2	285.0	333.5	319.4	336.6	307.0
Russia	2,530.0	2,430.0	1,470.0	1,210.0	1,610.0	1,340.0	1,650.0	1,370.0
Sweden	57.5	78.0	54.7	81.0	52.9	84.8	42.1	72.0

Source The Authors, based on Ritchie (2019)

of the business or other countries. This problem has two crucial consequences. Firstly, switching from production to imports of the emission-related goods (the Swedish case) enables to reduce the emissions without changes in the everyday life. Taxing the suppliers (exporters) should become even more popular. Secondly, the EU currently has substantially reduced its emissions. Each next euro spent in the EU is losing its competitiveness against the alternative use regarding climate change mitigation in Asia, in countries under 10,000 dollars GDP per capita, given that China may manage and finance climate policy by itself. In other words, the EU share in global emissions is lower each year, but both the shares and the amount of emissions of the other countries (in particular, the Asian ones) are growing. So, the EU finds itself in a paradoxical situation when its efforts are considered vital only within its borders. While their efficiency grows within the European Union, they are becoming less critical from the global perspective.

Energy Balances of the Baltic Sea Region Countries

The Baltic Sea countries experienced economic problems in 2008–2010 with the Great Recession (Slay & Pospíšilová, 2009). GDP growth rates in the region declined, and governments were focusing on immediate needs. Changes in the energy policies were coming later and mostly within the EU frameworks. So far, the energy balances of the countries are quite different. While Poland's primary consumption is driven by coal and oil, Denmark depends on oil and RES, and Estonia is highly dependent on oil, as Fig. 3.2 shows. As for natural gas, it is mostly consumed in Russia, Latvia, Lithuania and Germany. In addition, gas share in energy balances in Denmark, Estonia, Finland and Latvia declined in 2019 compared to 2010. However, in Germany, Lithuania, Poland, Sweden and Russia, the share has grown.

Being dependent on natural gas equals being dependent on Russian gas exports, which is the leading supplier in the region. Although the share of coal in all the countries, excluding Lithuania, has declined, we still witness impressive coal consumption in Estonia, Germany, Lithuania and Poland. It is especially true for electricity generation, i.e. in Estonia share of coal is 70.3%, in Germany—30.0%, in Poland—73.7% (IEA, 2020b). All the countries mentioned above are members of the EU, and will have

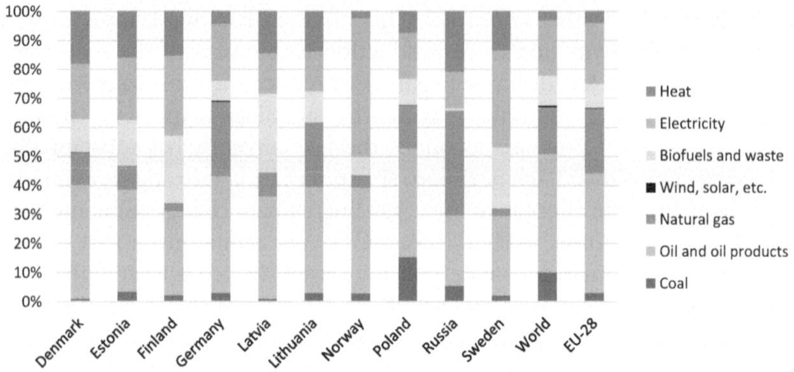

Fig. 3.2 Total final energy consumption by source in 2018 (%) (*Source* The Authors, based on IEA [2020b])

to adopt the same climate policy trends. So, energy balances of the countries, now depending on coal, leave space for both RES and natural gas, the latter as a bridge fuel for a decade or more. Russia does not only export natural gas, it also has the chief share of gas in the energy balance with much less coal and oil than the world, the EU, and most Baltic Sea region countries (Fig. 3.2).

Gas share in total primary energy consumption of the region has grown from 19% in 1990 to 27% in 2017 (IEA, 2020b). Although total energy consumption in 1991–2017 has declined by 0.6% annually, gas consumption grew by 0.7%, which indicates an essential role of natural gas for the region. Russia and Norway are the only countries abundant with natural resources, while others rely on imports mainly of natural gas and oil. Table 3.6 indicates that the average share of natural gas in primary energy consumption was around 18% in the Baltic Sea region, excluding the main exporters (Norway and Russia), in 2000. The relevant share was less than 17% 19 years later, indicating that the significance of natural gas has remained relatively unchanged.

Gas consumption in the region, excluding Norway and Russia, has grown by 30 bcm since 1990. The largest consumers are Germany and Poland. Compared to the EU, which consumed nearly 500 bcm in 2019, the amount consumed by the Baltic Sea region countries remains relatively low. The only exception is Germany—the leading consumer of Russian gas both in the region and in the EU (BP, 2020) (Fig. 3.3).

Table 3.6 Energy balances in the Baltic Sea region countries (share in total, %) and GDP per capita (PPP, constant 2017 US dollars)

	2000						*2010*						*2019*					
	Oil	*Gas*	*Coal*	*RES*	*Other*	*GDP per capita*	*Oil*	*Gas*	*Coal*	*RES*	*Other*	*GDP per capita*	*Oil*	*Gas*	*Coal*	*RES*	*Other*	*GDP per capita*
Denmark	52.1	21.7	19.6	6.5	0.0	49.0	43.5	22.7	19.5	14.3	0.0	50.9	47.8	15.1	5.6	31.5	0.0	57.2
Estonia	24.6	14.3	61.0	0.0	0.1	17.8	23.1	9.2	63.7	3.9	0.1	26.2	26.9	6.5	59.1	7.5	0.1	36.7
Finland	36.7	11.1	16.4	6.8	29.1	39.9	33.7	11.2	21.4	8.4	25.4	45.9	35.3	6.6	13.3	16.2	28.6	48.6
Germany	39.5	20.9	25.0	1.1	13.6	42.9	35.7	23.1	23.5	6.6	11.1	46.9	35.6	24.3	17.5	16.1	6.5	53.8
Latvia	40.6	34.2	4.1	0.0	21.1	12.9	42.3	35.1	2.6	0.0	20.0	21.0	49.2	29.7	1.9	7.3	11.8	30.8
Lithuania	36.2	31.0	1.4	0.0	31.4	13.9	47.7	44.2	3.7	2.3	2.1	24.0	56.4	31.7	3.5	9.3	0.0	37.0
Norway	19.2	7.6	2.1	0.1	71.0	56.1	25.7	8.5	1.8	0.9	63.1	60.3	21.9	9.2	1.9	3.9	63.2	63.6
Poland	23.7	11.4	64.3	0.0	0.6	16.2	27.8	14.0	55.1	2.4	0.7	24.0	31.4	17.2	44.7	5.8	1.0	33.1
Russia	20.4	51.0	17.1	0.0	11.4	14.6	20.6	54.5	13.5	0.0	11.3	24.0	22.0	53.7	12.2	0.1	12.1	27.0
Sweden	31.0	1.3	4.8	2.0	60.9	41.2	30.4	2.6	5.3	7.8	54.0	48.5	25.6	1.7	3.8	16.1	52.8	53.2
World	39.1	21.9	25.0	0.7	13.3	11.1	34.2	22.5	29.9	1.9	11.5	13.9	33.1	24.2	27.0	5.0	10.7	16.9
EU	40.9	22.4	18.1	0.9	17.7	34.7	37.9	25.3	15.8	4.6	16.4	39.1	38.4	24.6	11.2	11.0	14.9	44.4

Note RES = renewable energy sources
Source The Authors, based on BP (2020) and World Bank (2020)

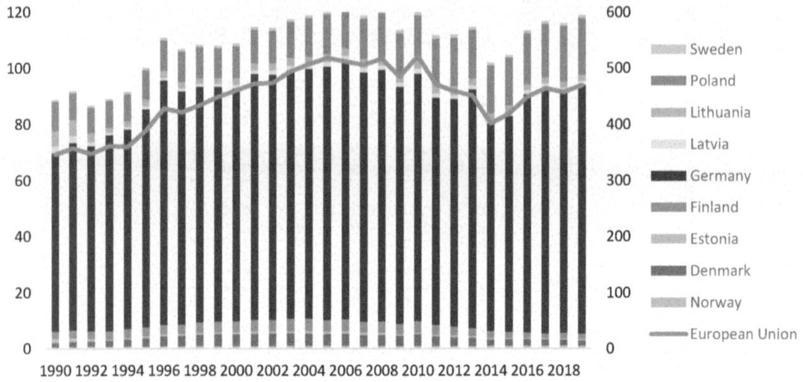

Fig. 3.3 Gas consumption in the Baltic Sea region countries and the EU (bcm) (*Note* The Baltic Sea region countries see the left axis and the EU see the right axis. The figure excludes the major natural gas exporters of the region, namely Norway and Russia. *Source* The Authors, based on BP [2020])

It is widely acknowledged that GDP per capita growth is associated with reducing coal's share in the energy balance. This statement is relevant for the region, as the share of coal has grown only in Lithuania in 2000–2019. A bright example of coal's reduction is Denmark. As RES replaced coal, the share of the latter was reduced from 20% in 2000 to only 6% in 2019. While the share of RES grew from 7% in 2000 to 32% in 2019. This dramatic decrease became possible due to wind power development (Mendonça et al., 2012). Still most Baltic countries are heavily dependent on fossil fuels, including coal. For example, the Estonian energy balance in 2019 included coal (59%), oil (27%) and natural gas (6%), while renewable energy sources had a share of only 8%. In Poland coal is not only widely consumed but also produced. Although the country reduces coal's share (from 64% in 2000 to 45% in 2019), the process is slow, and the state policy aims to switch to 'clean coal' (Kuchler & Bridge, 2018). Currently, the Polish energy system has coal at the very heart of its energy strategy (Hafner & Raimondi, 2020). It is a significant obstacle if Poland wants to achieve stated targets on GHG emissions.

Energy mix varies from one country to another. While Poland and Estonia still rely on coal, Sweden relies on nuclear energy (more than 30% of the energy consumption). Although the share of RES increased from 2% in 2000 to 16% in 2019, even more investment and political will are needed to replace fossil fuels and nuclear energy with wind power, solar energy and biomass (Hong et al., 2018; Podobnik, 2006).

The gas supply picture in the region is much simplier. Two suppliers give the most of the input: Norway and Russia. Russia is the leading exporter (over 50% of total exports) for Estonia, Finland, Germany, Latvia, Lithuania and Poland. Norway exports gas to Germany, Lithuania, Poland, Sweden and Finland.

Interdependence between the exporters (mainly Russia) and the importers is huge. In 2019, the Russian gas exports to Europe (including the EU) via pipeline reached 188 bcm, which equals 87% of Russia's total pipeline exports and 73% of Russia's total natural gas exports (Gazprom, 2020). Furthermore, pipeline gas seems to be more competitive than the LNG, given the existing infrastructure. Although it is costly to build the infrastructure (i.e. capital investment amount is significant), operational costs are low, and pipelines do not require regasification (which gives additional emissions). Several pipelines connect Russia and the European countries: the Urengoy-Pomary-Uzhhorod, Brotherhood, the Nord Stream 1 (the North Stream 2, which is under construction, faces severe sanctions) and the Yamal-Europe pipelines.

Russia's obligations—or to be precise—Gazprom's contracts on the European market will stay in force mainly until the 2030s. Regardless of the current political events, Gazprom must deliver to Central Europe (Germany, for example) more than 120 bcm on 'a normal basis' and even more in case of cold weather, weekends, et cetera. It creates a peculiar relation between the supplier and consumers. The key long-term supplier has significant investment obligations by legally binding contracts. On the other hand, consumers plan to reduce gas consumption as much as possible during this period. Still, a specific curve of import reduction is not clear. In other words, although carbon-neutrality is set as a goal, Gazprom is not yet aware of the particular amount of gas consumption reduction planned in the EU.

Transit countries (for example, Belarus and Ukraine) frequently have been suing the supplier, mostly attempting to avoid paying the increasing rents for transit. Also, the transit countries are trying to prevent the supplier from turning into seas instead of ground pipelines. This complex relationship comes along with two processes: (1) the EU's radical decarbonisation and (2) the US LNG exports. The US LNG exports have been growing since 2016, peaking in January 2020. During the pandemic the demand went down worldwide because of the economic crisis and a series of lockdowns. In 2019, the USA was still building new infrastructure (five large-scale liquefaction projects) and became the third-largest LNG supplier globally, behind Qatar and Australia (GIIGNL, 2020). Nevertheless, the future of the US LNG is questionable. The major uncertainty roots in the future policy of the new President Joe Biden regarding oil and gas companies. The second factor is the demand side, as economic activity weakened and oil and gas prices fell. Although during 2021 oil and gas demand is slowly restoring, it has not reached pre-crisis level yet.

As one may see, the global oil and gas consumption is similar to that of the EU and the Baltic Sea region countries (Table 3.6). Furthermore, the shares of fossil fuels have not changed much from 2000 to 2019. Coal is globally on retreat, but its share in 2019 is still above the level of 2000. The EU and some countries of the region seem to be more successful in terms of low coal and high RES shares in their balances. From this standpoint, one may see the tremendous task of going carbon–neutral by 2050 for the EU, while the rest of the world has much less ambitious plans (Grigoryev & Medzhidova, 2020).

Optimistic scenarios are typically based on the technological innovations and high growth rates during early stages of implementation of the new policies. Transition policies are often supported by subsidies, as in Norwegian electric cars industry. These measures are typical for the early stages of technological transformation. At the same time, the transformation of physical assets in the energy sector historically took decades. Moreover, intensive financing is needed due to the complicated matter of modernising (or rebuilding) the whole chain—from upstream to dowstream sector. Irreversibility of the fixed capital and social costs of the human capital adaptation also make the transition path more time and money consuming. Energy balances give an adequate picture since their sizes and compositions are based on the commercially viable investments made by numerous economic agents during extensive periods.

Table 3.6 gives a snapshot of the colossal task of the transition in the world and the Baltic Sea region. Before going into details, we should underline that radical decisions on eliminating fossil fuels, used in the EU, have at least one obvious consequence. They lead to doubts in profitability of any long-term investments into fossil fuels industries, upstream, midstream and downstream segments alike. What type of fossil fuel would be eliminated earlier: gas or coal—may depend on two types of decision-making: climate and economic efficiency ('rational') or political reasons ('political'). While the first one considers future profit and environmental concerns, the second one promotes energy security and the reduction of energy dependence from Russia by any means.

Gas and LNG, Different Roles for Different Objectives

In the present-day political and economic situation the role of LNG is undoubtedly 'controversial'. It appears that LNG may replace Russian pipeline gas in the region and absolutely secure supplies with the current level of costs and some additional investments. We believe that the shift to LNG cannot be carried out in a fast and a cheap way. The possible hazards should be discussed (maybe even inflated) broadly, so there is time and money left to finance the alternative sources of energy, if the pessimistic scenario evolves.

We will analyse the problem in economic terms and from the viewpoint of efficiency and rationality. LNG plays an increasingly important role in the world energy markets and balances. LNG exports gave additional income to many developing countries, such as Egypt, Indonesia and Qatar. The shift from coal to LNG in big cities like Beijing reminds us natural gas consumption growth in the twentieth century in European cities (London after smog). Both situations derive from ecological and health concerns. The LNG role is still mostly limited and complimentary, except for Japan, Taiwan, Korea and some other isolated markets.

LNG as an instrument of gas supply to the regions with no or limited access to the pipeline gas has several features: long-range (overseas) delivery, flexible supply, intense competition, security of supplies. In addition, natural gas (both pipeline and LNG) is a part of the transition as a coal substitute. Moreover, LNG supplies are used as a political instrument, for they are an alternative to pipeline supplies. A good example is Nord Stream 2, which would not face any sanctions if LNG deliveries were impossible.

A global gas market has not formed yet. For now, we can mention three vast regional markets, namely Europe, North America and Asia–Pacific. These markets have different price formation, stage of liberalisation, length of contracts, size and chief transportation method. North American market is the most liberalised with 'gas-on-gas' prices and Henry Hub spot trade. The contracts are typically short, and financial instruments are ubiquitously used. The European market is a hybrid one, as hubs coexist with oil-linked contracts for 15–20 years, and both

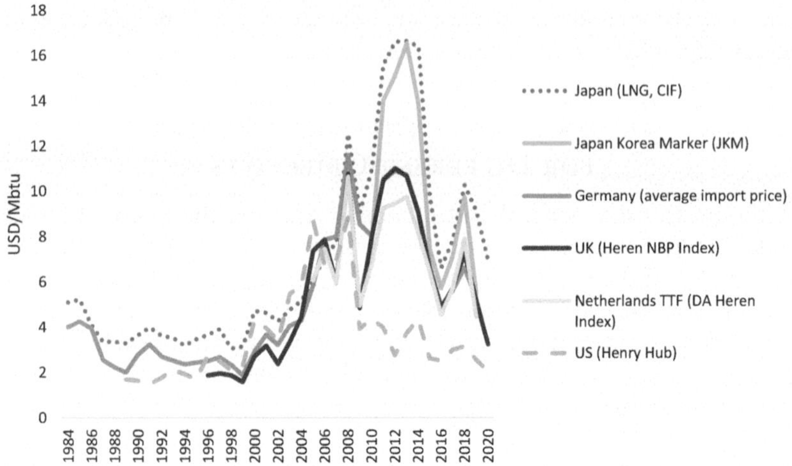

Fig. 3.4 Natural gas prices (USD/MBtu) (*Source* The Authors, based on BP [2020], IEA [2020c] and Rystad Energy [2021])

new pipelines and LNG terminals are being built simultaneously. The geographic features of the Asia–Pacific region led to massive LNG imports. The absence of significant hubs leads to oil-indexed contracts of long duration, and the prices in the region are historically the highest due to transportation costs. LNG prices in Japan almost reached USD17/MBtu in 2012 but have significantly declined since then. Liquefied natural gas serves as a connecting link (Kryukov & Medzhidova, 2019). As the volume of LNG grows, we witness regional price convergence, which may be treated as a step towards formation a global natural gas market (Fig. 3.4).

The European Commission intends to reach a complete liberalisation of the EU natural gas market (European Commission, 2020b). For now, there are several hubs in the region. The largest of them in terms of market participants, traded products and volumes, tradability index, and churn rate (Heather, 2019) are TTF (the Netherlands) and NBP (the UK).[5] According to BP (2020), Europe's gas imports reached 591 bcm in 2019, and almost 80% was imported via pipelines. The leading exporters

[5] The churn rate describes how many times the same physical gas is exchanged on the hub.

were Russia (around 46% of total imports of the EU) and Norway (19%), whose share is declining. Gas hubs become mature, promoting short-term trade, which is often associated with LNG, while pipeline gas is mostly traded on a long-term basis. We can conclude that, for now, the European market is a hybrid one. However, there is a strong trend for growth in short-term contracts, gas-on-gas price formation and development of spot trade.

LNG is undoubtedly a more flexible means of transportation, as pipelines connect a particular buyer and a specific seller, while LNG tankers can be sent to any destination. Although long-term contracts are still circulating, development of the LNG market has raised the share of short-term trade to approximately 34% in 2019 (GIIGNL, 2020). Many LNG exporters—Qatar, USA and Australia—have built additional capacities to react at once if demand exceeds the contracted volumes.

The volumes of LNG trade are rapidly growing. In 2019, they reached 482 billion cubic metres (13% growth compared to 2018). The growth is mainly driven by China and Europe (International Gas Union, 2020). Besides, the number of LNG market participants (both countries and companies) is growing every year. LNG might also seem like a good backup option even for countries with already developed pipeline infrastructure. In this case LNG enables price competition, bargaining power and security of supply. The flexibility of supplies makes LNG complementary to any other energy source, requiring backup energy capacities and storing cost minimisation. LNG plays an essential role in the global gas market formation. The crisis of 2008–2009 and an excess of LNG volumes caused price drop in the EU. So far, costs of upstream operations, processing and delivery on the biggest regional natural gas markets are too diverse. For example, delivery costs to the Baltic Sea shores from Norway, Yamal (potentially also from the Russian shore in the Baltic Sea) are modest, while transportation costs from the USA and Qatar are the same wide at the time of Sinbad.

In the Baltic Sea region, LNG has several functions. Firstly, it is more flexible than pipeline gas as short-term trade evolves. LNG can be received and regasified in Germany (when the infrastructure is built), Lithuania or Poland, and transported via pipelines through the region. Secondly, LNG is associated with a higher level of competition, as the number of exporting countries steadily grows, involving nearby countries. It prevents the monopoly of pipeline suppliers. So, LNG offers a cut in transportation costs in time, as markets grow and new participants enter every year.

Thirdly, natural gas, in general, is a part of the transition policy. Although it is still associated with more emissions than RES, some countries, such as Poland, could use it as a bridge fuel. Natural gas could force out coal in Polish energy balance, if the government eventually decides to abandon the lignite. Furthermore, LNG contributes to the European energy security. With new possible means of transportation, energy dependence on the Russian pipeline gas diminishes.

We should note here that Estonia, Latvia and Lithuania inherited gas infrastructure from the Soviet Union, and Russia remained their sole supplier for an extended period. Moreover, these countries were isolated from the European energy market. In other words, the issue of energy security, considered vital in the EU, is rather critical for these three Baltic states. Furthermore, according to the BEMIP, the regional gas and electricity market has been built. The members of this initiative are Denmark, Estonia, Finland, Germany, Latvia, Lithuania, Poland and Sweden, while Norway participates as an observer.

We may underline two issues to reduce energy dependence on Russian gas. The first one is to build pipeline infrastructure. Such projects are a part of the BEMIP: the Gas Interconnection Poland—Lithuania (GIPL) and the Balticconnector between Finland and Estonia. Balticconnector started to operate in December 2019, and GIPL is expected to be built shortly. Although the gas supplier remains the same (Russia), the pipeline will contribute to energy security if LNG infrastructure is developed. The latter might enlarge the list of suppliers to the region. The second way is to diversify imports via LNG projects. In 2014, Lithuania became the second (after Sweden) LNG importer due to Klaipeda LNG project. It is both a floating storage and a regasification unit, which can cover up to 90% of the total demand of the Baltic States (Mišík & Prachárová, 2016).

Nevertheless, in 2019 the usage of Klaipeda was a little over 44%, while Świnoujście utilisation in 2018 was the highest in the EU—around 60%. The economic efficiency of the project depends on LNG prices globally. However, some researchers have found out that such diversification can still be profitable from the viewpoint of the nation's welfare due to a decrease in prices (Shulte & Weiser, 2019). In sum, while building pipeline infrastructure will let Baltic Sea region countries develop a market, LNG projects' realisation can contribute to their energy security and bring down the prices (Table 3.7). However, both options are related to high additional costs and would be impossible without the EU financial support.

Table 3.7 LNG terminals in the Baltic Sea region, excluding Denmark, Norway and Russia, in 2020

Country	*LNG terminal*	*Current status*	*Capacity (mtpa)*	*Capital cost (EUR million)*	*Country's gas consumption (bcm)*
Estonia	Tallinn	Planned	2.7	250	0.4
	Paldiski	Planned	1.8	370	
Finland	Hamina-Kotka	Under construction	30,000 m^3 (storage terminal)	150	2.0
	Rauma	Planned	10,000 m^3 (storage capacity)		
	Tahkoluoto/Pori	Operational	0.1		
	Tornio Manga	Operational	0.4		
Germany	Brunsbüttel	Planned	8.0	500	88.7
	Stade	Planned	3.7	567	
	Wilhelmshaven	Planned	7.3	622	
Latvia	Skulte	Planned	1.1	110	1.3
Lithuania	Klaipeda	Operational	2.9	151	2.2
Poland	Świnoujście	Operational	5.0	950	20.4
Sweden	Brunnsviksholmen	Operational	20,000 m^3	2,857	1.0

Note None of the German LNG terminals mentioned in the above table is located on the shores of the Baltic Sea but on the shores of the North Sea
Source The Authors, based on LNG terminals' websites and BP (2020)

The volume of gas consumption in the region, excluding Denmark, Norway and Russia, in 2019 has reached 116 bcm, of which LNG had a minor share. LNG prices fluctuate along with the pipeline gas prices, so there are no stable price advantages. Two terminals (Świnoujście and Klaipeda) probably had external financing to the extent that they do not need to pay back the loan. In this case, political investment costs have already been paid, and one may expect their role as a security backup may continue regardless of the market situation. Another floating LNG terminal belongs to Gazprom. Its capacity is up to 2.7 bcm, designed to cover all needs of the particular region. The estimated costs were 86 billion Russian roubles (approximately one billion euros), invested in ensuring energy security of the Kaliningrad region. Essentially, Russia decided not to put at risk pipeline deliveries if another transit problem occurs. The case demonstrates the cost of an energy supply security risk elimination.

The factor of US LNG supplies so far is primarily important for the exporter—it needs a market in the future. It is not bringing substantial price gains and may be treated more in the geopolitical context. LNG by itself is just a gas. The conflict of political interests and dramatic changes in the EU climate policy brings more controversies into the LNG biography.

Energy security is a trendy theme in the region, while almost nothing dramatic related to Russian gas supplies has ever happened in the Baltic Sea region. However, we must mention the dispute between Russia and Belarus in 2004 as the most important. The issue of increasing gas prices for Belarus (Beltransgaz) resulted in one-day cut-off by Gazprom, Itera and Transnafta on 18 February 2004. In response, Belarus cut off Russian supply to Europe via the Yamal pipeline (Bruce, 2005). Eventually, the dispute was settled. However, a series of oil disputes between Russian and transit countries (primarily Ukraine and Belarus) followed. Although this cut-off lasted less than a day and no other cut-offs took place later, new pipelines were built to ensure energy security. This dispute worked as a factor of instability in the political discourse.

However, politics and political perceptions matter. The latter is connected with geopolitics and relations between Russia and other countries of the region. The twenty-first century has more history of price conflicts than stoppages of delivery (the most controversial was the event of January of 2009 in Ukraine). The formation of the global gas market with has not completed. Business cycle dynamic, COVID-19 and Greater Recession 2020 are changing the energy transition background and climate policy.

Fast Energy Transition and Destruction of the EU Gas Market

Nowadays, the European countries enlarge their efforts against global climate change. These efforts include energy transition from fossil fuels to renewables and reaching carbon-neutrality in 2050. However, this decision will take political will, significant investments and concordance between the countries with different energy balances.

Natural gas was regarded as a less noxious fuel at the beginning of the transition process. It was considered that natural gas would serve as a bridge from coal to renewables. In Asia, coal still dominates the power sector in many countries. Actually, the share of coal in the global energy balance in 2019 was at the same level as gas (respectively: 27.0 and 24.2%) (BP, 2020). Depletion of the coal generation in the world (outside the EU) in the short time horizon will probably be based on increasing natural gas consumption. Replacement of coal was always stated as the main contribution of natural gas to climate change mitigation (Kerr, 2010; Levi, 2013; Podesta & Wirth, 2009). Although the idea was a popular one, we are far away from there by now.

Natural gas is believed to be less harmful for the environment than other fossil fuels, however, there are necessary clarifications we would like to note. LNG supply chain includes liquefaction, storage, transportation via LNG tankers and regasification. Some of the stages are associated with GHG emissions, which results in additional emissions from LNG compared to pipeline gas. Liquefaction emissions occur mainly due to fuel gas combustion to power refrigeration compressors and electrical generators, fired process heat generators, venting of low-pressure carbon dioxide, fugitive losses of other GHG used in the facility, fugitive losses of natural gas from the process due to leakage. Furthermore, the more proximate is the delivery destination, the lesser is the harm to the environment (Goldthau, 2016). In many regions of the world coal latter may still play an essential role in the forthcoming decades. It is particularly true for Asian or African countries with high economic growth rates and critical dependence on the cheap local coal. To reduce the stock of emitted GHG it is vital to fasten coal generation replacement by RES or gas. The success of Paris Agreement is determined by the timing of climate change mitigation (Sanderson et al., 2016).

Zhang et al. (2016) note that the environmental safety of gas and coal varies in the short term (20 years) and the long term. To be more precise, methane from natural gas is more noxious than CO_2 from coal. Another disadvantage of using natural gas as a bridge fuel is its impact on the carbon-neutrality policy adaption (Hausfather, 2015). Gas is believed to delay such policies, which is inpermissible for climate change mitigation.

Nevertheless, we are currently witnessing the emergence of natural gas decarbonisation plans. According to Stern (2019), there exist three options for natural gas decarbonisation: (1) biogas/biomethane, (2) synthetic natural gas from gasification and (3) hydrogen options. All of them require modernisation of the existing infrastructure and building of a new one. Besides, Stern (2020) states that net-zero targets will influence gas demand in Europe and lead to its decline: '*The potential disadvantage would be that all networks and customers in those regions would need to be converted to hydrogen unless a further step was taken to methanise the hydrogen into syngas onshore ("power-to-methane" in Fig. 4) which would add to efficiency losses and therefore to costs*' (Stern, 2020, 396). We could not agree more: as the climate issue has become more critical, new challenges are posed for both exporters and importers of natural gas in Europe. The real choice in the coming decade may be not only between RES and gas but also between 'cleaner gas' (pipeline) and LNG on ecological grounds.

All in all, it becomes more and more evident that the 'traditional' natural gas era has almost ended, and gas could be regarded as 'a missed bridge'. This statement is proved by the EU hydrogen strategy (European Commission, 2020c), as low-carbon hydrogen is an option only until 2030. Later on, the EU is supposed to rely on renewable hydrogen.

We believe that the Green Deal is becoming the game-changer, and it's about time to recognise the strategies and decide on plans. The Green Deal has at least three main implications. Firstly, the EU wants to reduce its dependence on Russian gas for political reasons. Natural gas and low-carbon hydrogen cannot contribute to success in achieving this goal. So, no LNG bridge is needed anymore, and European countries stress the necessity to develop renewables. Secondly, energy security implies avoiding dependence on the USA gas supply as well. It also has political motives, connected to pursuing some sort of independent policy. The whole strategy of exporting American LNG to the EU is losing steam due to nullifying gas demand for the power sector roughly about the same time as Gazprom's long-term contracts will end. Thirdly, Brussels seeks the centralisation of the power. The latter is limited by the national specifics of Poland, Hungary and even by climate and other issues in Germany.

'The big leap' of the EU to renewables may have some severe consequences for the Baltic Sea region. Likewise, LNG projects, which include building (not leasing) of infrastructure, may now have low chances for economic efficiency in the long term. The EU climate policy's success is apparent, and it is only a question of time (and technology) when renewables will mostly replace fossil fuels. The Russian supply is guaranteed for another 15–20 years, basing on long-term contracts, and this period is vitally needed to rebuild the energy balances of the European countries. However, we should admit that a complete reduction of fossil fuels consumption so far looks highly unlikely, even in a longer perspective. Nevertheless, natural gas consumption is doomed to decline with oil and coal in the same process gradually. In other words, whether it is necessary to invest in LNG infrastructure in the Baltic Sea region becomes even a more questionable issue regarding the energy transition of the EU.

The rational position of LNG on the world market is for supplies of relatively clean low-carbon energy. In the EU, LNG's role focused on increasing competition, undermining monopolies and lowering prices. Nevertheless, now it is all about climate policy, the Green Deal. Originally, LNG's role in the Baltic Sea region was about prices, but then it turned to be a security of supply issue. New EU decisions on zero-carbon Europe are surprisingly playing against investing both in LNG (more emissions and more costly) and the pipeline gas. Reaching carbon-neutrality would take 30 years, but the targets of 2030 are already relatively high (making the power sector free of fossil fuels).

At that point, the political considerations and costs are entering the picture. From the perspective of economists, they are 'political costs' (Stern et al., 2014). If political elites are ready to pay for security or politically motivated projects, the cost/effectiveness approach is useless. These decisions would be outside economic context or climate policy contexts since gas is much cleaner than the rest of fossil fuels. By the same approach, the expected transition from fossil fuels in the power sector puts LNG supplies in a worse situation than existing pipelines. Furthermore, according to some estimates, the carbon footprint from Russian Nord Stream 2 is 2.6–4.6 times less than the EU's LNG imports from the USA, Algeria, Qatar and Australia (ThinkStep, 2017).

The matter looks rather controversial for us. On the one hand, the EU's energy security creates incentives for cutting dependence on Russian gas. On the other hand, the very same security issue promotes a shift to renewables, with little space left for natural gas, including LNG. German position of North Stream 2 is often ignored in debates on the project. While in all other economic matters, most European countries are heavily relying on German support. After intense discussions, sanctions and demonstrations of the conflict of interests it seems that the Nord Stream 2 project will be finally completed, as some specialists predicted (Yafimava, 2020). It took a joint statement of the French President and the German Chancellor that the pipeline is a matter of energy security for Europe to clarify the European position on American sanctions on the companies participating in the project (Delfs et al., 2021). This outcome would give the EU the supply chain with investment costs already paid. The rest depends on a huge investment programme in the EU to reach the declared targets. We expect that debate on these matters may slowly fade: serious recession, low demand for gas and low gas prices. Maybe the Green Deal just deprived natural gas of its long-term future in the EU, and even worse—it deprived LNG of its controversial role in the Baltic Sea region, sending LNG to the 'forced pension'.

Conclusions

Ten years ago, one of the authors of this chapter had written a sceptical piece in the Baltic Rim Economies review (Grigoriev, 2010) on North Steam 1. Our point was that too many 'inventions' were made to stop the first project, and these 'inventions' were somewhat artificial, and they are not even remembered now. Nothing wrong was caused by the North Stream 1 operation in these ten years, as we expected. It should also be noted two decades ago that importing countries have been dreaming of the anti-exporters sanctions (Mitchell et al., 2001, 2): '*The threat of political sanctions has been reversed. It is exporting countries that now need to be concerned about sanctions aimed at their domestic and foreign policies by governments and public opinion in developed countries*'.

We might also add that nowadays, these sanctions are imposed by other exporters as a part of the competitive strategy. Of course, the political and economic situations in ten years need to be reconsidered dramatically. By now, in 2020, we have the corona pandemic and the Greater Recession, and enormous resources are rededicated to ensure the very survival of peoples and economies. In times like these, it would be reasonable for the international community to concentrate on immediate survival needs.

References

Avelino, F., Grin, J., Pel, B., & Jhagroe, S. (2016). The politics of sustainability transitions. *Journal of Environmental Policy & Planning, 18*(5), 557–567. https://doi.org/10.1080/1523908X.2016.1216782

Bobylev, S., & Grigoryev, L. (2020). In search of the contours of the post-COVID Sustainable Development Goals: The case of BRICS. *BRICS Journal of Economics (BjE), 1*(2), 4–24. https://doi.org/10.38050/2712-7508-2020-7

BP. (2020). *Statistical review of world energy*. https://www.bp.com/en/global/corporate/energy-economics/statistical-review-of-world-energy.html. Accessed 3 September 2020. Accessed 5 April 2021.

Bridge, G., Bouzarovski, S., Bradshaw, M., & Eyre, N. (2012). Geographies of energy transition: Space, place and low-carbon economy. *Energy Policy, 53*, 331–340. https://doi.org/10.1016/j.enpol.2012.10.066

Bruce, C. (2005). *Fraternal friction or fraternal fiction? The gas factor in Russian-Belarusian relations*. The Oxford Institute for Energy Studies.

Climate Action Network Europe. (2018, June 17). *EU countries off target in fighting climate change*. https://www.caneurope.org/docman/climate-energy-targets/3357-off-target-ranking-of-eu-countries-ambition-and-progress-in-fighting-climate-change/file. Accessed 5 September 2020.

Delfs, A., Ruitenberg, R., & Colitt, R. (2021, February 5). *Merkel, Macron to put aside differences on Russian gas pipeline*. Bloomberg. https://www.bloomberg.com/news/articles/2021-02-05/merkel-macron-to-put-aside-differences-on-russian-gas-pipeline. Accessed 5 April 2021.

European Commission. (2020a). *2020 climate & energy package*. https://ec.europa.eu/clima/policies/strategies/2020_en. Accessed 2 August 2020.

European Commission. (2020b). *Gas market liberalisation*. https://ec.europa.eu/energy/content/gas-market-liberalisation_en. Accessed 22 November 2020.

European Commission. (2020c). *A hydrogen strategy for climate-neutral Europe*. Communication from the Commission to the European Parliament, the Council, the European Economic and Social Committee and the Committee of the Regions. https://ec.europa.eu/energy/sites/ener/files/hydrogen_strategy.pdf. Accessed 24 November 2020.

European Commission. (2021). *2030 climate target plan*. https://ec.europa.eu/clima/policies/eu-climate-action/2030_ctp_en. Accessed 29 July 2021.

European Council. (2019). *European Council meetings (12 December 2019) Conclusions*. https://www.consilium.europa.eu/media/41768/12-euco-final-conclusions-en.pdf. Accessed 5 September 2020.

Fouquet, R., & Pearson, P. J. G. (1998). A thousand years of energy use in the United Kingdom. *The Energy Journal, 19*(4), 1–41. https://doi.org/10.5547/ISSN0195-6574-EJ-Vol19-No4-1

Gazprom. (2020). *Delivery statistics*. http://www.gazpromexport.ru/en/statistics/. Accessed 5 September.

Geels, F. W., & Schot, J. (2007). Typology of sociotechnical transition pathways. *Research Policy, 36*(3), 399–417. https://doi.org/10.1016/j.respol.2007.01.003

GIIGNL. (2020). *Annual report*. https://giignl.org/sites/default/files/PUBLIC_AREA/Publications/giignl_-_2020_annual_report_-_04082020.pdf. Accessed 15 August 2020.

Goldthau, A. (2016). *Assessing Nord Stream 2: Regulation, geopolitics & energy security in the EU, Central Eastern Europe & the UK* (Strategy Paper, 10). European Centre for Energy and Resource Security.

Grigoriev, L. (2010). *Happy end of pipeline conflicts?* (p. 13). Baltic Rim Economies (BRE), 1/2010.

Grigoryev, L., & Medzhidova, D. (2020). The global energy trilemma. *Russian Journal of Economics (RuJec)*, *5*(4), 437–462. https://doi.org/10.32609/j.ruje.6.58683

Grubb, M., & Neuhoff, K. (2006). Allocation and competitiveness in the EU emissions trading scheme: Policy overview. *Climate Policy*, *6*(1), 7–30. https://doi.org/10.1080/14693062.2006.9685586

Hafner, M., & Raimondi, P. (2020). Priorities and challenges of the EU energy transition: From the European green package to the new green deal. *Russian Journal of Economics (RuJec)*, *6*(4), 374–389.

Hausfather, Z. (2015). Bounding the climate viability of natural gas as a bridge fuel to displace coal. *Energy Policy*, *86*, 286–294. https://doi.org/10.1016/j.enpol.2015.07.012

Heather, P. (2019). *European traded gas hubs: A decade of change*. The Oxford Institute for Energy Studies.

Hong, S., Qvist, S., & Brook, B. W. (2018). Economic and environmental costs of replacing nuclear fission with solar and wind energy in Sweden. *Energy Policy*, *112*, 56–66. https://doi.org/10.1016/j.enpol.2017.10.013

IEA. (2020a). *European Union 2020. Energy policy review*. https://www.iea.org/reports/european-union-2020. Accessed 9 November 2020.

IEA. (2020b). *Data & statistics*. https://www.iea.org/data-and-statistics?country=WORLD&fuel=Energy%20supply&indicator=TPESbySource. Accessed 10 September 2020.

IEA. (2020c). *Gas 2020*. https://www.iea.org/reports/gas-2020/annex#abstract. Accessed 31 March 2021.

IMF. (2020). *Fiscal monitor*. https://www.imf.org/en/Publications/FM/Issues/2020/09/30/october-2020-fiscal-monitor/. Accessed 15 August 2020.

IMF. (2021a). *World Economic Outlook database*. https://www.imf.org/en/Publications/WEO/weo-database/2021/April/. Accessed 21 May 2021.

IMF. (2021b). *Drawing further apart: Widening gaps in the global recovery*. https://blogs.imf.org/2021/07/27/drawing-further-apart-wideninggaps-in-the-global-recovery/. Accessed 29 July 2021.

International Gas Union. (2020). *Global gas report*. https://igu.org/resources/global-gas-report-2020/. Accessed 15 August 2020.

Kander, A., & Lindmark, M. (2006). Foreign trade and declining pollution in Sweden: A decomposition analysis of long-term structural and technological effects. *Energy Policy*, *34*(13), 1590–1599. https://doi.org/10.1016/j.enpol.2004.12.007

Kerr, R. A. (2010). Natural gas from shale bursts onto the scene. *Science, 328*, 1624–1626.

Kryukov, V., & Medzhidova, D. (2019). The influence of the relationship 'specificity of key assets—Human capital' on the development of the US gas industry. *Journal of Institutional Studies, 11*(3), 39–53. https://doi.org/10.17835/2076-6297.2019.11.3.039-053

Kuchler, M., & Bridge, G. (2018). Down the black hole: Sustaining national socio-technical imaginaries of coal in Poland. *Energy Research & Social Science, 41*, 136–147. https://doi.org/10.1016/j.erss.2018.04.014

Leach, G. (1992). The energy transition. *Energy Policy, 20*(2), 116–123. https://doi.org/10.1016/0301-4215(92)90105-B

Lenzen, M. (1998). Primary energy and greenhouse gases embodied in Australian final consumption: An input-output analysis. *Energy Policy, 26*(6), 495–506. https://doi.org/10.1016/S0301-4215(98)00012-3

Levi, M. (2013). Climate consequences of natural gas as a bridge fuel. *Climatic Change, 118*, 609–623. https://doi.org/10.1007/s10584-012-0658-3

Makarov, I., & Sokolova, A. (2017). Carbon emissions embodied in Russia's trade: Implications for climate policy. *Review of European and Russian Affairs, 11*(2), 1–20.

Melsted, O., & Pallua, I. (2018). The historical transition from coal to hydrocarbons: Previous explanations and the need for an integrative perspective. *Canadian Journal of History, 53*(3), 395–422. https://doi.org/10.3138/cjh.ach.53.3.03

Mendonça, R., Barros, N., Vidal, L. O., Pacheco, F. S., Kosten, S., & Roland, F. (2012). Greenhouse gas emissions from hydroelectric reservoirs: What knowledge do we have and what is lacking? In L. Guoxiang (Ed.), *Greenhouse gases: Emission, measurement and management*. InTech.

Millar, R. J., Fuglestvedt, J. S., Friedlingstein, P., Rogelj, J., Grubb, M. J., Matthews, H. D., Skeie, R. B., Forster, P. M., Frame, D. J., & Allen, M. R. (2017). Emission budgets and pathways consistent with limiting warming to 1.5 °C. *Nature Geoscience, 10*, 741–750. https://doi.org/10.1038/NGEO3031

Mišík, M., & Prachárová, V. (2016). Before 'Independence' arrived: Interdependence in energy relations between Lithuania and Russia. *Geopolitics, 21*(3), 579–604. https://doi.org/10.1080/14650045.2015.1113402

Mitchell, J., Morita, K., Selley, N., & Stern, J. (2001). *The new economy of oil: Impacts on business, geopolitics and society*. Energy & Environmental Programme. Earthscan.

Peters, G. P., & Hertwich, E. G. (2006). Pollution embodied in trade: The Norwegian case. *Global Environmental Change, 16*(4), 379–387.

Podesta, J. D., & Wirth, T. E. (2009). *Natural gas: A bridge fuel for the 21st century*. Center for American Progress. https://www.americanprogress.org/

issues/green/reports/2009/08/10/6513/natural-gas-a-bridge-fuel-for-the-21st-century/. Accessed 24 November 2020.

Podobnik, B. (2006). *Global energy shifts: Fostering sustainability in a turbulent age*. Temple University Press.

Ritchie, H. (2019). *How do CO_2 emissions compare when we adjust for trade?* Our World in Data. https://ourworldindata.org/consumption-based-co2. Accessed 3 August 2020.

Rystad Energy. (2021). *Rystad Energy UCube database*. https://www.rystadenergy.com. Accessed 31 March 2021.

Sanderson, B., Tebaldi, C., & O'Neill, B. (2016). What would it take to achieve the Paris temperature targets? *Geophysical Research Letters, 43*(13), 7133–7142. https://doi.org/10.1002/2016GL069563

Shulte, S., & Weiser, F. (2019). LNG import quotas in Lithuania—Economic effects of breaking Gazprom's natural gas monopoly. *Energy Economics, 78*, 174–181. https://doi.org/10.1016/j.eneco.2018.10.030

Slay, B., & Pospíšilová, M. (2009, August). *The Baltic Conundrum*. CASE Network E-Brief.

Smil, V. (2005). *Energy at the crossroads: Global perspectives and uncertainties*. The MOT Press.

Smith, A., Voß, J.-P., & Grin, J. (2010). Innovation studies and sustainability transitions: The allure of the multi-level perspective and its challenges. *Research Policy, 39*, 435–448. https://doi.org/10.1016/j.respol.2010.01.023

Solomon, B. D., & Krishna, K. (2011). The coming sustainable energy transition: History, strategies and outlook. *Energy Policy, 39*(11), 7422–7431. https://doi.org/10.1016/j.enpol.2011.09.009

Stern, J. (2019). *Narratives for natural gas in decarbonising European energy markets*. The Oxford Institute for Energy Studies.

Stern, J. (2020). The role of gases in the European energy transition. *Russian Journal of Economics (RuJec), 6*(4), 390–405.

Stern, J., Rogers, H., Yafimava, K., Pirani, S., El-Katiri, L., Honore, A., Henderson, J., Hassanzadeh, E., & Dickel, R. (2014). *Reducing European dependence on Russian gas—Distinguishing natural gas security from geopolitics*. The Oxford Institute for Energy Studies.

The Finnish Government. (2020). *Annual Climate Change Report 2020: Emission reduction targets for the following years likely to be reached, carbon-neutral Finland by 2035 requires further action*. https://ym.fi/en/-/annual-climate-change-report-2020-emission-reduction-targets-for-the-following-years-likely-to-be-reached-carbon-neutral-finland-by-2035-requires-further-action. Accessed 5 September 2020.

The Russian Government. (2017). Об утверждении перечня основного технологического оборудования, эксплуатируемого в случае применения наилучших доступных технологий. http://government.ru/docs/28226/. Accessed 6 September 2020.

ThinkStep. (2017). *GHG intensity of natural gas transport. Comparison of additional natural gas imports to Europe by Nord Stream 2 pipeline and LNG import alternatives*. https://www.europeangashub.com/wp-content/uploads/attach_795.pdf. Accessed 28 July 2020.

von der Leyen, U., & Hoyer, W. (2021, March 22). *A global green deal. The world's opinion page*. Project Syndicate. https://www.project-syndicate.org/commentary/a-global-green-deal-through-european-climate-leadership-by-ursula-von-der-leyen-and-werner-hoyer-2021-03?utm_source=Project+Syndicate+Newsletter&utm_campaign=4161ffd8c1-sunday_newsletter_03_28_2021&utm_medium=email&utm_term=0_73bad5b7d8-4161ffd8c1-107189098&mc_cid=4161ffd8c1&mc_eid=52c43548f0. Accessed 5 April 2021.

World Bank. (2020). *World Development Indicators*. https://databank.worldbank.org/source/world-development-indicators/. Accessed 29 July 2020.

World Energy Trilemma Index. (2019). *World Energy Council in partnership with Oliver Wyman*. https://www.worldenergy.org/assets/downloads/WETrilemma_2019_Full_Report_v4_pages.pdf. Accessed 29 July 2020.

Yafimava, K. (2020). *Nord Stream 2: Delayed but unstoppable* (pp. 35–37). Baltic Rim Economies (BRE), 3/2020.

Zhang, X., Myhrvold, N., Hausfather, Z., & Caldeira, K. (2016). Climate benefits of natural gas as a bridge fuel and potential delay of near-zero energy systems. *Applied Energy, 167*, 317–322. https://doi.org/10.1016/j.apenergy.2015.10.016

CHAPTER 4

Russian LNG Exports

Andrey Shadurskiy

Introduction

The year 2020 with warm European and Asian winters followed by the global coronavirus crisis added even more uncertainties to the equation of success for the Russian LNG industry. Already before 2020, the feasibility of Russia's LNG ambitions has constantly been questioned. In its quest to become one of the leading LNG exporters in the world, Russia initially bet on extremely challenging projects in the Arctic. This choice became even riskier after the Western sanctions had limited Russia's access to both large-scale funding and crucial technical expertise. Despite all these challenges and calmly brushing away general woes about the future of oil and gas industries, Russia has stayed positive about the future of LNG markets and its own role in these markets.

In October 2020, the Russian Ministry of Energy assessed that the capacity of already functioning LNG facilities was 29.8 mt, and 22.2 mt is currently under construction. This should be followed by 24.5 mt of projects which are now being drafted and, finally, there are yet unspecified plans to launch 48.9 mt of future projects. Thus, the total capacity of

A. Shadurskiy (✉)
Vienna, Austria

K. Liuhto (ed.), *The Future of Energy Consumption, Security and Natural Gas*, https://doi.org/10.1007/978-3-030-80367-4_4

currently operating LNG facilities and LNG projects, which are under construction, under development, or planned, exceeds 125 mt.

The operational facilities at the end of 2020 are Yamal LNG (18.3 mt), Sakhalin 2 LNG (10.8 mt), and Vysotsk LNG (0.7 mt). The projects currently under construction are Arctic LNG 2 (19.8 mt), the 4th train of Yamal LNG (0.9 mt), and Portovaya LNG (1.5 mt)—totalling 22.2 mt of capacity.[1] The projects, which were under development in 2020, should add 24.5 mt of capacity. These are Ob LNG (5 mt), Baltic LNG (13 mt), and Far East LNG (6.2 mt). Finally, 'future projects' can add almost 50 mt of capacity,[2] including Arctic LNG 1 (18.9 mt), the 3rd train of Sakhalin 2 (5.4 mt), 2nd train at Vysotsk LNG (1.1 mt), Vladivostok LNG (1.5 mt), Pechora LNG[3] (4.3 mt), and Yakutsk LNG (17.7 mt) (Interfax, 2020c). All the major Russian LNG projects are summarised in Table 4.1 and Map 4.1.

The schedule and capacities of the listed projects approximately correspond to the targets for production and exports of LNG set in the most recent Russian Energy Strategy until 2035, which was adopted in 2020. The strategy forecasts production of 46–65 mtpa by 2024 and 80–140 mtpa of LNG by 2035. Annual exports are expected to increase from the base level of 26.9 bcm in 2018 to 59.8–65.1 bcm in 2024 and then to 108–189 bcm in 2035, with lower and higher value reflecting cautious and optimistic scenarios (Ministry of Energy of Russian Federation, 2020).

By the middle of the 2030s, Russia hopes to get hold of at least a fifth or even a quarter of the global LNG market (Tikhonov, 2020). However, the challenges of 2020, even if overcome in 2021, can at least postpone these plans. Russia already did set ambitious targets at the beginning of the second decade of the 2000s, when it had only a stake in a single foreign-designed LNG project—through Gazprom in Sakhalin 2.

This article commences with the history of LNG production in Russia and plans for its development as stipulated in the new strategy documents of 2020. Then the article analyses several distinctive clusters of LNG projects in Russia: (1) Far East, the cradle of large-scale LNG production

[1] LNG train is a single liquefaction plant at an LNG terminal or facility.

[2] The category of 'future projects' should be treated extremely cautiously, as all of them are unlikely to go online before 2030 and these projects have significantly different chances of being realised.

[3] Pechora LNG was re-purposed to a methanol facility in the very end of 2020.

Table 4.1 Russia's sending LNG facilities: operational, under construction, under development, and planned

Name, location	*Annual capacity (mt)*	*Status (year)*	*Operator/owner*
Operational			
Sakhalin 2, Sakhalin Oblast	10.8	Operational (2009)	Sakhalin Energy: Gazprom, Royal Dutch Shell, Mitsui, Mitsubishi
Yamal LNG, T1-T3, Yamalo-Nenets Autonomous Okrug	18.3	Operational (2019)	Novatek, Total, CNPC, Silk Road Fund
Vysotsk LNG, Leningrad Oblast	0.7	Operational (2019)	Cryogas-Vysotsk: Novatek and Gazprombank
Under construction			
Yamal LNG, T4, Yamalo-Nenets Autonomous Okrug	0.9	Under construction (2nd half 2021)	Novatek, Total, CNPC, Silk Road Fund
Portovaya LNG, Leningrad Oblast	1.5	Under construction (2021)	Gazprom
Arctic LNG 2, Yamalo-Nenets Autonomous Okrug	19.8	Under construction (2023–2026)	Novatek, Total, CNPC, CNOOC, Mitsui, JOGMEC
Under development			
Baltic LNG, Ust-Luga, Leningrad Oblast	13	Under development (2023–2024)	RusKhimAlyans: Gazprom and RusGazDobycha
Ob LNG, Yamalo-Nenets Autonomous Okrug	5	Under development (2024–2025)	Novatek
Far East LNG, De-Kastri, Khabarovsk Krai	6.2	Under development (2027)	Exxon Neftegaz: ExxonMobil, Rosneft, SODECO, ONGC
Planned			
Vysotsk LNG, T2, Leningrad Oblast	1.1	Planned (2021)	Cryogas-Vysotsk: Novatek and Gazprombank
Arctic LNG 1, Yamalo-Nenets Autonomous Okrug	19.8	Planned (after 2026)	Novatek

(continued)

Table 4.1 (continued)

Name, location	*Annual capacity (mt)*	*Status (year)*	*Operator/owner*
Sakhalin 2, T3, Sakhalin Oblast	5.4	Planned (after 2026, conditional to the reassessment of available resources in 2021)	Sakhalin Energy: Gazprom, Royal Dutch Shell, Mitsui, Mitsubishi
Vladivostok LNG, Primorsky Krai	1.5	Planned (pre-FID completed in 2020, no specific schedule available)	Gazprom
Least likely or currently re-purposed			
Yakutsk LNG, Khabarovsk Krai	17.7	Planned (2025)	Globaltek
Pechora LNG, Nenets Autonomous Okrug	4.3	Cancelled—repurposed to the production of methanol	Ruskhim

Note Receiving facilities, such as Marshal Vasilevskiy FSRU (Kaliningrad), or planned Novatek'stransshipment facilities in the Murmansk Oblast and the Kamchatka Krai are exempt from the table
Source The Author

and a conflict area for Gazprom and Rosneft, (2) the Arctic cluster—so far the most successful LNG case ruled by Novatek, but contested by Gazprom and Rosneft, and (3) the Baltic Sea region—a unique case given the importance of small-scale and medium-scale LNG projects and complex geopolitical environment. Finally, there is a cluster not linked to geography: that of attempted independent projects, which can tell a lot about the underlying logic of developing LNG industry in Russia.

The article proceeds with a brief analysis of selected small-scale and medium-scale LNG projects together with domestic demand for LNG in Russia. These are not only important indirectly influencing the Russian LNG exports, but are directly a part of Russian LNG exports, often overlooked, but important in regional contexts. At the end of the chapter, there is an analysis of one of the most important issues: competition between Russia's LNG and pipeline gas, a rivalry of major Russian energy companies when it comes to the LNG exports, a role of the state in resolving these conflicts and the meaning of potential liberalisation of the LNG exports as stipulated in Russia's new energy strategy.

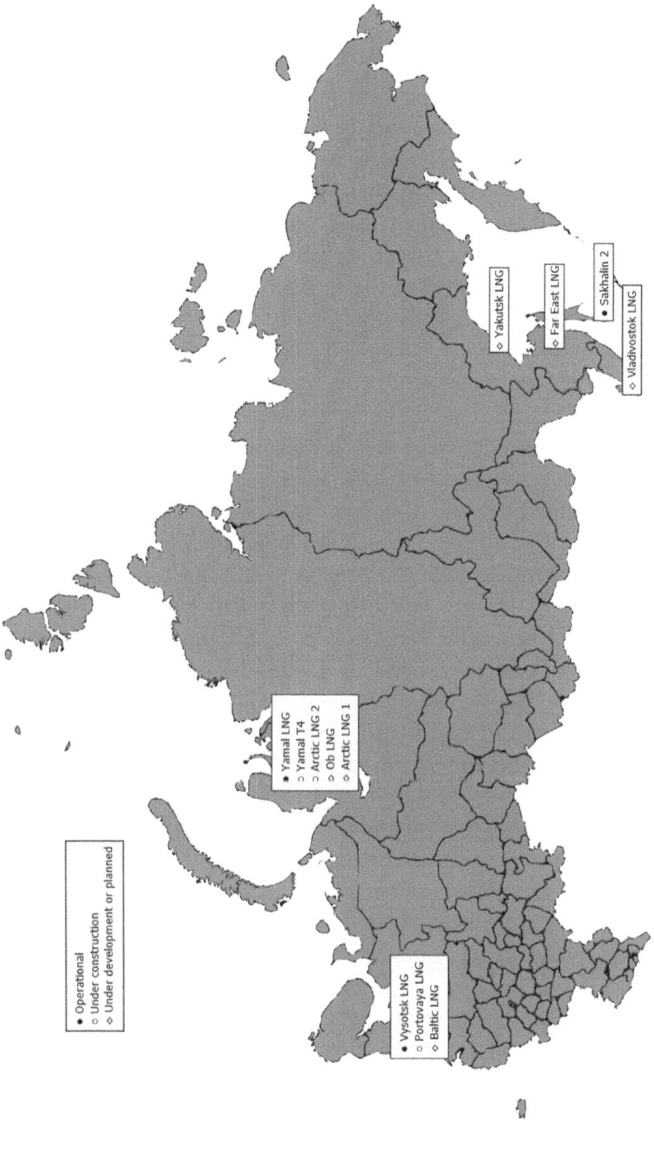

Map 4.1 Russian LNG facilities: operational, under construction, under development, and planned (*Source* The Author)

History and the Current State of Russia's LNG Ambitions

Pipelines, Shtokman, and the American Dream

Russia has long been relying on pipelines as the means of foreign energy trade and foreign influence alike—hence was coined the term 'pipeline diplomacy'. Diplomacy apart, pipelines have often been the only viable method of delivering hydrocarbons from the distant areas of production to main customer markets in Europe. Given previously strictly regional nature of gas markets, pipelines were tightly and securely binding what looked like two worlds apart during the Cold War.

The first project of a gas liquefaction facility was drafted in the USSR immediately after World War II. The LNG plant was to be located near Moscow and meant even to supply of gas from the Volga region. That project had to be postponed with the beginning of the Cold War as the USSR did not have the necessary technology for storing liquefied gas, which was already then mastered by the USA.

The 1950s did however see the first small-scale LNG plant being constructed in the USSR as well as the first plans to export gas as LNG—the latter to no avail. During the détente period of the Cold War between the 1960s and the 1970s, new ideas surfaced—to co-operate with the USA in producing LNG in the Russian North and then exporting it or to export LNG from Eastern Siberia to Japan. None of the aforementioned plans advanced beyond the ideation stage, neither did smaller-scale attempts to produce or use LNG in the USSR. Russia returned to considering the technology at the end of the 1990s when a couple of small-scale facilities were constructed in the Leningrad region (Karpov et al., 2020).

On the large scale, the first prominent LNG project in Russia was linked to the planned development of the Shtokman mammoth gas field in the Barents Sea. In the middle of the 2000s, before the shale revolution in the USA, one forecasted a world where the USA would become the largest driver of LNG and its consumer in the world, compensating for the depleting domestic resources (Yergin & Stoppard, 2003). Gazprom clearly had the lucrative US market in focus when it decided to engage in this project of unprecedented complexity, combining offshore, deepwater, and Arctic challenges. Still, the strategic value of the project was on par: LNG and Shtokman were perceived as an opportunity to diversify natural gas export routes from Russia.

At that time, Russia still had not come to the complete understanding of symmetric nature of energy security in case of pipeline connections and was dismissive of the danger of expanding LNG supplies to Europe, so the diversification in this regard was purely of a geographic nature. Despite the dwindling costs of new LNG facilities, expanding fleet of LNG tankers, and the growing number of exporters, there seemed to be no danger to what had long been posed as affordable and stable supplies via pipelines. After all, these could even stay the test of the collapse of the Soviet Union.

The first bell for Russia rang when its image was tarnished by 'the pipeline wars' with Ukraine (2005–2006) and Belarus (2006–2007). The second bell was overdue: however insignificant in capacity and isolated in terms of the European gas infrastructure the first LNG projects in the traditional Gazprom's market looked like, they happened to herald a new era of globalised LNG markets and had a drastic effect on Gazprom's market power in Europe. As soon as the effects of the globalising LNG market were obvious, Russia resolved to catch up. In 2013, it set a target of producing 40–45 mt of LNG by 2020, intending to occupy more than ten percent of the international LNG market. It also hoped to diversify exports by catering to dynamic and huge Asian market. Both targets have been missed: in 2019 Russia exported only 29.3 mt of LNG, which corresponded to eight percent of the world market (IGU, 2020).

The New Strategies of 2020

In June 2020, the Russian Government adopted the Energy Strategy of the Russian Federation until 2035 (Ministry of Energy of Russian Federation, 2020), replacing the previous strategy that was adopted in 2009 and covered the span until 2030. The strategy implies that until 2024 Russia must sustain natural gas production at the level of 795–820 bcm and then until 2035 at 860–1,000 bcm. The document lists the expanded use of LNG as one of the features of the expected structural diversification of energy technologies and policies. It forecasts a 2.4–3.4 times increase in production of LNG in Russia until 2024 compared with the base year of 2018 (18.9 mt) and puts a special emphasis on energy projects in the Arctic, Eastern Siberia, and Russia's Far East. Russia is expected to be one of the leaders in LNG markets and the strategy lists both general and very precise measures that should help to gain and hold that status.

Combining pipeline and LNG exports, there is the target of being either the largest or the second-largest exporter of LNG until 2035.

The strategy explicitly mentions creating an LNG production cluster at Yamal and Gydan peninsulas as well as the construction of Novatek's LNG hubs in the Murmansk region and Kamchatka. Specific Gazprom's projects are represented by the 3rd train of Sakhalin 2 and Baltic LNG facility (Ust-Luga). Rosneft's Far East LNG is also mentioned as one of the key projects. At the same time, there is nothing specific regarding independent projects despite the strategy admitting that further liberalisation of LNG exports may be necessary to achieve the targets set. Liberalisation is therefore meant to include only a very limited set of companies and be actually complemented with a control mechanism that would prevent excessive competition on one hand among the Russian LNG exporters and on the other hand—between LNG exports and pipeline exports of natural gas from Russia.

In general, by defining the latest strategy Russia bets on natural gas as a bridge fuel towards a lower-carbon economy in the second half of the century and expects growth of the globalised natural gas market with LNG rapidly increasing its share versus pipeline gas. There is no isolated reliance on the exports of LNG only. Domestic consumption of natural gas as a fuel is forecasted to increase from a mere 0.68 bcm in 2018 four-fold to 2.7 bcm by 2024 and about five-fold from the 2024 level to 10–13 bcm by 2035. LNG shall play a decisive role in this expansion too. The strategy stipulates broader domestic use of LNG as a fuel for marine, railway, and road transport and as a source of energy supply of settlements in regions that are not accessible or not covered by pipeline infrastructure.

The year 2020 saw one more strategy document published that is key for the LNG development in Russia. At the end of October 2020, President Putin signed the Strategy for Developing the Russian Arctic Zone and Ensuring National Security until 2035 (President of Russian Federation, 2020). This document is as important for Russian natural gas and LNG policy as the energy strategy, since the Russian Arctic continental shelf is thought to hold more than 85,100 bcm of natural gas and is home to the largest LNG projects meant to bring this gas to markets. The strategy implies that by 2024 production of LNG in the Russian Arctic will reach 43 mtpa, 64 mtpa by 2030, and 91 mtpa by 2035, compared with 8.6 mt in the base year of 2018. This will comprise a lion's share of all LNG produced in Russia as forecasted by the Russian Energy Strategy until 2035.

Like the Energy Strategy, the Arctic Strategy outlines several specific targets regarding LNG. For example, the Murmansk region is mentioned to host a centre for building and maintenance of large-scale constructions for the LNG industry in the Arctic—this is a Novatek's project. The strategy also implies that already by 2025 Russia shall build four new nuclear icebreakers Type 22220 that together with other new auxiliary ships will contribute to increasing the volume of goods transferred via the Northeast Passage. After 2025, two more icebreakers of the same type and two of the Leader type will ensure all-year-round navigation of the Northeast Passage.

Key Projects

Understanding the logic and future of Russian LNG projects are best done through analysis of both successful and failed projects, with the focus on the most recent ones. All of these cases not only shed light on the legal, financial, and technical background of the LNG industry in Russia. They are also a key to understanding practices and complex interactions of the major players in the Russian LNG industry, most notably Gazprom, Novatek, and Rosneft.

LNG in the Russian Far East: Gazprom Versus Rosneft

When in 2013 Russia unveiled ambitious plans of occupying more than ten percent of international LNG markets by 2020, there was only one functioning large-scale natural gas liquefaction facility in Russia, namely Sakhalin 2. Sakhalin 2 was launched in 2009 and it had the capacity of about ten million tonnes per year. Sakhalin 2 was initially a unique project, launched and run as a consortium of exclusively foreign companies under the ill-fated production sharing agreement (PSA) regime. As much as humiliating the PSA regime was to Russia, at the initial stage of LNG development in Russia, it allowed for the acquisition of valuable new experience in gas liquefaction and was later sweetened by a disputed takeover of the majority stake in the project by Gazprom (Bradshaw, 2010).

Gazprom has long tried to expand Sakhalin 2 with one more LNG train. Gazprom and Shell drafted a roadmap for expansion already back in 2014, but the project has not advanced since. Initially, expansion of Sakhalin 2 LNG was not an option, because of a lack of necessary volumes in the developed gas fields. Far from the expansion plans, from 2025 two already existing trains are forecasted to start experiencing deficit of natural gas. Constructing additional infrastructure to supply gas from the Sakhalin 1 fields could potentially be the easiest way of securing additional volumes for the existing and new trains at Sakhalin 2. However, Sakhalin 1's operator Exxon Neftegaz backed by Rosneft could not agree with Gazprom on price and are instead planning to construct their own liquefaction facility. Exxon Neftegaz' position may be indirectly backed by the Russian Government: using gas from Sakhalin 1 would also be the least preferred option for the Russian State, because of the PSA regime: project-related costs shall be compensated from the state budget.

Other than at Sakhalin 2, Gazprom's new LNG ambitions in the Far East of Russia have long been linked to the project of Vladivostok LNG. It was conceived in 2008 as a flexible outlet for prospective huge gas fields in Eastern Siberia, Chayandinskoye and Kovyktinskoye, with the planned total resource base of 2,800 bcm. At the same time, Vladivostok LNG could source natural gas from the Sakhalin-Khabarovsk-Vladivostok pipeline system that was launched in 2011 with the initial capacity of 5.5 bcm. By 2020, this pipeline was utilised only at around half of the capacity but was nevertheless being expanded by an additional 4.4 bcm of capacity. Gazprom justified the expansion with the plans to supply domestic chemical production, local companies, and population. The expansion also makes it possible to construct a new export route to China: Power of Siberia 3, the easternmost pipeline route to China.[4]

In 2012, Gazprom announced that Vladivostok LNG would be developed in co-operation with a Japanese consortium and the project was launched in 2017. It was supposed to reach the designed capacity of ten million tonnes per year by 2020. By the end of 2014, however, the project was far behind the schedule. First, Russia and Gazprom were hit by Western sanctions following the annexation of Crimea, which drastically

[4] Power of Siberia 1 was launched in December 2019 and has capacity of 38 bcm per annum. In 2020, only 4.1 bcm were exported through the pipeline. Gazprom hopes to double that figure in 2021. Power of Siberia 2 is planned pipeline that could link huge natural gas reserves in Western Siberia and major consumers in industrialised regions of China. The capacity of the pipeline that will cross Altai and Mongolia is projected to be 50 bcm per annum. The project can be realised after 2030 (Gazprom, 2020a; RIA Novosti, 2021).

limited funding and technological options. Secondly, the Chayandinskoye field became the source for the Power of Siberia pipeline to China. Therefore, in 2015 Vladivostok LNG was officially postponed.

Gazprom returned to the idea of Vladivostok LNG only in 2017, completely rethinking it in the process. The new project re-profiled the liquefaction plant from a large-scale to a medium-scale one, with the Asian market of LNG as a marine fuel in view. The new capacity was defined at the level of 1.5 mtpa and the sole source of gas would be delivered from Sakhalin via the Sakhalin-Khabarovsk-Vladivostok pipeline. In 2018, Alexei Miller, CEO of Gazprom, announced that there was an agreement with Mitsui regarding the project and its construction would be launched in 2020 (Mordushenko, 2017). But according to the 2019 annual report (Gazprom, 2019), Gazprom was still carrying out a pre-investment feasibility study for the project. Vladivostok LNG failed to be addressed in the report in any other way and was similarly not addressed in the 2020 Gazprom's Investor Day presentation (Gazprom, 2020c).

Nor is Vladivostok LNG mentioned in any way in the recently detailed press release of the agreement between Gazprom and Primorsky Krai on developing gas infrastructure in the region in 2021–2025 (Gazprom, 2020b). LNG could be a more flexible way of delivering gas to domestic consumers in Primorsky Krai in the Russian Far East: only 0.7% of companies and households had access to natural gas in this region as of the beginning of 2020. Vladivostok LNG would be completely justified in this scenario but given the sanctions and limited capacities of LNG equipment producers in Russia, the project does not currently look feasible. It seems that being unable to carry out a new large-scale LNG project in the region, Gazprom decided to postpone a small-scale project again and focus on another option with a high value-added: Amur gas processing plant—which will focus on producing helium.

Even if Vladivostok LNG is not totally cancelled, its reformatting means that Gazprom is left with the only option for the expansion of the LNG operations in the Russian Far East: that is through the long-planned expansion of Sakhalin 2 LNG with the 3rd train. Although the expansion plans have been discussed for over a decade, the future of this project is still unclear. Gazprom classifies this project among others where '*commissioning dates [are] subject to negotiations*' (Gazprom, 2020c), along with the Far Eastern Route (Power of Siberia 3) and Power of Siberia 2.

Difficulties to secure gas for Sakhalin 2 from Sakhalin 1 should be of no surprise given that Sakhalin has long been a battlefield for LNG ambitions between Gazprom and Rosneft. The Russian Government first intervened into the conflict in 2013, planning to set up a special commission that would resolve the issue to maximise strategic outcomes for the state. In 2014, when the decision was due, the solution was postponed again. One of the factors could have been the sanctions, which put the Russian energy policy into a new unknown, but the other could be self-distancing of the government from the two powerful energy corporations with nearly limitless lobbying opportunities given the structure of the Russian politics. In the apparent absence of high-level state arbitration, Rosneft resolved to use of a legal path, suing the Sakhalin 2 consortium to get access to its infrastructure. It claimed a right to transfer eight billion cubic metres per annum from the Sakhalin 1 production fields (485 bcm) in the northeast of Sakhalin to the planned location of liquefaction facility at the south-western shore of the island.

Despite Rosneft's efforts, the court also preferred to maintain the status quo and did not grant Rosneft access to the pipeline. This led Rosneft and its major partner in the project, ExxonMobil, to reconsider the project towards the construction of LNG export facilities (5 mtpa) next to its oil terminal at De-Kastri, the Khabarovsk region, one the mainland across the Nevelskoy Strait. This solution would induce substantial costs despite some existing infrastructure available, so Gazprom proposed to purchase gas from Sakhalin 1 and liquefy it at the 3rd train of Sakhalin 2. Gazprom's solution advanced by the end of 2017 when both parties were in detailed talks over the conditions of the deal but could not reach the final agreement.

The decision to go forward with own LNG facility at De-Kastri was probably influenced by Rosneft's leading partner ExxonMobil in an attempt to minimise political risks, which would definitely rise in the case of co-operation with Gazprom-controlled Sakhalin 2. Exxon already had to cancel its participation in several joint projects with Rosneft due to sanctions and did not want to risk Sakhalin 1, unique in the sense that it is the only large-scale hydrocarbons project in Russia not controlled by a Russian company. Construction of gas pipelines from the fields to the LNG plant will cost the project an additional USD1.3 billion, which is still less than 15% of the total costs of the Far East LNG project (TASS, 2019).

In 2019, Rosneft announced that Far East LNG would be realised not by 2023 as initially planned, but in 2027. Simultaneously, its projected capacity was increased from 5.0 mtpa to 6.2 mtpa. The costs of Far East LNG will be around USD6.1 billion. Even the distant target of completing the facility by 2027 is doubtful as ExxonMobil and the industry, in general, were hit hard by the market shrinking due to the COVID-19 pandemic and is increasingly pressured by environment-conscious investors. At the same time, Gazprom was reported to send yet another letter to the Russian Government outlining negative effects of Far East LNG for own export projects in the Far East and the Russian natural gas exports in general. A decision of Rosneft and ExxonMobil regarding the construction of own LNG infrastructure means that before constructing the 3rd train of Sakhalin 2, the Gazprom-led consortium will have to find additional natural gas resources to feed it—by 2019 it was not yet clear if there would be any available.

Novatek's LNG Projects in the Arctic

Even if it was Gazprom out of all Russian major oil and gas companies that ventured first into the LNG markets, it is Novatek that has become synonymous with the success of large-scale LNG projects in Russia. Novatek's maiden LNG project that has ultimately become the flagship for Russia was mulled already in the early 2000s by no other company than Gazprom. But the gas giant was too self-assured and inertial to have the project started, probably miscalculating extent of its own expertise and resources.

By the time of the international financial crisis, when the strategy could have been changed and necessary foreign help acquired, Yamal LNG's shares were amassed by Gennady Timchenko, one of the co-founders of Gunvor, a major Russian oil trader those years, and a reputed friend of Vladimir Putin. Parallel to taking control of Yamal LNG, Gennady Timchenko increased his share in Novatek and then sold Novatek a 51% stake in Yamal LNG's shares. Gazprom's easy partying with Yamal LNG could be explained by focusing on other more promising projects, such as Shtokman and Sakhalin 2, but after Yamal LNG had changed hands it suddenly became a top-priority project for the Russian Government.

Vladimir Putin personally endorsed the project in a meeting in Salekhard, the administrative centre of the Yamal region (the Yamalo-Nenets Autonomous Okrug), with heads of the leading international oil and gas companies. State guarantees and allocation of public investment into the costly Arctic infrastructure worth billions of dollars were rapidly secured, just a month after the endorsement of the project. It became clear that Yamal LNG was chosen not only to spearhead Russia's new LNG ambitions but also to become a powerhouse for not least ambitious projects of utilising and commercialising the Northeast Passage and developing Russia's new cargo fleet for that purpose. LNG in the meanwhile will be responsible for the bulk of the goods transferred via the Northeast Passage. Turning from a business project into a geopolitical one brought Yamal LNG as many preferences as new risks.

Despite all the technological challenges and issues with funding, partially due to the Western sanctions, Yamal LNG has been sticking to the originally planned schedule, gaining the trust of the Russian Government and of President Putin personally, who likes presenting the project as a major Russian success story. In 2019, Yamal LNG had the 3rd main train operational, one year ahead of the original schedule, and all the three trains did exceed the projected annual capacity by 11%, or by 1.9 mt.

The calamities of 2020 have however been felt even by Yamal LNG. Launching of its 4th train, a special LNG train with the planned capacity of 0.95 mtpa, was rescheduled three times throughout the year and, finally, postponed to the second half of 2021. The difficulties most probably arise from the unique character of this unit: the 4th train will use Novatek's proprietary gas liquefaction technology called 'Arctic cascade'—which exploits low ambient temperature of the Arctic climate to save as much as 30% of energy in the liquefaction process. According to the estimates of SKOLKOVO Energy Centre, capital costs for the 4th train are projected to be twice less per tonne of produced LNG than that of the larger trains at the site. The capacity of the 4th train will be used exclusively for the spot and short-term markets or bunkering purposes.

More important is the 4th train's role as the testing ground for the technology that will then be used at one of the next Novatek's projects in the region, namely Ob LNG. Ob LNG will use two trains of 'Arctic cascade', each with the annual capacity of 2.5 mt. Following the rescheduling of launching the 4th train at Yamal LNG, this project has also currently been rescheduled: the 1st train will be launched in 2024 and the 2nd one in 2025.

The next major Novatek's project will be Arctic LNG 2.[5] The final investment decision on Arctic LNG 2 was announced by Novatek at the Eastern Economic Forum in September 2019. Arctic LNG 2 will be fed by the Salmanovskoye (Utrenneye) gas field with proved and probable resources of more than 1,100 bcm. This field is located in the vicinity of the South-Tambeyskoye gas field, which feeds Yamal LNG—allowing for shared use of some marine infrastructure in the region. The liquefaction facility will have three trains, each with a capacity of 6.6 mtpa, which will be gradually launched during 2023–2026. The project costs will exceed USD21 billion. There are more prospective gas fields in the vicinity of both Yamal LNG and Arctic LNG 2 which can then potentially be used for the next project, Arctic LNG 1.

Utrenniy is a new terminal which will be used by Novatek's next Arctic LNG 2 project on the Gydan peninsula. The terminal is planned to be constructed until 2022 and two-thirds of it will be funded from the Russian National Wealth Fund.[6] Initially, Arctic LNG 2 project is designed to have three trains, but terminal Utrenniy will be able to accommodate up to six trains in the future, allowing project for subsequent expansion with the facilities of prospective Arctic LNG 1.

Success and profitability of the Arctic projects of Novatek are closely linked to the development of the Northeast Passage. As stipulated by the Russian Energy Strategy, Arctic LNG resources will mostly be exported to Asia via the Northeast Passage, potentially all year round. The route to the West, up to the transhipment facility in Murmansk can be serviced by either Arc7-class tankers or by Arc4-class tankers led by icebreakers using LNG as the fuel. The route to the East, up to the transhipment facility in Kamchatka can be, depending on the time of the year, be serviced by either Arc7-class tankers or Arc4-class tankers led by nuclear icebreakers of the new LK-60 type. In total, there is a plan to build five LK-60 icebreakers that will be responsible for the eastern leg of the Northeast Passage.

[5] Initially, Arctic LNG 2, as stipulated by the name, had to be the 3rd LNG project of Novatek in the region, after Yamal LNG and Arctic LNG, but then the sequence of the projects changed, without names of the projects updated—hence the confusion.

[6] Russian National Wealth Fund is funded by windfall profits from oil and gas industry. The fund guarantees stability of the pension system and the state budget. At the end of 2020, the size of the fund was estimated at about USD164 billion.

Novatek will be reloading LNG from ice-class Arc7 tankers to conventional tankers at each of the directions of the Northeast Passage. The LNG storage and transhipment facility in Murmansk (20 mtpa) is due to be completed in 2023. The parallel reloading facility in Kamchatka (21.7 mtpa) was supposed to be completed a year earlier but faced more uncertainty due to the resistance of the Russian military that is densely present in the region. The resistance was however overcome in autumn 2020 after Novatek guaranteed that it would contribute to improving public access to natural gas in the region, which has made some experts think that the resistance from the military was somewhat orchestrated from the very beginning as the means of pressuring Novatek into more of social responsibility, domestically. At the same time, Novatek gets regional preferences: in 2020 it could secure regional tax rebates in the Murmansk region.

In June 2020, Novatek ordered two floating barges from DSME, largest in the world of its kind, to be delivered in 2022. Before the transhipment facilities are constructed, Novatek will have to use Arc7 tankers all the way to key gas hubs or to temporary reloading facilities. Until the end of 2020, the transhipment operations took place in Norway. However, in November 2020 Novatek had the first transhipment of LNG done in the Murmansk region (Novatek, 2020), successful despite presumably more challenging marine conditions than in Norway.

One more way to save on transportation costs may be presented by continuing the rapid warming of the Arctic Ocean. In 2020, Sovkomflot's Arc7-class tanker Christophe de Margerie could make the eastern leg of the Northeast Passage as early as in May. Earlier, this way could be attempted only from July. If the warming trend continues, the navigation on the eastern leg of the route will be available for 9–10 months a year. This may lead Novatek to reconsider its plans to order four LNG-fuelled icebreakers (Interfax, 2020a).

The Baltic Sea Region Projects

Gazprom discussed constructing a large-scale LNG export facility in the Baltic Sea region as early as in the first half of the first decade of the twenty-first century. In 2006, Gazprom mulled a USD3.7-billion LNG project that would have five million tonnes per annum and could be completed by 2012. There were talks with technological partners and investors from Canada, Japan, and Italy. However, as soon as Gazprom focused on developing a huge Shtokman field (3,900 bcm) in the Barents

Sea, it was decided that the liquefaction facility for the project would be located in the immediate vicinity from the gas field, in the Teriberka locality of the Murmansk region, allowing for year-round ice-free access of tankers.

As Gazprom was not advancing with the development of Shtokman, ideas for Baltic LNG resurfaced at the end of 2013, this time as a large-scale facility (10 mtpa) with LNG bunkering capabilities. Gazpromplanned to attract its Shtokman's partner Total as a partner for the new project, but Total was not satisfied with the conditions of the deal, which would entail securing a long-term contract for half of the capacity of the LNG plant.

A preliminary investment decision regarding Baltic LNG was made in 2015 and the facility was pinpointed to be constructed in Ust-Luga. Following the Crimea-related sanctions on Russia, Gazprom was struggling not only with attracting investors but also with necessary technical expertise and equipment, which would previously be sourced in the USA and Germany, from Air Products and Linde respectively.

In 2016, Gazprom attracted Shell as the main partner in the project. The latter promised to localise liquefaction technology, hoping in exchange for tax rebates, albeit not at the level of the Arctic LNG projects. In 2018, however, Gazprom and its partner, RusGazDobycha decided to increase the project's capacity to 13 mtpa and to complement Baltic LNG with a gas processing plant that could produce significant volumes of ethane (4 mtpa) and liquefied petroleum gas (2.2 mtpa), and become a supplier to new chemical plants in the region. The decision to process natural gas and to develop a domestic chemical industry around the processing plant mirrors the new strategy of Gazprom in the East, where Gazprom's Amur gas producing plant is emerging parallel to expanding export projects.

The reconfiguration of the project has been reported to be the reason for Shell to leave the project, but Shell's concerns could be linked to implied links between RusGazDobycha and Arkady Rotenberg, who has been sanctioned by the West (Reuters, 2019; Toporkov, 2018). Following the changes in the project and departure of Shell, Baltic LNG was once again rescheduled—that time to the end of 2023 for the first train and the end of 2024 for the second.

In 2013, as Gazprom was mulling ideas for Baltic LNG, it also thought of developing a small-scale facility on the northern shore of the Finnish Gulf, in Vysotsk. The facility was planned to have a capacity of 0.66 mtpa and it was planned to come online already in 2017. Despite the promising market for bunkering, the construction of this facility was delayed as well. Finally, the Vysotsk LNG project was initiated by Cryogas, a company belonging to Gazprombank, in 2015, and then joined by Novatek in 2017, when the latter acquired 51% of the shares in the Cryogas-Vysotsk project. The project originally focused on the bunkering market, rapidly developing under the new ecological requirements for marine transport in the region. The two trains, each of 0.33 mtpa, were launched in 2019 and they took advantage of the Vysotsk port infrastructure located north of St. Petersburg, close to the border with Finland.

Vysotsk LNG can further be expanded with two additional trains similar to T1 and T2, bringing the total capacity to 1.32 mtpa. Another plan, voiced at the launch of the project, is to expand the facility not by 0.66 mtpa, but 1.1 mtpa. The plan for a larger expansion is, however, under pressure from Gazprom that feared additional competition to its project in Ust-Luga, or due to apparent oversaturation of the market in the Baltic Sea region (SKOLKOVO Energy Centre, 2019). Deliveries from Vysotsk LNG aim beyond the Baltic Sea region. Additionally, Novatek and Fluxys agreed back in 2018 to build a 0.3 mtpa transhipment terminal in Rostock, Germany, where Novatek has operated an LNG filling station since 2019.

Despite Gazprom being indirectly involved in the Vysotsk project and the company has gone ahead with Baltic LNG, there is one more project where it is a sole player, Portovaya LNG. Portovaya LNG is Gazprom's project to utilise excessive capacities at the compressing unit of the same name, which serves Nord Stream. The liquefaction facility has a capacity of 1.5 mtpa and utilises Linde's technology. The project was initiated in 2015 with the target to come online in 2018 but was later postponed, like many other LNG projects at that time. However, when Gazprom's plans for a large-scale LNG project in the Baltic Sea region stalled, it was planned that Portovaya LNG would at least be able to secure supplies of LNG to the Kaliningrad region. Portovaya LNG became a unique strategic project of national importance.

Instead of constructing a regasification terminal in the Kaliningrad region, Gazprom has opted for ordering a brand-new FSRU Marshal Vasilevskiy from Korea. Portovaya LNG and FSRU Marshal Vasilevskiy in the Kaliningrad region have basically become two parts of one system, a virtual pipeline. Both the sending and receiving units were planned to go online in 2017, but both were postponed until 2019 due to technical issues with construction and operation.

The FSRU offers better value for the Kaliningrad region than a shore terminal because even in case of disrupted natural gas supplies via pipelines, it can rely on extensive underground gas storage. The Kaliningradskoye underground gas storage facility has a capacity of 0.174 bcm as of 2020 and is expected to reach the designed capacity of 0.8 bcm by 2025 (Gazprom, 2020d). At the same time, the FSRU could be used as a regular LNG tanker. In the autumn of 2019, the FSRU was leased to OMV to be used in Rotterdam for the temporary storage of LNG and then it was leased again, that time to Gunvor, for deliveries of US and Nigerian LNG to Europe (Reuters, 2019, 2020).

Portovaya LNG will have its own operations diversified when it is expanded by another floating LNG storage facility. For this purpose, Gazprom has bought a tanker Excel, refitted it in Dubai, and renamed it to Portovaya. This new FSRU is likely to moor it in Portovaya LNG in 2021. Larger storage will allow for greater flexibility in serving the Baltic and North European regions with small and medium-sized LNG deliveries.

In the opinion of SKOLKOVO Energy Centre experts, FSRU Marshal Vasilevskiy could become a regional hub for deliveries to Lithuania and Poland, but that requires extensive changes in the Russian legislation on LNG exports and exemption from the 30% duty on natural gas (SKOLKOVO Energy Centre, 2019).

In the Baltic Sea region, Gorskaya LNG was an independent LNG project in Russia that ultimately failed, despite being designed to rely on domestic technology and cater the fast-growing market of marine and land LNG bunkering. One of the decisive drawbacks of Gorskaya LNG was that contrary to other independent projects it did not have access to own resources of natural gas, and hence it should have been fed from Gazprom's Unified Gas Supply System. The liquefaction facility would have three trains located in Ust-Luga, each of 0.42 mtpa—obviously, these ideas were made obsolete by Gazprom's own plans. This is not the most illustrative case of failing independent LNG projects in Russia.

Independent Large-Scale LNG Projects: Pechora LNG and Yakutsk LNG

Even though the development of LNG in Russia has mostly been driven by the three large companies—Gazprom, Novatek, and Rosneft—there have been a couple of prominent attempts to produce and export LNG by other Russian natural gas producers too. These cases display the limitations of what the Russian Government means by the liberalisation of LNG exports in the Energy Strategy until 2035.

Pechora LNG has been associated with a second-tier, independent company. It was proposed by a private Alltech Group back in 2010. The liquefaction facility would be linked to the gas fields of Korovinskoe and Kumzhinskoe in the Nenets Autonomous Okrug with the total reserves of 186 bcm and have a capacity of 2.6 mtpa (3.5 bcm per annum). Alltech Group hoped to complete the plant by 2015 with the help of Chinese or South Korean investors and technologies. At that time, Gazprom was still enjoying a monopoly on exports of gas and none of LNG projects could be fulfilled without Gazprom's agreement. The project was therefore very soon buried because of the resistance of Gazprom. The monopoly planned to go ahead with the Shtokman project and Gazprom was already serving Asian markets through Sakhalin 2, where it had the controlling stake. Despite the efforts of the regional administration to draw Gazprom to the project, there was no success in going forward.

However, at that time the Russian Government already started to realise the strategic significance of LNG. So did the major competitors of Gazprom—and there were only a couple of them that wielded enough of lobbying power to secure LNG export rights from the government. Novatek already focused on a much more ambitious Yamal project, so it was Rosneft that got interested in Pechora LNG. Rosneft decided to buy a major stake in it in spring 2014 and finalised the deal in 2015. By doing so, Rosneft hinted on the domestic focus of the project—in a likely attempt not to interfere with Gazprom. Simultaneously, however, there were obvious lobbying efforts, which resulted in an early legislation draft that could allow to include Pechora LNG into the list of projects authorised to independently export LNG from Russia.

Gazprom's resistance was extremely strong and very vocal. It sent a letter to the Russian Ministry of Energy explaining that only co-ordinated national LNG policy would allow preventing detrimental competition among several potential Russian LNG projects, and Gazprom implied that construction of Pechora LNG was therefore not in the national interests. Subsequently, the Russian Government strongly criticised the proposed legislation draft, deciding the fate of Pechora LNG among other independent projects (Podobedova & Dzyadko, 2014).

Probably, not only Gazprom's lobbying played a decisive role in the failure. As with Yamal LNG, Pechora LNG would hardly be possible without extensive public funding and support when it came to the Arctic infrastructure and further development of the area—and the public resources were already overloaded with the task of development of Yamal LNG. Rosneft left the Pechora LNG project in 2018. In 2019, Alltech Group decided to abandon the project and sell the rights to the gas fields, which seemed to put an end to Pechora LNG.

However, in 2020, after extensive transformation of Alltech Group's assets following the death of its main owner, plans for Pechora LNG resurfaced. Initially, its shares were consolidated to be presumably sold to Lloyds Energy, an obscure company based in Dubai, with links to both Gazprom and Rosneft. But in the end, half of the shares were sold to Vitaly Yuzhilin, a former co-owner of St. Petersburg Seaport and ex-member of the Russian State Duma (Forbes.ru, 2011). Another half was divided equally among two of his partners.[7] They initially planned to construct a methanol plant in Ust-Luga near St. Petersburg but promptly changed the location at the very end of 2020. Yuzhilin plans to produce two billion cubic metres per annum of natural gas from the available fields, export it via a 300-kilometre pipeline to the Indiga port and to produce there methanol, not LNG. By 2027, the company plans to increase natural gas production at Pechora twofold, to four billion cubic metres, respectively doubling the output of methanol to 3.4 mtpa (Interfax, 2020b). To realise the project, Yuzhilin hopes to attract support from the Russian Direct Investment Fund.[8] Gazprom's role in the fate of the project even in its new iteration can still be decisive. Gazprom controls adjacent gas fields that would be necessary to upscale the project in the future.

[7] According to Forbes Russia, both Alexey Miller and Alexander Dyukov were working for St. Petersburg Seaport at the same time when Yuzhilin co-owned the port, in 1999 (Forbes.ru, 2011).

[8] Russian Direct Investment Fund is a sovereign wealth fund that helps fast-growing Russian companies to attract direct investments, including investments from abroad. As of 2020, the fund was managing about ten billion dollars.

Another independent LNG project was announced in May 2020. Globaltek, a company owned by Albert Avdolyan, announced a pre-FEED for the Yakutsk gas project.[9] The project in the Republic of Sakha is planned to utilise gas from four gas fields with combined reserves of 367 bcm to pump gas 1,300 kilometres away to the shores of the Okhotsk Sea and liquefy there for subsequent exports. Expanding the resource base in the course of realising the project, Globaltek hopes to launch a liquefaction facility with a capacity of 13 mtpa already in 2025 (Alifirova, 2020). The project is assessed to cost more than ten billion dollars and looks extremely ambitious and questionable given this modest cost estimate (Rbc.ru, 2020).

Even if Globaltek raises more than the necessary funds, the project is still likely to follow the suit of other private large-scale LNG projects due to all the same set of issues. First, the Russian Government has so far been very conservative in issuing new permits to export LNG—and Globaltek does not have enough of lobbying power to change anything. Since 2013, there was only one amendment to the status quo on LNG exports, of purely formal nature. In April 2020, the Law on Export of Natural Gas was amended to allow exports from four further gas fields: Verkhnetiuteyskoye and Zapadno-Seyakhinskoye gas fields to feed Novatek's Ob LNG and Soletsko-Khanaveyskoye and Shtormovoye fields that are licensed to Novatek as well and will be developed in the subsequent Arctic LNG projects.

Second, the gas fields of Globaltek do not currently enjoy any special tax regime. Third, technical challenges of transporting gas via a pipeline from Yakutia will make it more expensive than the Russian shelf gas. Finally, despite the company now does not have access to the pipeline export infrastructure, namely Power of Siberia operated by Gazprom, it, however, may ultimately get access to this export route—especially if Gazprom will continue to experience difficulties with the expected capacity of own production in the Chayandinskoe field.

[9] The Yakutsk gas project should not be confused with a small-scale Gazprom project in the same region that has already succeeded in delivering LNG via rail to UlanBator, Mongolia (Gazprom Export, 2019).

Small-Scale and Medium-Scale Projects

Apart from the large-scale LNG project, the Russian Government clearly bets on the development of small-scale and medium-scale LNG facilities. They can be used for both exports as in the Baltic Sea region and bunkering domestically, especially along the Northeast Passage. The latter can be critical given possible changes in environmental regulations in the Arctic, as there have already been initiatives within Russia to ban using oil products as a fuel in the Arctic region. Small-scale LNG transported by railways or trucks can also be crucial in domestic switching to cleaner fuels, especially in Siberia. For example, the Russian Railways (RZD), plans to substitute a quarter of diesel fuel with LNG by 2030 (SKOLKOVO Energy Centre, 2018).

In 2018, the domestic demand for LNG in Russia was assessed at about 11 mtpa (SKOLKOVO Energy Centre, 2018). By the end of 2020, the Russian Government developed a draft roadmap for the development of small-scale LNG in the country. This document, expected to be approved in early 2021, will directly address the challenge of the void in the Russian legislation that was raised in Russia's new Energy Strategy until 2035.

Closing the legal gaps will start with the definition of small-scale LNG—these will be defined as projects with a yearly production capacity of fewer than one million tonnes. Prospective legislation will also remove a myriad of bureaucratic and regulatory burdens for both producing and consuming LNG: from simplifying fire safety requirements to rules for placement of small-scale LNG objects. The roadmap will lay a new foundation for supporting domestic demand—by encouraging local transport companies to switch from oil products to LNG and by supporting LNG bunkering infrastructure. In the draft version of the roadmap, there are currently some measures to simply exports from small-scale liquefaction facilities as well.

Overall, through the proposed measures the government plans to cut capital costs of constructing small-scale LNG objects by 30%. As in the case with larger objects, there must be a synergetic effect for the Russian industry from the plans: new objects shall predominantly rely on domestic technologies and components. In another synergetic effect, small-scale LNG should help Russia by providing industrial and private users across the country with more widespread access to natural gas. It has been assessed that LNG-based supplies are more effective than pipeline supplies if consumers are located within 400–600 kilometres from the source of gas. This could make LNG the primary way of bringing gas to most consumers in the Russian Far East. Rostec, the State Corporation for the Promotion of the Development, Manufacture, and Export of High Tech Products, have already come up with a plan to supply necessary energy equipment for this purpose.

Otherwise, beyond the typical use of LNG as a motor fuel for commercial long-haul trucks, there may be significant potential for LNG as both energy source and motor fuel in the extracting industry. This application for LNG will allow mineral extraction companies both to save costs and to contribute to the national targets for lowering greenhouse gas emissions (Volobuev, 2020).

However, despite all the potential advantages of switching to LNG, there is a significant drawback in the roadmap draft. It is an omission of tax rebates both for producers and consumers of small-scale LNG. It has been reported that the Ministry of Finance did not support any such exemptions. This is yet another reminder that large-scale LNG projects from the three large companies—Gazprom, Novatek, and Rosneft—are playing in a different league when it comes to state support. The tax rebates omission may also result in these companies dominating all probable independent players in the small-scale LNG sector.

Although Russia has currently several ships using LNG as fuel, including the domestically-built ones, there is still no dedicated marine bunkering infrastructure. To address this problem, the Russian Government discussed at the end of 2020 plans to build LNG bunkering facilities in the following fifteen ports, listed from the west to the east: Kaliningrad, Primorsk, Vysotsk, Ust-Luga, St. Petersburg, Murmansk, Novorossiysk, Tuapse, Kavkaz, Taman, Rostov-on-Don, Vladivostok, Vostochny, Vanino, and Nakhodka.

By 2030, the bunkering infrastructure should be available in all the key ports of the Northeast Passage and in the Russian Asian Pacific region. As with the large-scale projects, LNG producers expect public funding to support these plans—at least by providing the same level of support that is available to LNG fuelling stations for commercial transport (Lyvova & Podlinova, 2020). It is however most likely that the bunkering infrastructure will be following local demand, such as in the Baltic Sea region or along the Northeast Passage—where there are already many ships using LNG as fuel and more are expected to start using it in the nearest future.

Small-scale and medium-scale LNG projects are also important for exports and securing markets in regional contexts. Gazprom's LNG exports via rail to Mongolia has already been mentioned earlier in this article. Moreover, Cryogas' small-scale LNG facility in Pskov was supplying Tallink's LNG ferry Megastar in the Baltic Sea region until 2018. Tallink's current supplier, Elenger (EestiGaas) also sources at least part of its LNG from the Vysotsk LNG plant.

Co-ordination and Arbitration in the Russian LNG Policy?

So far, the arbitration between Russian LNG and pipeline gas has hardly been successful. In 2019, Russia delivered a little bit more of the exported LNG to the European markets (51%) than to the Asian and Middle Eastern (GIIGNL, 2020). For 2018, Gazprom assessed losses to the Russian budget from Novatek's LNG to be around 30 billion Russian roubles (USD392 million), as Russian media reported in 2019. This happened, according to Gazprom, because 4.9 mt out of Novatek's 7.6 mt of LNG deliveries ended up in Europe, squeezing out Gazprom's pipeline deliveries.[10] Novatek's reply to the claim was that more than 96% of LNG from Yamal had been delivered under contracts with Asian countries and Spain on the FOB basis (Barsukov, 2019). These claims can, in turn, be easily disputed given the increasing liquidity of international LNG markets and abundance of swap operations. In the end, it is often price and available infrastructure that decide the ultimate destination of an LNG cargo. The price dynamics in Europe and Asia in 2019 and 2020 could explain why Russian LNG may in fact cannibalise Gazprom's pipeline supplies in Europe (Fig. 4.1).

Novatek is likely to re-focus more on the eastern markets when the transhipment terminal is ready in Kamchatka in 2023, but a conflict with Gazprom is also inevitable in that destination. Gazprom already had to concede on the price of natural gas supplied via Power of Siberia, making it the cheapest imported pipeline gas in China. Increasing imports of LNG, including that from Russian projects, will make the project that is currently running at a little more than ten percent of the capacity, even more vulnerable.

Russia's Energy Strategy until 2035 leaves open, how independent producers may use the Gazprom-controlled pipeline system to export their gas (Ministry of Energy of Russian Federation, 2020). However,

[10] Novatek's LNG exports were exempted from the Russian mineral extraction tax and 30% export duty.

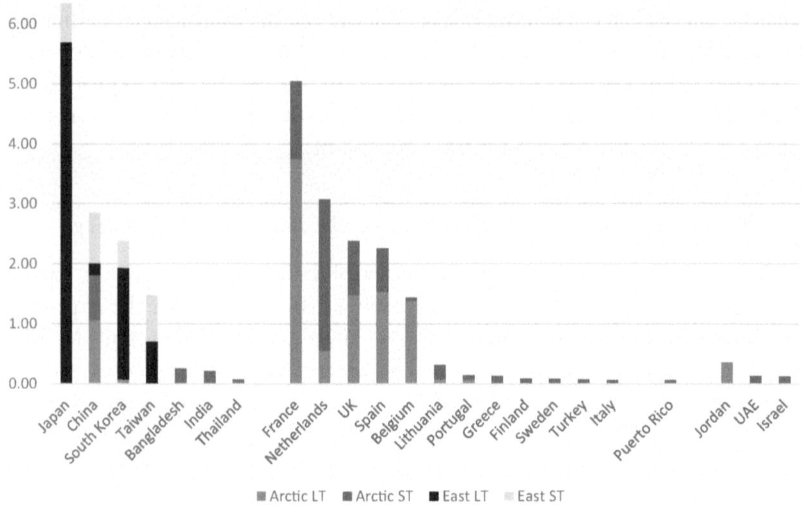

Fig. 4.1 Exports of Russian LNG under long-term and short-term contracts from the Arctic and the East LNG facilities (million tonnes) (*Note* LT = long-term contract; ST = short-term contract. *Source* The Author, based on GIIGNL [2020])

given existing tensions between Gazprom and Novatek, which are only going to become worse as new projects go online and Rosneft joins the LNG race, independent projects are extremely unlikely, at least at a scale other than micro-LNG. One more reason for highly restricted, manual mode of running Russia's LNG industry is that the Russian LNG industry highly depends on state support—technological, financial, and in infrastructure (Henderson & Yermakov, 2019).

Gazprom's criticism towards Novatek is justified in the sense that current large-scale LNG projects do not bring much income to the state budget, at least in the short term. These projects have rather more of a strategic value: to occupy a share in the international LNG markets and to serve as catalysts for development in the key domestic construction industries. Gazprom's own LNG projects will surely compete for comparable tax rebates, will use state-funded infrastructure, and rely on state-led technological solutions. The future of Russia's LNG is not solely defined by giant energy companies, but also by giant state corporations, such as Rostec, Rosatom, and Vnesh econom bank (VEB). Russia sees LNG as something larger than just a way to secure the status of an energy superpower in changing markets. These projects have become a catalyst for gaining new expertise and development in other key industries and a crucial factor for all-purpose development of the Arctic and Eastern Siberia.

References

Alifirova, A. (2020, May 6). А-Проперти планирует СПГ-проект с ресурсной базой в Якутии и строительством завода у берегов Охотского моря. Neftegaz.RU. https://neftegaz.ru/news/transport-and-storage/547071-a-properti-planiruet-spg-proekt-s-resursnoy-bazoy-v-yakutii-i-stroitelstvom-zavoda-u-beregov-okhotsk/. Accessed 19 March 2021.

Barsukov, Y. (2019, April 8). «Газпром» Видит в СПГ Источник Потерь Бюджета. Коммерсантъ. https://www.kommersant.ru/doc/3937997. Accessed 19 March 2021.

Bradshaw, M. (2010). A new energy age in Pacific Russia: Lessons from the Sakhalin oil and gas projects. *Eurasian Geography and Economics, 51*(3), 330–359. https://doi.org/10.2747/1539-7216.51.3.330

Forbes.ru. (2011). *Vitaly Yuzhilin.* https://www.forbes.ru//profile/vitalii-yuzhilin. Accessed 19 March 2021.

Gazprom. (2019). *PJSC Gazprom annual report 2019.* https://www.gazprom.com/f/posts/72/802627/gazprom-annual-report-2019-en.pdf. Accessed 19 March 2021.

Gazprom. (2020a, March 27). «Газпрому» поручено приступить к предынвестиционной стадии проекта «Сила Сибири — 2». Gazprom. https://www.gazprom.ru/press/news/2020/march/article502469/. Accessed 19 March 2021.

Gazprom. (2020b, October 6). «Газпром» и Приморский край в 2021–2025 годах продолжат развивать газификацию региона. Gazprom. https://www.gazprom.ru/press/news/2020/october/article514827/. Accessed 19 March 2021.

Gazprom. (2020c). *Next chapter: Balanced CFs. Higher shareholders returns.* Gazprom Investor Day 2020.

Gazprom. (2020d). *Kaliningradskoye UGS facility.* https://www.gazprom.com/projects/kaliningradskoye-ugs/. Accessed 10 December 2020.

Gazprom Export. (2019, November 6). *First Russian gas sent to Mongolia.* http://www.gazpromexport.ru/en/presscenter/press/2406/?year=2019. Accessed 19 March 2021.

GIIGNL. (2020). *GIIGNL annual report.* International Group of Liquefied Natural Gas Importers.

Henderson, J., & Yermakov, V. (2019). *Russian LNG: Becoming a global force* (NG 154. OIES). The Oxford Institute for Energy Studies.

IGU. (2020). *World LNG report 2020.* International Gas Union. https://www.igu.org/resources/2020-world-lng-report/. Accessed 19 March 2021.

Interfax. (2020a, October 28). Майские рейсы навели 'НОВАТЭК' на мысль отказаться от СПГ-ледоколов. https://www.interfax.ru/russia/734638. Accessed 19 March 2021.

Interfax. (2020b, November). 'Печора СПГ' сменил владельцев и перестраивается на метанол. https://www.interfax.ru/business/738910. Accessed 19 March 2021.

Interfax. (2020c, September 30). Минэнерго РФ оценивает потенциал СПГ-мощностей РФ в 125 млн т, из них почти 50 млн т - возможные проекты - Дальний Восток || Интерфакс Россия. https://www.interfax-russia.ru/far-east/news/minenergo-rf-ocenivaet-potencial-spg-moshchnostey-rf-v-125-mln-t-iz-nih-pochti-50-mln-t-vozmozhnye-proekty. Accessed October 10 2020.

Karpov, A., Mescherin, I., Kozlov, A., & Butyrskaya K. (2020, May 8). СПГ в России. Путь Производственных Мощностей. https://magazine.neftegaz.ru/articles/rynok/547774-spg-v-rossii-put-proizvodstvennykh-moshchnostey/. Accessed 19 March 2021.

Lyvova, A., & Podlinova, A. (2020, September 8). Правительству предлагают построить огромную сеть для заправки судов СПГ. Ведомости. https://www.vedomosti.ru/business/articles/2020/09/03/838793-pravitelstvu-postroit. Accessed 19 March 2021.

Ministry of Energy of Russian Federation. (2020). *Russia's energy strategy to 2035.*

Mordushenko. O. (2017, July 3). «Владивосток СПГ» теряет масштаб. Коммерсантъ. https://www.kommersant.ru/doc/3342085. Accessed 19 March 2021.

Novatek. (2020, November 25). «НОВАТЭК» совершил первую перевалку СПГ в Мурманской области. https://www.novatek.ru/ru/press/releases/?id_4=4116. Accessed 19 March 2021.

Podobedova, L., & Dzyadko, T. (2014, October 6). Решение по проекту «Печора СПГ» примет Путин. РБК. https://www.rbc.ru/business/06/10/2014/542ed64fcbb20fe29870b629. Accessed 19 March 2021.

President of Russian Federation. (2020). *Strategy for the development of the Arctic zone of the Russian Federation and provision of national security through 2035.*

Rbc.ru. (2020, May 5). Основатель Yota вложит более $10 млрд в СПГ-проект. https://www.rbc.ru/business/05/05/2020/5eb1170d9a794754a25c7a91. Accessed 19 March 2021.

Reuters. (2019, August). *Russia leases its rainy day LNG vessel to Austria's OMV*. https://www.reuters.com/article/us-russia-lng-tanker-idUSKCN1VJ1G6. Accessed 19 March 2021.

Reuters. (2020, January 14). *Russian tanker back in Kaliningrad Region after shipping U.S. LNG to Europe*. Reuters. https://in.reuters.com/article/russia-lng-tanker-idUKL8N29J4SO. Accessed 19 March 2021.

RIA Novosti. (2021, January 2). 'Газпром' поставил по 'Силе Сибири' в Китай 4,1 млрд кубов газа за год. РИА Новости. https://ria.ru/20210102/gaz-1591820386.html. Accessed 19 March 2021.

SKOLKOVO Energy Centre. (2018). Среднетоннажный СПГ в России: Между Небом и Землей. SKOLKOVO Moscow School of Management.

SKOLKOVO Energy Centre. (2019). Российский Мало- и Среднетоннажный СПГ. Региональная Серия: Балтика. 1. SKOLKOVO Moscow School of Management.

TASS. (2019, September 24). Минэнерго Оценило Стоимость Трех Новых СПГ-Проектов На Дальнем Востоке в $12,3 Млрд. TASS. https://tass.ru/ekonomika/6919877. Accessed 19 March 2021.

Tikhonov, S. (2020, January 8). Выгодное сжижение. Российская газета. https://rg.ru/2020/01/08/smozhet-li-rossiia-narastit-proizvodstvo-spg.html. Accessed 19 March 2021.

Toporkov, A. (2018, April 2). Для мегапроекта «Газпрома» на Балтике придется модернизировать газопроводы. Ведомости. https://www.vedomosti.ru/business/articles/2018/04/23/767601-megaproekta-gazproma?fbclid=IwAR0cRd6fKsX6oJV1z2DC_sApoBqPqK78exeYImPza7w1Hd4XUzrh-1GWSL4. Accessed 19 March 2021.

Volobuev, A. (2020, September 29). Минэнерго задумало резко увеличить мощности мини-СПГ в России. Ведомости. https://www.vedomosti.ru/business/articles/2020/09/29/841591-minenergo-zadumalo. Accessed 19 March 2021.

Yergin, D., & Stoppard, M. (2003). The next prize. *The Foreign Affairs, 82*(6), 110–121.

CHAPTER 5

Gas Logistics Between Russia and the EU: Case of Ukraine, Belarus, Nord Streams and Other Routes of Supply

Mykhailo Gonchar and Igor Stukalenko

Gas Logistics on the East–West Line: Genesis

Before the Soviet Union became an exporter of gas on the East–West line, gas in the USSR moved from west to east in the 1950s and the 1970s. Natural gas from the Dashava field in the west of Ukraine and the Shebelinske field in the east of Ukraine was supplied to Russia via the Dashava-Kyiv-Moscow gas pipeline. Through another route—the Dashava-Minsk-Vilnius-Riga, gas went to the number of western republics of the USSR, namely Belarus, Latvia and Lithuania.

The contemporary route of East–West natural gas flows from the giant fields of Central Asia, the Urals and Western Siberia to Europe was formed in the 1960s–the 1980s, i.e. during the Cold War. Initially, gas exports were directed only to certain satellite countries of the USSR in Eastern Europe, i.e. members of the Council for Mutual Economic Assistance

M. Gonchar · I. Stukalenko (✉)
Centre for Global Studies Strategy, Kyiv, Ukraine

K. Liuhto (ed.), *The Future of Energy Consumption, Security and Natural Gas*, https://doi.org/10.1007/978-3-030-80367-4_5

(CMEA) and the Warsaw Pact, and later on to countries not belonging to the Soviet bloc, i.e. Austria and Finland.

The escalation of the Soviet-Chinese relations until the armed conflict in March 1969 around the Damansky Island on the Amur River put the Soviet Union, according to the Kremlin's vision at the time, at risk of war on two fronts: the United States and the NATO in the west and China in the east. This encouraged the Soviet leadership to move to a policy of détente with the West, especially since the 1962 Cuban Missile Crisis ended in favour of the Soviet Union. The start of negotiations between the USSR and the USA in Helsinki in November 1969 on limiting strategic offensive weapons accelerated the signing of the famous 20-year-gas-pipeline contract between the governments of the Soviet Union and West Germany. With its signing, large-scale projects for the construction of transcontinental gas transmission systems began to be implemented, through which natural gas was to enter Western Europe, i.e. France, Germany and Italy.

The fact that the first export supplies of natural gas from the USSR were provided from the fields located in the western part of Ukraine remains little known. The exports of gas to the west, which began in Poland in 1956, were expanded by exports through a new gas pipeline with the symbolic name Brotherhood (Dolyna-Uzhhorod-Western Border). It began to supply Czechoslovakia with natural gas. Brotherhood was launched in 1967, and the following year the pipeline from Czechoslovakia was extended outside the Eastern Bloc and gas began to flow into a neutral country, Austria.

Ukrainian gas fields were the main ones that met the Soviet gas demand before exploration of the giant fields of Central Asia, the Urals and Western Siberia in the 1970s. To transport gas from these fields, interconnectors were built delivering gas to consumption areas within the USSR and for the exports to Western Europe and CMEA countries (Table 5.1).

It is worth recalling that these large-scale infrastructure projects were implemented in order to increase foreign currency earnings of the USSR, which needed them to achieve military parity with the United States and the NATO. This could be achieved by exporting energy to NATO member states and the European Economic Community. However, the Soviet leadership was not only guided by foreign currency needs. The goal of large-scale increase in oil and gas exports was the dependence of Western Europe on the USSR, its separation from the United States,

Table 5.1 The location of the Soviet gas fields and the main gas pipes

Location of gas fields	*The main gas pipes*
Turkmenistan and Uzbekistan	Central Asia-Centre (CAC)
The Urals region in Russia	Orenburg-Western Border (Soyuz)
West Siberian region in Russia	Yamburg-Western Border (Progress)

Source The Authors

while neutral countries, namely Austria and Finland, were to become more committed to Moscow.

Ivan Diyak, the Corresponding Member of the Academy of Mining Sciences of Ukraine, who held senior positions at the Ukrainian state-owned company Ukrgazprom in 1972–1998 and took a direct part in projects to build Soviet gas pipelines, highlights the period of the early 1980s as a particular one. According to his memoirs, then Soviet leadership finally formulated the strategic goal of creating East–West transcontinental gas transmission systems: "*The Central Committee of the CPSU sets the task of building gas pipelines that will supply Western Europe with up to 70% of the required gas, so it will be possible to ensure that European countries will be completely dependent on the Soviet energy resources. ... The USSR will be able to influence Western Europe economically and politically. In addition, it will make it possible to minimise US influence on European countries, which will help transform the Soviet Union into a world superpower*" (GolosUkrainy, 2018, 3).[1]

Russian experts also point to Soviet intentions to make one of Europe's largest economy dependent on gas supplies from the East, focusing on a fragment of a note from the Soviet Foreign Ministry entitled 'On the Policy Line and Some Practical Steps of the USSR in Relation to the Formation of Willy Brandt's Government in Germany', which was submitted to the Central Committee of the CPSU on the 1st of December 1969: "*The achievement of an agreement on the supply of Soviet natural gas to the FRG may be of great importance. We are talking about concluding a contract that would be valid for two decades and would make*

[1] A translation from the Ukrainian language to English conducted by the authors.

such an important sphere of the FRG national economy as energy, to a certain extent dependent on the Soviet Union" (Lipkin, 2016, 456–457).

Low oil prices in the period of 1985–1999 and the collapse of the Warsaw Pact, the CMEA, and finally the USSR, led only to a certain pause in Moscow's policy of energy expansion. It was re-created after Vladimir Putin came to power in Russia and the growth of demand and prices for oil and gas on the European market.

Post-Soviet Period: Reincarnation of the Old Plans

It is noteworthy that the official document 'Energy Strategy of the Russian Federation for the period up to 2020' began with the statement: "*Russia has significant reserves of energy resources and a powerful fuel and energy complex, which is the basis for economic development, a tool for domestic and foreign policy. The country's role in world energy markets largely determines its geopolitical influence*" (Government of the Russian Federation, 2003, 1).[2]

The approach 'energy resources and delivery infrastructure as a tool of foreign policy', was used by Russia to the fullest in its relations with post-Soviet Armenia, Belarus, Georgia, Moldova, Ukraine and the EU. Towards the EU, the gas leverage was used as soft power through the creation of business schemes for gas trade with a corruptive component. Towards the post-Soviet countries, Moscow also used gas as semi-hard power, blackmailing to restrict or close gas supplies, and as hard power, shutting off the gas tap and arranging a gas blockade. This was clearly evident in Russia's policy towards Ukraine in 2006, 2009 and 2014.

Russia aimed to restore full control over gas transmission systems in the post-Soviet countries between Russia and the EU. It succeeded in Belarus, when Beltransgaz became a part of Gazprom through a share repurchase mechanism in 2007–2011. As for Ukraine, Russia has made repeated attempts to gain control of the gas transmission system (GTS). In the 1990s, it tried to do so using the formula 'GTS assets in exchange for repaying Ukraine's gas debts'. In the 2000s, Russia tried to create an international gas transmission consortium to manage the Ukrainian GTS. This idea was first formulated in June 2002 in a joint statement

[2] A translation from the Russian language to English conducted by the authors.

by Ukrainian President Leonid Kuchma, German Chancellor Gerhard Schroeder, and Russian President Vladimir Putin at a tripartite meeting in St. Petersburg. But the idea was obstructed in Ukraine because, under the guise of an international management consortium, Russia was in fact trying to establish majority control over Ukraine's gas transmission system, to make it a part of Gazprom. Russia's long-standing efforts were successfully blocked by the Ukrainian Governments during the 2000s.

However, Russia did not stop in its attempts to gain control over the Ukrainian GTS. It is no coincidence that during the rule of pro-Russian President Viktor Yanukovych in Ukraine, the then-Prime Minister of Russia Vladimir Putin proposed a unification project at the talks in Sochi in April 2010: "*I propose to unite Gazprom and Naftogaz of Ukraine*" (Interfax, 2010).[3] Finally, this also failed, as Kyiv saw the example of Belarus as a gradual de-sovereignisation of the Ukrainian State due to the gradual loss of control over energy infrastructure assets. In the case of Ukraine, Russia failed.

Russian Non-transit Projects

Two projects bypassing Ukraine began to be implemented in the 1990s. The first was Yamal-Europe pipeline through the territory of Belarus and Poland, which at that time was not yet a member of the EU and the NATO, to Germany. Next was the trans-Black Sea pipeline, namely Blue Stream, to supply Russian gas to Turkey, bypassing the traditional route through Ukraine, Moldova, Romania and Bulgaria. With the coming to power of Vladimir Putin, Gazprom's corporate policy not only became the state policy of the Russian Federation, but also responsibilities for its implementation were delineated. The Kremlin acted as a decision-maker, Gazprom was given the role of provider, and the Russian Foreign Ministry and Russia's intelligence services were active supporters.

Russia's goal is still to disconnect Ukraine from the gas supply chain to Europe, to switch gas supplies directly to Germany via the Baltic Sea, and via the Black Sea through Turkey to Europe, to take the EU into the pipeline 'crimping pliers' and prevent implementation of alternative projects that were to bring gas to the EU from non-Russian sources. In this way, Russia is trying to make Germany and Turkey its allies, which

[3] The quote has been translated from the Russian language into English by the authors.

automatically leads to a split in transatlantic and European solidarity, a drift of individual EU and NATO member states towards Russia. This is exactly what has been observed in Europe in recent years on the example of the Nord Stream 2.

After another failure in 2003 to gain control of Ukraine's GTS under the guise of an international gas transmission consortium and a failed attempt to bring a pro-Russian president to power in Ukraine in the 2004 elections, Russia has stepped up gas bypass routes. The goal is to punish Ukrainians for the Orange Revolution, nullify Ukraine's transit role, deprive it of part of its income and, in general, weaken the country, making it marginal in the space between Russia and the EU (Naftogaz, 2021a).[4] And, of course, to increase the EU's dependence on Russia.

Russia's plans were fuelled by intense oil and gas prices in the 2000s and rising revenues of Russian state-owned energy companies, which became the basis of the Kremlin's kleptocracy within the country and the financial engine of external expansion, which increasingly took the form of hybrid aggression.

Against this background, Russia initiated the transformation of the North European Gas Pipeline project, which was to connect the giant Shtokman gas condensate field in the Barents Sea with the German market into the Nord Stream project for gas from Western Siberia, which traditionally entered the European market via Ukraine and Belarus.

It is worth noting the characteristics of the future Trans-Baltic Sea gas pipeline made by Vladimir Putin during his visit to Germany on the 8th of September 2005: "*The route of this gas pipeline should run along the bottom of the Baltic Sea – from Vyborg to the coast in Greifswald and with branches to Sweden, Finland and the Kaliningrad region of the Russian Federation, and will be 1,200 km. In the future, it is planned to lay a branch through the Netherlands to Beckton (UK). And then the total length can be 3,000 km. The total design capacity of the pipeline is almost 20 billion cubic meters annually. With a possible increase in 2011 to 55 billion a year*" (Presidential Executive Office of Russia, 2005).[5]

[4] Naftogaz' revenue from providing Gazprom with gas transportation services amounted to USD 2.1 billion in 2020. According to Energy Ministry of Ukraine (2021), this revenue amounted to 1.4% of Ukraine's GDP in 2020. For comparison: Naftogaz' transit revenue in 2012 was USD 3.3 billion, or 1.9% of GDP (Institute of Economics and Forecasting, 2021; Naftogaz, 2021b).

[5] The quote has been translated from the Russian language into English by the authors.

That is, the project was conceived in the Soviet style, with the aim of supplying not only Germany but also the key countries of the Baltic Sea region, including Finland and Sweden. But after it finally became clear that, on the one hand, Russia did not have the technological capabilities for exploration of the Shtokman field, and on the other hand, the Kremlin had a strong desire to reset transit through Ukraine, the project underwent a transformation. It became essentially a transit-free substitute for the transit route 'Northern Districts of the Tyumen Region-Dolyna-Uzhhorod' through Belarus and Ukraine, which Russia finally rejected for political reasons after the Orange Revolution in Ukraine.

Shortly after Putin's meeting with Schroeder in December 2005, Gazprom, together with Germany's Wintershall and E.ONRuhrgas, registered Nord Stream AG in Switzerland to implement the project of the same name. Such a Russian-German alliance for the pipeline provoked a negative reaction from Ukraine and Poland. Radoslaw Sikorski, Poland's Defence Minister, compared the project to create a transit-free gas transport corridor between Russia and Germany to the Molotov-Ribbentrop Pact: "*Poland has a particular sensitivity to corridors and deals above our head. That was the Locarno tradition, that was the Molotov-Ribbentrop tradition*" (Beunderman, 2006).

After the gas crisis in early 2006, which Russia used to demonstrate Ukraine's unreliability as a transit link on the East–West line, Gazprom stepped up efforts not only to build the Nord Stream gas pipeline. In 2007, the South Stream project with a capacity of 63 billion cubic metres annually (bcma) was initiated–for the same gas from the northern regions of Russia through the route from north to south, across the Black Sea to Bulgaria, bypassing Ukraine and Belarus.

The gas crisis of 2009 undoubtedly helped Gazprom accelerate the implementation of Nord Stream, the first line of which was put into operation in 2011 and the second in 2012. But it did not work out with the South Stream. The principled position of the then-European Commission regarding the need to comply with the Third Energy Package on the territory of EU member states, US pressure on Bulgaria and the West's negative reaction to Russia's aggression against Ukraine led to Russia's withdrawal from South Stream in December 2014. But later on, it was reported that Russia intends to implement another project, namely TurkStream, the capacity of which amounts to 31.5 bcma, i.e. exactly a half of the South Stream capacity.

Since the spring of 2014, Gazprom has been working in Europe to prepare for the Nord Stream expansion initiative, arguing it by the Ukrainian transit risks due to the 'civil conflict in Ukraine'. This narrative was actively disseminated by Russian propaganda to disguise the hybrid aggression against Ukraine (Gonchar, 2020). One of the goals of this aggression is to accelerate the implementation of Gazprom's bypass projects in the Baltic Sea and the Black Sea together with a pool of European companies to virtually zero transit through 'non-stable territory of Ukraine' where 'civil war' broke out. By Gazprom's logic, the non-transit gas pipelines will allow to avoid transit risks.

The surplus of pipeline capacity calculated in Table 5.2 is clearly excessive from the point of view of conducting gas business. In practice, Gazprom's export capacity surplus, including possible Nord Stream 2 capacities, is equal to its weighted average exports in recent years. This has become the main reason for criticising the economic viability of projects, such as Nord Stream 2 and TurkStream, their politically-motivated and geopolitically-oriented nature.[6] Experts and politicians from Ukraine, Poland, the Baltic States, the United Kingdom, the European Parliament and some independent Russian experts are constantly paying attention to this for governments of some European countries which support Nord Stream 2.

Therefore, it is no coincidence that the Nord Stream 2 project received the greatest opposition from Ukraine, Poland and especially the United States. Washington D.C. quickly realised Russia's real intentions. If Nord Stream 2 and TurkStream work, west–east and north–south interconnectors built in Central Europe for alternative supplies of non-Russian gas to the region will come under Gazprom's de facto control. The main reason for this is the dominance of Russian resources in this part of the

[6] Technical support and modernisation of the Ukrainian GTS is ongoing. The 2020–2029 plan provides for investments of UAH 38.8 billion (EUR 1.26 billion) over ten years. The plan is based on the transit volumes stipulated by the Naftogaz and Gazprom Agreement of 2019, according to which only 40 bcma will be ordered for transportation by 2024. Larger modernisation can be carried out while achieving greater demand for gas transportation services through the GTS of Ukraine. But in any case, the amount of investment is many times smaller compared to the Nord Stream 2 project. Taking into account the infrastructure built on Russian territory from the Yamal to the Baltic Sea, the total cost of the project is over EUR 40 billion, of which the cost of the underwater gas pipeline from Ust-Luga (Russia) to Greifswald (Germany) is only nine billion euros (DW, 2018).

Table 5.2 Transmission capacity for gas exports from Russia towards the west

Routes	*Capacity (bcma)*	*Remarks*
Ukrainian gas transmission system (Ukrainian GTS)	**146.0**	Total capacities of all routes operated by the Ukrainian transmission system operator (TSO)
Offshore non-transit routes	**102.5**	**Operated by Gazprom**
Blue Stream	16.0	Full capacity in operation
TurkStream	31.5	50% of utilisation, final stage for the 2nd line
North Stream	55.0	Overloaded (58.5 bcm in 2019)
Onshore transit pipelines	**49.3**	**Operated by Gazprom** (Gazprom Transgaz Belarus)
Yamal-Europe	32.9	Via Belarus and Poland to Germany
Kobryn-Brest-Warsaw	5.0	Via Belarus to Poland
Minsk-Vilnius-Kaunas-Kaliningrad (Königsberg)	11.4	Via Belarus to Lithuania and Kaliningrad (Königsberg)
Onshore non-transit pipelines	**15.1**	**Operated by Gazprom**
Valday-Pskov-Riga	7.4	Directly to Latvia
Izborsk-Tartu-Rakvere	1.2	Directly to Estonia
St. Petersburg-Kohtla-Järve-Tallinn	0.5	Directly to Estonia
Vyborg (Viipuri)-Imatra	6.0	Directly to Finland
Total export transmission capacity (TETC)	**312.9**	
Gazprom averaged annual exports (GAAE)	**184.7**	Averaged annual export volume in the western direction, provided by Gazpromexport during 2015–2020
TETC—GAAE	**128.2**[a]	Surplus of the transmission capacity

Note [a]If the Nord Stream 2 is completed and put into operation, the total export transmission capacity will reach 367.9 bcma, a surplus of the transmission capacity will be 183.2 bcma. Almost 100% excess capacity does not seem economically reasonable.
Source The Authors, based on East European Gas Analysis (2013), ENTSOG (2019), Gazprom (2021), Gazpromexport (2020a, 2020b), Gazprom Invest (2020), Nord Stream (2020) and TSOUA (2020c)

EU market and the reservation of pipeline capacities in the region by Gazprom-affiliated companies. Both Russian streams somehow converge in the Austrian hub Baumgarten. The route through Ukraine with the above-mentioned surplus of pipeline capacity becomes redundant and is excluded by Russia from the scheme of supplies to Europe. This means that Ukraine will not only lose revenues from the transmission of Russian gas to Europe, but also reverse gas supplies from Europe to the Ukrainian market will become problematic. The lack of physical flow of gas from east to west will mean the impossibility of taking a part of it for the return flow from the EU to Ukraine (via Poland, Slovakia, Hungary and Romania).

This situation will create an additional temptation for the Kremlin regime to act more aggressively towards Ukraine, which, in its opinion, will no longer be of serious importance to the EU, as it no longer has a transit function. Therefore, Ukraine's resistance to Russian bypass projects and its American support both have a vitally important security dimension.

EU-Ukraine-Russia Gas Triangle

Russia began to increase natural gas exports to Europe after the collapse of the Soviet Union. Gazprom export's data illustrate an almost steady upward trend. Some temporary decline took place only in the aftermath of the economic crisis of 2008–2009 (Gazpromexport, 2020b) (Table 5.3).

In the 1990s, 95% of Russian gas supplies to Europe were transited through Ukraine using a network of gas pipelines that transported not only transit gas from Russia, but also gas imported to Ukraine and domestic gas (Neftegaz.Ru, 2015).

Only supplies to the small markets of Finland and the Baltic States (Estonia, Latvia and Lithuania) were non-transit or bypassing Ukraine. Transit via Ukraine was in the range of 120–140 bcm with a maximum capacity of the GTS of Ukraine in transit was 146 bcm per annum (Fig. 5.1).

However, transit volumes also included exports to Moldova and Russian-Russian transit, i.e. gas supplies from the Russian mainland via

Table 5.3 The development of the Russian gas exports towards the European direction (bcma)

1990	*1995*	*2000*	*2005*	*2010*	*2015*	*2016*	*2017*	*2018*	*2019*	*2020*
110.0	117.4	130.3	154.3	138.6	158.6	178.3	192.2	200.8	198.9	179.3

Source The Authors, based on Gazpromexport (2020b) and Telegraph (2021)

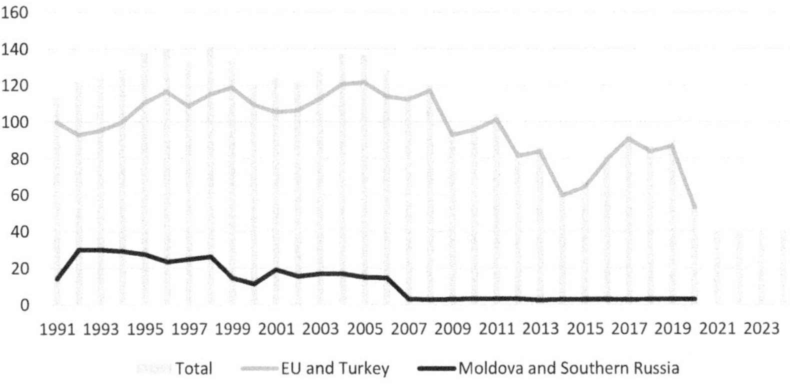

Fig. 5.1 Transmission of natural gas from Russia to the European countries and Turkey via Ukraine in 1991–2024 (bcma) (*Notes* The years 2020–2024 corresponds to the capacities ordered by Gazprom for transmission through the territory of Ukraine. The agreement between Ukraine's Naftogaz and Russia's Gazprom for the reservation of transit capacity by Gazprom in the amount of 65 bcm (178 million cubic metres per day) in 2020 and 40 bcm (110 mcm per day) in 2021–2024. Russia's gas transit via Ukraine to southern Russia stopped in 2007 due to Gazprom's construction of a bypass pipeline. *Source* The Authors, based on Naftogaz, 2021b; TSOUA, 2021a; Ukrtransgaz, 2020)

eastern Ukraine to another destination in Russia. In 2006, Gazprom built a 310-km bypass gas pipeline Sokhranovka–Oktyabrskaya worth USD 1,030 million, to save USD 36–40 million in annual costs for 250 km transit of 15–30 bcm of gas through Ukraine. This is a very illustrative case, which once again demonstrates the dominance of not commercial, but political and geopolitical approaches to the choice of energy routes.[7] The Sokhranovka–Oktyabrskaya gas pipeline was Russia's petty revenge for the Orange Revolution in Ukraine, which thwarted plans to bring Kremlin protégé Viktor Yanukovych to power. A larger revenge was the acceleration of the project to build the North European gas pipeline, renamed as Nord Stream.

[7] In 2002, a similar project to bypass Ukraine was implemented by the oil transport operator Transneft.

In 2019, Gazprom used all bypass routes, i.e. Yamal-Europe, Blue Stream and Nord Stream at maximum capacity, while through the territory of Ukraine to the EU, Turkey and the Balkans, it supplied only 45% of Russia's total gas exports (Gazpromexport, 2020b). In 2020, this figure dropped to 31%. This means that there is no monopoly of Ukraine for the transit of Russian gas to Europe. Nevertheless, the Russian side persistently continues to implement bypass projects—TurkStream and Nord Stream 2. At the same time, it is no secret that the goal is to null transit through Ukraine as soon as these gas pipelines are completed and put into operation.

Although the Russian aggression against Ukraine, which began in February 2014, did not affect the transit function of the Ukrainian GTS, it created serious problems for gas supplies to Ukraine. Russia effectively imposed a gas blockade on Ukraine in June 2014, suspending gas supplies due to Naftogaz' refusal to pay for a price that exceeded the market value.

Since the 25th of November 2015, Ukraine's gas imports from the aggressor country (Russia) have been suspended. The suspension was caused both by Gazprom's price dictates (its prices significantly exceeded the European price markers) and by the principled position of the Government of Ukraine to limit trade with Russia as much as possible. Gas imports from Russia have been set to zero. But transit via Ukraine was maintained as Ukraine tried not to harm its European neighbours and partners. However, from a legal point of view, Naftogaz, having no contractual obligations to European companies regarding the transit of Russian gas, could have stopped providing services to Gazprom as a state-owned company of the aggressor country. However, this did not happen.

During 2014–2015, Ukraine, thanks to co-operation with the EU and the USA, as well as Poland and Slovakia, and later Hungary, succeeded in diversifying gas supplies to the country, which dramatically reduced the risks of economic blackmail by Russia as a former monopoly exporter of gas.

Opportunities were created to receive gas through the GTS of three neighbouring countries: Poland, Slovakia, Hungary—and since 2019 from Romania. Against the background of a significant reduction in gas consumption in Ukraine, reverse supplies, i.e. gas flows from the west to Ukraine, fully met the country's gas import needs. Moreover, the total reverse supply capacity of 22.6 bcm has been created in 2016 that almost doubled the annual volume of required imports of 11 bcm. In 2019, the reverse capacity was increased to 29.8 bcm per annum, i.e. almost to the volume of annual gas consumption in Ukraine. This was done in the event of Russia cut off gas supplies to the EU via Ukraine.

It should be noted that Russian gas exports are quite tightly tied to Europe, both in terms of infrastructure and finance. Attempts to deploy it eastward–to China–are not commercially viable for Russia, given the much longer transport leg and the more complex terrain. It should also be taken into account that in Eastern Siberia, in contrast to Western Siberian, not gas but gas condensate fields are located. Russia cannot explore them effectively due to the lack of necessary technologies and already has made mistakes in deposit explorations. Due to this, gas production cannot reach the design target and the Power of Siberia gas pipeline is used at minimum capacity. But in Moscow, as usual, they preferred geopolitical approaches to commercial ones. If in the late 1960s the Kremlin used the Chinese threat as a factor in rapprochement with Europe and its separation from the United States, half a century later the Chinese factor was used to blackmail and force Europe to have no alternative to Russian gas projects. Only one thing remains unchanged–an attempt to tear Europe away from the United States and to minimise the American gas presence in the European markets.

Ukraine: From the Transit Country to an Integral Part of the EU Gas Market

After the collapse of the USSR and the restoration of Ukraine's independence, gas transmission through the territory of Ukraine was carried out under contracts concluded for the implementation of agreements between the governments of Ukraine and Russia. The transit route through Ukraine has become strategically important for Russia. Gazprom has become a monopoly customer of gas transmission capacities in Ukraine. The Russian exporter's gas entered the Ukrainian GTS on the Russian-Ukrainian border, was transported through Ukraine and on the EU-Ukraine border (with Poland, Slovakia, Hungary and Romania) was again transferred to Gazprom. Such a monopoly on the use of transit capacity was supplemented by dominance, and later by a monopoly on the supply of gas to the Ukrainian market. This contradicted the rules of the EU gas market. This situation persisted in fact during 1991–2015. An illustrative example is 2014, when Russia resorted to aggression against Ukraine, and Gazprom began to demand even higher prices for gas supplies to Ukraine (Fig. 5.2).

Russia's aggression against Ukraine led to a change in the post-Soviet status quo and accelerated the reform of both the gas market in Ukraine and the situation with the transit of Russian gas to Europe.

The concept of the European market provides for the achievement of a high level of its competitiveness and integration. A common regulatory environment, ensuring the physical interconnection of gas networks, avoiding the isolation of markets enhances security and security of supply. The EU gas standards are almost fully implemented in the national legislation of Ukraine, which strengthens the EU gas market from the east in terms of reliability, safety and integration.

Ukraine aspires to be a full participant in the EU's integrated gas market and has reason to be one of its most important links, including ensuring the transmission of gas supplies from the east and significantly enhancing overall security. Moreover, gas imports to Ukraine are carried out from the sources of the EU market since November 2015, i.e. Russian gas supplies for Ukrainian use have been completely suspended. The share

Fig. 5.2 Russian gas price increase for Naftogaz in April 2014 (USD per 1,000 cubic metres) (*Notes* *Fair price for Ukraine is based on export parity price (NCG) minus transportation from east border of Ukraine to German hub NCG and minus wholesale trade margin. **NCG hub is a gas trading hub in Germany. *Source* The Authors, based on Vitrenko Library, 2021)

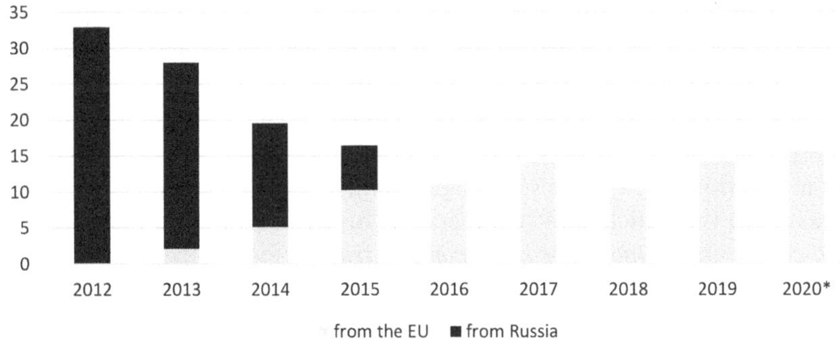

Fig. 5.3 The development of Ukraine's gas imports in 2012–2020 (bcma) (*Note* *Estimation. *Source* The Authors, based on data from TSOUA, 2020a, 2020b, 2020c, 2020d, 2021a, 2021b)

of natural gas in the Ukrainian primary energy balance increased from 28.9% in 2015 to 29.8% in 2019 (TSOUA, 2020a) (Fig. 5.3).

On its way to membership in the EU gas market, Ukraine has already overcome a long road of transformation. Ukraine's integration process in the field of gas is based, for example, on the following events:

(1) membership in the Energy Community Treaty since 2011 (Verkhovna Rada of Ukraine, 2005);
(2) organisation of a reverse scheme for gas imports from the EU to Ukraine since 2012;
(3) adoption of the Law of Ukraine on the natural gas market in accordance with the European Third Energy Package in 2015;
(4) the EU-Ukraine Association Agreement in 2017 (Eurointegration Portal, 2017);
(5) Naftogaz' 2018 victories related to lawsuits against Gazprom under sales and transit contracts of 2009 in the Arbitration Institute of the Stockholm Chamber of Commerce; and
(6) the establishment in 2019 of new relations between Naftogaz and Gazprom on the transmission of Russian gas to Europe, based on the EU legislation.

The EU-Ukraine Association Agreement, which contains effective instruments for integration in the energy sector as a whole, is of key importance (Verkhovna Rada of Ukraine, 2015).

Ukraine's and the EU's gas networks are of strategic importance to both parties. With this in mind, special attention is paid to co-operation and interaction of the parties in the planning and use of gas infrastructure. As stated in the Article 274 'Cooperation on infrastructure': "*The Parties shall endeavour to facilitate the use of gas transmission infrastructure and gas storage facilities and shall consult or coordinate, as appropriate, with each other on infrastructure developments. The Parties shall cooperate on matters related to trade in natural gas, sustainability and security of supply*" (European Union, 2014, 115).

The parties undertook to avoid disruptions in gas transmission. At the same time, neither Ukraine nor the EU should be held responsible for interrupting or reducing gas flows as a result of third-country actions. Pursuant to paragraph 3 of Article 276 "*The Parties agree that a Party shall not be held liable for an interruption or reduction pursuant to this Article where that Party is in an impossibility to supply, transit or transport energy goods as a result of actions attributable to a third country.*" (European Union, 2014, 116).

This is an important clarification and is an echo of Gazprom's actions in 2006 and 2009 to cut off natural gas flows to Europe through Ukraine. Now, even the term 'transit' is an anachronism, because, according to the law, between the countries of the EU single gas market, including the territory of Ukraine, the term 'transmission' is used. By the way, the term 'transit' is not used in the new agreement between Naftogaz and Gazprom in 2019.

The EU gas legislation is currently being implemented in both Ukraine and EU member states, but not always synchronously. Since the beginning of February 2011, before the Association Agreement was signed, Ukraine has acceded to the Treaty Establishing Energy Community (TEEC), which also implements European gas legislation.

As a result of the sectoral integration process, Ukraine must move from a transit country to a full participant in the EU gas market. Such transformations can take place even before EU membership. Association of Georgia, Moldova and Ukraine with the EU, the creation of the Energy Community has led to a situation where the space covered by European legislation becomes much larger than the territory of the EU itself. And this has a positive effect on the security of gas supply.

Ukraine: Changes in Positioning Towards the EU Gas Market

Ukraine is appearing more often in documents and reports of European institutions. In particular, data on the Ukrainian gas market are regularly published on the ENTSO-G Transparency Platform (ENTSOG, 2020) and the Gas Infrastructures Europe (GIE) platform. Leading gas agencies publish price indicators of the Ukrainian gas market, for example the ENTSO-G Transparency Platform and GIE platform AGSI + (ENTSOG, 2020; European Commission, 2020b).

After the unbundling of Naftogaz, which caused separation of the underground gas storage (UGS) facilities into a separate enterprise, the business opportunities for underground gas storage have significantly expanded.

The short-haul service which has been provided by the GTS operator of Ukraine since the beginning of 2020 means the ability to transport gas between cross-border entry/exit points without providing access to the Ukrainian virtual trading point (UAVTP) and the domestic market. It can be used together with the service of the UGS operator Customs Warehouse, which is provided by the UGS operator—Ukrtransgaz.[8]

Gas in the Customs Warehouse mode can stay in the UGS of Ukraine for 1,095 days without paying taxes and customs duties. Organisational and legal opportunities for the functioning of the Customs Warehouse regime are created based on the following Ukrainian UGS (Table 5.4).

As a matter of interest, these underground gas storage facilities are former gas fields that were depleted during the period of active production in the 1960s and the 1970s and were adapted for gas storage. First, it was important from the point of view of uninterrupted exports of Siberian gas to Europe at the peak of its consumption in the winter. Gas from Ukrainian UGS facilities has traditionally ensured the reliability of Soviet and then Russian exports to Europe.

Since 2020, there has been a significant reduction in Russian gas transmission. Thus, most of the transport and storage capacity can be offered to participants in the gas market of Ukraine and EU countries.

[8] Customs Warehouse is a special customs regime, allowing to temporary store natural gas in Ukrainian underground gas storages for 1,095 days without paying taxes and customs duties (TSOUA, 2021c; Ukrtransgaz, 2021b).

Table 5.4 Ukrainian underground gas storage facilities (in an alphabetical order)

Name	*Region*	*Working volume (million cubic metres)*
UGS Bilche-Volytsko-Uherske	Lviv	17,050
UGS Bohorodchanske	Ivano-Frankivsk	2,300
UGS Dashavske	Lviv	2,150
UGS Hlibivske[a]	Crimea	1,000
UGS Kehychivske	Kharkiv	700
UGS Krasnopopivske	Luhansk	420
UGS Mrynske (Chervonopartyzanske)	Chernihiv	1,500
UGS Olyshivske	Chernihiv	310
UGS Oparske	Lviv	1,920
UGS Proletarske	Dnipropetrovsk	1,000
UGS Solokhivske	Poltava	1,300
UGS Uherske (XIV-XV)	Lviv	1,900
UGS Verhunske[a]	Luhansk	400
Total		31,950

Note [a]Marked underground gas storages are located on the territories occupied by Russia, temporarily not controlled by Ukraine
Source The Authors, based on data from Ukrtransgaz (2021a)

The new services allowed engaging European gas companies into gas storage and as a result in 2020 Ukraine storage facilities contained maximum filling level in the last ten years (Fig. 5.4). In addition, these new products have a positive impact on Europe's security of gas supply

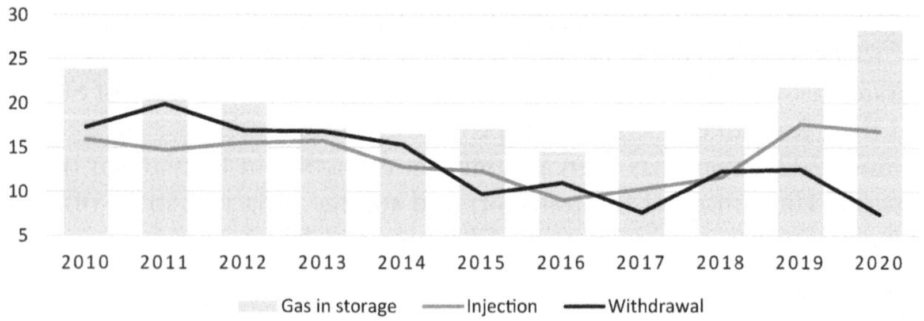

Fig. 5.4 Historical data on Ukraine's UGS in 2010–2020 (bcm) (*Source* The Authors, based on data from Ukrtransgaz, 2021b)

(SoS) and can be also used in case of need to cover additional demand in case of crisis situations in the EU gas market.

When transporting gas between EU countries (Poland, Romania, Slovakia and Hungary) via the Ukrainian GTS, tariffs may be more attractive than on alternative routes in the EU. At the same time, the interconnection between the networks of neighbouring countries is improving, additional transport capacities that significantly exceed the existing ones are becoming available, as well as UGS of Ukraine for seasonal gas storage. Tariffs for the Short-haul + Customs Warehouse service are clearly lower than the level of tariffs for gas storage in UGS in neighbouring member states of the European Union (Table 5.5).

Most of the gas volume in the short-haul mode is sent to underground storage. Since its launch, the Short-haul service has been used by 24 non-resident customers and five Ukrainian companies (Expro Consulting, 2020).

Thus, the introduction of European rules has allowed new services, new choices, which fosters competition and strengthens the load of gas infrastructure and energy security in Central and Eastern Europe.

Table 5.5 A comparison of tariffs for Short-haul + Customs Warehouse service in Ukraine and for underground gas storage in neighbouring EU countries

Connection	*Tariff for Short-haul + Customs Warehouse service (EUR/MWh)*	*Country*	*Tariff for storage (EUR/MWh)*
Hungary–Ukraine Ukraine–Hungary	1.67	Hungary	2.45–6.14
Poland–Ukraine Ukraine–Poland	1.70	Poland	4.20–4.70
Romania–Ukraine Ukraine–Romania	1.63	Romania	3.12–5.51
Slovakia–Ukraine Ukraine–Slovakia	1.62	Slovakia	3.65

Source The Authors, based on Ukrtransgaz https://utg.ua/utg/media/news/2020/05/informaciini platformy-operatoriv-gts-ta-psg-obednuyt-poslugi-short-haul-ta-mytnij-sklad.html

Reliability of Gas Infrastructure and Security of Supply

The implementation of EU gas legislation in Ukraine contributes to the improvement of the operation and development of gas infrastructure, and thus to the reliability and security of supply. The Law of Ukraine 'On the Gas Market' stipulates that the gas market is founded on "*principles of free competition, due protection of consumers and security of supply...*" and is based on European gas legislation (Ukrtransgaz, 2015, 1).

The law imposes responsibility on GTS operator for reliable and secure operation. The operator is obliged to maintain and develop the gas transmission infrastructure, including new construction and reconstruction of the network. The operator is obliged to annually develop and submit for approval to the regulator and implement the Gas Transmission System Development Plan for the next ten years (NKREKP, 2020).

In March 2020, the NKREKP approved the GTS Development Plan of Ukraine for 2020–2029, which for the first time had been developed the GTS operator of Ukraine, a new independent operator. It evolved as a result of the Naftogaz unbundling (TSOUA, 2020a).

The annual updates of the plan continue. A project for 2021–2030 has been developed, which addresses the problem of overcapacity, although such excess has existed for a long time (TSOUA, 2020c). For example, the capacity utilisation at the entrance from the Russian Federation from 2012 to 2019 did not exceed 35% on average (Fig. 5.5). Capacities at entry points from Belarus (Mozyr and Kobryn interconnection points) were used by 7.5%, and gas transmission through these points has been stopped altogether since the year 2016.

The prospect of loading the Ukrainian GTS after the termination of the contract with Gazprom in 2024 will depend primarily on whether gas pipeline projects will affect both the Ukrainian GTS and the entire European market—the second line of TurkStream and Nord Stream 2—will be completed or closed down.

After the commissioning of the first line of the TurkStream in the beginning of 2020, the transmission of Russian gas through the Orlivka cross-border interconnection point (IP) was basically stopped. Thus, the capacities for transmission of about 15 bcm per year became unloaded.

The second line of the TurkStream in the case of its completion and commissioning in Bulgaria, Serbia and Hungary is expected to be influencing the GTS of Ukraine from 2022. This will reduce gas transmission

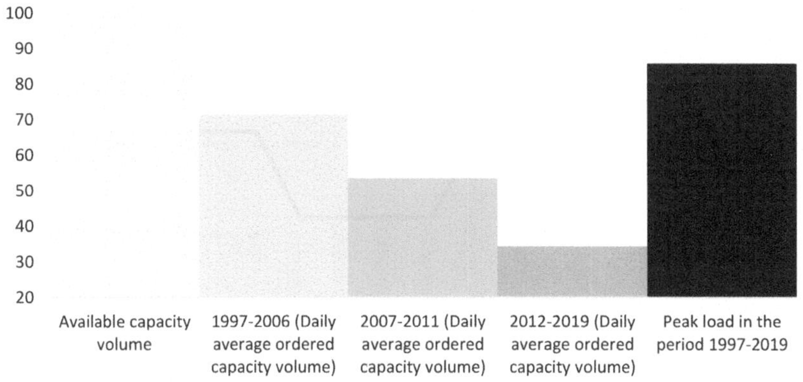

Fig. 5.5 Use of capacities at the Ukraine-Russia entry points in 2012–2019 (%) (*Source* The Authors, based on TSOUA, 2020c)

through the Beregovo IP by 11 bcm and the Orlivka IP by four billion cubic metres per year.

The Nord Stream 2 project with a design capacity of two branches—55 bcma, if implemented, will influence the loading of Uzhhorod, a cross-border interconnection point, and carries the risk of complete cessation of supply to the European Union via Slovakia.

Thus, the forecast load options of the GTS of Ukraine are reduced to three scenarios, reflected in the Development Plan of LLC Gas Transmission System Operator of Ukraine for 2021–2030 (Fig. 5.6).

Thus, there is a certain probability that from 2025 even more gas infrastructure facilities of Ukraine will not be used for natural gas transmission to Europe. At the same time, Ukraine is making efforts to block the implementation of Nord Stream 2 and the second line of the Turk-Stream, to unblock the traditional route for gas from Central Asia to the EU via Russia and Ukraine, and to keep the level of gas transportation to Europe via Ukraine within 50–80 bcm per annum depending on the volume of the EU's imports from the east, which is estimated at 180–210 bcm per year till the end of 2020s.

The assessment of domestic peak demand for transport services also shows an excess of capacity for which no additional demand is expected

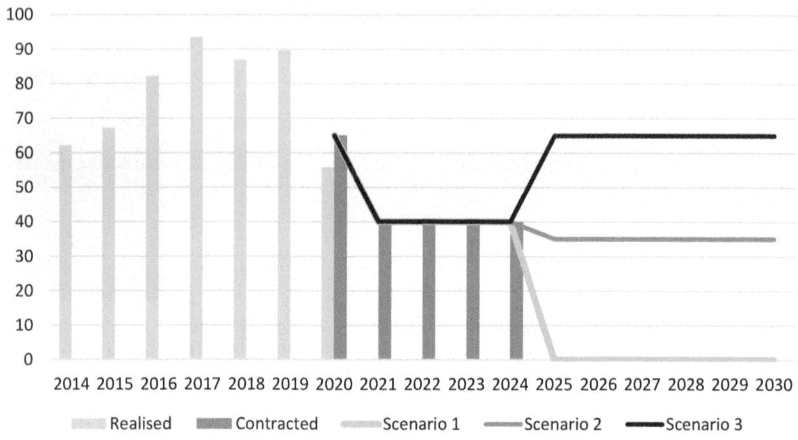

Fig. 5.6 Prospects of gas transportation via Ukraine in 2020–2030 (bcma) (*Source* The Authors, based on TSOUA, 2020c)

even in the future. This situation requires certain measures to adapt infrastructure facilities to the conditions when significant GTS capacity will not be used.

The GTS operator of Ukraine has developed a list of infrastructure facilities not involved in gas transportation. A part of the compressor stations will be in reserve to ensure the reliability of the system at peak loads. This means that the facilities will be supported in working mode but without technical re-equipment and modernisation (Fig. 5.7).

The draft plan until 2030 also forecasts that many gas pumping units may be decommissioned, including 272 gas compressor units (GCUs), according to preliminary estimates (TSOUA, 2020c). About 180 GCUs can be transferred to the reserve, and 267 GCUs will remain in operation. The exact number of units to be decommissioned will be determined after a detailed study of each facility. In general, it is possible to drop 60–70% of the GTS capacity if Russian bypass projects are not suspended (TSOUA, 2020b).

Thus, the TurkStream project and the Nord Stream 2 project increase the negative impact on Ukraine's gas infrastructure as a part of the European network. In view of the monopoly on gas exports from the Russian Federation and the control of transport routes, Gazprom distorts the

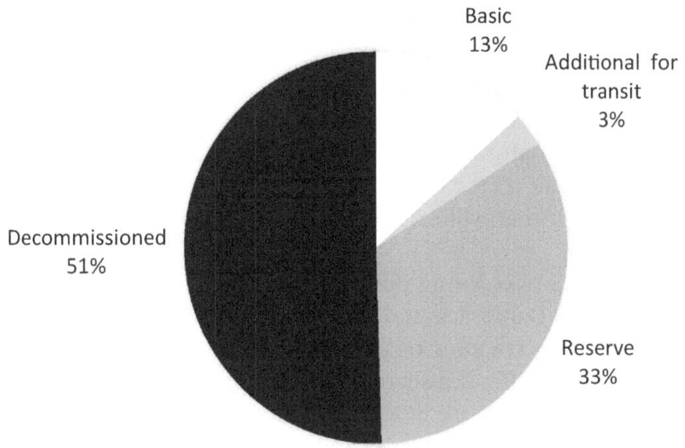

Fig. 5.7 The structure of the gas compressor units in accordance with the draft decommissioning plan (%) (*Source* The Authors, based on TSOUA, 2020c)

market environment and hinders market competition in the provision of gas transportation services.

On the 6th of May 2019, Naftogaz filed a complaint to the European Commission against Gazprom for abuses of dominance in European gas markets (Ukrinform, 2019). Gazprom has been accused of violating/distorting market rules, obstructing competition, conducting discriminatory practices, and blocking access of Russian independent producers and producers from Central Asia to the European market. Naftogaz' complaint also calls on Gazprom to allow European buyers to buy gas on both Ukraine's eastern and western borders.

Gazprom must stop abusing its dominant position and agree to transfer gas at points on the Ukraine-Russia border (for example, the Sudzha IP) and unblock gas from Central Asia. Moreover, Gazprom must stop abusing its dominant position and agree to transfer gas at interconnection points on the Ukraine-Russia border (for example, the Sudzha IP) and unblock gas from Central Asia.

The implementation of Russian projects that contradict the concept of the EU market puts the GTS operator of Ukraine in a state where the available capacity exceeds the demand, which is limited by Gazprom on the grounds of non-economic nature. Market distortions created by

Gazprom increase the likelihood of decommissioning a part of Ukraine's gas transmission infrastructure, which reduces the opportunity of the most reliable route for gas transportation to the EU market and worsens security of gas supply. The EU already has a large excess of capacity to import Russian natural gas. The construction of Nord Stream 2 and TurkStream will lead to the destruction of the Ukrainian route (pipelines and UGS facilities) that will increase Gazprom's dominance and threaten security of supply.

The EU market risks losing flexibility and Russian gas imports will be dependent on the Baltic Sea and Black Sea bypass pipelines, which can only transport basic volumes of gas and will not be able to balance the market flexibly. In 2019, the share of Russian gas, including pipeline and LNG, was 46%, furthermore in the third quarter it reached maximum of 49%, including 45% of pipeline gas and four percent of LNG (European Commission, 2019).

New projects within the EU gas market should not harm existing gas infrastructure. Therefore, the ten-year network development plans, which are being developed in the EU (ENTSO-G) and in Ukraine (GTS operator of Ukraine), need the closest possible co-ordination. Requirements for the co-ordination of strategies and plans are set out in Article 274 of the EU-Ukraine Association Agreement.

Belarus on Gas Routes

The development of gas infrastructure in Belarus began in the early 1960s with the Ukrainian routes Dashava-Minsk-Vilnius-Riga and Dashava-Kyiv-Bryansk-Moscow with a branch to the Belarusian Gomel. It supplied gas from the Dashava gas field for the needs of the Soviet Belarus and Soviet Russia and went in transit to Soviet Lithuania and Soviet Latvia. In the mid-1970s, after the development of gas fields in Western Siberia, a new gas transmission system Torzhok-Smolensk-Minsk-Ivatsevychi-Kobrin-Dolyna was built, through which gas came not only to Belarus, but also in transit to Ukraine and further for the exports to Western Europe. The USSR's attempts to increase gas exports were accompanied by the emergence of additional route projects. One of them was supposed to be a large-diametre gas pipeline Torzhok-Smolensk-Mozyr-Dolyna, which would supply gas to the main Soviet export corridor through Ukrainian Uzhhorod in a more direct way.

The construction of a direct pipeline between Torzhok and Dolyna (through Russian Smolensk and Belarusian Mozyr) began in 1989, during the economic decline of the USSR. With the collapse of the Soviet Union, the project turned into a never-ending construction, and the construction of a pipeline (without compressor stations) on the territory of the already new independent states—Russia, Belarus and Ukraine, was completed only in 1996. However, the lack of compressor stations did not allow the countries to use the gas pipeline with a design capacity of 28 bcm per annum.

As far back as in the early 2000s, the Ukrainian side proposed to complete the construction of the pipeline through further construction of four compressor stations in Ukraine. The Ukrainian Government was ready to consider the transfer of the Ukrainian parts of both Torzhok-Smolensk-Mozyr-Dolyna and Torzhok-Smolensk-Minsk-Ivatsevychi-Kobrin-Dolyna transit gas pipelines to Russia's Gazprom to repay a debt for previously supplied Russian natural gas. If all 11 compressor stations were completed according to the project plan, the total capacity of both pipelines would have been 57 bcm (Neftegaz, 2001).

Belarus would benefit from the aforementioned pipes as well, as they would increase the volume of transit through its territory. The proposal also fits into the development of the Russian gas transport corridor 'Northern Districts of the Tyumen region-Torzhok'. In fact, Torzhok became an internal Russian hub from which gas flowed in different directions.

But Russia already had other priorities, namely the Yamal-Europe pipeline bypassing Ukraine through the territory of Belarus with a capacity of 33 bcm. It is there where 'Northern Districts of the Tyumen region-Torzhok' gas pipeline was to supply gas to, as the gas fields on the Yamal Peninsula had not yet been developed in the 1990s. In fact, gas supplies from Yamal only became possible since 2012, when the Bovanenkovo field was put into operation and the Bovanenkovo-Ukhta gas pipeline was built, that is, almost 20 years later, when Gazprom initiated the construction of a gas pipeline to export gas reportedly from Yamal to Europe. This, together with the refusal to bring the corridor from Torzhok to Uzhhorod via Dolyna to design capacity, points to Moscow's political decision to create 'a Northern Districts of the Tyumen region-Europe' route bypassing Ukraine, disguised as Yamal-Europe, almost immediately after Ukraine's Declaration of Independence.

Initially Belarus was seen by Russia as an ally in projects of building gas transmission systems bypassing Ukraine. The Yamal-Europe 2 gas pipeline was to appear too. In fact, it was not a full-fledged gas pipeline project from Yamal to Europe, as a parallel string, but an interconnector to connect Belarus' existing gas transmission facilities with the main export corridor for Russian gas in Slovakia through Poland bypassing Ukraine.

The Polish Government took the principled stand against implementation of the project as harmful for Ukraine and the Ukrainian-Polish relations. In addition, the strategic goal in Poland was to diversify gas supplies. For these reasons, the Government of Poland initiated the Baltic Pipe project in 2001 to obtain gas from Norway via Denmark. Although the project had been criticised as not economically feasible enough, after the first Russian-Ukrainian gas crisis in early January 2006 and the famous Munich speech by Russian President Vladimir Putin in 2007, the project was revived, and the second gas crisis in 2009 added to Poland's confidence in the necessity of its implementation. Gazprom made numerous attempts to revive Yamal-Europe 2 with another government change in Warsaw but failed.

Unlike Ukraine, which by any means did not allow the transfer of strategic gas transmission infrastructure to Russia as compensation for debts for gas supplied or a discount on the price of gas imported from Russia, Belarus chose another strategy for its relations with Gazprom. This was not a voluntary decision of the Lukashenko regime. The Lukashenko regime was forced under pressure from Russia through gas blackmail. Moscow threatened to cut supplies or raise prices. Beltransgaz, a state-owned gas transmission and supply company, was offered to Gazprom in exchange for cheap gas.

Gazprom became the owner of all the Beltransgaz shares. In 2013, the relevant re-organisation of the company was completed, and as a result, Beltransgaz became an integrated part of the Russian monopoly called GazpromTransgaz Belarus, as a wholly-owned subsidiary of Gazprom (Gazprom Transgaz Belarus, 2020).

Gazprom Transgaz Belarus includes approximately 8,000 kms of gas pipelines, 13 compressor stations, three underground gas storage facilities (Mozyrske, Osipovychske and Pribuzke), 226 gas distribution stations and seven gas measuring stations. It also operates the 575-km-long section of the Yamal-Europe gas pipeline and five compressor stations (Gazprom Transgaz Belarus, 2020).

Belarus and Ukraine have two points of interstate connection—Mozyr and Kobryn on both gas pipelines of the Torzhok-Dolyna corridor. In fact, this corridor is not used. If Belarus had not transferred its gas transmission system to Gazprom, it would retain the possibility of reverse gas supplies from the EU gas market both through Ukraine and directly from Poland. Attempts of the GTS operator of Ukraine to conclude a co-operation agreement and to create the opportunity of transporting natural gas in both directions were unsuccessful due to the position of Gazprom Transgaz Belarus, i.e. due to the position of Gazprom (TSOUA, 2020c).

LNG in the Central and Eastern Europe

Russia's use of gas as an instrument of political influence over governments of neighbouring countries and the two Russian-Ukrainian gas crises of 2006 and 2009 have sharply increased attention to LNG in Europe. Particularly, the two-week interruption of gas pipeline supply from Russia to Europe in transit through Ukraine in 2009 affected it. This opened a new window of opportunity for LNG producers, Qatar in particular, and the following year 2010 saw a spike in its exports (Fig. 5.8).

The shale gas revolution in the United States became no less a stimulus for LNG development. Russia's aggression upon Ukraine in 2014 and fears in the EU about the future of transit through Ukraine in the context

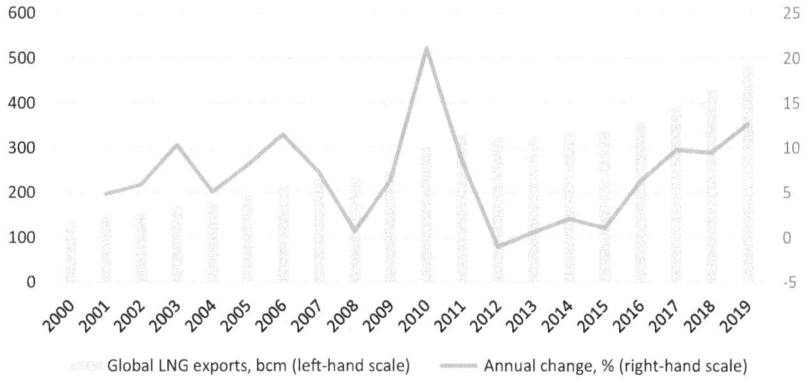

Fig. 5.8 The development of global LNG exports (bcm and %) (*Source* The Authors, based on BP, 2020)

of the Russian-Ukrainian conflict have also stimulated interest in LNG, whose supply to Europe does not depend on the East–West gas pipeline routes.

The rapid development of the LNG market is both a global and European trend. Currently, LNG terminals are now an important gateway to most key gas markets in Europe (CEER, 2020). Projects for the construction of LNG regasification terminals in the EU have received the status of projects of common interest (PCIs) and enjoy the right for funding from the Connecting Europe Facility (CEF), the EU fund of EUR 30 billion. The fund has been created to improve energy, transport and digital infrastructure, to boost security of supply, to eliminate isolated markets, to promote interaction of gas networks and to achieve the Green Deal goals.

The shale gas revolution in the United States became no less a stimulus for LNG development. Russia's aggression upon Ukraine in 2014 and fears in the EU about the future of transit through Ukraine in the context of the Russian-Ukrainian conflict have also stimulated interest in LNG, whose supply to Europe does not depend on the East–West gas pipeline routes.

The rapid development of the LNG market is both a global and European trend. Currently, LNG terminals are now an important gateway to most key gas markets in Europe (CEER, 2020). Projects for the construction of LNG regasification terminals in the EU have received the status of PCI and enjoy the right for funding from the CEF, the EU fund of EUR 30 billion. The fund has been created to improve energy, transport and digital infrastructure, to boost security of supply, to eliminate isolated markets, to promote interaction of gas networks and to achieve the Green Deal goals.

The development of the single European gas market and the strengthening of network interconnection open promising opportunities for access to the global LNG market, even for countries that do not have the appropriate infrastructure for receiving tankers. Natural gas in regasified form in Central and Eastern Europe can be obtained from LNG terminals in Poland, Lithuania and Croatia, and in Southern Eastern Europe–from Turkey, Greece and Croatia.

A successful experiment to supply Ukraine with a consignment of liquefied natural gas from the United States through a Polish LNG terminal in regasified form was conducted on the 19th of November 2019.

In this context, the Croatian LNG terminal on the Adriatic island of Krk, commissioned in the beginning of 2021, is important for the Balkans and Central and Eastern Europe. Although the LNG terminal is designed according to the FSRU scheme and the terminal has a rather small capacity (2.6 bcm), it is able to play the role of a regional compensator for possible deficits and provoke competition to Gazprom's supplies, which until recently dominated the market of the Balkans and Central and Eastern Europe. This means in practice the emergence of the North–South corridor, which was initiated by Poland and supported by the Visegrad Four (V4) back in 2007 and was to connect the Polish LNG terminal in the Baltic Sea and the Croatian one in the Adriatic Sea via several network interconnectors. The emergence of the North–South corridor corresponds to the strategic vision of the Polish-Croatian Three Seas Initiative and opens new opportunities for Central and Eastern Europe.

The huge volume of Ukrainian UGS 31 billion cubic metres, its convenient location of the main facilities near the border with the EU, and their transition to EU rules provide new opportunities for the development of gas business in the region, using underground storage capacity. New LNG receiving facilities in Poland and Croatia, the expected appearance of Norwegian gas in Poland after 2022 through Baltic Pipe and the Ukrainian UGS create an eastern configuration (V4 + Ukraine) in addition to the western configuration of the North–South corridor (V4 + Croatia). It can be expanded by means of the Eastern Partnership countries bordering the EU, in addition to Ukraine.

Given the importance of LNG for safety and the environment, in the framework of the Eastern Partnership the European Commission initiated in 2019 a study of possible options for access to liquefied gas markets in partner countries, including Belarus, Moldova and Ukraine (Publications Office of the EU, 2020).

According to the European Commission's study on LNG in the Eastern Partnership, the availability of developed infrastructure provides a link with EU countries and technically enables the imports of regasified LNG. In particular, it enables deliveries from terminals in Świnoujście (Poland), Klaipeda (Lithuania) and other European liquefied gas tanker collection points.

Ukraine's energy strategy until 2035 stipulates that Ukraine should receive no more than 30% of primary energy resources from one source of supply (Energy Ministry of Ukraine, 2017). Liquefied natural gas can be an important factor in achieving the goals of diversifying gas imports. In Ukraine, there is an LNG terminal project near Odesa, but its realisation is complicated by Turkey's position, which does not allow methane tankers traffic to the Black Sea through the narrow Bosporus Strait.

However, LNG for Central and Eastern Europe is quite promising. LNG is becoming a game changer in the region, because:

(1) gaining access to the LNG market is seen as a factor in market flexibility and enhanced security of supply;
(2) new LNG terminals in Poland, Lithuania, Croatia, Greece, Turkey, together with the development of cross-border connections, open opportunities to receive LNG in regasified form to enhance energy security; and
(3) Ukraine and Moldova are on the way to full integration into the EU gas market, which will allow them to take advantage of European opportunities to access the global LNG market. Belarus, subject to changes in the political regime in the country, has the opportunity, thanks to the gas infrastructure of neighbouring countries—Lithuania, Poland, Ukraine, to receive both pipeline and regasified liquefied gas from the EU.

Ukrainian GTS in the Context of the European Green Deal and Hydrogen Strategy

A hydrogen strategy for a climate-neutral Europe provides for the abandonment of fossil fuels in industrial sectors and their replacement by RES and hydrogen (European Commission, 2020a). Hydrogen requires not only its industrial production capacity, but also transmission infrastructure. The strategy provides for several stages in the spread of hydrogen use in the EU.

The GTS operator of Ukraine and other Ukrainian organisations, such as National Nuclear Energy Generating Company Energoatom, Regional Gas Company, Ukrainian Danube Shipping Company, Igor Sikorsky Kyiv Polytechnic Institute and Ukraine Hydrogen Council, have already become members of the European Clean Hydrogen Alliance, formed by the European Commission in accordance with the Hydrogen Strategy.

Since 2021, the GTS operator of Ukraine is also launching in cooperation with the institutes of the National Academy of Sciences of

Ukraine a large-scale two-year project of scientific and technical research to determine the boundaries and conditions of gas transmission infrastructure for transporting methane-hydrogen mixtures to Europe in accordance with the EU Hydrogen Strategy (TSOUA, 2021b). Pavel Stanchak, Deputy Director General for Development and Transformation of the GTS operator of Ukraine, notes that given the official recognition by the European Commission of Ukraine as the main potential site for hydrogen production and exports to Europe, "*we need to analyse all opportunities to offer appropriate services*" (TSOUA, 2021b, 1).[9]

Potential producers of green hydrogen—companies engaged in solar and wind generation—have an increased interest in the use of GTS. The green energy boom in Ukraine during 2015–2020 led to the appearance of 6.133 GW of installed RES capacity (5.062 GW of solar and 1.071 GW of wind (Ukrenergo, 2020). This is the equivalent of the capacity of the Zaporizhzhya nuclear power plant (NPP), the largest in Europe. For comparison–in Russia, which declares itself a future supplier of hydrogen to the EU, Ministry of Energy of Russian Federation (2020) indicates a total RES capacity as of 2019 of about 1.1 GW, but it should be borne in mind that this figure includes the capacity of solar and wind power plants in occupied Crimea, which were built by Ukraine in the pre-occupation period (approximately 0.36 GW). Official documents indicate that Russia does not intend to develop the RES sector, unlike the EU. Therefore, it will not be able to become a large producer of green hydrogen. At the same time, it can produce grey and blue hydrogen, which can be obtained by steam-methane reforming technology from natural gas, as well as pink hydrogen from NPP electricity.

On the 24th of September 2020, the national nuclear power company Energoatom and Naftogaz signed a memorandum of understanding and co-operation for the study and use of the potential of hydrogen energy. Energoatom shall study the possibility of producing pink hydrogen, and the oil and gas holding shall study its transmission to the EU via the GTS.

The Green Hydrogen Investment and Support Report of the Hydrogen Europe Association provides for EUR 20.1 billion of investments to create 10 GW of solar power plant and wind power plant capacities in Ukraine. This will produce one million tonnes of hydrogen per year out of the 16.6 million tonnes that the EU will need in general by

[9] A translation from the Ukrainian language to English conducted by the authors.

the beginning of 2030 (European Union, 2020). Appropriate investments in the adaptation of the GTS to the transmission of methane-hydrogen mixtures, construction of hydrogen storage facilities are also envisaged.

The EU Association Agreement with Ukraine provides the political basis for participation in joint hydrogen research and development programmes with the EU. The requirement of the Agreement on the coordination of gas network development plans should be met considering the need to load and possible re-design and transformation of the existing GTS of Ukraine. It can take on a new quality and significance for the EU in the context of a decarbonised future of the continent.

Conclusions

Gas logistics between the EU and Russia is characterised by an excessive surplus of gas transmission capacity created by Gazprom in the direction of gas supplies to Western Europe from the East. Building extra gas transmission capacity serves political and geopolitical purposes of Russia and goes beyond the logic of gas business.

Further implementation of Nord Stream 2 and the second line of TurkStream, which harm the concept of an all-European competitive gas market and the principles of solidarity, and threaten the energy security of Central and Eastern Europe, does not seem appropriate.[10] Instead, the European Union needs to seek a resumption of gas supplies to the EU from Central Asia, blocked by Gazprom, and the exports of independent gas producers from Russia. This would increase gas flow competition.

LNG is a game changer for both the EU gas market and gas infrastructure. It is able to limit the use of natural gas and pipelines as weapons by suppliers who have gained a monopoly position in a particular area of exports.

Creating a combined pipeline and LNG supply system in combination with underground gas storage is the most flexible and commercially

[10] "... the Court notes that the principle of solidarity is a fundamental principle of EU law, which is mentioned in several provisions of the EU and FEU Treaties and which finds specific expression in Article 194(1) TFEU." "... the spirit of solidarity mentioned in Article 194(1) TFEU extends to any action falling within the European Union's energy policy." The Court of Justice of the European Union. PRESS RELEASE No 129/21 Luxembourg, 15 July 2021, Judgment in Case C-848/19P Germany v Poland.https://curia.europa.eu/jcms/upload/docs/application/pdf/2021-07/cp210129en.pdf.

viable option for diversification and security of supply. One may offer two examples:

(1) Trans-Baltic corridor–integration of Baltic Pipe, Polish LNG terminal, Lithuanian LNG terminal through GIPL interconnectors (Poland-Lithuania) and Balticconnector (Estonia-Finland) with the Inčukalns UGS in Latvia; and.
(2) Baltic-Carpathian corridor–integration of Baltic Pipe, Polish LNG terminal through the PLUA interconnector (Poland-Ukraine) with the UGS in western Ukraine.

The integration of Ukraine's gas sector into the EU gas market significantly enhances the interconnection of gas infrastructure, transparency and security of gas supply. Ukraine's gas infrastructure, in particular its large UGS units, is serving common market purposes and may be the basis for a regional East European gas hub.

References

Beunderman, M. (2006). Poland compares German-Russian pipeline to Nazi-Soviet pact. *Euobserver*. May 2, 2006. https://euobserver.com/foreign/21486. Accessed January 15, 2021.

BP. (2020). *Statistical review of world energy—All data, 1965–2019*. https://www.bp.com/en/global/corporate/energy-economics/statistical-review-of-world-energy.html. Accessed March 27, 2021.

CEER. (2020). *Webinar: The future role of LNG in Europe*. Council of European Energy Regulations. September 21, 2020.

DW. (2018). Во сколькоо бойдется России и Европе "Северный поток-2". https://p.dw.com/p/2tsVN. Accessed February 15, 2021.

East European Gas Analysis. (2013). Единая система газоснабжения России и мощности экспортных газопроводов. April 20, 2013. https://eegas.com/fsu_r.htm. Accessed June 10, 2015.

Energy Ministry of Ukraine. (2017). Енергетична стратегія України на період до 2035 року "Безпека, енергоефективність, конкурентоспромож ність" http://mpe.kmu.gov.ua/minugol/control/publish/article?art_id=245234085. Accessed November 25, 2020.

Energy Ministry of Ukraine. (2021). http://mpe.kmu.gov.ua/. Accessed March 26, 2020.

ENTSOG. (2019). *Transmission capacity map*. https://www.entsog.eu/. Accessed December 18, 2020.

ENTSOG. (2020). *Transparency platform*. https://transparency.entsog.eu/#/map. Accessed January 28, 2021.

Eurointegration Portal. (2017). РОЗДІЛ IV. ТОРГІВЛЯ І ПИТАННЯ, ПОВ'ЯЗАНІ З ТОРГІВЛЕЮ. October 24, 2017. http://eu-ua.org/tekst-uhody-pro-asotsiatsiiu/rozdil-iv-torhivlia-pytannia-poviazani-z-torhivleiu/. Accessed January 15, 2021.

European Commission. (2019). *Quarterly report on European gas markets, 12*(4). https://ec.europa.eu/energy/data-analysis/market-analysis_en. Accessed February 19, 2021.

European Commission. (2020a). *A hydrogen strategy for a climate-neutral Europe*. Communication from the Commission to the European Parliament, the Council, the European Economic and Social Committee and the Committee of the Regions. July 8, 2020 COM(2020) 301 final. https://ec.europa.eu/energy/sites/ener/files/hydrogen_strategy.pdf. Accessed January 20, 2021.

European Commission. (2020b). *Quarterly report on European gas markets, 13*(3). https://ec.europa.eu/energy/sites/default/files/documents/quarterly_report_on_european_gas_markets_q3_2020.pdf. Accessed March 27, 2021.

European Union. (2014). *Association agreement between the European Union and its member states, of the one part, and Ukraine, of the other part*. https://trade.ec.europa.eu/doclib/docs/2016/november/tradoc_155103.pdf. Accessed April 2, 2021.

European Union. (2020). *Green hydrogen investment and support report hydrogen Europe's input for a post COVID-19 recovery plan*. http://profadvanwijk.com/green-hydrogen-investment-and-support-report/. Accessed 20 January 2021.

Expro Consulting. (2020). Компанії розпочали ре-експорт природного газу в режимі short-haul. November 6, 2020. https://expro.com.ua/novini/kompan-rozpochali-re-eksport-prirodnogo-gazu-v-rejim-short-haul. Accessed January 15, 2021.

Gazprom Invest. (2020). Газопровод «Минск—Вильнюс—Каунас—Калининград». https://invest.gazprom.ru/about/projects/mvkk/. Accessed October 20, 2020.

Gazprom Transgaz Belarus. (2020). О компании. https://belarus-tr.gazprom.ru/about/. Accessed September 22, 2020.

Gazprom. (2021). «Ямал—Европа»: Поставки российского газа в Западную Европу. https://www.gazprom.ru/projects/yamal-europe/. Accessed January 15, 2021.

Gazpromexport. (2020a). Транспортировка. http://www.gazpromexport.ru/projects/transportation/. Accessed September 20, 2020.

Gazpromexport. (2020b). Статистика поставок. http://www.gazpromexport.ru/statistics/. Accessed December 21, 2020.

GolosUkrainy. (2018). Газзавжди був геополітичною зброєю Кремля. No. 76 (p. 6831). April 24, 2018. http://www.golos.com.ua/article/302286. Accessed April 2, 2021.
Gonchar M. (2020). *Putin's streams: 'Perpetuum mobile' of state terrorism. How Girkin and Malofeev contributed to the Nord Stream 2.* December 2, 2020. https://geostrategy.org.ua/en/media/articles/putins-streams-perpetuum-mobile-of-state-terrorism-how-girkin-and-malofeev-contributed-to-the-nord-stream-2. Accessed January 15, 2021.
Government of the Russian Federation. (2003). Энергетическая стратегия Росс ии на период до 2020 года. http://www.energystrategy.ru/projects/ES-28_08_2003.pdf. Accessed January 15, 2021.
Institute of Economics and Forecasting. (2021). http://ief.org.ua/?lang=en. Accessed March 27, 2021.
Interfax. (2010). *To unite Gazprom and Naftogaz.* April 30, 2010. https://www.interfax.ru/business/135073. Accessed January 15, 2020.
Lipkin M. 2016. *The Soviet Union and integration processes in Europe: Mid-1940s–late 1960s* (pp. 457–458). M. Russian Fund for Educational Promotion. ISBN 9785912441813.
Ministry of Energy of Russian Federation. (2020). ОБ ОТРАСЛИ: Система госу дарственного стимулирования хранения электроэнергии в России. https://minenergo.gov.ru/node/489. Accessed January 20, 2021.
Naftogaz. (2021a). Нафтогаз надав Газпрому у 2020 році послуги з організа ції транспортування газу на $2,11 млрд. https://www.naftogaz.com/www/3/nakweb.nsf/0/E750445E0B0C320EC225865D0036EF6E?OpenDocument&year=2021&month=01&nt=%D0%9D%D0%BE%D0%B2%D0%B8%D0%BD%D0%B8&/. Accessed February 15, 2021.
Naftogaz. (2021b). https://www.naftogaz.com/. Accessed January 15, 2021.
Neftegaz. (2001). Украина отдает газопроводы за долги. April 13, 2001. https://neftegaz.ru/news/transport-and-storage/326641-ukraina-otdaet-gazoprovody-za-dolgi/. Accessed January 20, 2021.
Neftegaz.Ru. (2015). Закат эры украинского транзита. April 17, 2015. https://neftegaz.ru/science/transportation/331701-zakat-ery-ukrainskogo-tranzita/. Accessed February 20, 2021.
NKREKP. 2020. *National energy and utilities regulatory commission.* Ukraine. http://www.nerc.gov.ua. Accessed January 15, 2021.
Nord Stream. (2020). В 2019 году по газопроводу «Северныйпоток» было транспортировано 58,5 млрд куб. метров природного газа. January 29, 2020. https://www.nord-stream.com/ru/informatsiya-dlya-pressy/press-relizy/v-2019-godu-po-gazoprovodu-severnyi-potok-bylo-transportirovano-585-mlrd-kub-metrov-prirodnogo-gaza-510/. Accessed August 30, 2020.
Presidential Executive Office of Russia. (2005). Совместная пресс-конференц ия с Федеральным канцлером ФРГ Герхардом Шрёдером. September 8,

2005. http://kremlin.ru/events/president/transcripts/23161. Accessed May 5, 2006.

Publications Office of the EU. (2020). *Prospects of LNG markets in the Eastern partner countries*. Final report. January 2020. https://op.europa.eu/en/publication-detail/-/publication/52ff7d53-882e-11ea-812f-01aa75ed71a1/language-en?WT.mc_id=Searchresult&WT.ria_c=37085&WT.ria_f=3608&WT.ria_ev=search. Accessed February 21, 2020.

Telegraph. (2021). Председатель Правления ПАО «Газпром» Алексей Миллер:. January 2, 2021. https://telegra.ph/itogi-2020-01-02. Accessed January 15, 2021.

TSOUA. (2020a). План розвитку газотранспортної системи Оператора газотранспортної системи Товариства з обмеженою відповідальністю «Оператор газотранспортної системи України» на 2020–2029 роки. https://tsoua.com/wp-content/uploads/gas-quality/files/TYNDP_2020-2029_18-03-2020.pdf. Accessed January 8, 2021.

TSOUA. (2020b). Аналітична розмова: Сергій Макогон, генеральний директор Оператор газотранспортної системи України. Інтерв'ю S&P Global Platts. October 19, 2020. https://tsoua.com/news/analitychna-rozmova-sergij-makogon-generalnyj-dyrektor-operator-gazotransportnoyi-systemy-ukrayiny/. Accessed October 29, 2020.

TSOUA. (2020c). ПЛАН РОЗВИТКУ ГАЗОТРАНСПОРТНОЇ СИСТЕМИ Оператора газотранспортної системи Товариства з обмеженоювідповідальністю «ОПЕРАТОР ГАЗОТРАНСПОРТНОЇ СИСТЕМИ УКРАЇНИ» на 2021–2030 роки. https://tsoua.com/wp-content/uploads/2020/10/TYNDP-2021-2030-TSO-4.1.pdf. Accessed 15 January 2021.

TSOUA. (2020d). *Shorthaul service*. https://tsoua.com/en/news/starting-from-the-beginning-of-the-year-6-1-billion-cubic-meters-of-gas-has-been-transported-to-ukraine-in-the-shorthaul-mode/. Accessed January 15, 2021.

TSOUA. (2021a). *Gas transmission system operator of Ukraine*. https://tsoua.com/en/. Accessed January 16, 2020.

TSOUA. (2021b). Оператор ГТС України залучає дослідні інститути до масштабного проєкту з вивчення аспектів транспортування водню. January 4, 2021. https://tsoua.com/news/operator-gts-ukrayiny-zaluchaye-doslidni-instytuty-do-masshtabnogo-proyektu-z-vyvchennya-aspektiv-transportuvannya-vodnyu/. Accessed January 5, 2021.

TSOUA. (2021c). *Introducing short-haul*. https://tsoua.com/wp-content/uploads/2020/02/broshure-short-haul-2020.pdf. Accessed March 27, 2021.

Ukrenergo. (2020). Встановлена потужність енергосистеми України на 12/2020. December 2020. https://ua.energy/vstanovlena-potuzhnist-energosystemy-ukrayiny/. Accessed January 3, 2021.

Ukrinform. (2019). Єврокомісія отримала скаргу Нафтогазу на Газпром. May 17, 2019. https://www.ukrinform.ua/rubric-economy/2695466-evr

okomisia-otrimala-skargu-naftogazu-na-gazprom.html. Accessed March 27, 2021.

Ukrtransgaz. (2015). *Law of Ukraine on the natural gas market*. http://utg.ua/law-on-natural-gas-market.PDF. Accessed April 2, 2021.

Ukrtransgaz. (2020). *Naftogaz*. http://utg.ua/en/. Accessed January 15, 2020.

Ukrtransgaz. (2021a). *Real time data*. http://utg.ua/en/utg/business-info/live.html. Accessed March 27, 2021.

Ukrtransgaz. (2021b). *Historical data*. http://utg.ua/en/utg/business-info/historical-data.html. Accessed March 27, 2021.

Verkhovna Rada of Ukraine. (2005). Договір про заснування Енергетично го Співтовариства. https://zakon.rada.gov.ua/laws/show/994_926#Text. Accessed January 15, 2021.

Verkhovna Rada of Ukraine. (2015). Угода про асоціацію міжУкраїною, з однієї сторони, та Європейським Союзом, Європейським співтовариством з ато мної енергії і їхніми державами-членами, з іншої сторони. https://zakon.rada.gov.ua/laws/show/984_011#Text. Accessed January 15, 2019.

Vitrenko Library. 2021. https://www.vitrenkolibrary.com/data-library/. Accessed January 13, 2021.

https://curia.europa.eu/jcms/upload/docs/application/pdf/2021-0/cp210129en.pdf

CHAPTER 6

Norwegian Gas in Europe in the 2020's

Jakub M. Godzimirski

Introduction

The aim of this chapter is to contribute to a better understanding of the role of the Norwegian natural gas in the European market in the 2020's. This chapter is divided into four parts. In the first section, a brief history of Norway as a major energy producer and exporter is presented, outlining the main features of the Norwegian energy policy and its impact on energy situation in Norway's neighbourhood. Key data on Norway's energy production, consumption and exports are also examined presenting Norway as an energy actor. The second section narrows the scope of examination to the role of Norwegian gas in the broader European context in a historical perspective. Here we examine some historical data on Norway's role as a gas supplier to Europe and the broader international context of Norway's gas co-operation with the EU. The third section presents some assessments of how Norway's role in the European gas market may change in the 2020's. Here the focus is on the role of structural factors that may influence the future position of Norway as a gas supplier to the broadly understood Europe. The factors

J. M. Godzimirski (✉)
The Norwegian Institute of International Affairs, Oslo, Norway
e-mail: JMG@nupi.no

K. Liuhto (ed.), *The Future of Energy Consumption, Security and Natural Gas*, https://doi.org/10.1007/978-3-030-80367-4_6

examined in this part include the role of the EU as an energy agenda setter, the role of other gas suppliers in this market, including the impact of LNG supplies, as well as the question of the resource base that could secure Norway's future position as an important actor in the European gas market. Finally, the fourth section sums up the main findings.

Norway as an Energy Actor in 2020

According to the most recent available data (IEA, 2020a), in 2018 Norway's total energy production reached 207 million tonnes of oil equivalent (mtoe), which gave Norway 15th place globally, behind Qatar, but before Kazakhstan. In the same year, Norway exported 177 mtoe more energy than it imported. Only five countries—Russia, Saudi Arabia, Australia, Canada and Indonesia—had a better energy import/export balance. Total domestic energy supply (TES) reached in the same year 28.3 mtoe. Norwegian primary energy consumption in 2019 was dominated by domestically available hydropower which made Norway unique among major global producers and consumers of energy as demonstrated in Table 6.1.

Table 6.1 Primary energy consumption by fuel

	Norway's energy consumption in 2019 (exajoules)	*Share in Norway in 2019 (%)*	*Share in the EU in 2018 (%)*	*Share in the world in 2019 (%)*
Oil	0.39	22.0	34.1	33.1
Natural gas	0.16	9.0	22.0	24.2
Coal	0.03	1.7	14.2	27.0
Nuclear energy	0.00	0.0	13.2	4.3
Hydroelectricity	1.12	63.3	2.0	6.4
Renewables	0.07	4.0	13.0	5.0
Total	1.77	100	98.5 (waste + others 1.5)	100

Exajoule = 1 quintillion joules (1×10^{18}). 1 Exajoule is equal to 278 terawatt hours
Sources The Author, based on BP (2020) and European Commission (2020b)

Norway's Petroleum Resources

After discovery of deposits of oil and gas in the North Sea Norway has entered European and global stage as a major producer and exporter of petroleum products, mainly crude oil and natural gas. By the end of 2019, total production of oil reached 4,431 Sm^3o.e. and for gas the figure was 2,571 Sm^3o.e. (Norskpetroleum.no, 2020c).[1] This means that oil represented 59% of the total production and gas 34%, the rest being condensate and natural gas liquids. Production and sales of petroleum commodities generated also huge revenues for the Norwegian state—by the end of 2019 the market value of the Government Pension Fund Global reached 10,088 million Norwegian Krones (NOK), or approximately 1,000 billion US dollars (USD), which was almost three times more than the country's gross domestic product (GDP) in the same year (Norskpetroleum.no, 2020a).

Figure 6.1 presents a synthetic picture of Norway's increasingly important role as a key European and global petroleum actor. History of Norway as a major producer and exporter of oil and gas can be divided into several sub-periods. Oil dominated the production mix until 2000 when oil production peak was reached with production of 181 Sm^3o.e. General peak production came four years later in 2004 when total production reached 264 Sm^3o.e. The share of gas in total production was increasing constantly and in 2010 was for the first time in history higher than the share of oil when it went up to 46.19% of the total production against 45.26% share of the latter (Norskpetroleum.no, 2020b).

By the end of 2019, basic estimate of total proven and unproven petroleum resources is about 15.7 billion Sm^3o.e. Of this, 7.6 billion Sm^3o.e., or 48%, has been sold and delivered. The estimate for undiscovered resources is 3.9 billion Sm^3o.e. The Norwegian Petroleum Directorate (NPD) estimates that 8.2 billion Sm^3o.e. are left to produce. Of this, 4.3 billion Sm^3o.e. are proven resources (Norskpetroleum.no, 2020c).

What is more important to understand when discussing the future of the Norwegian petroleum sector is the volume of recoverable petroleum reserves that are not yet produced, but for which a production decision

[1] Standard cubic metres of oil equivalents abbreviated as Sm^3o.e. is a standard volume unit of petroleum products—for oil, it equals 6.29 barrels of oil, or 0.858 metric tonnes. For gas, it equals 1,000 m^3 of natural gas.

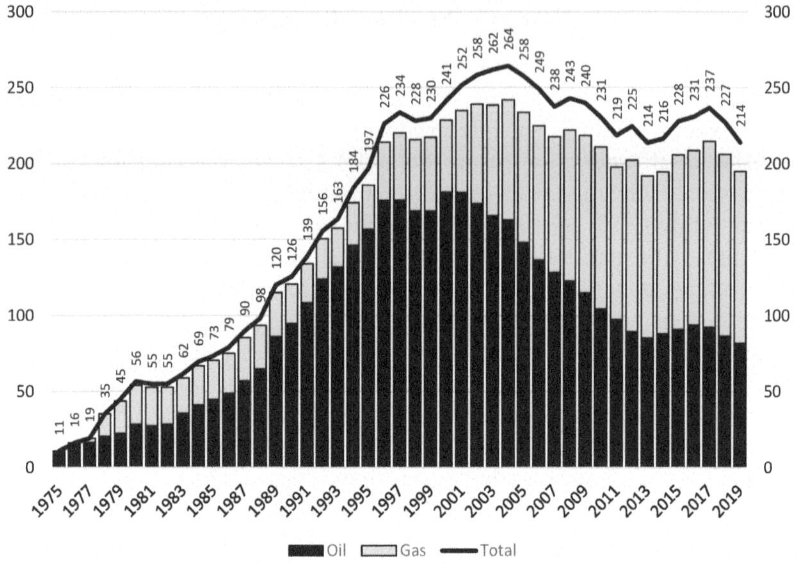

Fig. 6.1 Norwegian crude oil and natural gas production in 1975–2019 (Sm^3o.e.) (*Source* The Author, based on Norskpetroleum.no, 2020b)

had been made. By the end of 2019, these reserves totalled 2.9 billion Sm^3o.e. and 53% of these was natural gas (Norskpetroleum.no, 2020c).

Norway has 1,500 bcm in gas reserves, which represented 0.8% of global gas reserves. With these known reserves, gas production that reached 114 bcm in 2019 could be maintained at the same level for the next 13.4 years. Production of gas in 2019 was 5.7% lower than in 2018 and represented 92.8% of gas production in the top year 2017 when 123.2 bcm of natural gas was produced. Norway's gas output in 2019 represented 2.9% of the global gas production. Domestic consumption of natural gas in Norway was very low—4.5 bcm per year—and represented only 3.9% of production in 2019. This has made huge volumes of gas available for exports. Most of the Norwegian gas reached foreign markets through an extensive network of pipelines linking Norwegian production sites with national markets in Europe (BP, 2020).

Most of energy resources that have already been produced have been exported to European market and this market will also take a lion's share of energy to be produced in Norway in the coming years. It is therefore important to understand how the developments in this market will influence Norwegian energy producers.

What Makes Norway Special as an Energy Exporter?

There are several factors that make Norway an important and special actor in the global and regional energy markets. First, Norway is better endowed with locally available energy resources that are used to cover the country's own energy needs than any other major exporter of energy as illustrated in Table 6.2. To cover its own energy needs expressed as TES Norway uses nearly 14% of energy produced within its borders which is

Table 6.2 Share of total domestic energy supply in national energy production and net exports of energy in 2019

Country	*Net energy exports (mtoe)*	*TES/Production (%)*
Russia	701.3	51.2
Saudi Arabia	449.1	32.1
Australia	279.5	31.1
Canada	227.6	56.2
Indonesia	220.6	51.3
Norway	177.0	13.7
Iraq	175.5	26.7
Qatar	172.5	19.8
United Arab Emirates	142.2	29.2
Iran	138.5	65.4
Kuwait	131.8	20.7
Kazakhstan	101.6	42.7
Nigeria	97.2	62.4
Algeria	93.7	39.3
Colombia	87.8	32.3
Venezuela	73.0	36.3
Angola	70.3	18.1
Oman	53.6	31.3
Libya	52.0	25.5
Turkmenistan	51.3	34.7
Azerbaijan	40.7	26.0

Note Countries are ranked in descending order starting with those with the highest net exports of energy
Source The Author, based on IEA (2020a)

the lowest share among the countries that according to IEA (2020a) had more than 40 mtoe in energy trade surplus.

Second, relatively small size of the Norwegian economy results in a relatively low domestic demand for energy that is covered by domestically available renewable energy sources, mainly hydropower, which helps Norway reduce its environmental footprint.

Third, relatively high per capita demand for energy—5.33 toe per capita (16th position globally)—is balanced by an even higher per capita production of energy—more than 39 toe per capita (Norway ranked 4th globally, with only Qatar, Brunei and Kuwait ranked higher) and by a relatively high energy efficiency of the Norwegian economy, especially compared with other major producers and exporters of energy (IEA, 2020a).

Fourth, Norway is the last Western European country to have substantial energy resources to be produced and exported to other European members of the Western community with which Norway shares liberal norms organising co-operation among like-minded states and economic interests strengthened by increasingly important mutual energy interdependence (Andersen & Sitter, 2019; Austvik, 2019). In other words, Norway is the only full-fledged European democracy with which other members of the European Western clubs—the EU and the NATO—can embark on fruitful energy co-operation without having any second thoughts or political concerns. In addition, Norway's energy co-operation with the EU is regulated, through membership in the European Economic Area (EEA), by the same set of regulations and norms as the ones other EU members must play by, which should make this co-operation even smoother and more predictable (Austvik & Claes, 2011; Ministry of Foreign Affairs Norway, 2012).

Gas Exports—Current Directions and Trends

The WTO estimated that in 2008 alone Norway had a 4% share in global exports of fuels, earning almost USD 114 billion from sales of fuels, or more than USD 23,000 per capita (World Trade Organization [WTO], 2010). In the same year, the share of gas production in petroleum production in Norway reached for the first time 41% and only two years later gas became the most important petroleum commodity produced in Norway. In the following years gas production represented more than 50% of the overall petroleum production in Norway, and even in years when oil production slightly re-bumped, gas share went only slightly below that magic 50% (Norskpetroleum.no, 2020b).

In Norway, gas is produced and exported by various actors operating on the Norwegian continental shelf but it is the Norwegian state-owned company Gassco that is responsible for shipments of piped gas to Norway's gas customers in Europe. Gassco operates an 8,000-km-long network of gas pipelines connecting Norwegian gas production sites with buyers of Norwegian gas in the EU and in the UK. Construction of this extensive pipeline network came at ca USD 26 billion, but the network needs to be extended to connect new production fields to the existing infrastructure and increase transport capacity. The pipeline system was used to deliver 107 bcm of gas to receiving terminals in 2019 and 114 bcm in 2018 (Gassco, 2020).

SSB estimated that in 2019 Norway produced 119 bcm of natural gas, which made it the 8th largest global producer of that commodity (SSB, 2019). Norway was 'beaten' by the USA, Russia, Iran, China, Canada, Qatar and Australia, but produced more gas than Saudi Arabia and Algeria. Norway exported 95% of its gas production, most as piped gas to consumers in the European Union. In 2019, Norway was ranked the 3rd among global gas exporters, behind Russia, that exported 265 bcm of gas and Qatar (124 bcm), but ahead of Australia (95 bcm), the USA (54 bcm), Turkmenistan (52 bcm) and Canada (51 bcm) (IEA, 2020a) (Table 6.3).

BP (2020) figures show that after the Brexit the share of the EU in Norwegian gas exports will be substantially reduced, if we take 2019 figures as the basis for calculations. With the UK as the EU member the

Table 6.3 Importers of Norwegian gas in 2019 (bcm)

Country	*Piped gas*	*LNG*
Germany	27.8	0.0
UK	26.6	0.5
Netherlands	25.3	0.0
France	19.3	1.5
Belgium	5.1	0.0
Italy	2.7	0.2
Spain	1.8	0.7
Other EU	0.4	3.1

Source The Author, based on BP (2020)

share of the EU in gas export from Norway was 99%, after the UK withdrawal from the EU this will be reduced to 76%. However, the EU will continue to be the most important gas partner of Norway and Norway will retain its position as one of the two major suppliers of gas to the EU (Fig. 6.2).

The importance of the EU should be therefore factored in all examinations of the future of Norway as an energy producer and supplier of gas because for obvious structural reasons, such as the existence of the well-developed rigid pipeline infrastructure and the lack of substantial LNG capacity, Norway is somehow 'doomed' to supply its gas primarily to the European customers. From the point of view of a major gas exporter the question of security of demand in the main available market is therefore of the utmost importance.

The future demand for Norwegian gas in the EU will depend on several factors such as: domestic EU gas production, demand for gas as a source of energy and input to industry, price level on the European and global gas market, competition from other gas suppliers to the EU market, competition from other sources of energy, adaptation and implementation of various EU energy, climate and market regulations, national

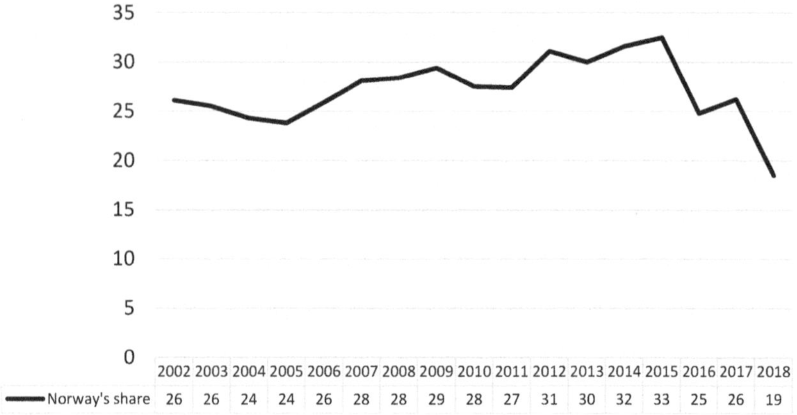

Fig. 6.2 Share of Norwegian gas in the EU's total gas imports in 2002–2018 (%) (*Sources* The Author, based on European Commission, 2020a and earlier editions)

energy policies and, finally, on the availability of the Norwegian gas to be supplied to the EU.

The Future of Norwegian Gas in Europe—Opportunities and Challenges

What are the prospects for Norwegian gas in Europe in the 2020's if all the above examined issues are factored in? This part is divided into two sub-sections. In the first sub-section the focus is on new opportunities that can help extend the lifespan of the Norwegian gas in the European market, while in the second section the emerging challenges are discussed. When conducting this examination special attention is paid to what policy instruments Norway has at its disposal and in what ways Norway can help buyers of Norwegian gas address some of their energy security concerns related to availability, affordability, acceptability and accessibility of energy resources.

Opportunities

The UK

The UK is already an important Norwegian gas customer and gas co-operation between Norway and the UK will continue in many years to come. The UK relies on supply of huge volumes of Norwegian gas which is also facilitated by construction and extension of necessary infrastructure connecting Norwegian gas production sites with the UK gas marked. Domestic production of natural gas has been dwindling in the UK and went down from 98 mtoe in 2000 to 35 mtoe in 2018. While in 2000 the UK was a net exporter of gas, in 2018 the UK's net imports of gas reached impressive 33 mtoe, making it one of the key gas importers in Europe. In 2000, the UK's exports of gas were almost 11% higher than its imports but by 2018 the UK had to import almost 50% of consumed gas. Gross inland consumption of gas in the UK went down from 87 mtoe in 2000 to 68 mtoe in 2018 and gas share in final energy consumption went from 37% in 2000 to 32% in 2018 (European Commission, 2020b). Norway has 'profited' from this situation and increased its gas exports to the UK from some one billion cubic metres in 2000 to almost 27 bcm in 2019 (BP, 2020). In 2019, Norwegian gas had 34% share in the UK gas consumption.

Supplies of Norwegian gas to the UK were facilitated greatly by several factors, such the falling domestic production in the UK and not least the construction of new elements of infrastructure, first and foremost the Langeled pipeline that is the main artery for transport of Norwegian gas to the UK.[2] Having in mind the high level of trust between the UK and Norway and mutual interest in continuing this mutually beneficial energy co-operation it can be expected that this co-operation will continue in the future and that the Brexit will not have any direct negative impact on this gas relationship.

Another factor that will secure Norway's dominant position on the UK gas market is the lack of a long-term alternative for supplies of piped gas from other sources. Although some UK-based actors have some time ago expressed interest in buying higher volumes of gas from Russia, this has become more controversial an option after the crisis in Ukraine that has demonstrated Russia's aggressive designs in Europe. Also other events, such as the poisoning of Alexander Litvinenko in 2006 and Sergei Skripal and his daughter in 2018 have most probably reduced 'appetite' for Russian gas in the UK. Although according to Gazprom its sales of gas in the UK soared from 34.2 bcm in 2018 to 59.0 bcm in 2019 (Gazprom, 2020), Gazprom Export reported that only 10.32 bcm of Russian gas reached the UK in 2019 (Gazprom Export, 2020).

Germany

Germany is another country that can provide some extended opportunities to Norwegian gas in the coming years. Germany must address several energy-related problems in the coming decades (Westphal, 2019) and Norwegian gas can be a part of the solution, at least in some years to come. The challenges faced by Germany are:

- the need to replace the highly polluting and less acceptable hard coal and lignite as the source of energy with some other sources especially after 2038 when all coal mines in Germany are going to be closed;
- the need to replace nuclear energy as a part of the energy mix after 2022 when the last nuclear power plants in Germany are going to be closed down; and

[2] Langeled is a 1,166-km-long pipeline constructed to carry gas from the Ormen Lange field in the Norwegian Sea to the UK with transport capacity of ca 72/75 mcm per day or ca 27 bcm per year.

– the need to add back up capacity to address the problem of intermittency of the German energy system that is increasingly relying on renewable energy sources.

Although there is a clear preference in Germany that has launched its Energiewende programme for renewable energy sources, natural gas, including gas from Norway, may play an important part in this transition towards a greener energy system in Germany. Seeking greater diversification of gas suppliers and facing dwindling production of gas in the Netherlands that has been traditionally an important gas partner, it can be expected that Germany will be interested in increased imports of gas from Norway, especially in the light of controversies caused by Germany's promotion of the Nord Stream 2 pipeline that is by many German partners perceived as highly controversial (Lang & Westphal, 2017; Westphal et al., 2017).

German domestic production of gas went down from 18 bcm in 2000 to some five billion cubic metres in 2019 while the domestic gross consumption of gas increased in the same period from 79 to 81 bcm. Imports of gas increased in this period from 63 to 78 bcm and net import dependence increased from 79 to 97% (European Commission, 2020b).

Norpipe, Europipe and Europipe II pipelines connect Norwegian production sites and gas infrastructure with market in Germany and facilitate trade in gas between Norway and Germany, making Germany the most important market for Norwegian gas. In 2019, Norway exported 27.8 bcm to Germany, covering 31% of the country's gas consumption and supplying 32% of its gas imports. Germany and Norway have also established close political co-operation and Germany is defined as one of Norway's strategic partners. Continued gas co-operation between Norway and Germany can therefore alleviate some problems in the period of German transition to a greener economy and help Germany diversify its gas supplies. This will also make Germany less exposed to over-reliance on gas coming from Russia (see Gustafson, 2020 for a historical overview, and Westphal, 2020 on the current state of Russian–German gas relations) with which relations have suffered several setbacks in the aftermath of the crisis in Ukraine in 2014 and in connection with poisoning of Alexei Navalny and Russian hacking of the German Bundestag that have resulted in imposition of sanctions against Russia and in the general worsening of bilateral relations (Fischer, 2020).

New Gas Relationships

Norwegian gas can be used not only to cement or extend old relationships, helping traditional partners to address various energy related challenges, but also to establish new energy relationships. There are at least three new emerging relationships in which Norwegian gas can play a positive role.

First, after the crisis in 2014, Ukraine expressed interest in replacing Russian gas supplies with supplies from other countries. Norway saw this new opening and was able to help Ukraine by supplying small but symbolically important volumes of gas—0.9 bcm in 2014 and two billion cubic metres in 2015 (Eurostat, 2020).

Second, Lithuania that wanted to reduce its gas dependence on Russia joined as a new gas customer when the floating LNG gas terminal in Klaipeda with a highly symbolic name FSRU Independence—owned by the Norwegian company Höegh, built in South Korea with support of the Norwegian State bank guarantees—made it possible to import gas in the LNG form from other suppliers. Norway was among the countries that used this opportunity exporting 0.1 bcm of gas in 2014, 0.5 bcm in 2015 and 1.4 bcm in 2016. Some affordability-related questions hampered this promising co-operation and imports of gas from Norway went slightly down to 0.9 bcm in 2017 and one billion cubic metres in 2018 (Eurostat, 2020). Supplies from Norway represented 4% of gas consumption in Lithuania in 2014, 21% in 2015, 66% in 2016, 41% in 2017 and 45% in 2018. These supplies have helped reduce the country's dependence and reliance on Gazprom and forced Gazprom to rethink its pricing policy on this small national market where it until 2014 had a monopolist position.

The third and most promising gas relationship that is about to be established is the one involving Poland, Denmark and Norway that work together to open a new transport route for Norwegian gas to reach new customers and help Norway diversify its markets. The Baltic Pipe project that is to allow for exports of up to ten billion cubic metres of Norwegian gas to Poland via Denmark is in fact no less than a third attempt to connect Norwegian production sites with a promising gas market in Poland, and more broadly in Central Europe. If implemented as planned by 2022 it will improve energy security in Poland in many ways. First, it will reduce dependence on imported energy from Russia which is perceived as an unreliable partner trying to use energy supplies as a political leverage (Gawlikowska-Fyk, 2019; Korteweg, 2018; Naimski, 2015). The Baltic Pipe project (BalticPipe, 2020) is the third of series of gas-related measures taken by the Polish policymakers interested in diversifying supplies and reducing Poland's energy dependence on Russia.

The first of these measures was the plan to turn Poland into a European shale gas power, but after some overly optimistic prognosis it turned out that this was not to happen (Godzimirski, 2016). The second one was the construction of an LNG terminal in Świnoujście that enabled Poland to import LNG, including some small volumes from Norway (0.3 bcm in 2018 and 0.25 bcm in 2019). To increase gas import capacity Polish authorities have also given a green light to construction of a floating LNG terminal close to Gdańsk.

Baltic Pipe and the two LNG terminals will help Poland realise its plan to become a gas hub in Central Europe from which gas—including Norwegian gas—could be supplied to other regional customers, such as Lithuania, Slovakia or Ukraine. Increased imports of gas will also help Poland deal with another serious energy security-related problem—the question of the (in)acceptability of coal as a major energy source in Poland. Being a member of the EU and facing a huge air pollution problem in major urban areas Poland has joined the project of reducing the EU climate footprint. To achieve its goals it must phase out coal and lignite as the main energy sources. Natural gas, including gas from Norway, can help Poland deal with this challenge by making it possible to replace polluting coal with gas in the period of transition towards a greener energy system (Ministry of Energy Poland, 2019).

Two-Edged Technologies

An issue that deserves a closer scrutiny when discussing the future of Norwegian gas in Europe is the question of the technological change that can provide both some new opportunities and pose some challenges. From the point of view of a major producer and supplier of fossil fuels to the most attractive global energy market where a serious attempt is made to build a fossil free energy system as a way of dealing with the problem of climate change several technological transformations can be viewed as crucial. Two of these possible technological transformations can have direct and indirect impact on the situation of Norwegian gas in Europe in the short-term, mid-term and long-term perspective.

The first of these technological transformations has to do with the ability of the increasingly greener energy system to be coupled with new more effective energy storage technology that could help address the question of intermittency of renewable energy. A cost-effective solution to this energy storage challenge can speed up energy transformation and reduce the need to have gas as a convenient transition fuel (O'Sullivan et al., 2017; Scholten & Bosman, 2016; Shivakumar et al., 2019).

But new cost-effective technological solutions can also help extend the lifespan of natural gas as an acceptable, affordable, accessible and available energy source. The most promising way of making gas—and some other fossil fuels—an acceptable energy solution with an extended lifespan is the success of large-scale CCS technology (Benson et al., 2012). This could give natural gas a new lease of life, for instance by making it a part of a new energy value chain in the form of green hydrogen that can replace other more polluting sources of energy in transport, heating or in other energy-related contexts. The fact that Norway has relatively voluminous gas reserves, well-developed energy infrastructure, access to renewable hydropower that can help it cover its own energy needs and have established many strong energy relationships with key European economic powers can make Norway a dream partner in a new era of green hydrogen (Mench, 2015; Overland, 2019). However, the success or failure of this possible reinvention of Norway will depend on the success or failure of the technological CCS revolution and as we in Norway have learnt it is much easier to proclaim CCS Moon landing than make it happen in reality. This makes it even more important to examine what real challenges Norwegian gas may face in the coming years.

Challenges

In this examination of challenges faced possibly by the Norwegian gas, we will focus on the developments in the 2020's and beyond 2030. We will also assess these challenges along two axes—the probability of them emerging, and how serious a challenge they can pose to the situation of the Norwegian gas on the European gas market.

The EU Focus on Climate Change and Decarbonisation

The success or failure of the EU launched policy of decarbonisation of the EU energy system should be viewed as the most important factor influencing the future of gas on the European market. This policy is to help the EU address the issue of climate change identified as an existential threat not only to the EU, but also in the global context (European Commission 2020c, 2020e; Goldstein, 2016; Luterbacher & Sprinz, 2018; Sartor et al., 2014; Skjærseth, 2015). The EU has at its disposal four types of power and it is expected that all those types of power will be used in the EU's promotion of its approach to the climate change challenge (Goldthau & Sitter, 2019).

The core idea shaping the EU energy policy and thus its ability to project normative power is the idea of market and trade liberalisation as the best response to specific energy market-related challenges. Approaching the issue of gas market predominantly from a consumer perspective the EU aims to pursue a set of international rules that are somehow value-neutral but are shaped by the EU's overall approach to trade liberalisation. The EU seeks to shape international energy co-operation not by pursuing its own narrow economic interests but by building rules and regulations intended to be attractive to all market-oriented global players. This is also clearly visible in the EU's approach to how to mitigate climate change that could be understood as an effort to develop a regulatory regime that can serve as a model for global governance or a model for other national or regional regimes. Especially the introduction of the ETS can have direct bearing on fossil fuels, including Norwegian gas, in the European energy market. By 'imposing' an additional fee on consumption of fossil fuels the competitive edge of renewable fuels is strengthened which in turn may make them more attractive to energy consumers in the EU, and elsewhere.

To make both member states and external energy players play by the set of rules regulating the market the EU can in addition use its regulatory, market and economic power. Application of these three types of power by the EU has already had and is going to have a huge impact on the situation of fossil fuels, including natural gas, in the area where the EU is able to project its power. The EU's regulatory power shapes both the internal markets within the confines of the EU and exerts influence on external suppliers of energy to the EU.

For instance, publication and implementation of EU directives on gas market liberalisation is the best example of how this regulatory power is 'translated' into market rules and practices that have a huge impact on the functioning of the gas market in the EU and elsewhere. The most visible change in the gas market over the past decades is the departure from long-term contracts with many rigid options and provisions to daily market-based spot prices as basis for trade decisions. All actors wanting to have access to the EU gas market have been forced to accept this change of the rules of the gas game, not least because the EU regulatory power is meant to build and manage markets in ways that favour EU itself by putting in place regulatory regimes that generate consumer benefit.

Having in mind increased EU focus on mitigation of climate change and EU priorities in development of energy market that are to reduce its environmental footprint we should expect that various types of climate, competition and trade related regulations will have a direct and indirect impact on gas producers' and exporters' access to the EU internal gas market also in the coming decades. In addition, the EU can also use its market and economic power to make actors play by the normative and regulatory rules set by the EU—or to eliminate them as suppliers of energy to the EU, if they refuse to comply with EU energy market rules and regulations. The EU's market and economic power is targeted at selected actors to get them to pursue or not pursue a given course of action (Goldthau & Sitter, 2019). In the area of gas '*the market power strategy is based on the idea that gas is a strategic good and that security of supply must be a paramount concern for a specific group of states that rely on a neighbouring empire for almost 40 percent of their gas imports*' (Goldthau & Sitter, 2019, 34). Finally, the economic power of the EU can be used as a tool in foreign policy to support selected industries or policies for political or economic reasons.

In this situation, Norwegian gas can have a limited role as a part of the solution in a short-term and mid-term perspective, but can face some problems in the long-term perspective. Being the second largest external supplier of gas to the EU, Norway can alleviate some risks related to the EU's in general and some EU countries more specific, overdependence on gas supplies coming from Russia. This is already the case when Norway decided to supply gas to Ukraine, Lithuania or Poland and has plans about increasing these supplies to represent almost 10% of its total export of gas when the Baltic Pipe project becomes operational by 2022. In a similar way, Norwegian gas can help countries, such as Poland or Germany, to achieve climate and emissions goals outlined in national documents and agreed at the EU level by replacing coal in national energy mixes.

However, realisation of climate and emission goals may also force phasing out of fossil fuels, including Norwegian gas, from energy mixes. For instance, according to prognoses presented in the last edition of the IEA World Energy Outlook (IEA, 2020b) some scenarios see demand for gas both globally and in the EU fall due to more focus on combatting climate change and phasing in new renewable energy resources replacing fossil fuels. According to Stated Policies Scenario, gas demand in the

EU is to be reduced by 30 bcm in 2030 compared with 2019 (IEA, 2020b). However, it may turn out that for various political and market-related reasons Norwegian gas will suffer lesser losses on this shrinking EU energy market in transition towards a greener energy system than gas coming from other suppliers with a more complicated relationship with the EU than Norway.

When dealing with the EU and trying to influence its energy policy and priorities to promote its energy interests Norway that is in many respects a de facto member of the Union (Austvik & Claes, 2011), has a limited arsenal of instruments at its disposal (Godzimirski, 2019). Energy relationship between Norway and the EU can be best described as an asymmetric interdependence, with the EU having the upper hand in most of the areas and Norway forced to adapt to changing political, market, economic and normative framework conditions (Andersen & Sitter, 2019; Gawlikowska-Fyk et al., 2015; Godzimirski & Nowak, 2018). This asymmetry is even more clear in a situation when the EU aims at removing all fossil fuels, including gas, from its energy mix while Norway, as a major gas supplier is interested in having access to the EU gas market. When commenting on strategic choices made by the EU in 2018 Norwegian media painted therefore a rather bleak picture for the future of Norwegian gas in Europe. One of the leading Norwegian newspapers argued for instance that although according to some EU estimates demand for gas in the EU will be reduced only by ca 15% by 2030 and Norwegian gas will have an important role in the EU in the coming decade, the situation will change dramatically in the following decades. According to two EU scenarios, the EU that plans to become climate neutral by 2050 will reduce its consumption of gas by 85% by 2050 and Norwegian and other gas suppliers will therefore face hard time in this key energy market (Dagbladet, 2018).

Especially after 2025 the prospects for gas will start to deteriorate in established markets as a result of environmental considerations, increasing competition from renewables, efficiency gains, growing electrification of end-use demand and improving prospects for alternative low-carbon gases, including hydrogen (IEA, 2020b). A possible way of extending the lifespan of natural gas is the implementation of effective CCS technology that will help turn natural gas into green hydrogen, a prospective fuel with almost no direct negative environmental footprint.

Changing Competition Landscape

Another challenge Norwegian gas can face in Europe is the coming of new gas suppliers who can offer more affordable, and thus more acceptable gas supplies. Although today some of the gas supplied to the EU from further away comes already as LNG, it is believed that LNG will see its share increased in the EU market. The future role of the USA as the emerging gas supplier to the EU draws a lot of attention. Some EU members, such as Poland, are enthusiastic about these prospects and have already signed contracts for LNG supplies from the USA, while others, such as Germany, are more reluctant, but it is expected that the ongoing LNG revolution that is about to change the global gas market will also have huge impact on gas trade in Europe and indirectly on Norway's position in this market. It is expected that huge volumes of the US produced LNG will press gas prices in Europe down and this will also have consequences for other gas producers and suppliers (Barstad, 2016).

Norway itself has experienced how gas from the USA can change gas trade in Europe. Already in March 2016, a giant gas vessel fully loaded with ethane extracted from American shale gas arrived in Norway to deliver gas to the Ineos facility in Rafnes (Sørheim & NTB, 2016). This gas was meant to be used in production of plastic but this shipment was also viewed as a highly symbolic sign of the new gas era emerging in Europe where traditional gas producers and suppliers were challenged by newcomers who intended to change the rules of the gas game not only in Europe but globally. The emergence of new LNG suppliers, first and foremost the USA, Qatar and Australia is often interpreted as a new step in creation of a truly global single gas market where piped gas will be facing increased competition from LNG. Since more than 95% of gas produced and exported from Norway has the EU countries as the main customers the emergence of LNG competition poses a challenge to Norway's position as the second most important gas supplier to the EU. The volume of LNG supplies to Europe is not for the time being huge, and demand for gas saw a slump in the aftermath of the COVID-19 pandemic, but in the short-term, medium-term and long-term LNG can compete with Norwegian gas on many markets in Europe. However, for the time being this competition is limited to the UK where LNG has been arriving in increased volumes and to some other national markets where the Norwegian gas is one of available options.

In 2019, the last pre-COVID year, the EU imported the highest volume of LNG in its history—108 bcm that represented 27% of total gas imports and 22% of gas consumption (European Commission, 2020f) which was purely by chance almost the same volume of gas Norway exported to the EU in the same year. Qatar supplied 30 bcm of LNG to the EU in 2019, and was followed by Russia with 21 bcm and the USA with 17 bcm.

Situation changed in 2020 as EU LNG imports kept on increasing, up by 26% year-on-year in the 1st quarter of 2020. The USA remained the most important LNG supplier to Europe, ensuring 30% of the EU's total LNG imports in the 1st quarter of 2020, ahead of Russia (22%) and Qatar (15%). In the 1st quarter of 2020, the EU imported 25 bcm of LNG, and the three largest importer countries were: Spain (6 bcm), France (5 bcm) and Belgium (4 bcm) (European Commission, 2020f).

This list of major LNG suppliers reveals some interesting developments—Qatar has been the major global LNG player for some time and has supplied LNG to Europe in many years, but the emergence of Russia on this list is a relatively new phenomenon caused by opening of the Yamal LNG in the Russian Arctic run by main Gazprom's Russian gas competitor Novatek that has managed to break Gazprom's monopoly for gas exports from Russia, while the US supplies are a result of the ongoing shale gas revolution turning USA into a major global LNG player and the number one global producer of oil and gas combined.

Although this LNG 'expansion' was slowed down by the COVID-19 related developments that have reduced demand for energy in Europe, it is expected that LNG will continue to play an increasingly important role both on the European and on the global market, posing in that way a challenge to suppliers of piped gas (Analiticheskii tsentr pri pravitelstve Rossiyskoy Federatsii, 2020a).

Price Volatility

The volatility of gas price in Europe is one of the key structural factors all gas suppliers must factor in their plans. In December 2019, the price of natural gas at Europe's largest terminal—the Title Transfer Facility (TTF) in the Netherlands—fell by 10.3% to USD 4.62 per MBtu. In the 3rd quarter of 2019, the average sale price of thousand cubic metres (tcm) of gas to the EU was USD 170 which was 32% lower than in the 3rd quarter of 2018. In the 3rd quarter of 2019, natural gas prices in Europe fell to the level not seen since 2004 when the average price amounted to USD 138 per tcm (Volovik, 2020). This trend continued in the 1st half of 2020, when the COVID-19 pandemic resulted in massive lockdowns and

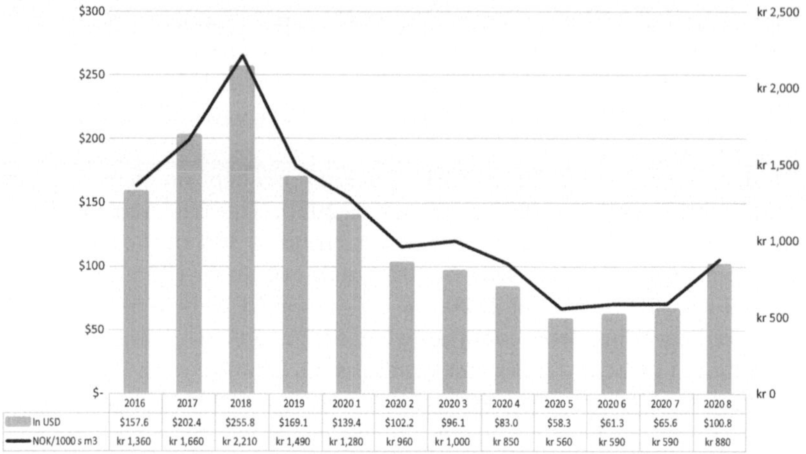

	2016	2017	2018	2019	2020 1	2020 2	2020 3	2020 4	2020 5	2020 6	2020 7	2020 8
In USD	$157.6	$202.4	$255.8	$169.1	$139.4	$102.2	$96.1	$83.0	$58.3	$61.3	$65.6	$100.8
NOK/1000 s m3	kr 1,360	kr 1,660	kr 2,210	kr 1,490	kr 1,280	kr 960	kr 1,000	kr 850	kr 560	kr 590	kr 590	kr 880

Fig. 6.3 Price of Norwegian gas on the European market 2016–2020 (NOK and USD/1000 Sm^3o.e.) (*Note* kr = Norwegian Krone (NOK). *Source* The Author, based on Brenna, 2020b)

a far lower demand for energy. Both global and regional European gas markets were hard hit and the gas price collapsed. In May 2020, gas was traded for USD 37 per tcm in Europe and for USD 66 per tcm in Asia (Analiticheskii tsentr pri pravitelstve Rossiyskoy Federatsii, 2020b). After the end of the first phase of the COVID-19 pandemic, gas price in Europe went up by nearly 60% from July to August 2020, but was still below USD 100 per tcm, both in Europe and the USA (Analiticheskii tsentr pri pravitelstve Rossiyskoy Federatsii, 2020c). However, cold weather in the first weeks of January 2021 contributed to skyrocketing of gas price in Europe where it reached USD 252 per tcm at TTF, but this seems to be a short-lived price spike and not a long-term trend (Lenta.ru, 2021) (Fig. 6.3).

Will Norway Be Able to Maintain the Current Level of Gas Production in the Future?

To remain an important energy producer and exporter, Norway needs to have enough energy resources to cover its own energy needs and to send the surplus of energy to other actors. A recently published examination of the resource situation paints a rather disturbing picture of that future, describing the Norwegian continental shelf where most of the discovered and undiscovered resources are located as a squeezed lemon. According to the recent estimate, the production of petroleum is to increase until 2024 and to decrease in the following years. It is also estimated that approximately 50% of all discovered and not yet discovered resources are still to be produced and that most of these resources are in the Barents Sea. What is however more problematic is that most of these resources are in natural gas in the fields that are located far away from the existing infrastructure. This means that only the largest fields to be discovered in this promising region will be considered as marketable, but so far the discoveries in the region have been disappointing. The main conclusion from this rather realistic study was that the deposits that are discovered today are far smaller than before and the prospects for new major discoveries are becoming increasingly uncertain (SSB, 2019). This can in the longer perspective put an end to Norway's role as a major gas producer and exporter.

With the current level of production—ca 120 bcm of natural gas per year—that is not expected to grow substantially in the coming years this would secure the same level of supplies in the coming thirteen years. The situation could change into a more positive direction if the levels of contingent and undiscovered gas resources were to increase. Contingent resources of gas are proven resources for which a production decisions have not yet been made. Undiscovered gas resources are those resources that will most likely be discovered and can be produced, but which have not yet been proven through drilling. At the end of 2019, contingent resources totalled 1,378 million Sm^3o.e. while the undiscovered resources were at that moment estimated at 3,910 million Sm^3o.e. According to official NPD data, there are additional 310 million Sm^3o.e. of gas in contingent resources in fields, similar volume of gas—310 million Sm^3o.e.—in contingent resources in discoveries, and 1,805 million Sm^3o.e. in undiscovered resources. If all the estimated volumes of gas in all categories are added they total 3,955 million Sm^3o.e. This in theory could secure production of gas from Norwegian fields at the current level in the coming 33 years—in other words, until the year 2053.[3]

[3] The author's calculations based on data from Norskpetroleum.no (2020c).

Acceptability and Affordability Question

The future of the Norwegian resource base will depend not only on development of known and yet undiscovered fields, but also on the outcome of the political discussion on how Norway could and should reduce its environmental footprint to help mitigate problems caused by the climate change not only in Norway but globally. There are strong voices both in Norway and elsewhere, calling for putting an end to production from some existing or newly discovered fields, for stopping development of new fields as well as exploration in some areas deemed too vulnerable environmentally.

A good example of how difficult decisions on petroleum activity in Norway could be was provided recently when the debate on the so-called marginal ice zone in the Barents Sea was concluded, leading to a lot of controversy. The so-called constitutional climate controversy—Klimasøksmålet—taken by Norwegian environmental NGOs to the Supreme Court of Norway that wanted to stop exploration and production of fossil fuels in the Arctic part of Norway is another good example of how the issue of acceptability can influence the future of the gas industry in Norway (Klimasøksmal, 2020). Yet another good example with direct bearing on possible access to some important but yet undiscovered petroleum resources is the ongoing discussion on exploration and possible petroleum activity in the marine areas of Lofoten, Vesterålen and Senja located in the northern part of the country far away from the EU market (Åslie & Mansouri, 2020).

The future of Norwegian gas production will therefore depend not only on the availability of resources, but also on whether exploration and development of these resources will be acceptable and affordable, not only in purely economic but also in political and environmental terms. Depending on what choices in this area will be taken by Norwegian policymakers, and how strong such decisions will be pushed on Norway by the EU that is seriously concerned with the negative impact fossil fuels have on climate, we cannot completely rule out the possibility of some known and undiscovered gas assets ending as stranded assets.

Also quickly falling costs of renewable energy, increasing costs of CO_2 emissions and availability of cheaper gas with lower break even costs can undermine the economic viability of some of the projects located in those vulnerable areas. The fate of the huge Russian Shtokman gas field—the second largest offshore gas field in the world—located in the same area where many yet undiscovered Norwegian fields are expected to be found is a good example illustrating technological, economic, market and even political challenges to be faced by Norwegian gas producers in years to come.

Norwegian Hydropower Versus Norwegian Gas?

The role of hydropower in Norway needs to be examined for at least two reasons in the context of discussion on the current and future role of Norway as a gas supplier to Europe. First, the availability of hydropower and its central role in the Norwegian energy consumption contribute to limited demand for gas in the domestic market, which makes huge volumes of gas of Norwegian provenience available to other consumers in the neighbourhood. Second, there is a growing interest in both Norway and in the EU in strengthening the connection between Norwegian power grid and production facilities and the European electricity consumers. The idea is to turn Norway into an important element of the European power generation system to help it cope with the challenge of intermittency caused by the more prominent role of renewable energy resources in the European energy mix. The idea of turning Norway into a green battery of Europe is being translated into policy of building interconnectors linking Norwegian power grid with several national grids. This means that Norwegian supplies of electricity can in fact compete with Norwegian gas on some national energy markets. This trend may become even more important in the future when new grid interconnectors between Norway and Europe will be added to the existing ones and gas will no longer be treated as a convenient transition fuel but as a less harmful but still a fossil fuel to be removed from the European energy mix.[4]

In 2019, Norway produced 125 TWh of hydroelectricity (3% of the global hydropower) and had 33 GW of installed capacity which helped generate 95% of all electricity produced in Norway. However, even if the production of electricity in Norway were to increase substantially in the coming years it would be impossible to replace gas with electricity as the main Norwegian contribution to energy security of Europe. According to realistic calculations, energy value of the Norwegian gas exported to Europe—1,200 TWh—was almost ten times higher than the total production of electricity in Norway—125 TWh in 2019 (Brenna, 2020a). The

[4] See IEA (2019) on the role of gas in energy transition.

main conclusion here should therefore be that Norwegian electricity can play a certain balancing role in the European context, but gas—and oil—will remain the main energy commodities to be supplied to Europe—at least until they will be replaced by other, less harmful sources of energy in the EU that has an ambition to reduce its environmental energy footprint to zero (Gullberg, 2013; Schjøtt-Pedersen, 2016).

Concluding Remarks

The aim of this chapter was to contribute to a better understanding of the role of the Norwegian natural gas in the European market in the 2020's. To be able to draw any conclusions on the future role of the Norwegian gas we decided to examine its historical role in the most important market in Europe and factors that have had and will have impact on the evolution of the strong energy relationship developed between Norway and the EU. The main conclusions from this examination are as follows:

- Norwegian gas has become the main energy commodity exported from Norway to the EU and will remain so due to the composition of the resource base in Norway, a short re-bump in oil production in Norway notwithstanding.
- Several structural factors that have been influencing gas relations between Norway and the EU are going to influence these relations also in the coming decade, but their influence will be weighted differently. This has to do with the changing energy priorities in the EU. More focus now is on the sustainability of the energy system and closely related issue of climate change caused by the use of fossil fuels and less on the security of supply, with the need to have access to competitively priced energy that will make the EU more competitive globally being viewed as less acute. Once climate change has been defined as a an existential threat not only to the EU, but to the whole mankind, the EU embarked on policy of reducing environmental footprint of energy to zero, which bodes ill for all fossil fuels, including Norwegian gas.
- Norwegian gas is perceived as a politically safer commodity than the Russian one, especially after the 2014 conflict in Ukraine that has provided additional motivation to look for new sources of gas by those actors who perceive energy dependence on Russia as a serious security challenge (Van de Graaf & Colgan, 2017). This has opened

some new market opportunities to Norwegian gas and the construction of the Baltic Pipe that is to be concluded as planned in 2022 will redirect some 10% of Norwegian gas production to new markets. Construction of new LNG terminals has also provided some new market opportunities in countries, such as Poland or Lithuania, but the volume of LNG from Norway is relatively small due to limited production capacity.

- The depletion of existing gas fields in the UK, the Netherlands and Denmark opens also some new market opportunities for the Norwegian gas. Also decision on phasing out of nuclear power by 2022 and coal by 2038 taken by the German authorities will open some new possibilities in the relatively saturated German gas market even if the Nord Stream 2 project is completed.
- The availability of gas to be shipped from Norway to markets abroad is one of the structural uncertainties as the known reserves allow for maintaining production at the current level for some thirteen years and new large discoveries are uncertain and are expected in the areas far away from the existing infrastructure and markets.
- Norwegian gas will face growing competition from new, renewable sources of energy and if the EU climate plans are implemented, it should be phased out by 2050. The only possible but maybe less probable rescue for all fossil fuels could be development of the cost-effective large-scale CCS technology that would help address the question of their environmental footprint. However, it remains to be seen how economically viable such a technological solution will be in a situation when the costs of renewable energy are getting lower due to technological innovations and effects of economies of scale. The CCS technology will also be crucial and help extend the lifespan of the Norwegian gas turning it into an important input in green hydrogen, a new promising energy source combining the best of the two energy worlds—the fossil one and the green one (European Commission, 2020d). Finding a viable solution to elimination or substantial reduction of the environmental footprint will also silence critics of fossil fuels and make them less unacceptable.

References

Analiticheskii tsentr pri pravitelstve Rossiyskoy Federatsii. (2020a). Novaya konfiguratsiya gazovykh marshrutov v YeS. Energeticheskiy byulleten'(nr 81 February). 14–18.

Analiticheskii tsentr pri pravitelstve Rossiyskoy Federatsii. (2020b). Energostrategiya v epokhu peremen. Energeticheskiy byulleten' (nr 85 June). 14–19.

Analiticheskii tsentr pri pravitelstve Rossiyskoy Federatsii. (2020c). Atomnaya energetika v yubileynyy god. Energeticheskiy byulleten' (nr 88 September).

Andersen, S. S., & Sitter, N. (2019). The EU's strategy towards external gas suppliers and their responses: Norway, Russia, Algeria and LNG. In J. M. Godzimirski (Ed.), *New political economy of energy in Europe: Power to project, power to adapt* (pp. 49–72). Palgrave Macmillan.

Åslie, Ø. J. C., & Mansouri, M. (2020). Is petroleum activity in the marine areas of Lofoten, Vesterålen and Senja desirable for Norway?—A case study in the oil and gas industry. *INCOSE International Symposium, 30*(1), 1280–1293.

Austvik, O. G. (2019). Norway: Small state in the great European energy game. In J. M. Godzimirski (Ed.), *New political economy of energy in Europe: Power to project, power to adap* (pp. 139–164). Palgrave Macmillan.

Austvik, O. G., & Claes D. H. (2011). *EØS-avtalen og norsk energipolitikk. Europautredningen*. Utvalget for utredning av Norges avtaler med EU.

BalticPipe. (2020). *Baltic Pipe Project*. https://www.baltic-pipe.eu/. Accessed 22 October 2020.

Barstad, S. (2016). Skipet med skifergass er dårlig nytt for Norges største næring. Aftenposten 27 September 2016.

Benson, S. M., Bennaceur, K., Cook, P., Davison, J., de Coninck, H., Farhat, K., Ramirez, A., Simbeck, D., Surles, T., Verma, D., Wright, J., & Ahearne, J. (2012). Carbon capture and storage. *Global energy assessment—Toward a sustainable future* (pp. 993–1068). Cambridge University Press. Cambridge.

BP. (2020). *Statistical review of world energy 2020* (69th ed.). BP.

Brenna, A. L. (2020a). *Dette koster det å produsere strøm med norsk gass*. https://enerwe.no/gass-gasspris-kommentar/dette-koster-det-a-produsere-strom-med-norsk-gass/351041. Accessed 12 October 2020.

Brenna, A. L. (2020b). *Gassprisen tok seg kraftig opp i august. Prisen på gass traff bunnen i mai*. https://enerwe.no/gass-gasspris/gassprisen-tok-seg-kraftig-opp-i-august/380048. Accessed 12 October 2020.

Dagbladet. (2018, November 30). *EU med både godt og dårlig nytt for norsk gass*.

European Commission. (2020a). *Energy production and imports*. https://ec.europa.eu/eurostat/statistics-explained/index.php/Energy_production_and_imports. Accessed 16 October 2020.

European Commission. (2020b). *EU energy in figures. Statistical pocketbook 2020*. European Commission.

European Commission. (2020c). *A European Green Deal. Striving to be the first climate-neutral continent*. https://ec.europa.eu/info/strategy/priorities-2019-2024/european-green-deal_en. Accessed 12 January 2021.

European Commission. (2020d). *A hydrogen strategy for a climate-neutral Europe*. European Commission.

European Commission. (2020e). *Methane emissions*. https://ec.europa.eu/energy/topics/oil-gas-and-coal/methane-emissions_en. Accessed 12 October 2020.

European Commission. (2020f). *Quarterly Report on European Gas Market Q1 2020*. European Commission. Market Observatory for Energy.

Eurostat. (2020). *Database updated in October 2020*. https://ec.europa.eu/eurostat/. Accessed 12 January 2021.

Fischer, S. (2020). *What Russia doesn't get about Germany*. Carnegie Moscow Center.

Gassco. (2020). *Gassco*. https://gassco.no/en/. Accessed 15 October 2020.

Gawlikowska-Fyk, A. (2019). Poland: Coping with the challenges of decarbonization and diversification. In J. M. Godzimirski (Ed.), *New political economy of energy in Europe: Power to project, power to adapt* (pp. 195–214). Palgrave Macmillan.

Gawlikowska-Fyk, A., Nowak, Z. & Puka, L. (2015). *The EU gas game: Time to redefine the rules? Case studies of Russia and Norway and lessons for the EU, Norway and Poland* (PISM Goodgov Report). PISM.

Gazprom. (2020). *Gazprom in figures 2015–2019 factbook*. Gazprom. https://www.gazprom.com/f/posts/72/802627/gazprom-in-figures-2015-2019-en.pdf. Accessed 12 January 2021.

Gazprom Export. (2020). *Foreign partners*. Great Britain. http://www.gazpromexport.ru/en/partners/gb/. Accessed 12 June 2021.

Godzimirski, J. M. (2016). Can the Polish shale gas dog still bark? Politics and policy of unconventional hydrocarbons in Poland. *Energy Research & Social Science*, 158–167. http://dx.doi.org/10.1016/j.erss.2016.06.009

Godzimirski, J. M. (2019). Channels of influence, or how non-members can influence EU energy policy. In J. M. Godzimirski (Ed.), *New political economy of energy in Europe: Power to project, power to adapt* (pp. 105–137). Palgrave Macmillan.

Godzimirski, J. M., & Austvik, O. G. (2019). Introduction: The EU and the changing (geo)politics of energy in Europe. In J. M. Godzimirski (Ed.), *New political economy of energy in Europe: Power to project, power to adapt* (pp. 1–24). Palgrave Macmillan.

Godzimirski, J. M., & Nowak, Z. (2018). EU gas supply security: The power of the importer. In K. Szulecki (Ed.), *Energy security in Europe: Divergent perceptions and policy challenges* (pp. 221–249). Palgrave Macmillan.

Goldstein, J. S. (2016). Climate change as a global security issue. *Journal of Global Security Studies., 1*(1), 95–98. https://doi.org/10.1093/jogss/ogv010

Goldthau, A., & Sitter, N. (2019). Regulatory power or market power Europe? Leadership and models for external EU energy governance. In J. M. Godzimirski (Ed.), *New political economy of energy in Europe: Power to project, power to adapt* (pp. 27–47). Palgrave Macmillan.

Gullberg, A. T. (2013). The political feasibility of Norway as the 'green battery' of Europe. *Energy Policy, 57*, 615–623. https://doi.org/10.1016/j.enpol.2013.02.037

Gustafson, T. (2020). *The bridge: Natural gas in a redivided Europe*. Harvard University Press.

IEA. (2019). *The role of gas in today's energy transitions*. International Energy Agency.

IEA. (2020a). *Key world energy statistics 2020*. International Energy Agency.

IEA. (2020b). *World energy outlook 2020*. International Energy Agency.

Klimasøksmal. (2020). *Outrage after judgement in favour of the Norwegian oil state*. https://www.xn--klimasksml-95a8t.no/en/2020/12/22/outrage-after-judgement-in-favour-of-the-norwegian-oil-state/. Accessed 13 January 2021.

Korteweg, R. (2018). *Energy as a tool of foreign policy of authoritarian states, in particular Russia*. Policy Department for External Relations, Directorate General for External Policies of the European Union.

Lang, K.-O., & Westphal, K. (2017). *Nord Stream 2—A political and economic contextualisation* (SWP Research Paper). SWP.

Lenta.ru. (2021). *Tseny na gas dostigli maksimuma*. https://lenta.ru/news/2021/01/11/gas/. Accessed 13 January 2021.

Luterbacher, U., & Sprinz, D. F. (Eds.). (2018). *Global climate policy: actors, concepts, and enduring challenges*. MIT Press.

Mench, M. M. (2015). High hopes for hydrogen: Fuel cells and the future of energy. *Foreign Affairs, 94*, 117–123.

Ministry of Energy Poland. (2019). *Polityka eneregetyczna Polski do 2040*. Ministry of Energy Poland.

Ministry of Foreign Affairs Norway. (2012). *Utenfor og innenfor: Norges avtaler med EU* (Vol. NOU 2012:2). Ministry of Foreign Affairs Norway.

Naimski, P. (2015). *Energia i niepodległość*. Ośrodek Myśli Politycznej.

Norskpetroleum.no. (2020a). *Management of revenues*. https://www.norskpetroleum.no/en/economy/management-of-revenues/. Accessed 20 October 2020.

Norskpetroleum.no. (2020b). *Production forecasts*. https://www.norskpetroleum.no/en/production-and-exports/production-forecasts/. Accessed 20 October 2020.

Norskpetroleum.no. (2020c). *Resource accounts for the Norwegian shelf at 31.12.2019*. https://www.norskpetroleum.no/en/petroleum-resources/resource-accounts/. Accessed 20 October 2020.

O'Sullivan, M., Overland, I., & Sandalow, D. (2017). *The geopolitics of renewable energy* (Working Paper). Columbia University Press, Harvard Kennedy School, NUPI.

Overland, I. (2019). EU climate and energy policy: New challenges for old energy suppliers. In J. M. Godzimirski (Ed.), *New political economy of energy in Europe: Power to project, power to adapt* (pp. 73–102). Palgrave Macmillan.

Sartor, O., Spencer, T., Bart, I., Julia, P.-E., Gawlikowska-Fyk, A., Neuhoff, K., Ruester, S., Selei, A., Toth, B., Szpor, A., & Tuerk, A. (2014). The EU's 2030 climate and energy framework and energy security. *Climate Strategies*. https://www.osti.gov/etdeweb/biblio/22376382

Schjøtt-Pedersen, K. E. (2016, February 27). Gass er Europas batteri. *Dagens Næringsliv*, p. 23.

Scholten, D., & Bosman, R. (2016). The geopolitics of renewables; Exploring the political implications of renewable energy systems. *Technological Forecasting and Social Change, 103*(Supplement C), 273–283. https://doi.org/10.1016/j.techfore.2015.10.014

Shivakumar, A., Dobbins, A., Fahl, U., & Singh, A. (2019). Drivers of renewable energy deployment in the EU: An analysis of past trends and projections. *Energy Strategy Reviews., 26*, 100402. https://doi.org/10.1016/j.esr.2019.100402

Skjærseth, J. B. (2015). EU climate and energy policy: Demanded or supplied? In G. Bang, A. Underdal, & S. Andresen (Eds.), *The domestic politics of global climate change: Key actors in international climate cooperation* (pp. 71–94). Edward Elgar Publishing.

Sørheim, T. I., & NTB. (2016). *Gigantskip med skifergass fra USA inntar Norge*. https://e24.no/naeringsliv/i/jPy10w/gigantskip-med-skifergass-fra-usa-inntar-norge. Accessed 21 October 2020.

SSB. (2019). Ettermiddagsbyger eller væromslag for norsk sokkel? SSB Analyse 31. https://www.ssb.no/energi-og-industri/artikler-og-publikasjoner/ettermiddagsbyger-eller-vaeromslag-for-norsk-sokkel. Accessed 12 January 2021.

Van de Graaf, T., & Colgan, J. D. (2017). Russian gas games or well-oiled conflict? Energy security and the 2014 Ukraine crisis. *Energy Research & Social Science, 24*, 59–64. https://doi.org/10.1016/j.erss.2016.12.018

Volovik, N. (2020). Russia-EU trade development under the sanctions. *Baltic Rim Economies*. https://sites.utu.fi/bre/russia-eu-trade-development-under-the-sanctions/. Accessed 10 December 2020.

Westphal, K. (2019). Germany's energiewende: Climate change in focus—Competitiveness and energy security sidelined? In J. M. Godzimirski (Ed.),

New political economy of energy in Europe: Power to project, power to adap (pp. 165–194). Palgrave Macmillan.

Westphal, K. (2020). German-Russian gas relations in face of the energy transition. *Russian Journal of Economics, 6*(4), 406–423.

Westphal, K., Bros, A., & Mitrova, T. (2017). *German-Russian gas relations: A special relationship in troubled waters* (Vol. 2017/RP 13).

World Trade Organization (WTO). (2010). *World trade report 2010. Trade in natural resources*. World Trade Organization.

CHAPTER 7

Development of the LNG Terminal in Świnoujście, Poland

Dariusz Zarzecki

Introduction

Today, natural gas is considered by many as the fuel of the future. Years ago, when oil companies drilled for oil and found gas, their effort was deemed a failure. Gas, if associated, often had to be either reinjected or flared or, if dry, left for another day. When flaring was branded as wasteful by producing countries, companies had to find an alternative use for gas. Consequently, LNG projects were evaluated, and if viable, pursued. As oil prices rose and production costs fell, LNG became economically more feasible. Consuming nations with long-term vision were willing to pay a premium to secure clean energy from diverse and reliable producers (Tusiani & Shearer, 2007).

The decarbonisation policy, which is undoubtedly one of the most important, long-term, joint actions undertaken by the vast majority of countries, will probably lead to a reduction in the global consumption

D. Zarzecki (✉)
University of Szczecin, Szczecin, Poland
e-mail: dariusz.zarzecki@usz.edu.pl

K. Liuhto (ed.), *The Future of Energy Consumption, Security and Natural Gas*, https://doi.org/10.1007/978-3-030-80367-4_7

of natural gas.[1] In the short term and medium term, natural gas will continue to play a large role, and in countries moving away from highly polluting coal, the importance of gas will be even greater.

Some countries have problems with ensuring gas supplies via gas pipelines (e.g. Japan). In others, own deposits have depleted (e.g. Western Europe). According to the Paris Agreement, it is necessary to move away from hard hydrocarbons in favour of less harmful energy sources. As a result, the role and importance of LNG is increasing. Moreover, tremendous technological advances in natural gas extraction, compression, transport and decompression have contributed to a significant cost reduction, making the use of LNG an attractive and profitable option. Nowadays, LNG is an increasingly important part of the world's energy mix. It is actually the fastest-growing segment of the world's hydrocarbon industry.

The LNG industry is based largely on a series of virtually self-contained projects made up of interlinking chains of large-scale facilities, requiring huge capital investments, bound together by complex, long-term contracts and subject to intense oversight by host governments and international organisations at every stage of the process (Tusiani & Shearer, 2007).

The objective of the article is to describe the growing importance of LNG in Poland's energy system and to analyse an impact of the LNG terminal in Świnoujście on diversification of energy supply and improvement of energy security. The first part of the article presents the energy mix of Poland, and how Poland intends to replace coal with natural gas. Then, the genesis and the expansion the LNG terminal in Świnoujście are presented. Further on, other investments in infrastructure supporting LNG imports to Poland are presented, in particular the purchase of gas carriers and the investment in the FSRU in the Gulf of Gdańsk. The last part of the chapter describes the most important challenges and opportunities in the field of energy. The article ends with a summary and final remarks.

[1] One of J. Biden's first decisions after taking the presidency was to sign in January 2021 the executive order, which assumed that the USA was returning to the principles of the Paris Agreement.

The Energy Mix in Poland: Gas Replaces Coal

Poland's energy import dependence was historically low and accounted merely to 10.7% in 2000. Such a low level of dependence on imports resulted from the very high extraction of hard coal and lignite. For many decades, Poland was a significant producer and exporter of coal. The country's energy mix was mainly based on coal, the vast majority of power plants used this raw material. Gradually, coal production decreased and since 2008 Poland has been (except for two years) a net importer of coal. The continuous reduction in coal production in Polish mines resulted in a systematic, significant increase in the dependence of the Polish economy on fuel imports. In 2010, the ratio of dependence on energy imports increased to 31.6%, and in 2018 to 44.8% (European Commission, 2020).

In Europe, natural gas is increasingly replacing coal. It is no different in Poland, where, thanks to the gradual transformation of the domestic energy sector towards cleaner energy sources, the role and consumption of gas are gradually increasing. Particularly noteworthy is the paradox of the domestic coal market. On the one hand, the share of coal in electricity production in 2019 was nearly five percentage points lower than in the previous year. The trend of declining hard coal mining in domestic mines, which has been visible for years, is also maintained. In 2020, electricity consumption amounted to 171 TWh and was 2% lower than in 2019. Hard coal is still dominant in electricity production in Poland with a share of 46%. The second source of electricity is lignite (24%). It is followed by natural gas (10%), wind energy (10%), biomass/biogas (5%) and other sources (5%). In total, coal (hard coal and lignite) is the raw material for the production of as much as 70% of electricity in Poland. Never theless, the share of coal is systematically and significantly decreasing and is currently the lowest in the over 100-year history of the Polish power industry (wysokienapiecie.pl, 2021).

On the other hand, however, the demand for hard coal remains high. In 2020, coal consumption was 109 mt. A large part of it, almost 20% of domestic consumption, is supplemented with imported coal. Ten million tonnes came from Russia, and the remaining three million tonnes arrived mainly from Colombia, the USA and Kazakhstan (wysokienapiecie.pl, 2021).

According to forecasts, electricity consumption in Poland in 2021 should remain at a level similar to previous years. Due to further increases in prices of CO_2 emission allowances, which are very likely to remain above EUR 35 per tonne, production in coal-fired power plants will decline for another year in a row, while renewable energy production and imports will increase (wysokienapiecie.pl, 2021).

The share of oil in Poland's primary energy consumption was 31% in 2019. The respective share for natural gas was 17%. Poland does not produce any significant amounts of oil but the country produces 20% of its natural gas (BP, 2020). Poland imported 68% of its oil and petroleum products from Russia in 2019. The relevant share for natural gas was 60%. The aforementioned figure takes into account LNG imports. These figures mean that Russian oil covered 21% of Poland's primary energy consumption in 2019. The relevant share for Russian natural gas was just 10%. It may suggest that Russian oil plays a more strategic role in Poland's energy mix than Russian natural gas (Liuhto, 2020). However, imports of gas from Germany (about 17% of total Poland's imports) should be added to imports from Russia as it is still Russian gas. Poland buys it cheaper than directly from Russia. Therefore, total imports of gas from Russia reaches effectively almost 80% and Russian gas covered about 14% of Poland's primary energy consumption in 2019. It can be concluded that the role of oil and gas in the Polish imports of energy resources from Russia is similar, although with a clear predominance of oil. However, with the expiry of the Yamal contract, direct imports of gas from Russia will decrease dramatically.

Statistics on gas consumption, production and import vary depending on the data source. Table 7.1 presents data for the year 2000 and the period 2010–2020 relating to consumption, production and imports, taken from BP, the Central Statistical Office of Poland (GUS) and PGNiG (a major producer, importer and trader of gas in Poland). The differences result from the different methodology and scope of data used by the mentioned institutions. The indicators describing the share of imports in consumption were calculated on the basis of consumption and production from the BP report (BP, 2020) and imports from the Central Statistical Office report (GUS, 2021).

In the period 2000–2020, the share of imports in gas consumption in Poland was between 67–87%. The share of imports remains high, because with a stable level of domestic production (about 4.0 bcm per year), imports are growing at a pace similar to consumption. On the other hand, the growing imports of LNG cause a gradual reduction in gas imports via gas pipelines. In 2020, the share of LNG in consumption was 17.9% (Table 7.1 and Fig. 7.1). The share of LNG in the imports of gas handled

Table 7.1 Natural gas production, consumption and imports in Poland in 2000–2020

Year	*Consumption (bcm)*		*Production (bcm)*			*Imports (bcm)*		*Share of imports in consumption (%)*		
	BP	*GUS*	*BP*	*PGNiG*	*GUS*	*Total*	*LNG*	*Total*	*Excl. LNG*	*LNG*
1	2	3	4	5	6	7	8	9 (7:2)	10 (7–8:2)	11 (8:2)
2000	11.10	13.35	3.7	3.80	5.20	8.10	0.00	73.0	73.0	0.0
2010	16.20	17.16	4.3	4.22	6.08	10.90	0.00	67.3	67.3	0.0
2011	16.50	17.18	4.5	4.33	6.25	11.79	0.00	71.5	71.5	0.0
2012	17.40	18.10	4.5	4.32	6.32	12.25	0.00	70.4	70.4	0.0
2013	17.40	18.23	4.4	4.21	6.21	12.49	0.00	71.8	71.8	0.0
2014	17.00	17.66	4.3	4.03	6.08	11.82	0.00	69.5	69.5	0.0
2015	17.10	18.20	4.3	4.01	6.08	12.12	0.00	70.9	70.9	0.0
2016	18.30	19.02	4.1	3.88	5.79	14.68	0.97	80.2	74.9	5.3
2017	19.20	20.08	4.0	3.84	5.75	15.73	1.72	81.9	73.0	9.0
2018	19.90	20.20	4.0	3.81	5.68	15.77	2.71	79.2	65.6	13.6
2019	20.40	20.74	4.0	3.81	5.65	17.67	3.43	86.6	69.8	16.8
2020[a]	21.00	21.47	3.9	3.75	5.64	17.35	3.76	82.6	64.7	17.9

[a]Preliminary data

Source The Author, based on BP (2020), Gaz-System (2021), GUS (2021), and PGNiG (2021)

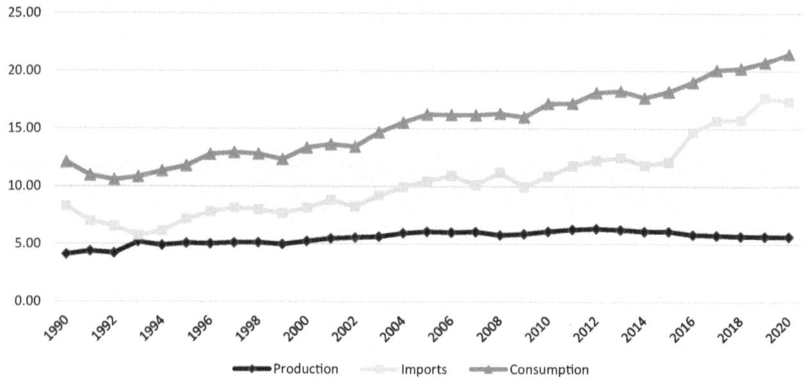

Fig. 7.1 Natural gas production, consumption and imports in Poland in 1990–2020 (bcm) (*Source* The Author, based on GUS, 2021)

by PGNiG is 25% (Biznes Alert, 2021), and the share of LNG in the total gas imported to Poland is 22%.[2]

As the purest fossil fuel, natural gas is used in many sectors of the economy. The level of natural gas penetration may vary from one country or region to another. In Poland, chemical industry is a large natural gas consumer for the production of plastics or artificial fertilizers. Industry, commercial and non-energy use account for more than 64% of the total demand for gas. Also the residential sector (almost 32%) is a major consumer of natural gas for heating and gas cookers (Polish Geological Institute, 2020). The use of gas for household needs in Poland is similar to the corresponding structure index in the world (29.3%). On the other hand, it is lower than in the EU (Fig. 7.2).

The shape of the Polish energy mix is one of the most important problems facing the domestic energy sector today. Looking from the perspective of the European Union countries, today Poland has the sixth largest energy sector. Nevertheless, it belongs to the group of the least energy-diversified countries of the old continent. As shown by the data from the Energy Forum published in the report 'Energy transformation in Poland, 2020 edition', the 2020 energy structure of Poland was based mainly on coal, which is responsible for 70% of electricity generated in

[2] In addition to PGNiG, a leading entity on the gas market in Poland, there are also smaller entities operating on this market.

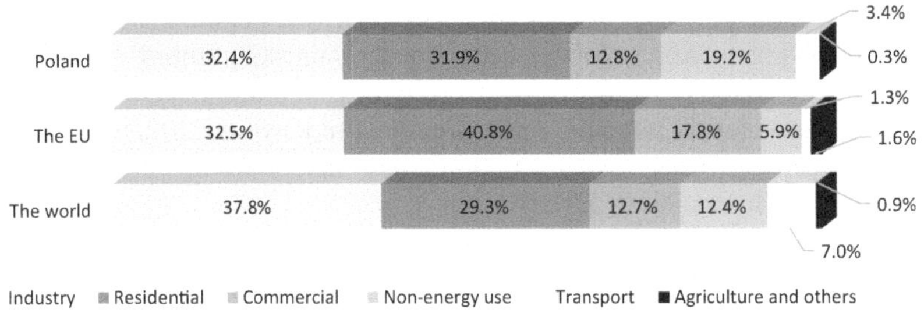

Fig. 7.2 Natural gas consumption by sector in Poland, the EU and the world in 2019 (*Source* The Author, based on Polish Geological Institute, 2020)

the country each year. RES accounted for 18%, natural gas 10% and other sources the remaining 2%. For a comparison, two years earlier, the share of coal was close to 80%, RES accounted for 8.6% and gas 5.8% respectively (wysokienapiecie.pl, 2021).

Such a large dependence of the Polish energy sector on coal—at a time when the EU expects the member states to transform towards climate neutrality and opt for cleaner energy sources—causes a number of challenges and complications for Poland. Hence, in the next decade, significant changes are planned in the structure of raw materials used to generate electricity. And these changes include successively increasing the share of renewable energy sources in the energy mix, for which natural gas would be the stabilising fuel. This was confirmed by Piotr Naimski, Secretary of State in the Chancellery of the Prime Minister and the government plenipotentiary for strategic energy infrastructure, who told the Rzeczpospolita daily: '*We assume that gas will be an important supplement to the system—complementing wind or photovoltaic sources. Therefore, gas installations are to be built, including two in Dolna Odra, 700 MW each. Gaz-System is already working on connecting the gas source to this power plant. Perhaps one or two more blocks will be built. Therefore, there will be more gas in the mix, it will play a stabilising role*' (Biznes Alert, 2019).[3]

The increased demand for gas is to be met thanks to additional sources, which will increase supplies by more than eight billion cubic metres by 2030. As explained by Piotr Naimski, ten billion cubic metres will reach Poland via Baltic Pipe, approximately 7.5 bcm from the Świnoujście

[3] A translation from the Polish language to English by the author.

LNG terminal and four billion cubic metres from Poland's own sources (domestic production). At the same time, Naimski pointed out that a decision has already been made to invest in a floating LNG terminal in the Gulf of Gdańsk, which is to be implemented around 2025, and from this source, approximately four billion cubic metres are to be supplied to the system (Biznes Alert, 2019).

Poland plans not only to increase purchases of sea-borne LNG, but also to secure natural gas pipeline deliveries from Norway through the Baltic Pipe. The construction of the pipeline has begun and it is the result of a joint venture between Poland's Gaz-System and Norway's Energinet. The pipe will have a potential capacity of up to ten billion cubic metres per year to Poland and up to three billion cubic metres per year to Denmark and Sweden. Baltic Pipe is expected to be completed in October 2022 (Gaz-System, 2021). Ultimately, the imports from Norway are to reach the level of the capacity reserved by PGNiG in Baltic Pipe, i.e. 8.3 bcm annually (PGNiG, 2021).

Poland will soon gain new connections with Lithuania and Slovakia. At the beginning of 2022, a connection with Slovakia is to be ready, which will enable imports from the southern direction up to 5.7 bcm per year. The gas pipeline connecting Poland and Lithuania should be put into operation soon after. The transmission capacity of this pipeline is to be 1.9 bcm of gas. GIPL is a bi-directional gas pipeline between Poland and Lithuania. The length of the pipeline is 508 kms (316 miles) and it will run from the Jauniūnai GCU in Lithuania to the Hołowczyce GCU on the Polish side. GIPL will also connect the Baltic States to the European natural gas pipeline system. The project is being implemented by gas transmission system operators Amber Grid (Lithuania) and Gaz-System (Poland). The construction of the gas pipeline started in October 2019. It is projected that the pipeline will be ready for operation by the end of 2021. Its commissioning is planned in stages in 2022 (GIPL, 2021).

The estimated value of the GIPL project is EUR 500 million. The project is financed by Gaz-System and Amber Grid, and it is co-financed with a significant grant from the EU. In addition, a part of investments in Poland is compensated by Estonia, Latvia and Lithuania. When GIPL will be established Lithuania together with other Baltic States and Finland will be integrated into the European Union gas transmission system (GIPL, 2021).

Entities from the Polish energy sector also undertake many activities aimed at achieving low-emission goals. For example, PGNiG promotes natural gas as a way to clean air. Natural gas is a relatively inexpensive, safe fuel that contributes to the development of a sustainable economy of the future and addresses the assumptions of the Paris Agreement. Generating electricity from natural gas practically does not emit sulphur dioxide or dust. Minor amounts of nitrogen oxides appear in the combustion process. Therefore, companies from the PGNiG Group implement a number of programmes encouraging customers and business partners to use gas. In addition to educational and informational programmes, co-financing for people interested in replacing heating sources from solid fuels to gas or implementing anti-smog measures, public transport powered by compressed natural gas (CNG) and LNG is also developing intensively (PGNiG, 2019).

The EU climate policy reform project proposed in December 2019 by Ursula von der Leyen assumes, inter alia, climate neutrality by 2050 and CO_2 reduction by 2030 by another 10–15%. In reducing emissions by the energy sector, an important role is played by the dissemination of renewable energy sources, in particular the use of solar and wind energy. According to PSE, the installed capacity of wind farms in Poland was 6.26 GW as of the beginning of September 2020 (Bojanowicz, 2020).[4] The earlier version of the draft 'Polish Energy Policy until 2040' assumed that all wind farms operating in Poland today will be scrapped by 2035, and no new windmills will be built in their place. The modified version of this document restores the possibilities of wind energy development—both on land and in the Baltic Sea.

After a period of stagnation, several entities started building new wind farms. For example, the Lithuanian energy concern the Ignitis Group is building a wind farm (the Pomerania power plant) with a capacity of 94 MW in the Pomeranian Voivodship (a Polish region). In June 2020, Polenergia signed a contract for the construction of a 121-MW Dębsko wind farm, and in July 2020, the Energa Group launched a 31-MW wind farm near Toruń. The companies Orlen, PGE and Polenergia declared that by 2025 they will build turbines in the Baltic Sea with a total capacity of 3,400 MW (Bojanowicz, 2020).

The updated draft of the 'Polish Energy Policy until 2040' assumes that construction of the first nuclear unit with a capacity of 1.0–1.5 GW

[4] PolskieSieciElektroenergetyczne (PSE), a sole proprietorship of the State Treasury, associated with the power industry in Poland, owner of the highest voltage (LV) grids in Poland.

is to begin in 2026 and will start operations in 2033. Subsequent blocks will be implemented every 2–3 years until 2043, and the entire nuclear programme involves the construction of six blocks (Polski Atom, 2021). Nuclear is to play an important role in a zero-emission energy system. The construction of 6–9 GW units in 2022–2043 is to cover approximately 14% of Poland's annual electricity demand in 2050. Unfortunately, one can have serious doubts as to the feasibility of this plan, as the first decision to build a nuclear power plant in Poland was made already in 1971. The investment started in 1982, but the project was closed in 1990. The topic of building at least two nuclear power plants returned in 2008. In 2010, the special purpose vehicle PGE EJ1 was established. Its task was to build the first Polish nuclear power plant with a capacity of three gigawatts at a cost of PLN 40–60 billion (some USD 10–16 billion). Electricity from nuclear power plants was supposed to start in 2020. Nothing came out of the aforementioned plans—despite incurring significant costs for preparatory works.

Construction of the LNG Terminal in Świnoujście

The LNG terminal in Świnoujście is a liquefied natural gas import terminal. It was developed by Gaz-System, a designated natural gas transmission system operator in Poland. Gas transmission operator Gaz-System has been operating since the 16th of April 2004. Upon its establishment, the company took over the responsibility for the transmission of natural gas and the management of the transmission network in Poland. In June 2004, President of the Energy Regulatory Office granted the company a gas transmission and distribution concession for the years 2004–2014, and on the 23rd of August 2010, extended the company's gas transmission concession until the 31st of December 2030. The company was set up as a wholly-owned subsidiary of PGNiG but in 2005 Gaz-System became a 100% state-owned company. Gaz-System owns and operates all gas transmission and distribution pipelines in Poland, except the Yamal-Europe pipeline owned by EuRoPol GAZ.[5]

[5] EuRoPol GAZ is the owner of the Polish part of the Yamal-Europe transit gas pipeline, one of the most advanced pipes and at the same time the largest energy investment in Europe at the turn of the twentieth and twenty-first centuries. The Polish section of the gas pipeline, approximately 684 kms long, transports natural gas for the needs of domestic and foreign customers. The company provides the free transmission capacity of the gas

The separation of the natural gas transmission operator resulted from the provisions of the Gas Directive adopted in 2003 by the Council and the European Parliament, which required technical separation of gas transmission from gas trading. Thus, this provision allows other economic entities to use the transmission network on an equal basis, i.e. the third party access (TPA). Under the Resolution of the Council of Ministers of the 19th of August 2008, Gaz-System became the owner of Polskie LNG—the company responsible for the construction and operation of the liquefied natural gas terminal in Świnoujście.

Discussions about the LNG terminal project started already in 2006. The project was originally developed by PGNiG. In January 2008, SNC-Lavalin was chosen for the front-end engineering design. The engineering, procurement and construction contract was signed with a consortium of Saipem, Techint, Snamprogetti and PBG. After the establishment of Gaz-System and its separation from PGNiG, the newly created company took over the project.

The terminal has unloading jetty for large LNG tankers, two storage tanks and a regasification train. The terminal's initial regasification capacity was five billion cubic metres per annum (180×10^9 cubic feet/annum), and with the construction of the third tank its capacity is due to expand to reach 7.5 bcm per annum (260×10^9 cubic feet/annum) (Zarzecki, 2015).

LNG terminals work as safety buffers which is why their capacities may not always be used in full. There is a margin of free capacity which can be used in emergency situations. For instance, in 2011, the British LNG import potential was used in 47%, and in France in 58%. Between 2008 and 2014, European LNG terminals experienced low utilisation rates, some below 20%. The year 2016 saw an average utilisation rate of 20%, with the European Commission stating that the LNG infrastructure in the EU was under-utilised and not optimally distributed (European Commission, 2016).

Needless to say that the use of LNG terminals also depends on gas prices (importer may expect lower prices of this commodity and wait for a more favourable economic situation) and on the season. Similar mechanisms apply in the LNG terminal in Świnoujście. Poland decided to

pipeline to the operator Gaz-System, which offers gas transmission services within the Transit Gas Pipeline System. The company's shareholders are PGNiG (48%), Gazprom (48%) and Gas-Trading (4%) (EuRoPol GAZ, 2021).

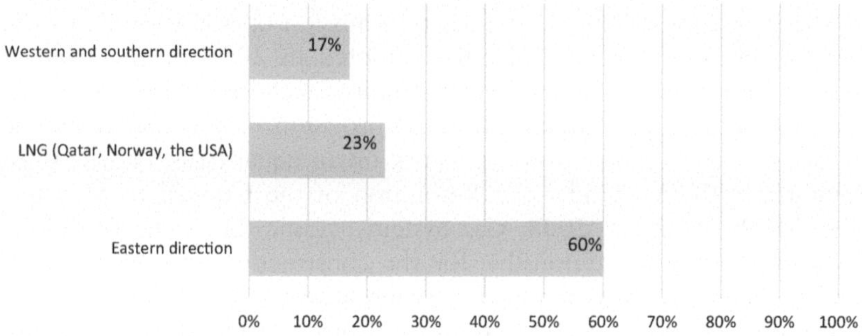

Fig. 7.3 The structure of Poland's supply of natural gas in 2019 (*Source* The Author, based on PGNiG, 2020; Polish Geological Institute, 2020)

build the LNG terminal in Świnoujście mainly for strategic reasons, as the facility allows diversification of national gas supplies. Therefore, Poland is able to develop its gas-based energy industry, modernise the chemical and fertilizer industry as well as expand transport using the advantages of LNG fuel. With the LNG terminal, it is easier and safer to enhance the development of ambitious economic plans (Polskie LNG, 2021a).

Owing to the LNG terminal in Świnoujście, is improving energy security of Poland and the region in Europe, which previously used supplies mainly from one direction. The surplus of gas fuel from the Świnoujście LNG terminal may be transported to the Baltic States and other countries.

Gas imports are still dominated by supplies from Russia, whose share in total imports in 2019 amounted to 60%.[6] Imports from the western and southern direction accounted for 17%, and sea-borne LNG imports were 23%, respectively (Fig. 7.3). These proportions remained almost the same in 2020: Russia 60%, LNG 25%, and the western and southern direction 15%. After the expiry of the Yamal contract, Russia's share will dramatically decrease in favour of the other two, i.e. LNG and imports via Baltic Pipe (Biznes Alert, 2021).

Interestingly, the longer the distance over which natural gas has to be moved, the more favourable are the economics of LNG over pipelines. Where producers have a choice between the two, the tendency to favour

[6] These numbers apply only to imports handled by PGNiG.

LNG has in practice been even stronger than a straight economic calculation might suggest. Price levels and regional market dynamics have been shifting rapidly over the past decade, so the option to switch destination that comes with LNG is increasingly seen as a critical advantage. Meanwhile, the interruptions to Russian supply to Europe since 2006, because of Russia's disputes with Ukraine and Belarus, have increased the perception of the risks associated with cross-border pipeline supply, particularly when transit through third countries is involved (IEA, 2014).

As already mentioned, in August 2008, the Polish Government adopted a resolution in which the construction of the LNG terminal was considered a strategic investment for the country's interest, in line with the plans to diversify the sources and routes of natural gas supply and to guarantee Poland's energy security. The launch of the LNG terminal in Świnoujście in 2016 was a revolutionary change on the Polish gas market. The diversification of the directions and sources of supplies of this raw material initiated a fundamental turn. This change is complemented by the investments undertaken by Gaz-System. First of all, a further expansion of the terminal and construction of the Baltic Pipe gas pipeline to create the so-called North Gate (Brama Północna) to change the direction of gas imports.

While LNG supply volumes are falling across Europe, the LNG terminal in Świnoujście enjoys 100% occupancy. Also before the pandemic, the terminal accepted more gas than similar installations in Europe and the world. In 2017, Gaz-System announced that the LNG terminal in Świnoujście had the highest level of utilisation in Europe, even though it was only 35%. A year later, the same happened again. Paweł Jakubowski, CEO of Polskie LNG, announced that the use of the terminal was 60–65%. This level was maintained in the following year, keeping the Polish gas terminal in the leading position. In 2020, despite the globally lowered demand for energy, including gas, the terminal had 100% reserved commercial capacity. On the 29th of May 2020, an agreement was signed for the regasification service between the company operating the terminal, Polskie LNG and PGNiG. No wonder that a decision was recently made to expand the facility, thanks to which it will increase the capacity from 5.0 bcm to 7.5 bcm per year. Analyses are even underway for further expansion to ten billion cubic metres (Energetyka24, 2020; Polskie LNG, 2021a).

In 2020, there were 36 LNG deliveries for PGNiG. Since its launch, a total of 114 deliveries of liquefied natural gas have taken place to the

Świnoujście terminal. The 100th gas delivery at the terminal was received in July 2020. The first commercial delivery was picked up in June 2016. The previous two loads, which arrived here at the turn of 2015 and 2016, were used for the technical start-up of the installation.

PGNiG's import portfolio currently includes contracts for the purchase of LNG from the Qatargas company from Qatar and four long-term contracts for the purchase of LNG produced in terminals located in the USA, concluded with Cheniere Energy, Venture Global LNG and Port Arthur LNG. The contract with Cheniere has been implemented since July 2019, and the implementation of further contracts with US companies is to begin in 2022–2024. As of today, PGNiG has signed contracts for supplies reaching around 12 bcm, starting from 2024. This is more than the maximum capacity of the Świnoujście gas terminal, therefore PGNiG intends to sell a part of the contracted gas on other markets (Furman, 2020).

On the 31st of March 2021, Gaz-System and Polskie LNG merged. The integration of entities carried out by Gaz-System should increase the efficiency of investment projects that were managed separately by both companies before the merger. The existing undertakings and activities of Polskie LNG will be continued by Gaz-System as the legal successor of Polskie LNG (WNP, 2021).

The Expansion of the LNG Terminal in Świnoujście

The expansion of the LNG terminal in Świnoujście is a part of the larger investment plan of the Gaz-System Capital Group called North Gate, under which the Polish gas system is to be prepared to reverse the direction of supply from the East–West relationship to the North–South. The gate also includes Baltic Pipe and North–South Corridor, as well as a number of accompanying investments. The construction of North Gate is inextricably linked with the Expansion Programme. Their joint implementation will significantly increase the security and energy independence of Poland and Central and Eastern Europe. Gaz-System implements the LNG Terminal Expansion Programme, which includes the following projects (Polskie LNG, 2021b):

(1) The SCV (submerged combustion vaporiser) project: The existing regasification installation will be expanded by two additional security vulnerability assessments (SVAs). The devices were ordered by Polskie LNG as a part of investor deliveries in October–November 2019. The selection of the contractor for the SCV project and signing the contract with the consortium of PORR companies and TGE Gas Engineering GmbH took place in February 2020. The scheduled completion date of this project is the end of 2021.
(2) The tank project: This project involves construction of a new LNG tank with a capacity of approximately 180,000 gross cubic metres with accompanying installations and devices and technological connection with the existing infrastructure. The contract for the implementation of this installation was signed in June 2020, and the investment completion date is the end of 2023.
(3) The quay project: A new quay will be built for unloading, loading and bunkering LNG along with a dedicated transmission flyover. The project is scheduled for completion by the end of 2023.
(4) The railway project (optional scope): In the longer term, it is planned to build a new LNG loading infrastructure in the onshore part (LNG reloading installation to rail tankers and ISO containers) along with a railway siding.[7]

There are many benefits of the expansion. First of all, the LNG Terminal Expansion Programme will contribute to the improvement of Poland's energy security and will make it possible to increase the level of diversification of natural gas supply sources for Poland and its neighbouring countries. In particular, the Expansion Programme will allow for (Polskie LNG, 2021b):

- increasing the amount of natural gas imported to Poland by at least 2.5 bcm/year from various directions of the world;

[7] An ISO container is an international intermodal container that is manufactured according to the specifications outlined by the International Organization for Standardization (ISO). ISO containers are suitable for ship, rail and truck. Container capacity is usually communicated in twenty-foot equivalent units (TEUs). ISO intermodal containers are used to transport cryogenic bulk liquids (argon, carbon dioxide, ethylene, LNG, methane, nitrogen, nitrous oxide and oxygen) worldwide by ship, rail or road (LaGore, 2020).

- increasing the nominal shipping capacity to 856,000 Nm^3/hour to the National Transmission System (a maximum target regasification capacity of the installation is 984,000 Nm^3/hour);
- improving the flexibility of operation of the LNG terminal by increasing the LNG process storage capacity to approximately 500,000 gross cubic metres;
- increasing the level of reliability and flexibility of receiving LNG deliveries;
- increasing the volume of LNG shipped by land and enabling shipment by sea;
- increase in revenues from the provision of new services: ship bunkering, LNG loading on small-scale, medium-scale and large-scale LNG vessels, LNG transshipment from ship to ship, LNG loading onto rail tankers and ISO containers (option); and
- development of infrastructure enabling greater use of LNG in the region.

Other benefits of the Expansion Programme include (Polskie LNG, 2021b):

- strengthening regional security of supply through diversification of supplies (an access to new sources of gas supplies);
- increasing the possibility of importing LNG on the spot market when there are seasonal price reductions;
- increasing competition on regional gas markets and facilitating price convergence between markets, enabling new participants to enter the market and a potential increase in gas demand in the regions affected by the expanded LNG terminal;
- increasing the technical reliability of gas supplies to customers by diversifying the methods of supplying imported gas;
- securing gas supplies in crisis and emergency situations;
- increasing the negotiating position in relation to current gas suppliers;
- significant increase in the operational reliability of the terminal by building an independent connection of the new quay with the terminal's onshore infrastructure, reducing harmful emissions to the environment by ensuring and increasing the availability of clean fuel;

- development of infrastructure related to bunkering of vessels in the Baltic Sea and Polish inland waters;
- development of infrastructure supporting the logistics of LNG supplies in the region;
- the basis for the development of local gas distribution networks in non-gasified areas of the country;
- avoiding the cost of interruptions in gas supplies to users;
- the possibility of Polish entities entering the LNG re-export market in the Baltic Sea basin;
- acquiring and educating qualified staff, thanks to which it will be possible to effectively implement further investments in the development of the LNG market in Poland; and
- the expansion of the LNG terminal may make Poland a leader in the LNG market in the Baltic Sea basin and indirectly contribute to the gasification of new areas of Poland (by creating conditions for LNG supplies to small regasification stations).

The expansion of the terminal is an important stage in the implementation by the Polish Government of a consistent, long-term and coherent strategy of actual diversification of energy supply sources. The extensive infrastructure for importing LNG will be used at least in the medium-term, making Poland independent of gas supplies from the East.

From the perspective of 2021, it is difficult to predict how the demand for gas in Europe will develop in the future. However, there are visible phenomena on the global market related to the process of decarbonisation and liberalisation of the market (EU Gas Directive), which may make it possible to satisfy the growing domestic demand with imports from more competitive sources. The ongoing expansion of the LNG terminal in Świnoujście offers more options for PGNiG to obtain gas on the global market.

Construction of New Gas Carriers for PGNiG

As a part of the continuation of the policy of strengthening the country's energy security, Poland has taken another important step towards securing the availability of a modern gas carrier fleet, which primarily services LNG imports to the terminal in Świnoujście. The Norwegian shipowner Knutsen OAS has just ordered gas carriers from the South Korean shipyard Hyundai Heavy Industries in Ulsan, intended for charter to the Polish PGNiG Group.[8] The ships ordered by Knutsen OAS Shipping, which are to be chartered to a company from the PGNiG Group, are to have a cargo capacity of 174,000 m^3. Gas carriers built for the needs of PGNiG will have a modern cargo re-liquefaction system. They will be the first in the world to receive a new generation Wärtsilä production system. The project of cryogenic membrane loading tanks has already been ordered for the new Knutsen gas carriers to which the charter agreement signed with the PGNiG Group applies (Stareńczak, 2020).

The PGNiG Group signed an agreement for a long-term charter of two gas carriers on the 3rd of November 2020. Chartered gas carriers will be used for trading in liquefied natural gas contracted with American producers, and the commissioning date will coincide with the commencement of operation of the Calcasieu Pass terminal, the first of two LNG exporting installations built by the American company Venture Global LNG, with which PGNiG has one of the long-term contracts signed.

At the beginning of November 2020, PGNiG announced that two modern tankers will enter service in 2023. The direct charterer is PGNiG Supply & Trading from London, which is part of the PGNiG Group. According to the contract with Knutsen OAS Shipping, the chartering period of both ships is ten years with an option to extend. The Norwegian shipowner will be responsible throughout the term of the contract for manning ships and taking care of the technical condition of the ships among other things (Stareńczak, 2020).

Floating Storage Regasification Unit in the Gulf of Gdańsk

Another key investment for Poland's energy security is also getting closer. In September 2020, a letter of intent was signed on the implementation of the programme for the construction of a floating LNG terminal in the Gulf of Gdańsk. FSRU is a ship that has the functions of LNG storage and regasification. For example, Lithuania has such a vessel in the port of Klaipeda, which has been operating since December 2014. Lithuania then became the fifth country in the world to use the FSRU. The investment in

[8] Gas carrier ships (gas tankers) are especially designed ocean-going vessels that are dedicated for transporting all types of liquefied natural gases and liquefied petroleum gases to their destinations. These ships are inbuilt with tankers of plain surface, spherical or cylindrical shape to carry the gas.

the FSRU in the gulf will enable the development of the LNG market in Central Europe and the Baltic Sea basin and contribute to strengthening Poland's energy security as well. The location of the FSRU unit in the Gulf of Gdańsk will increase the economic importance of this part of the Polish coast.

At the present stage, Gaz-System has assumed the construction of a unit with a capacity of 4.5 bcma in the Gulf of Gdańsk. The construction of the FSRU terminal as a new entry point to the national transmission system is a response to the growing domestic demand for natural gas. In 2020, the construction of a floating LNG terminal was placed on the fourth list of investments that received the status of PCI in the energy sector.[9]

Current Challenges and Opportunities in the Field of Energy

The role of gas will grow with the closure of more coal mines in Poland. In September 2020, representatives of the government and trade unions signed an agreement on the pace of transformation in the hard coal mining industry. In accordance with the adopted provisions, the closure of the mines will last until 2049. The social contract with the full schedule of the shutdown of mining was to be signed in December 2020. A month later, the government submitted a draft decommissioning 13 mines (Bankier.pl, 2021).

In the opinion of experts and trade unions, this document is full of gaps and inaccuracies, which calls into question the further transformation in the mining industry (Inwestycje.pl, 2021). The trade unions rejected the assumptions of the government's coal mining restructuring programme and they presented their own proposals in January 2021. Politically motivated keeping unprofitable mines alive for many years have resulted in a collapse in the Polish hard coal mining industry. The situation is dramatically bad at the moment. Many years have been wasted and there has been no planned, orderly restructuring and phasing out of this declining sector. The necessity to close coal mines results from the EU's decarbonisation policy but also from the increasing unprofitability of coal mining

[9] PCI projects are key infrastructure projects aimed at increasing the level of security on the European energy market. Their implementation is to support the energy policy and climate challenges in the EU.

in Polish mines. Of course, the shift away from coal is favourable to the use of natural gas. The trend of replacing coal with gas is already clearly visible in Poland and will continue to grow stronger.

Poland has gas storage facilities with a total capacity of 2.985 bcm. These include gas storage facilities in depleted gas fields: Wierzchowice (1.2 bcm), Husów (0.5 bcm), Strachocina (0.360 bcm), Brzeźnica (0.1 bcm) and Swarzów (0.090 bcm), as well as in leached caverns from salt deposits: Mogilno (0.598 bcm) and Kosakowo (0.145 bcm). Due to the reduction in Russian gas supplies via the Yamal gas pipeline, it will be necessary to ensure greater flexibility of the transmission system in the event of interruptions in supplies from the East. Therefore, the expansion of gas storage facilities should be another element of the diversification of gas sources and ensuring the security of gas supply. It will also be important for the operational flexibility of Baltic Pipe going ashore in Niechorze, the LNG terminal in Świnoujście and the FSRU in the Gulf of Gdańsk. Therefore, storage capacity should be increased with an emphasis on the greatest possible use of caverns. Poland intends to expand its storage capacity. The storage system operator—Gas Storage Poland from the PGNiG Group—plans to expand the gas storage facilities in Mogilno to 0.8 bcm in 2028 and Kosakowo up to 0.3 bcm around 2035. The operator of gas storage facilities in Poland, Gas Storage Poland (a subsidiary of PGNiG), also intends to expand the Wierzchowice storage facility to as much as 2–3 bcm (Biznes Alert, 2020).

Competition for the continued use of natural gas, including LNG, is the development of other energy sources that may replace the current sources in the near or distant future. One of such energy sources is hydrogen. This technology is gaining more popularity in many countries. Japan is a good example here. Japan's goal of transforming into 'a hydrogen society' became closer in October 2020, when Prime Minister Yoshihide Suga announced that the country would strive to become carbon neutral by 2050. While renewable energy solutions are seen worldwide as the answer to carbon emissions, Japan has also been striving to build a hydrogen-based society. The high cost of hydrogen power generation also put the fuel at a disadvantage to LNG, which has long been touted as the bridging fuel to a green energy future. Bloomberg New Energy Finance's Hydrogen Economy Outlook found that green hydrogen production in Australia could cost USD 8–14/MBtu by 2050. While LNG prices soared to new highs in the last decade, driven partially by the Fukushima NPP disaster, they have since retreated and are currently around USD 7.50/MBtu. There are other power generation alternatives, including nuclear, but the wholesale and retail gas markets will face increasing pressure from 2030 because of emissions targets. By embracing methanation, the gas sector would be able to adapt and convert existing infrastructure and create a long-term business model. The catalytic methanation process uses hydrogen and CO_2 to create synthetic methane, which can be piped into existing gas grids. Takeo Kikkawa, Professor of International Management studies at the International University of Japan, has stated: '*This is a very important technology and could pave the way for a switch to 100% hydrogen use in the gas grids*' (Kemp, 2020, 55).

Poland also intends to implement hydrogen as an important energy source in the future. On the 14th of January 2021, the Ministry of Climate and Environment of Poland submitted for public consultation the draft of 'Polish Hydrogen Strategy until 2030 with a perspective until 2040'. This document sets ambitious goals for the development of the use of hydrogen technologies in Poland. The project defines goals and activities related to the development of national competences and technologies to build a low-emission hydrogen economy. They relate to the three sectors of hydrogen use: (1) energy, (2) transport and (3) industry, as well as to its production, distribution and the necessary legal changes and financing (MinisterstwoKlimatuiŚrodowiska, 2021).

Different decarbonisation options, such as gas switching to biomethane or hydrogen, will vary across regions. If the solution is switching to hydrogen, it will be less costly for distribution companies to make the necessary adjustments to the distribution network than it will be for the larger long-distance transmission systems. At the same time, an upgrade or refurbishment of transmission grids would almost certainly require the simultaneous upgrade or refurbishment of all the networks they supply. Based on the future potential of hydrogen production (especially if only green hydrogen is considered), it remains to be seen to what extent substantial transmission infrastructure would be used for transporting hydrogen over long distances (MinisterstwoKlimatuiŚrodowiska, 2021).[10]

[10] Green hydrogen is the production of hydrogen from renewable energy through electrolysis. It is a process that splits water into its basic elements—hydrogen and oxygen—using an electric current. The electricity used in the process comes from renewables. As the greenhouse gasses are captured, this mitigates the environmental impacts on the

Gas continues to increase its share of the global energy market. In fact, it is the only fossil fuel whose share is increasing. Even when considering significant sensitivities, gas demand remain robust within a ± 3-percent-range until 2035. In the long term (after 2035), gas demand will probably decline overall. It is particularly under pressure in the power sector, where the share of total demand is expected to drop from 41% in 2015 to 33% in 2050 (McKinsey, 2019).

Up until 2030, the demand for natural gas is projected to remain stable or to decrease slightly. Switching to natural gas-fired power plants can represent a short-term or medium-term solution for countries going through a coal phase-out. Gas can also contribute to the flexibility in the power sector necessitated by the increasing share of variable renewables, such as wind and solar. The demand projections for 2050 show more significant differences between results. The higher the assumed 2050 GHG emissions reduction target in the scenario, the lower the projected demand for natural gas will be. As the EU moves towards its 2050 targets, a mix of low and zero-carbon gaseous fuels, such as biogas, biomethane, blue and green hydrogen, and synthetic methane, are expected to replace natural gas. Biogas and biomethane are currently the most commercially ready alternatives to natural gas and require no major infrastructural upgrades. However, their production will be limited by the availability of feedstock and regional contexts. Hydrogen can also be produced to replace the use of natural gas (Catuti et al., 2019).

Projections of demand for gas in 2040 and 2050 vary significantly between scenarios, but the majority indicate a continuous decline in gas consumption. The share of natural gas will strongly decrease, while the overall demand for gas, including multiple other 'gaseous fuels' (biogas, biomethane, hydrogen and synthetic methane) will depend on a number of factors including costs, availability, acceptability, end-uses, infrastructure developments and policy decisions. The results of scenario projections vary based on the assumptions made about the levels of GHG

planet. Blue hydrogen is derived from natural gas through the process of steam methane reforming (SMR) or auto thermal reforming (ATR). SMR mixes natural gas with very hot steam, in the presence of a catalyst, where a chemical reaction creates hydrogen and carbon monoxide. Additional water is added to the mixture converting the carbon monoxide to carbon dioxide and creating more hydrogen. The carbon dioxide emissions produced are then captured and stored underground using carbon capture, utilisation and storage (CCUS) technology leaving nearly pure hydrogen (Haynes, 2021).

emissions reduction. Scenarios targeting at least minus 80% GHG emissions foresee a strong decrease in natural gas consumption, but only scenarios consistent with a 95–100% reduction in GHG emissions project a near-complete phase-out of natural gas. Achieving net-zero GHG emissions in the EU by 2050 will almost certainly require the development of renewable and low-carbon forms of gases, such as biogas, biomethane, hydrogen or synthetic methane to replace much of the natural gas consumption. The future position of natural gas in the fuel mix beyond the 2040–2050 period (for example for the production of blue hydrogen) will be linked with the large-scale deployment of carbon capture and storage technology (Catuti et al., 2019).

Any new investments in natural gas also need to consider the developments in the sector after 2030. Despite its advantages compared to coal, natural gas is also a fossil fuel and its combustion still produces CO_2 emissions, which may not be fully eliminated even with the use of CCS (carbon capture and storage). This may become more problematic in the context of stricter future GHG emissions reduction targets. Consequently, in a 2050 net-zero emissions energy system, the future of the gas industry is linked with its ability to be fully decarbonised. Without this, the future of gas demand may decline sharply after 2030. In the long term, renewable methane and hydrogen can provide carbon emissions-free alternatives to natural gas (Catuti et al., 2019).

As shown by the IEA (2019), given the existing infrastructure, the EU has one of the highest potentials in the world for switching from coal to gas-fired power generation, which can provide rapid emissions reductions. However, the window of opportunity for such a choice is limited. After 2030, natural gas investments are increasingly facing the risk of stranded assets, given the long lifetime of gas infrastructure projects. New gas-powered generators have a lifespan of 20 years, large pipelines and LNG projects are normally designed to run more than two decades, while storage can potentially be functional for up to 40–50 years (Stern, 2019). In a list of Projects of Common Interest published by the Commission in 2017, 53 PCIs were gas projects (European Commission, 2017). This raised questions about the long-term implications of these gas infrastructure investments, both in terms of potentially stranded assets and value added, for decarbonisation efforts in a long-term perspective. Most projections indicate a decline in demand for gas by 2040 and 2050. There may be increases in demand in individual sectors, but overall, the future consumption of gas is generally predicted to fall (Catuti et al., 2019).

Increasingly on the agenda when companies plan their futures and assess their financial results, is decarbonisation and low carbon targets, and the LNG sector is not detached from these goals. LNG is frequently described as a clean fuel, due to the fact it produces the lowest levels of greenhouse gas emissions and air pollutants than those of other fossil fuels. Consequently, LNG is forecast to be increasingly utilised as companies strive to reduce their carbon footprints and emit less harmful emissions.

Most projections indicate a decline in demand for gas by 2040 and 2050. There may be increases in demand in individual sectors, but overall, the future consumption of gas is generally predicted to fall. Europe's choice of promoting energy efficiency measures and the electrification of end-users will create further pressures on gas demand. As a result of forecasting a decreased demand for gas, some studies do not recommend any large-scale natural gas infrastructure investments (with the exception of a few LNG terminals), as all future consumption needs can be served using the existing infrastructure. New projects may be able to improve security of supply and improve the functioning of the internal market, but investments would need to be made based on careful evaluation (IEA, 2019). Future investments will also need to take into account not only the future demand for gas, but also the type of gaseous fuels that need to be developed in the context of a decarbonised European economy (Catuti et al., 2019).

Summary and Final Comments

As of the 1st of January 2019, the total world proved reserves of natural gas reached approximately 200,000 bcm (EIA, 2020). At current rates of production and consumption, the worldwide reserves of natural gas are sufficient to last about 50 years at the current consumption level, excluding unproved reserves.

Global gas demand fell by an estimated 2.5% or 100 bcm in 2020—its largest drop on record. Amid this slowdown, gas demand for power generation remained resilient owing to fuel switching, while the whole supply chain showed strong flexibility in adjusting to demand variations. Gas trade globalisation progressed with increasing liquidity, while prices experienced historical lows and extreme volatility. The COVID-19 crisis and a well-supplied market put investment on hold, whereas gas market reforms and clean gas policy initiatives gained momentum in major consuming markets (IEA, 2021).

Global LNG trade reached 360 mt in 2020, an increase of 5.3 mt since 2019 and 46.2 mt since 2018. LNG demand is expected to grow steadily with a supply–demand gap estimated to emerge in the middle of the present decade. With an increasing number of buyers and suppliers, the industry has evolved to offer a wider choice of commercial structures to meet changing needs. Against a backdrop of increasing net-zero emissions targets, the industry will need to further innovate to offer cleaner energy supply. It was the seventh year of consecutive growth in LNG trade. It goes without doubt that gas and LNG have a key role to play in a decarbonising world. LNG demand continued to grow despite the global pandemic and ensuing economic crisis. Global LNG prices hit a record low before rebounding to hit a record high in January 2021.[11] New LNG supply investment decisions ground to a halt. Nearly half of gas demand growth in the next 20 years expected to come from Asia (RD Shell, 2021).

In April 2016, the LNG terminal in Świnoujście was put into operation. It was the first large onshore LNG import terminal in Poland and in the Baltic Sea basin as a whole. The commercial operation of the terminal was launched on the 1st of June 2016. The construction of infrastructure in Świnoujście, enabling the collection of liquefied natural gas from any direction in the world, means that Poland currently has the most modern LNG receiving infrastructure with the highest development potential among the countries of the Baltic Sea basin.

In recent years, Poland has taken active measures to diversify its natural gas supplies. The gas contracts signed between PGNiG and American companies are of strategic importance, as they allow for a change in the strategic supplier of natural gas to Poland after 2022, or at least to somehow balance the situation, which will probably enable the effective renegotiation of gas supply conditions from the eastern direction. It would not be possible if the LNG terminal in Świnoujście had not been built.

[11] Asian spot LNG prices have risen to unprecedented levels due to the February 2021 cargo shortages, transportation bottlenecks, supply outages and record winter temperatures boosting end-user demand. The S&P Global Platts JKM for February was assessed at a record high of USD 32.494/MBtu on 12th of January 2021. This was the highest for the LNG benchmark for Asian spot LNG since it was launched in early 2009 (Yep, 2021).

During 2021–2022, Poland will be able to import from Russia up to 10.2 bcm of gas annually under the Yamal contract. This is half of Poland's demand. From the beginning of 2023, supplies from the East are to be replaced mainly by imports via Baltic Pipe and the LNG terminal in Świnoujście. Baltic Pipe is currently at the construction stage. The implementation of this project is in line with the assumptions adopted by Gaz-System. Thus, the date of putting it into operation, set for the 1st of October 2022 is not threatened. Thanks to the investment worth approximately EUR 1.6 billion, Poland and Denmark will gain access to Norwegian deposits. This will enable Poland to import up to ten billion cubic metres of gas. The second key diversification project concerns the expansion of the LNG terminal. Also in this case, the implementation of the project is proceeding according to the schedule. The first stage of the investment is to be completed in December 2021. Already then, as mentioned earlier, the terminal's handling capacity will increase from 5.0 bcm to 7.5 bcm. In the second stage, the completion of which is planned for the end of 2023, the import capacity is to reach 8.3 bcm (Furman, 2020).

Poland definitely and consistently focuses on the use of LNG. This source of energy will play an increasingly important role in the Polish energy mix—at least in the medium term. This is evidenced by the very high level of utilisation of the current handling capacity of the terminal in Świnoujście. Despite the already implemented programme of its expansion, an option of further expansion to ten billion cubic metres is being considered. Moreover, it is planned to launch a floating storage regasification unit in the Gulf of Gdańsk with a transshipment capacity of 4.5 bcm. Therefore, Poland is likely to increase its LNG import infrastructure from five billion cubic metres at present to even 14.5 bcm.

The already completed and planned investments in the LNG terminal in Świnoujście and in the floating LNG terminal in the Gulf of Gdańsk indicate the government's determination to make LNG an important source of energy in Poland for at least the next 20 years. The actual use of natural gas in Poland, including that imported in a liquid form via LNG terminals, is obviously an open question and will depend on many factors, which were mentioned earlier. There is no doubt, however, that having a modern LNG terminal in Świnoujście with a transshipment capacity of 7.5 bcm (and ultimately even 10.0 bcm) and a planned new floating terminal in the Gulf of Gdańsk with a regasification capacity of 4.5 bcm provides Poland with a real diversification, both in terms of energy sources and directions of supply. Investments in LNG infrastructure thus serve to strengthen Poland's energy security. At the same time, basing the country's energy strategy on the extensive use of LNG is in line with the current trends in the world and the policy of the European Union.

References

Bankier.pl. (2021, January 13). *Górnicze związki odrzuciły rządowy projekt umowy społecznej*. https://www.bankier.pl/wiadomosc/Gornicze-zwiazki-odrzucily-rzadowy-projekt-umowy-spolecznej-8036185.html. Accessed 1 March 2021.

Biznes Alert. (2019, August 20). *Naimski: Nie przestawimy energetyki na gaz*. https://biznesalert.pl/namiski-energetyka-gaz/. Accessed 2 February 2021.

Biznes Alert (2020, January 16). *Jakóbik: Polska potrzebuje większych magazynów gazu (ANALIZA)*. https://biznesalert.pl/magazyny-gazu-polska-rozbudowa-damaslawek-mogilno-kosakowo-energetyka-gaz/. Accessed 23 March 2021.

Biznes Alert. (2021, February 4). *Jedna czwarta importu PGNiG to LNG. Kontrakt jamalski blokuje głębsze zmiany*. https://biznesalert.pl/pgnig-import-gaz-2020-25-procent-lng-60-procent-z-rosji-energetyka-gaz/. Accessed 3 April 2021.

Bojanowicz, J. (2020, November 1). Energetyka w rozkroku. *Przegląd Techniczny*, pp. 18–19.

BP. (2020). *Statistical review of world energy*. https://www.bp.com/content/dam/bp/business-sites/en/global/corporate/pdfs/energy-economics/statistical-review/bp-stats-review-2020-full-report.pdf. Accessed 14 March 2021.

Catuti, M., Egenhofer, C., & Elkerbout, M. (2019, August). *The future of gas in Europe: Review of recent studies on the future of gas* (CEPS. Research Report. No. 2019/03).

EIA. (2020). *What is the volume of world natural gas reserves?* U.S. Energy Information Agency. https://www.eia.gov/tools/faqs/faq.php?id=52&t=8. Accessed 2 February 2021.

Energetyka24. (2020, June 5). *Nadzwyczajne wykorzystanie terminala LNG w Świnoujściu na tle Europy* [KOMENTARZ]. https://www.energetyka24.com/terminal-lng-w-swinoujsciu-z-najwiekszym-wykorzystaniem-w-europie-komentarz. Accessed 23 March 2021.

European Commission. (2016). *Liquefied Natural Gas and gas storage will boost EU's energy security*. https://ec.europa.eu/commission/presscorner/detail/hu/MEMO_16_310. Accessed 2 February 2021.

European Commission. (2017, November 23). *Staff Working Document accompanying the document Commission Delegated Regulation amending Regulation (EU) No 347/2013 of the European Parliament and of the Council as regards the Union list of projects of common interest* (SWD [2017] 425 Final). Brussels.

European Commission. (2020). *EU energy in figures 2020: Statistical pocketbook 2020.* https://op.europa.eu/en/publication-detail/-/publication/87b16988-f740-11ea-991b-01aa75ed71a1/language-en?WT.mc_id=Searchresult&WT.ria_c=37085&WT.ria_f=3608&WT.ria_ev=search. Accessed 21 March 2021.

EuRoPol GAZ. (2021). https://www.europolgaz.com.pl/o-firmie/informacje-podstawowe. Accessed 21 March 2021.

Furman, T. (2020, December 30). *Polsce nie zabraknie gazu po zakończeniu importu z Rosji. Parkiet.* https://www.parkiet.com/Surowce-i-paliwa/312309995-Polsce-nie-zabraknie-gazu-po-zakonczeniu-importu-z-Rosji.html. Accessed 15 March 2021.

Gaz-System. (2021). https://www.gaz-system.pl. Accessed 3 April 2021.

GIPL. (2021). *Gas interconnection Poland–Lithuania*. https://en.wikipedia.org/wiki/Gas_Interconnection_Poland%E2%80%93Lithuania. Accessed 15 March 2021.

GUS. (2021). *Zużycie, produkcjai import gazu w Polsce w okresie 1990–2020.* Badania GUS i Ministerstwa Klimatu i Środowiska.

Haynes, A. (2021). *The difference between green hydrogen and blue hydrogen.* https://www.petrofac.com/en-gb/media/our-stories/the-difference-between-green-hydrogen-and-blue-hydrogen/. Accessed 14 March 2021.

IEA. (2014). *World energy investment outlook 2014.* OECD/International Energy Agency.

IEA. (2019). *The role of gas in today's energy transitions.* International Energy Agency. https://www.iea.org/reports/the-role-of-gas-in-todays-energy-transitions. Accessed 2 February 2021.

IEA. (2021). *Gas Market Report, Q1-2021.* https://www.iea.org/reports/gas-market-report-q1-2021. Accessed 22 March 2021.

Inwestycje.pl. (2021, January 13). *Strona związkowa przedstawi własny plan restrukturyzacji górnictwa węgla.* https://inwestycje.pl/biznes/strona-zwiazkowa-przedstawi-wlasny-plan-restrukturyzacji-gornictwa-wegla/. Accessed 1 March 2021.

Kemp, A. (2020). Japan's hydrogen plans may need creative touch. *Global Voice of Gas, 1*(2), 53–55.

LaGore, R. (2020). *ISO container definition and facts in 100 words.* https://blog.intekfreight-logistics.com/iso-container-defined-and-facts. Accessed 21 March 2021.

Liuhto, K. (2020, August 1). *Natural gas in the Baltic Sea region: A special emphasis on liquefied natural gas (LNG). A slide package.* https://www.res

earchgate.net/publication/343350581_Natural_gas_in_the_Baltic_Sea_region_A_special_emphasis_on_liquefied_natural_gas_LNG. Accessed 26 March 2021.

McKinsey. (2019, January). *Global energy perspective 2019: Reference case*. Energy Insights by McKinsey. https://www.mckinsey.com/~/media/McKinsey/Industries/Oil%20and%20Gas/Our%20Insights/Global%20Energy%20Perspective%202019/McKinsey-Energy-Insights-Global-Energy-Perspective-2019_Reference-Case-Summary.ashx. Accessed 2 February 2021.

Ministerstwo Klimatu i Środowiska. (2021). *Rozpoczęły się konsultacje publiczne projektu „Polskiej Strategii Wodorowej"*. https://www.gov.pl/web/klimat/rozpoczely-sie-konsultacje-publiczne-projektu-polskiej-strategii-wodorowej. Accessed 2 February 2021.

PGNiG. (2019). *W kierunku energii przyszłości. Innowacje w sektorze gazu, paliw i energii*. https://www.cire.pl/pokaz-pdf-%252Fpliki%252F2%252F2019%252Fraport_innowacje_2019.pdf. Accessed 2 February 2021.

PGNiG. (2020). *Polskie Górnictwo Naftowe i Gazownictwo SA*. https://pgnig.pl/documents/10184/2776740/Company+Overview_PL_Wrzesie%C5%84_2020.pdf/8636c0ca-7958-472c-8ddf-ef2d6dc2c355. Accessed 23 March 2021.

PGNiG. (2021). *Investor relations*. https://en.pgnig.pl/investor-relations. Accessed 21 March 2021.

Polish Geological Institute. (2020). *Crude oil and natural gas*. https://www.pgi.gov.pl/dokumenty-pig-pib-all/foldery-instytutowe/foldery-surowcowe-2020/8049-folder-gaz-i-ropa-2020/file.html. Accessed 3 April 2021.

Polski Atom. (2021). *Uchwała w sprawie „Polityki energetycznej Polski do 2040 r"*. https://www.gov.pl/web/polski-atom/uchwala-w-sprawie-polityki-energetycznej-polski-do-2040-r. Accessed 26 March 2021.

Polskie LNG. (2021a). https://en.polskielng.pl/. Accessed 1 March 2021.

Polskie LNG. (2021b). *Informacje o spółce*. https://www.polskielng.pl/o-firmie/polskie-lng-sa-informacje-o-spolce/. Accessed 3 April 2021.

RD Shell. (2021). *Shell LNG outlook 2021*. https://www.shell.com/promos/energy-and-innovation/download-the-shell-lng-outlook-2021/_jcr_content.stream/1614823770264/2b5b3fdaa9feba85dadc9b3408c200f26eadf85f/lng-outlook-2021-final-pack-updated.pdf. Accessed 26 March 2021.

Stareńczak, P. B. (2020, December 14). *Takie będą pierwsze gazowce LNG czarterowane przez PGNiG*. PortalMorski.pl. https://www.portalmorski.pl/m-zegluga/47078-jak-beda-wygladaly-pierwsze-gazowce-lng-czarterowane-przez-pgnig. Accessed 3 April 2021.

Stern, J. (2019). *Narratives for natural gas in decarbonising European energy markets* (OIES Paper: NG 141/2019). The Oxford Institute for Energy Studies.

Tusiani, M. D., & Shearer, G. (2007). *LNG: Nontechnical guide*. PennWell.

WNP. (2021). *Połączenie spółek Gaz-System i Polskie LNG*. https://www.wnp.pl/gazownictwo/polaczenie-spolek-gaz-system-i-polskie-lng,459879.html. Accessed 2 April 2021.

wysokienapiecie.pl. (2021, February 12). *Źródła energii w Polsce w 2020: mniej węgla, więcej gazu i OZE*. https://wysokienapiecie.pl/35619-zrodla-energii-w-polsce-w-2020-mniej-wegla-wiecej-gazu-oze/. Accessed 23 March 2021.

Yep, E. (2021, January 13). *Factbox: Asian spot LNG prices hit record highs on supply glitches, demand spike*. S&P Global. https://www.spglobal.com/platts/en/market-insights/latest-news/natural-gas/011321-factbox-asian-spot-lng-prices-hit-record-highs-on-supply-glitches-demand-spike. Accessed 23 March 2021.

Zarzecki, D. (2015). The role of the Świnoujście LNG terminal in security of gas supplies. In K. Liuhto (Ed.), *Natural gas revolution and the Baltic Sea region* (BSR Policy Briefing 1/2015). Centrum Balticum Foundation. https://www.centrumbalticum.org/files/1910/BSR_policy_briefing_1_2015.pdf. Accessed 2 February 2021.

CHAPTER 8

The Klaipeda LNG Terminal and Its Impact on the Baltic States' Gas Market

Tadas Jakštas

Introduction

The Baltic States are often considered as "energy islands" in the EU. The concept of the "island" implies exclusion and isolation as well as a lack of choice in terms of origins of supplies. As "energy islands" these countries are physically disconnected from the EU energy market, meaning there are no interconnecting energy infrastructure between those countries and the rest of the European Union, and in the case of energy, this includes a factor of dependence either from a single supplier or from a single type of fuel. This issue of single supplier has been especially crucial in the gas sector. Until recently, the Baltic States depended almost entirely on Russia for their natural gas imports (Directorate-General for Energy, 2018; Eurostat, 2019).[1] This dependence meant that Russia was in the

[1] In 2018, 11 EU member states, namely Austria, Bulgaria, Czechia, Estonia, Finland, Hungary, Latvia, Poland, Romania, Slovakia, and Slovenia imported more than 75% of their natural gas imports from Russia (Eurostat, 2019).

T. Jakštas (✉)
Vilnius, Lithuania

K. Liuhto (ed.), *The Future of Energy Consumption, Security and Natural Gas*, https://doi.org/10.1007/978-3-030-80367-4_8

position to politically dictate gas prices and manipulate conditions of gas supplies in the Baltic States.

Nevertheless, in the past half a decade, the three Baltic States, namely Estonia, Latvia, and Lithuania, have made important progress towards diversifying their energy supplies, especially of natural gas. This progress was brought about because of remarkable political will as well as improved regional co-operation has resulted in considerable economic benefit while decreasing these countries' vulnerability to outside pressure.

For example, the security of gas supply and gas supply resilience in the Baltic States has considerably improved since 2015 as the result of the opening of the LNG terminal "Independence" in Klaipeda, Lithuania. The construction of the LNG terminal in Lithuania was an important milestone for the implementation of other important internal gas infrastructure projects, which all contributed to increase in the security of gas supply in the region. For example, with the opening of the LNG terminal in Klaipeda, the enhancement of the Klaipeda-Kiemenai pipeline's capacity, which is essential for trading gas between Lithuania and Latvia was implemented.[2] Therefore, with the construction of the LNG terminal and other gas infrastructure as well as the adoption of new EU energy laws, the Russian gas monopoly in Lithuania and other Baltic States has been broken. In addition, LNG raised a feeling of the consumer's self-confidence.

However, despite evident progress in ensuring the security of gas supplies in recent years, the LNG saga also raises some questions for the Baltic States. One of the challenges is that the construction and operation of the LNG terminal in Klaipeda raises some political tensions among the Baltic States. Sharing infrastructure and related benefits or burden could become acceptable for Estonia, Latvia, and Lithuania only if consumers accept related costs naturally. According to Molis (2016, 93), "*this would be possible if LNG terminal in Klaipeda, Inčukalns underground gas storage and other facilities offer services or commodity (natural gas) under acceptable conditions or there is an agreement to use and maintain infrastructure jointly*". Another challenge is that the burden of the infrastructure maintenance compromised the whole idea of the gas consumption. The problem is that despite huge investments in gas infrastructure, the consumption of natural gas in the past 3–5 years

[2] The length of the pipeline is around 110 kms. Maximum technical capacity is up to 11 million Nm^3 of gas per day.

has gradually been falling in the region due to the comparatively high prices and increased consumption of biofuels in the heating sector (Molis, 2016). Moreover, there is a growing uncertainty of the role of gas in the EU as the European Commission is trying to enforce new stricter environmental and climate laws in support of new Green Deal.

Despite the evident progress in ensuring the security of gas supplies, much remains to be done to complete the three countries' internal gas markets into one competitive regional market. There are certainly signs of excellent co-operation on a working level among the three Baltic States as well as Poland and Finland. On the other hand, there is a lack of consensus on some of important steps that need to be implemented. For example, the Baltic States and Finland need to find an agreement over market design of the regional gas market as well as the development of new regional infrastructure.

Recently signed Memorandum of Understanding between gas transmission operators in Finland, Latvia, and Estonia aims to set up a single gas transmission tariff zone for the three countries from the start of 2020 which is an important step to implement plans in time for the creation of a common market in 2022. Because of common entry–exit zone, these three countries will have common entry points for pipeline access. Nevertheless, disagreements remain over the exact design of the future gas market in the region, especially with regard to the inter-transmission system compensation mechanism, partly concerning the sharing revenues of the Baltic TSO (Jegelevicius & Powell, 2019).

For example, Lithuania participated in single gas transmission tariff zone negotiations until 2017. Nevertheless, at the later stage of these negotiations, Lithuania decided to discontinue its participation in the entry-exit zone. According to some Lithuanian officials from the Ministry of Energy, Lithuania decided to discontinue its participation in the entry–exit zone as the current market design proposed by its neighbours do not ensure fair and balanced economic gains to all countries in the region. According to spokesman of Lithuania's Energy Ministry, "… *under the current conditions Lithuania would suffer significant financial losses*" (Jegelevicius & Powell, 2019).

Moreover, Lithuania proposes to set the tariffs for the entry capacity products from Belarus at the same level as the Finland–Estonia–Latvia entry/exit zone. A discount would be applied at the entry point from the LNG terminal in Klaipeda to the Lithuanian entry/exit zone. However, Latvia disagrees, claiming a zero tariff is not in its interest (Jegelevicius &

Powell, 2019). According to spokesman of Lithuania's energy ministry, "*Lithuania remains open to the idea that a separate cost-benefits analysis should be performed by an independent body such as the European Commission. Such analysis would determine, what would be the most balanced and correct inter-transmission system mechanism to expect from the perspective of all four countries*" (Jegelevicius & Powell, 2019).

The aim of this chapter is to assess the impact of the construction of the Klaipeda LNG for the security of supply and the development of gas market in the Baltics. The author starts by providing a historical overview of energy security situation in the Baltic States. Then, he shortly explores the technical specifications of the Klaipeda LNG terminal. Thereafter, the author assesses the contributions of the LNG terminal to energy security and creation of gas market in the region. Then, he analyses current and future challenges and uncertainties with regard to the usage of LNG in the Baltic States. Finally, the main conclusions are drawn.

Historical Insecurity and Asymmetrical Gas Dependence

Dependence on Monopolistic Gas Supplier

For years, Lithuania and its Baltic neighbours, Estonia and Latvia, have been extremely vulnerable to Russia's gas pressure. The Baltic States have relied on Russia for 100% of their natural gas (receiving Russian gas via the Soviet-era pipeline system). Moreover, Russia repeatedly has increased its gas prices to Lithuania and other Baltic States at times of political tension with them. For example, Gazprom boosted its price to Lithuania to one of the highest in Europe when the Lithuanian Government showed its determination to implement the European Union's anti-monopoly regulation, specifically the Third Energy Package that forces gas supply companies, such as Gazprom, to divest from their ownership of pipeline systems (Grigas, 2014). For example, in 2013, Lithuania paid the highest gas price in the EU. Interestingly in 2013, Lithuania and two other Baltic States paid around USD 500 per 1,000 cubic metres well beyond the average price paid by such countries as Austria, France, and Germany. As James Henderson, an oil and gas industry expert at the Oxford Institute for Energy Studies, pointed out that "*Gazprom prices according to what the alternatives in those countries. It essentially acts as a discriminating monopolist. If it has a significant market share in a country, or if it can see that a country has limited alternatives, then it prices accordingly*" (Kates & Luo, 2014).

Liberalisation and Diversification of Energy Markets

The EU Energy Union declared the core framework for energy policy objectives that seek to bring about a more diversified, better connected and more sustainable energy sector. In 2015, European Commission (EC) adopted Energy Union strategy setting out five key targets, which incorporate market objectives as well as put in place the guidelines of the common EU energy policy (European Commission, 2015). The energy security strategy addresses measures both for short-term security, mainly focusing on resilience to energy supply disruptions, and for long-term security, i.e. diversification of energy supply and finally reduction of energy dependence on external energy supplies. The aims of common energy policy include ensuring the functioning energy market and security of energy supply by diversification of energy sources and promoting interconnection of all member states' energy networks (Hermanson, 2018).

Even before the Energy Union Strategy, the EU energy market liberalisation packages, adopted in 1998, 2003 and 2009, have been at the core of the common gas market creation in the EU. All of them were agreed with the intention to increase short-term transactions and gas-to-gas or electricity-to-electricity competition. With the adoption of relevant directives and regulations the EC set a goal to finalise (with few exceptions) the internal energy market by 2014, notably, by enforcing the unbundling of networks away from the competitive parts of the electricity and gas business. The EU Third Energy Package mandates the EU member States to unbundle natural gas and electricity distribution networks: transmission should be separated from supply and distribution. This would reduce the monopoly power of energy suppliers.

Unbundling requirements envisaged that the independent TSO should not be associated with the gas supply business and instead should ensure the best use of the infrastructure it operates (Molis, 2016). Earning from selling the capacity of pipelines and related services (but not gas), the TSO would be interested in attracting new suppliers, this way diversifying gas supply, investing into new grids, expanding trading hubs and integrating gas storage facilities into liquid trading systems based on trading hubs. To achieve these goals, the EU Third Energy Package provided three models for unbundling: "*Ownership unbundling, establishment of the Independent System Operator or creation of the Independent Transmission System Operator. Lithuania was among the first countries implementing the Third Energy Package and adopting the strictest option—ownership unbundling*" (Molis, 2016, 99). Following Lithuania's decision, Estonia implemented its unbundling legislation. Latvia, on the other hand, postponed the implementation until April 2017 (European Commission, 2017). In addition, gas market in Finland was opened to competition at the beginning of 2020 with the creation of Gasgrid Finland which is responsible for operation of the gas network.

The work and achievements of regional co-operation in the energy sector in the Baltic Sea region has been conducted within the framework of the BEMIP initiative, which was launched by the EU in 2009. The main objective of the BEMIP is to create an open and integrated regional electricity and gas markets between EU countries in the Baltic Sea region, ending energy isolation of the Baltic States and Finland (European Commission, 2018). The BEMIP initiative was further reinforced through reforms launched by the EC at the BEMIP High Level Group meeting on the 31st of October 2014, and the Declaration on Energy Security of Supply signed on the 14th of January 2015 by the Energy Ministers of the Baltic States (BEMIP, 2015).

As it is stated in the action plan: "*Efforts should be continued to implement the most economically viable solution to connect Finland and the three Baltic States to the continental European gas network and to new gas supply sources, and to accelerate market opening in the Member States applying derogations from the Union's third energy legislative package*" (BEMIP, 2015, 7). The BEMIP concerns the plans to build pipelines between Poland and Lithuania and Finland and Estonia to connect gas systems of these countries together with the EU. If successfully implemented, these projects would contribute to region's security of supply.

Contribution to Energy Security and Development of Regional Gas Market

Current and New Infrastructure

The national gas infrastructure in the Baltic States is inherited from the Soviet period. Gas was separately supplied to each Baltic State during that period (Belyi, 2019). As it was designed for much larger population, the

Soviet gas grid took advantage of local strengths, such as, for example, the unique geological properties of Latvia's Inčukalns area was used to meet the needs of St. Petersburg (former Leningrad) heating during winter time. Today, the main gas storage facility in the Baltic States, the Latvian UGS in Inčukalns is connected to both the Lithuanian and the Estonian gas networks and constitutes an important balancing point for south-to-north gas flows from Latvia to Estonia. Finland receives supplies from Russia via Imatra and from Estonia via Balticconnector, a gas pipeline connecting Estonian and Finnish gas markets, which was opened in December 2019.

The Baltic States have already completed some important internal and regional projects to facilitate the creation of integrated regional gas market. As already explained, at the end of 2014 a new LNG terminal in Lithuania (Klaipeda) was opened. The terminal for the first time ensured alternative gas supply routes and sources to the Russian gas delivered by pipelines.

The Klaipeda LNG Terminal: Technical Characteristics

The LNG terminal operates in the southern part of Klaipeda Seaport, in the Curonian Lagoon at the Kiaulės Nugara Island. Put into operation in December 2014, the LNG terminal consists of an FSRU named "Independence", a berth, and a gas pipeline (Klaipedos Nafta, 2019).

"Independence" is the world's first new-build LNG floating storage regasification unit. It has been built at the Hyundai Heavy Industries' shipyard in Ulsan, South Korea, for floating LNG services provider Höegh LNG. The vessel is chartered to Klaipedos Nafta under a ten-year lease agreement signed in March 2012, which also includes an option for purchase (Ship Technology, 2019). Moreover, the Lithuanian Parliament in December 2018 decided to allow the Lithuanian Government to acquire the Klaipeda LNG terminal "Independence" (Lapienyte, 2018). Lithuania intends to repurchase the storage vessel by the end of 2024, when its lease agreement from the Norwegian company Höegh LNG expires. In addition, the EC has approved a state aid scheme for Klaipedos Nafta to acquire the currently leased LNG terminal-storage facility "Independence" or another similar LNG vessel by the end of 2024 (Ministry of Energy of the Republic of Lithuania, 2020b).

"*The LNG FSRU incorporates a double hull built of mild steel. She has an overall length of 294 m, a width of 46 m and a depth of 26 m. She*

Table 8.1 The Klaipeda LNG terminal value chain

	2015	*2016*	*2017*	*2018*	*2019*
Regasification (billion normal cubic metres)	0.5	1.3	1.1	0.77	1.67
Usage of the terminal (%)	13	35	30	21	45
Terminal users	Litgas	Litgas, Lituvos Dujos Tiekimas, Achema	Litgas, Lietuvos Dujos Tiekimas, Achema	Achema, Lietuvos Energija Tiekimas	Achema, Eesti Energia, Implitex, Ignitis

Source The Author

has a maximum draught of 12.6 m and capacity to store 70,000 tonnes of chilled natural gas. The vessel is of the Det Norske Veritas (DNV) class with a storage volume of 170,000 m^3 *of LNG in thermally insulated membrane tanks. The LNG stored at −162 °C will be heated up to very high temperatures in the regasification system onboard the ship so that it evaporates to form natural gas. The gas will be then delivered to the vessel through pipelines to be supplied to consumers in Lithuania*" (Ship Technology, 2019).

If running at full capacity of almost four billion cubic metres, the terminal could cover 80% of demand of the Baltic States. The usage of the terminal has increased from 13% in 2015 to 45% in 2019 (Table 8.1).

> The FSRU is permanently moored near the jetty to receive LNG from LNG carriers. Other facilities to be erected on the jetty include a high gas pressure platform, a servicing platform, mooring decks, berthing decks, communication bridges, observation towers, a control room, fire safety equipment, cranes for technical maintenance and high-pressure gas transmission loading arms. (Ship Technology, 2019)

Contribution to Energy Security

LNG terminal in Klaipeda has also significantly improved security of supply and ended the sole reliance on Russian gas supplies. First, the LNG terminal allowed the Baltic States to diversify supplies and to connect to global markets. Juris Ozolins, a Latvian energy expert, praised the opening of the terminal as follows: "*Now we'll have a link with global gas trading markets for the first time during the Baltic States' history. Besides, from now on, we will have alternative is spite of relying on a single participant of the market, and the consumers will be able to choose one*" (Jegelevicius, 2014). Moreover, with LNG terminal operating in Lithuania, the Baltic States are now much more protected against a major gas supply disruption from the east. Security is provided by a combination of key infrastructure elements, including diversification of gas import routes via the Klaipeda LNG terminal (Sabanas, 2018).

For example, a Pan-European gas system resilience stress test conducted by the EC in 2014 showed that with LNG terminal supplies for the protected consumers (all households, small and medium-sized enterprises, essential social services, and/or district heating installations) would be ensured in all three Baltic States in all scenarios of hypothetical disruption of gas supplies from Russia. Even in the scenario of a one-month disruption of all Russian gas flows, there would be important gas shortages for non-protected customers in Estonia and Lithuania. In the absence of the Klaipeda LNG terminal, the situation would be more dramatic in Estonia as there would be no gas in their system, including for protected customers, within 4–5 days (Postimees, 2014). Based on stress test results, the European Commission provided a specific recommendation to Estonia to finalise an agreement with Lithuania for the supply of protected customers in case of an emergency from the Klaipeda LNG terminal (European Commission, 2014).

In a similar way, the importance of LNG terminal for resilience in case of gas supply disruption was also proven by Coherent Resilience (Core 19) Tabletop Exercise, which was co-organised by the European Commission's Joint Research Centre and the NATO Energy Security Centre of Excellence. The goal of the exercise was to support the national authorities and gas TSO of the Baltic States in ensuring supply of gas to consumers and mitigating the disruption over the Baltic States. The result of the exercise clearly demonstrated that the LNG terminal in Klaipeda would be indispensable instrument to mitigate supply disruptions via pipelines from the east (Kopustinskas et al., 2019).

Contribution to the Development of Local and Regional Gas Market

The Klaipeda LNG terminal has helped to reduce wholesale market prices and introduce competition into wholesale gas supply. Interestingly in

2014, Gazprom agreed to cut gas price for Lithuania around 23% amid new LNG supplies. It could be argued that one of the major reasons for sudden change in Gazprom's pricing attitude towards Lithuania has been Lithuania's strong determination to build its new LNG gas terminal. According to Grigas (2014), "*...the main factor was that Lithuania is poised for the first time to buy from an alternate supplier*". In other words, back in 2014 Lithuania successfully used its LNG option as a bargaining power in new price negotiations with Gazprom. Similar price reductions were also agreed in other Baltic States (Jegelevicius & Powell, 2019). Therefore, the construction of LNG terminal put pressure on Gazprom's pricing strategy towards the Baltic States resulting in further price decreases for Gazprom's natural gas.

The utilisation of LNG terminal in Klaipeda for gas supplies to the Baltic States is increasing. For example, in 2019, Lithuania transported the highest ever-recorded amount of gas to the Baltic States. Lithuania's well-developed gas infrastructure, i.e. the Klaipeda LNG terminal and a developed and properly maintained gas transmission system ensured that the transmission to the Baltic States increased 2.6-fold last year if compared to 2018 and reached almost six TWh (0.6 bcm) of gas in 2019. As far as the competitiveness of LNG in the market is concerned, the gas transportation via Klaipėda LNG terminal also reached its record level.

In 2019, the gas imports via the LNG terminal reached 65% 19.6 TWh (2.0 bcm) of the total amount of gas transported to the EU market via Lithuania. In 2018, this indicator reached only 35% of the 2019 level (Ministry of Energy of the Republic of Lithuania, 2020a).

Moreover, the LNG terminal's value for regional gas market development is clearly demonstrated by the significant increase in terminal users from other Baltic States in recent years. For example in August 2019, Estonian energy trader EestiEnergia has signed an agreement to start using services of the Klaipeda LNG terminal in Lithuania. According to Eero Sirendi (2019), Head of Energy Trading at Eesti Energia, "*... Klaipeda LNG terminal...enables us in a given market situation to purchase LNG at a competitive price, to regasify and bring it to our clients in the Baltics*". Moreover, in November 2020, another Estonian energy company Elenger (Eesti Gaas) become the fifth company to start importing gas via Lithuania's Klaipeda LNG terminal.[3] As Margus Kaasik,

[3] The users of LNG gas terminal are Achema, Eesti Energia, Elenger, Ignitis, and Implitex.

a board member of the company commented the decision: "*This grants us access to the global market and means more reasonable prices to our clients as there are more sources of supply available*" (Murphy, 2019). In addition, gas procured from the Klaipeda LNG terminal was used by the company to supply clients in Estonia and Latvia. According to Juris Ozolins, a Latvian energy expert, "*I don't see any legal hindrances preventing the largest Latvian consumers from buying LNG in other markets through the Klaipeda LNG terminal and Lithuanian infrastructure*" (Jegelevicius, 2014). Furthermore, in 2019 Polish gas company PGNiG signed a five-year contract for the full capacity of the LNG reloading facility for trucks in Klaipeda, Lithuania, which will allow the company to import liquefied natural gas from various sources by sea and sell it to recipients. Piotr Wozniak, CEO of PGNiG, pointed out that "*PGNiG will...be able to access better the small-scale LNG market in the Baltic countries and be more competitive for customers in northeast Poland and central and eastern Europe*" (PGNiG, 2019).

The LNG import terminal in Lithuania provides an open access infrastructure platform that encourages optimal usage of the entire gas infrastructure operated by the Baltic States and creation of an efficient gas supply chain in the region. For example, the Klaipeda LNG import terminal is a proven alternative supply route for seasonal storage in the Inčukalns UGS, the main gas storage facility for the region. In 2017, regional gas supplies reached an important historical milestone as for the first time natural gas received from the Klaipeda LNG was injected into the Inčukalns UGS. Moreover, the development LNG terminal has also facilitated the development of other important regional infrastructure, such as the Klaipeda-Kiemenai pipeline, which is essential for cross-border supplies between Lithuania and Latvia. According to Ozolins, the common Baltic gas market is formally working. "*We have the ever-increasing flows of gas through the local interconnectors, the gas for the Klaipeda LNG terminal is stored in Incukalns, the Baltic gas exchange GET has entered Finnish market and so on*" (Jegelevicius & Powell, 2019).

The Klaipeda LNG Terminal: Past, Current, and Future Challenges

Political Disagreements and a Lack of Regional Solidarity

Intra-regional co-operation in energy security among the Baltic States has often been hindered by the domination of self-interests and the lack of understanding of regionalism among the states. This creates the duplication of projects and expansion of excessive energy infrastructure in neighbouring states, leading to inefficient or irrational use of financial resources. The infrastructure which could service the whole region is not accepted by neighbouring countries as such.

For example, the development and operation of the LNG terminal in Klaipeda has been surrounded by a lack of intra-regional co-operation and solidarity. There have been clear political and economic disagreements among the Baltic States with regard to LNG options in the region. According to Kustova (2014), "*the case of construction of an LNG terminal in the Baltic Region is an example when a high level of solidarity for the EU common goals has not been reflected in the implementation of EU regulations*".

The idea of building a regional LNG terminal in the Baltic region was initiated in parallel with the BEMIP back in 2007–2009 as a way of ensuring diversification of gas from Russia as a monopolist supplier. The National Energy Strategy of Lithuania in 2007 mentioned the possibility to conduct regional assessment on the development of LNG terminal. The European Commission has been providing consultations to ensure that the terminal should be built to support the needs of all the three Baltic States. As it was indicated in the BEMIP plan in 2009 "*…relatively small gas markets in Estonia, Finland, Latvia and Lithuania do not generate scope for more than one terminal*" (BEMIP, 2009, 20).

Despite the determination of the European Commission, clear signs of intra-regional competition for LNG terminal quickly appeared. For example, the BEMIP regional plan envisaged one plan for the terminal in Lithuania with capacity of 3.0 bcm per year (Pakalkaite & Posaner, 2019). In Estonia, LNG terminal was envisaged in Paldiski or Tallinn with capacity of 2.5 bcm per year. Latvia also discussed LNG option on the shore of the country. None of these visions moved forward as the agreement on one terminal would mean that other Baltic States would have to drop plans of building their own.

Therefore, between 2008 and 2012 struggling to handle higher gas import prices from Gazprom, the Lithuanian Government had actively pursued their own initiative outside the priority schemes of the European Commission. As a result, in 2010 under the leadership of Energy Minister the Government created a high-level working group to analyse the construction of LNG terminal (Pakalkaite & Posaner, 2019). Moreover, without waiting for the report of the group, the Lithuanian Government in 2010 announced that state-led energy company Klaipedos Nafta will develop LNG terminal. Consequently, 2012 Lithuania signed a ten-year lease contract agreement for an FSRU.

An example of regional rivalry became especially evident when in 2013 Latvia reportedly attempted to block EUR 87 million European Investment Bank's loan for LNG terminal in Lithuania. According to Lithuania's officials, Latvia's motive for blocking the loan was a wish to build its own LNG terminal (Pakalkaite & Posaner, 2019). In addition, some argued that Latvia's actions could have been provoked by promises which were not fulfilled by Lithuania's side. For example, Antanas Valionis, Lithuania's former ambassador to Latvia, in his latest memoirs argued that the Lithuanian Government at the end of the 2000s promised to a Latvian counterpart to support its plans to build LNG terminal near Riga in exchange of undersea electricity cable construction from Sweden to Lithuania, Klaipeda (Valionis, 2018).

According to Lithuania's former ambassador, "*I had no serious arguments in defense of Lithuania's policy. I do not know why it was decided not to fulfil the promises made to the Latvians*" (Jegelevicius, 2018). In addition, the fact of disagreements over Klaipeda LNG terminal is also supported by some energy experts in the region. According to Rytas Staselis, "*the Latvians and particularly Estonians are still irked by the fact that Lithuania operates a liquefied gas terminal it sees as regional. There are still expectations, especially in Estonia, that the topic of a regional Baltic liquefied natural gas terminal will pop up anew in the future*" (Jegelevicius & Powell, 2019). As a result, the construction of the LNG terminal in Klaipeda is a good example of a lack solidarity and co-operation with regard to the development of regional energy infrastructure.

Disagreements Over Sharing Operational Costs of the LNG Terminal

The operational model of the LNG terminal in Klaipeda based on subsidised gas tariff raised concerns over possible gas market distortion in the Baltic States. For example, commenting on Lithuania's wish to get Estonia to recognise the Klaipeda terminal as a regional facility, Ando Leppiman, Deputy Secretary General for Energy and Construction at the Ministry of Economic Affairs and Infrastructure of Estonia, pointed out that "*Estonia has taken the position that it doesn't want to support the establishment of LNG terminals* via*the gas tariff. The regional LNG terminal should evolve on the basis of market logic. In order to provide our market with the solution that is the most sustainable in the long term, one must assess whether the Lithuanian terminal is more advantageous than a regional LNG terminal in Paldiski; we are not convinced of this today*" (Vahtla, 2016). Moreover, concerns over market distortion were also expressed by companies seeking to make investments in the construction of an LNG terminal in Estonia's largest cargo harbour. According Arnout Lugtmeijer, CEO of Vopak E.O.S., "*it is Estonia's interest to keep the transport prices of liquid natural gas low, but the terminal in Klaipėda, on the other hand, will make this much more expensive*" (Cavegn, 2017).

The LNG terminal's maintenance model when Estonia and Latvia do not contribute to terminal's maintenance costs was also criticised by Lithuania's energy authorities. For example, Virginijus Poderys, Chairman of Energy Committee at the Parliament of Lithuania, argued the current maintenance model goes against the interests of Lithuania's energy consumers as it distorts market conditions in the Baltic States. As Poderys argued, "*there are situations when [Lithuania's neighbours] buy gas from the LNG terminal, produce electricity in their country, and then sell the power on the Baltic market*" (Lrt.lt, 2019). According to Poderys, based on its output and size, the terminal is built for all the three Baltic States, which now do not contribute to its upkeep (Lrt.lt, 2019). Therefore, Lithuania's running costs of the terminal could be decreased if the other Baltic States were to get involved.

Concerns over the maintenance cost model of the terminal were expressed by some energy experts in the region. According to Rytis Staselis, a Lithuanian energy expert, "*Yes, the terminal has had a positive impact on the gas market, but the prices are too high for it to be able to stimulate a competitive Baltic gas market. … Latvia does not want to share the costs Lithuania incurs in operating the facility. As a result, the price of the gas at the terminal is uncompetitive, especially so in winter with low gas prices on spot markets. The fact that state companies are in charge of the market also contributes to the drag in drawing common rules and conditions for a single Baltic gas market*" (Jegelevicius & Powell, 2019).

Moreover, some experts pointed out that the LNG terminal in Lithuania has not contributed to a genuine regional LNG market as the price is too high. According to Belyi (2019, 14), "*the Klaipėda LNG terminal illustrates the pernicious effects of state aid arrangements on the markets. It is in Estonia's interests to argue in favour of a market-based approach at EU level. The provision of state aid to Klaipėda LNG FSRU should be viewed as impediment to Lithuania's access to the entry-exit zone*".

Disagreements Over the Role of the Russian LNG Supplies

The availability and purchase of Russian LNG via LNG terminal in Lithuania has raised some security concerns, especially in Lithuania. For instance in 2019, Lithuania's state-owned natural gas supplier UAB Lietuvos Energijos Tiekimas has sparked a controversy over the purchase of LNG from a plant owned and operated by the Russian gas company Novatek. Some politicians in Lithuania's expressed public outcry over the purchase of gas from the company, which belongs to people from President Putin's inner circle urging legal and national security investigations (Jokubatis, 2019). Moreover, in the yearly National Threat Assessment report, Lithuania's intelligence services expressed some risks that Novatek can start dictating conditions for LNG consumers after they get hooked on its supplies (Pakeniene & Viluckas, 2020).

Despite the aforementioned, some regional energy experts claimed that Lithuania's reaction was highly exaggerated and underlined the economic logic of LNG purchase from Russia. Vidmantas Jankauskas, former Head of Lithuania's Energy Pricing Commission, argued that "*I don't see a big difference if the gas comes from Gazprom or Novatek. It would be very foolish to prevent national gas traders from buying Novatek gas. As it is cheaper ... any ban would affect them adversely. Furthermore, they could lose competitiveness in spot gas markets*" (Jegelevicius, 2019). In addition, Virginijus Poderys, Chairman of Energy Committee at the Parliament of Lithuania, pointed out restrictions over the shipments of Russian gas via terminal will lead to higher prices (Lrt.lt, 2019). This position was supported by the director of international expansion of Lietuvos Energija, who pointed out "*clear rules need to be set both for state and private energy companies' gas purchases, in a very competitive environment. Any (gas) acquisition, regardless of its origin, means more competition for Gazprom and lower prices. Even if Lietuvos Energija does not do so, other companies will continue buying gas including from Novatek, and selling it directly to consumers on the gas exchanges, meaning Lietuvos Energija would lose out*" (Jegelevicius, 2019). Moreover, limited Russian LNG volumes are supplied to Estonia across the Lake Peipsi. Therefore, the availability of a competitive supply of small-scale LNG from Russia has become a reality and may certainly contribute to the development of the regional gas market (Belyi, 2019).

Uncertainty Over the Future Role of Gas

Another challenge for the future utilisation of LNG terminal in Lithuania is presented by the low and declining gas consumption volumes involved in regional countries. According to Belyi (2019, 1), "*competition cannot be promoted where the volumes in question are limited*". Moreover, the decline in gas demand has been evident in many European countries, especially from 2011 to 2014. The Baltic States and Finland are not an exception as, for example in 2017, the largest falls in gas consumption among the EU member States were recorded in Latvia (a 9.6% decline), Finland (a 6.8% decline) and Estonia (a 5.0% decline) (Eurostat, 2018). Moreover, in the past ten years, there was a large decrease in the final gas consumption in all the Baltic States. For example, according to statistical information provided by International Energy Agency (IEA), the final consumption of natural gas decreased from 23,316 terajoules (TJ) in 2008 to 16,025 TJ in 2018 (International Energy Agency, 2020).[4] Similar tendencies could be seen in other Baltic States. For example, in Estonia the consumption of natural gas decreased from 16,234 TJ in 2008 to 11,707 TJ in 2018 (International Energy Agency, 2020). Lithuania had also experienced contraction of gas consumption, from 69,625 TJ in 2008 to 67,671 TJ in 2018 (International Energy Agency, 2020).

Moreover, gas constitutes less than 10% of Estonia's primary energy supply and its gas demand is the lowest of the three Baltic States. As Belyi (2019, 26) pointed out that "*in order to achieve a competitive gas market, Estonia needs to further stimulate gas demand in the power sector and in transport*". Furthermore, the potential for increased demand exists, given the fast evolution of new technologies relating to gas usage, comprising CNG, LNG and biomethane in transport and industries. As Belyi (2019,

[4] The calculations have been made on the basis of gross calorific values.

1) pointed out that "*gas-driven transport together with a potential shift to gas-fired power plants represent a significant incremental increase in demand for natural gas*". Nevertheless, despite significant potential of new technologies, the ultimate consumption of gas will depend on the actual implementation of policies, such electrification of economic sectors including the road transport sectors. Another potential area for increasing gas demand is the transport sector where gas could be used in the form of either CNG or LNG. The Finnish gas fuelling station network is one of the fastest-growing ones in Europe as Gasum is expanding its Nordic gas filling station network by several new stations a year (Gasum, 2019). Furthermore, a growing trend in natural gas consumption is expected in the transport sector (Elering, 2018). In addition, Estonian CNG distribution companies have indicated that the Estonian CNG market is already competitive and is set to gradually increase in scale. Furthermore, Eesti Gaas recently announced about company's plans to expand to neighbouring countries, such as Latvia and Lithuania (PetrolPlaza, 2019).

The future role of natural gas of fossil fuel origin in Europe has never been more uncertain than it is today. Gas is under increasing scrutiny as the EC adopted a new green deal with a stronger than ever backing of carbon neutrality by 2050 (Simon, 2019). The European Commission's 2050 long-term climate strategy foresees up to 90% less fossil gas demand compared to today. This strategy has already delayed European Commission's new reforms over EU gas market rules. According to van Renssen (2019), "*the Commission has gone quiet recently over a highly-anticipated reform of EU gas market rules. Its new director-general for energy, Ditte Juul-Jørgensen, did not mention it at a first high-level meeting of member states in September. Nor is it cited in von der Leyen's mission letter to her would-be energy commissioner, Kadri Simson*". Moreover, there is a clear change in the terminology. As van Renssen (2019) argued "*...what EU officials once called the 'gas package' has been rebranded the 'gas decarbonisation package' or simply the 'decarbonisation package'*". According to Klaus-Dieter Borchardt, the European Commission's director for the internal energy market, the aim of the package is to create Europe's first regulatory framework for green—renewable or decarbonised—gas (van Renssen, 2019). In addition, Florian Ermacora, a senior official at the European Commission's energy directorate, stressed the key principle of the European Commission's attitude towards gas—"*no lock-in into natural gas*" (van Renssen, 2019). According to Ermacora, "*it's clear that, if we want to go for a carbon neutral Europe in 2050, natural gas* *will not be able to do the job of decarbonisation. The EU's 2050 climate neutrality goal also means that we cannot rely for decades on imports of natural gas. Any investment which is done now, including new LNG facilities, needs to put this question: is this decarbonisation-fit?*" (van Renssen, 2019).

In the context of the EU transition to a low-carbon economy, the gas industries, including LNG operators, could face significant uncertainties and transformations over the next decades. For example, whether the existent LNG infrastructure could be used to transport and store green gases? How competitive LNG gas will be in case the European Commission puts decarbonisation premium of LNG imports from Russia, Norway or the USA? Unless industry and policy makers will find effective answers to these questions, the prospects of LNG look uncertain.

Importance of Poland as Gas Hub

Looking towards the future, the economic viability of the Klaipeda LNG terminal depends very much on the broader gas market development in Poland. Poland has ambitions to become the gas hub of Central and Eastern Europe, and its interconnection plans in all directions have significantly progressed (Tuohy, 2019). Poland can—or soon will be able to—draw on storage capacities in Ukraine, additional import possibilities via interconnections with the Czech Republic, Slovakia, Ukraine, and Lithuania (Map 8.1).

In addition, having signed both spot, medium-term and long-term contracts respectively with Qatar and the USA, Poland is also expanding its LNG infrastructure in Świnoujście to boost its regasification capacity from 5.0 bcm to 7.5 bcm (then possibly up to 10 bcm/year following further extension). Moreover, Poland's Gaz-System and its Danish counterpart, Energinet, agreed to proceed with the Baltic Pipe project, a long-held-PCI-funded project to link Poland with Norway's gas fields (Shotter, 2019). According to Jakubowski, CEO of Polskie LNG, "*Poland is working on interconnectors with Lithuania, Ukraine, Slovakia and the Czech Republic to be able to deliver surplus volumes to neighbouring markets to create a regional gas hub. … The Baltic pipe can give us very stable supplies to the Polish gas market on a long-term basis. The LNG terminal can give us flexibility and price arbitrage*" (Shotter, 2019).

As a result, Poland is in the process of significant diversification of gas supply options in the region. The construction of new interconnections

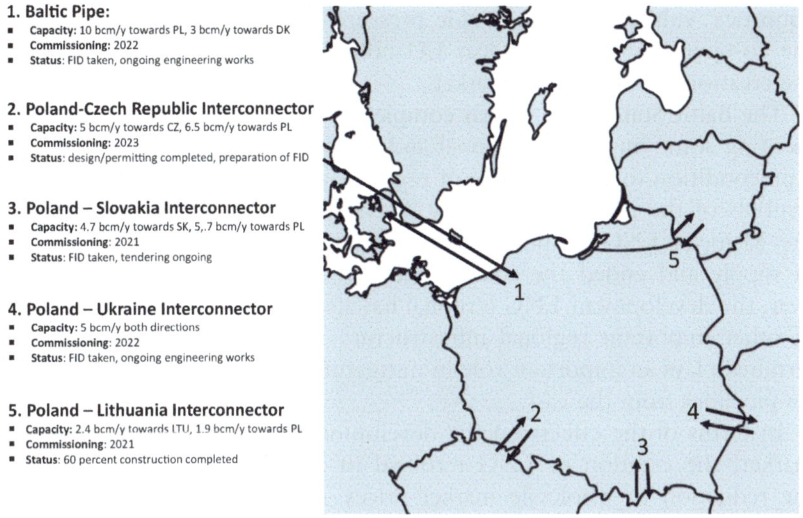

Map 8.1 Major infrastructure projects between Poland and its neighbouring countries (*Abbreviations* CZ = the Czech Republic, DK = Denmark, FID = final investment decision, LTU = Lithuania, PL = Poland, and SK = Slovakia. *Source* The Author)

will not only strengthen the attractiveness of the Polish gas market but also potentially spur the growth of trading and market liquidity. Nevertheless, the prospects of these developments will very much depend on whether all regional countries involved will find common ground over the regional gas market design.

Conclusions

The Baltic States have often been considered being one the most exposed to energy supply problems in the EU. Most of the dangers resulted from their strong dependence on gas delivered from one supplier, namely Russia. Despite that, in the past ten years, countries in the region have made an important progress towards diversifying their energy supplies, especially of natural gas. This progress was brought about because of remarkable political will as well as improved regional co-operation has resulted in considerable economic benefit while decreasing the three countries' vulnerability to outside pressure. The important stimulus for the co-operation has been clear EU policies and legislation concerning the creation of internal gas market.

The Baltic States have already completed or are in the process of implementing some important national and regional projects, which serves as a precondition for the creation of regional gas market. One of the main symbols of the progress of energy diversification is the development of the Klaipeda LNG terminal, which has significantly improved security of supply and ended the sole reliance on Russian gas supplies. Moreover, the development LNG terminal has also facilitated the development of other important regional infrastructure. In addition, Klaipeda LNG terminal plays an important role in mitigating possible supply disruptions via pipelines from the east.

In terms of the effects on the development of local and regional gas market, the creation of LNG terminal in Klaipeda has contributed to the reduction of wholesale market prices. Moreover, the utilisation of the LNG terminal in Klaipeda for gas supplies to the Baltic States is increasing. In addition, LNG terminal's value for regional gas market development is clearly demonstrated by the significant increase in terminal users from other Baltic States in recent years.

Despite the importance of diversification of infrastructure and the development of local and regional gas market, the construction of the Klaipeda LNG terminal has also been affected by the domination of self-interests and the lack of understanding of regionalism among the states. There have been clear political and economic disagreements among the Baltic States with regard to LNG options in the region. Moreover, the operational model of the LNG terminal in Klaipeda based on subsidised gas tariff raised concerns from other Baltic States over possible gas market distortion in the Baltics.

Another issue for the utilisation of LNG terminal in Lithuania is presented by the low and declining gas consumption volumes in the Baltic States. Moreover, the future role of natural gas of fossil fuel origin in Europe has never been more uncertain than it is today. Gas is under increasing scrutiny as the EC adopted it new green deal with a stronger than ever backing of carbon neutrality by 2050. In the context of the EU transition to a low-carbon economy, the gas industries, including LNG operators, could face significant uncertainties and transformations over the next decades.

References

Belyi, A. (2019). *Stepping on the gas: Future-proofing Estonia's energy market and security*. ICDS Report: 1–44. https://icds.ee/wp-content/uploads/2019/05/ICDS_Report_Stepping_on_the_Gas_Belyi_May_2019.pdf. Accessed September 29, 2020.

BEMIP. (2009). *Baltic energy market interconnection plan: Final report*. Final report of the HLG. https://ec.europa.eu/energy/sites/ener/files/documents/2009_11_25_hlg_report_170609_0.pdf. Accessed September 22, 2020.

BEMIP. (2015). *PA energy—BEMIP action plan (for competitive, secure and sustainable energy)*. https://elering.ee/sites/default/files/attachments/Action_Plan_FINAL_DG%20REGIO.PDF. Accessed September 18, 2020.

Cavegn, D. (2017). *Businesses concerned EU gas infrastructure investments will distort market*. October 30, 2017. https://news.err.ee/639514/businesses-concerned-eu-gas-infrastructure-investments-will-distort-market. Accessed October 12, 2020.

Directorate-General for Energy. (2018). *EU energy in figures*. European Commission. https://publications.europa.eu/en/publication-detail/-/publication/99fc30eb-c06d-11e8-9893-01aa75ed71a1/language-en. Accessed September 12, 2020.

Elering. 2018. *Estonian gas transmission network development plan 2018–2027*. https://elering.ee/sites/default/files/attachments/Estonian_gas_transmission_network_development_plan_2018_2027.pdf. Accessed October 15, 2020.

European Commission. (2014). *Annexes to the communication from the commission to the European parliament and the council on the short-term resilience of the European gas system*. COM (2014) 654. Accessed October 2, 2020.

European Commission. (2015). *A framework strategy for a resilient energy union with a forward-looking climate change policy, energy union package*. COM (2015). https://setis.ec.europa.eu/system/files/Communication_Energy_Union_en.pdf. Accessed September 16, 2020.

European Commission. (2017). *Latvia's gas market now liberalized*. https://ec.europa.eu/energy/en/news/latvias-gas-market-now-liberalised. Accessed October 5, 2020.

European Commission. (2018). *Antitrust: Commission imposes binding obligations on Gazprom to enable free flow of gas at competitive prices in Central and Eastern European gas markets*. Press release. May 24, 2018. https://europa.eu/rapid/press-release_IP-18-3921_en.html. Accessed September 12, 2020.

Eurostat. (2018). *Natural gas supply statistics: Statistics explained*. https://ec.europa.eu/eurostat/statistics-explained/pdfscache/10590.pdf. Accessed September 24, 2020.

Eurostat. (2019). *EU imports of energy products—Recent developments: Statistics explained*. https://ec.europa.eu/eurostat/statistics-explained/pdfscache/46126.pdf. Accessed September 16, 2020.

Gasum. (2019). *The Nordic gas filling station network is expanding—A new station opens in Norrköping. Sweden*. June 18, 2019. https://www.gasum.com/en/About-gasum/for-the-media/News/2019/the-nordic-gas-filling-station-network-is-expanding--a-new-station-opens-in-norrkoping-sweden/. Accessed September 16, 2020.

Grigas, A. (2014). *Standing up to Gazprom: What Ukraine can learn from Lithuania*. Atlantic Council. June 23, 2014. https://www.atlanticcouncil.org/blogs/new-atlanticist/standing-up-to-gazprom-what-ukraine-can-learn-from-lithuania/. Accessed September 19, 2020.

Hermanson, A.-S. (2018). Energy security in a multi-level governance perspective. *Marine Policy, 98*, 301–308. https://doi.org/10.1016/j.marpol.2018.09.025. Accessed September 16, 2020.

International Energy Agency. (2020). *Data and statistics*. https://www.iea.org/data-and-statistics/data-tables/?country=WORLD&energy=Natural%20gas. Accessed November 18, 2020.

Jegelevicius, L., & Powell, W. (2019). *Finding common ground in the Baltics*. Natural Gas World. June 25, 2019. https://www.naturalgasworld.com/finding-common-ground-in-the-baltics-ngw-magazine-70847. Accessed September 22, 2020.

Jegelevicius, L. (2014). *FSRU independence a historic milestone for Lithuanian energy security*. Natural Gas World. October 28, 2014. https://www.naturalgasworld.com/lithuania-fsru-independence. Accessed September 24, 2020.

Jegelevicius, L. (2018). *Lithuania and Latvia: The tale of two sisters marked with rivalry*. Baltic News Network. February 22, 2018. https://bnn-news.com/lithuania-and-latvia-the-tale-between-two-sisters-marked-with-rivalry-180480. Accessed October 2, 2020.

Jegelevicius, L. (2019). *Lithuania's Russian LNG cargo sparks row*. Natural Gas World. April 29, 2019. https://www.naturalgasworld.com/novateks-lng-sparks-baltic-discord-69647. Accessed October 2, 2020.

Jokubatis, M. (2019). KuorizikuojaLietuva, pirkdamadujasišsankcijųsąrašeesančiorusųoligarcho? *15min.lt*. April 18, 2019. https://www.15min.lt/verslas/naujiena/energetika/kuo-rizikuoja-lietuva-pirkdama-dujas-is-sankciju-sarase-esancio-oligarcho-664-1132874. Accessed October 2, 2020.

Kates, G., & Luo, L. (2014). *Russian gas: How much is that?* RadioFreeEurope. July 1, 2014. https://www.rferl.org/a/russian-gas-how-much-gazprom/25442003.html. Accessed September 25, 2020.

Klaipedos Nafta. (2019). *About LNG terminal*. https://www.kn.lt/en/our-activities/lng-terminals/klaipeda-lng-terminal/559. Accessed September 20, 2020.

Kopustinskas, V., Šikas, R., Walzer, L., Vamanu, B., Masera, M., Vainio, J., & Petkevičius, R. (2019). *Tabletop exercise: Coherent Resilience 2019 (CORE 19).* JRC Technical Report. Luxembourg: Publications Office of the European Union. https://publications.jrc.ec.europa.eu/repository/bitstream/JRC118083/core_19_ttx_final_report_online.pdf. Accessed October 2, 2020.

Kustova, I. (2014). *Bridging the energy Islands*. Natural Gas World. August 2, 2014. https://www.naturalgasworld.com/energy-island-baltic-states-gas-market. Accessed October 2, 2020.

Lapienyte, J. (2018). Seimas palaimino Independence pirkima. *15min.lt*. December 18, 2018. https://www.15min.lt/verslas/naujiena/energetika/lietuva-pirks-independence-664-1076258. Accessed October 2, 2020.

Lrt.lt. (2019). *Five years ago Lithuania broke Russian gas monopoly—But at what cost?* October 29, 2019. https://www.lrt.lt/en/news-in-english/19/1111346/five-years-ago-lithuania-broke-russian-gas-monopoly-but-at-what-cost. Accessed October 5, 2020.

Ministry of Energy of the Republic of Lithuania. (2020a). *In 2019, Lithuania transported the highest ever recorded amount of gas to the Baltic States*. January 14, 2020. http://enmin.lrv.lt/en/news/in-2019-lithuania-transported-the-highest-ever-recorded-amount-of-gas-to-the-baltic-states. Accessed September 24, 2020.

Ministry of Energy of the Republic of Lithuania. (2020b). *The European Commission approves state aid measures to secure long-term operation of Klaipėda LNG terminal*. November 23, 2020. https://enmin.lrv.lt/en/news/the-european-commission-approves-state-aid-measures-to-secure-long-term-operation-of-klaipeda-lng-terminal. Accessed October 12, 2020.

Molis, A. (2016). Towards a regional gas market in the Baltic states: Political, economic and legal aspects. *Humanities and Social Sciences Latvia., 24*(1), 91 125.

Murphy, J. (2019). *Lithuanian LNG terminal signs up fifth buyer*. Natural Gas World. November 5, 2019. https://www.naturalgasworld.com/lithuanian-lng-terminal-signs-up-fifth-buyer-74290. Accessed October 12, 2020.

Pakalkaite, V., & Posaner, J. (2019). The Baltics: Between competition and cooperation. In J. Godzimirski (Ed.), *New political economy of energy in Europe: Power to project, power to adapt* (pp. 215–237). Palgrave Macmillan.

Pakeniene, R., & Viluckas, P. (2020). *Lithuania could take 'legal measures' to restrict Russian gas imports*. February 5, 2020. https://www.lrt.lt/en/news-in-english/19/1139778/lithuania-could-take-legal-measures-to-restrict-russian-gas-imports. Accessed October 16, 2020.

PetrolPlaza. (2019). *EestiGaas: We want to expand our CNG operations to neighbouring countries*. March 1, 2019. https://www.petrolplaza.com/news/20423. Accessed October 16, 2020.

PGNiG. (2019). *PGNiG enters small scale LNG market in Lithuania*. November 29, 2019. http://en.pgnig.pl/news/-/news-list/id/pgnig-enters-small-scale-lng-market-in-lithuania/newsGroupId/1910852?changeYear=2019&currentPage=1. Accessed October 5, 2020.

Postimees. (2014). *European Commission recommends Estonia to conclude gas agreement with Lithuania*. Accessed September 22, 2020.

Sabanas, M. (2018). *Integration of LNG terminal in the Lithuanian gas system*. May 22, 2018. https://erranet.org/wp-content/uploads/2018/02/Day-2-KN-LNG-terminal-in-Klaipeda-2018-05-22c.pdf. Accessed September 28, 2020.

Ship Technology. (2019). *Independence LNG floating storage regasification unit (LNG FSRU)*. Ship-Technology.com. https://www.ship-technology.com/projects/independence-lng-floating-storage-regasification-unit-lng-fsru/. Accessed September 28, 2020.

Shotter, J. (2019). Poland aims to break dependence on Russian gas. *Financial Times*. January 27, 2019. https://www.ft.com/content/d1b9d764-febd-11e8-aebf-99e208d3e521. Accessed October 21, 2020.

Simon, A. (2019). Let's get real about the future role of gas. *Foresight Climate & Energy*. June 5, 2019. https://foresightdk.com/lets-get-real-about-the-future-role-of-gas/. Accessed October 21, 2020.

Sirendi, E. (2019). *EestiEnergia to begin using Klaipeda LNG terminal from September*. LNG World News. August 26, 2019. https://www.lngworldnews.com/eesti-energia-to-begin-using-klaipeda-lng-terminal-from-september/. Accessed October 5, 2020.

Tuohy, E. (2019). *Going past monopoly: Developing a balanced Baltic sea regional gas market*. ICDS Policy Paper, 1–15. https://icds.ee/wp-content/uploads/2019/03/ICDS_Policy_Paper_Going_Past_Monopoly_Emmet_Tuohy_March_2019.pdf. Accessed October 25, 2020.

Vahtla, A. (2016). *Estonian ministry: Lithuanian LNG terminal has no advantages over Paldiski now*. December 28, 2016. https://news.err.ee/120172/estonian-ministry-lithuanian-lng-terminal-has-no-advantages-over-paldiski-now. Accessed October 12, 2020.

Valionis, A. (2018). *Politikossūpuoklės. Diplomatijos arena iružkulisiai*. Lithuania: Tyto alba. Accessed October 12, 2020.

van Renssen, S. (2019). *EU rethinks future gas strategy in light of 'European Green Deal'*. Euractiv. October 2, 2019. https://www.euractiv.com/section/energy-environment/news/eu-rethinks-future-gas-strategy-in-light-of-european-green-deal/. Accessed October 21, 2020.

CHAPTER 9

Energy and Climate Policy: Driving Factors Affecting the Future of LNG in Latvia

Reinis Āboltiņš

Introduction

LNG is entertaining a special role globally, regionally and locally as a fuel that is freely available, that can have very competitive price and that is seen as a temporary solution to climate issues associated with energy and transport sectors. The specifics of LNG lie in the role of infrastructure: presence or absence of LNG import facilities can be either a factor facilitating energy independence and a breakthrough in fuel change in transportation or an obstacle to gas supplies altogether. It is a rather complex set of factors that is going to determine the future of LNG in Latvia, but the main conclusion is that wherever there is potential to use natural gas, there is also potential for LNG.

This article examines possibilities of developing LNG import infrastructure in Latvia considering the context of the local and regional energy market and the potential impact of climate and energy policy on the

R. Āboltiņš (✉)
Riga Technical University, Riga, Latvia

K. Liuhto (ed.), *The Future of Energy Consumption, Security and Natural Gas*, https://doi.org/10.1007/978-3-030-80367-4_9

local and regional energy portfolio. Since the regional context is relevant for this analysis, for comparative purposes most of the figures include reference to data describing situation in Finland and Poland as well.

Next section of the article explains the relevance of the structure of energy production capacities in national as well as regional context of the three Baltic States. Thereafter, the article discusses how the regional gas market development can affect potential LNG supplies and decisions about building new LNG infrastructure in Latvia. It illustrates the role of the Inčukalns underground gas storage after gas market liberalisation in Latvia and elaborates about the Skulte LNG import terminal project explaining current developments and factors affecting the project. Section on energy demand provides a short overview of the dynamics of energy demand and what influence it can have on natural gas demand in future. It is followed by sections discussing factors that may have a positive effect on gas demand in Latvia and providing a more global backdrop to the gas market development in the Baltic States. A dedicated section highlights how European energy and climate policy plays into the local context. Section on the geopolitical context to the potential LNG flows to the Baltic States shows things into a bigger picture before summarising conclusions at the end of the article.

Energy Portfolio and Regional Context

Natural gas still plays an important role in Latvia's energy portfolio as district heating in the capital city Riga largely depends on natural gas. The two larger natural gas combined heat and power plants (CHPPs) in Riga represent the second largest source of power generation (Latvenergo, 2021). They represent the largest source of natural gas consumption in Latvia.

On average, slightly more than one third of electricity in Latvia is produced by large hydroelectric power plants (HPPs), just under one third of electricity comes from natural gas (combined cycle gas turbine power plants or CCGTs) and the remaining one third of electricity is imported.[1] Key factors influencing domestic production of electricity are

[1] Combined cycle gas turbine is highly efficient energy generation technology that combines a gas-fired turbine with a steam turbine. The design uses a gas turbine to generate electricity and then captures the resulting waste heat to create steam, which in

hydrological conditions in the Daugava River and the need for heat, especially during the periods of the lowest demand, which usually coincide with the summer months (June–August). As the Daugava is a lowland river the HPPs are run-of-the-river type HPPs and can be very effective when the water flow is sufficient, and that usually happens during the spring flood season between the end of February and the beginning of May. The electricity generation data from Augstsprieguma tīkls, Latvia's electricity TSO, on power generation sources in 2020 illustrates that the share of electricity generated by large HPPs constitutes nearly a half of total generation during this period, while large CCGT combined heat-and-power plants account for 32% (Fig. 9.1).

Thus, natural gas plays an important role (fluctuating between 25 and 35% of total power production) in Latvia's domestic electricity production. Domestic production and the choice of technology to ensure scalable generation depends on demand and supply in the Baltic States as a region and Estonia and Lithuania in particular, and the situation in the region can have implications for the use of natural gas in electricity generation. In terms of power generation, the three Baltic States have close to equal capacity with Lithuania having had to downscale with the closure of the Ignalina nuclear power plant in 2009, which turned the table for the

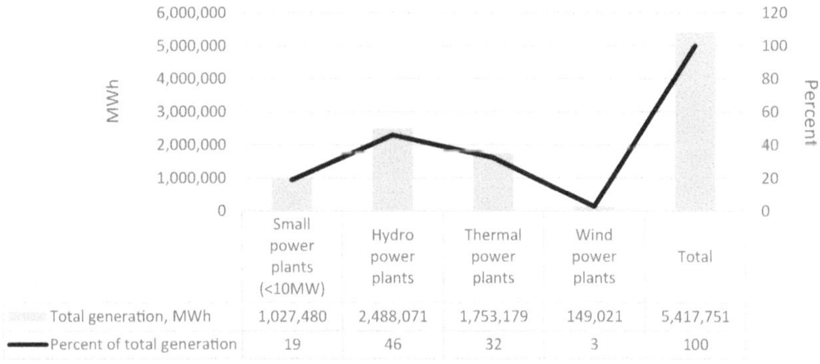

Fig. 9.1 Electricity generation in Latvia in 2020 (MWh) (*Source* The Author, based on Augstsprieguma tīkls [2021])

turn drives a steam turbine significantly increasing the system's power output without an increase in fuel consumption.

country and increased the role of natural gas. In other words, the closure of Ignalina pushed Lithuania to become the first among the Baltic States to liberalise its gas market and to create LNG infrastructure (LNG import terminal in Klaipeda) making possible alternative gas supply to Russian gas.

A role of natural gas in power and heat production has remained stable over the past 10 years in Latvia and Estonia, while the use of natural gas in Lithuania for power and heat production has been steadily decreasing since 2010 (Fig. 9.2). Natural gas consumption in Estonia has never been high, it has mostly fluctuated at around 0.7–0.8 bcm per annum and gas has covered district heating and industrial demand.

Figure 9.2 illustrates that among the five countries that are going to be interconnected by gas pipelines once the Gas Interconnection Poland - Lithuania (GIPL) linking the gas transmission systems of Poland (and thus with the rest of Europe) and Lithuania is completed, Poland has doubled its power production from natural gas between 2015 and 2019, which is indicative of the trend of switching over from the use of coal to natural gas in the light of the EU's energy and climate policies that have had rather cold reception by the Polish Government. Although a growing gas demand in Poland is likely going to be covered by pipeline supplies from various European destinations, including Russia, and LNG supplies through Poland's own LNG import terminal in Świnoujście, the

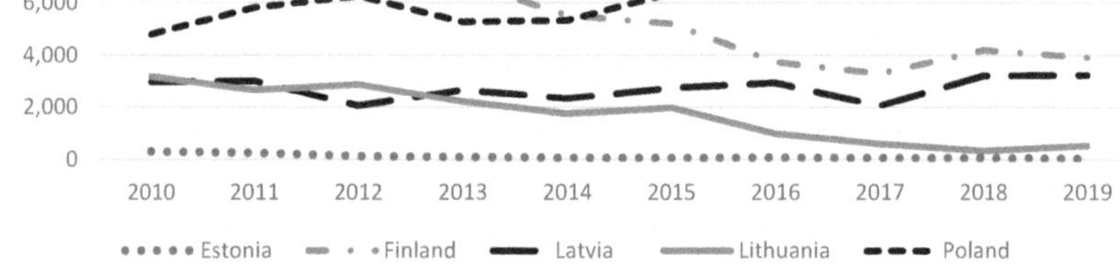

Fig. 9.2 Gross production of electricity and derived heat from natural gas (GWh) (*Source* The Author, based on Eurostat 2021)

GIPL interconnection would provide for elasticity of gas supplies in both directions across the Lithuanian–Polish border. It is not clear, what will be the impact of the GIPL on the gas market, and whether gas flows through the GIPL pipeline would have a negative impact on the LNG import terminal project in Gdańsk.

Hydro power plants in Latvia and Lithuania are another sizeable asset that provides important capacity that can supply low-cost electricity. However, hydro power plants can produce electricity at their maximum capacity in a cyclical way as topography in the Baltic States is flat and does not allow to accumulate significant water reserves. Hydro resources are particularly important in Latvia where HPPs can serve as an important balancing and peak-shaving asset along or by replacing natural gas (CCGT) capacities.

In terms of the dynamic of change in primary energy consumption, the trend has been stable showing a steady growth in all five interconnected countries. Lithuania experienced a reduction just after the closure of the Ignalina nuclear power plant, but afterwards the trend has been similar to the trajectories in the rest of the quintet (Fig. 9.3). The data on primary energy consumption in absolute figures confirms the trend and illustrates the convergence of consumption trends in the three Baltic States and the different scale of primary energy consumption in Finland and Poland. As noted above, only one country among the five, namely Poland, can potentially expect growth in primary energy consumption and increase in the use of natural gas for power and heat production.

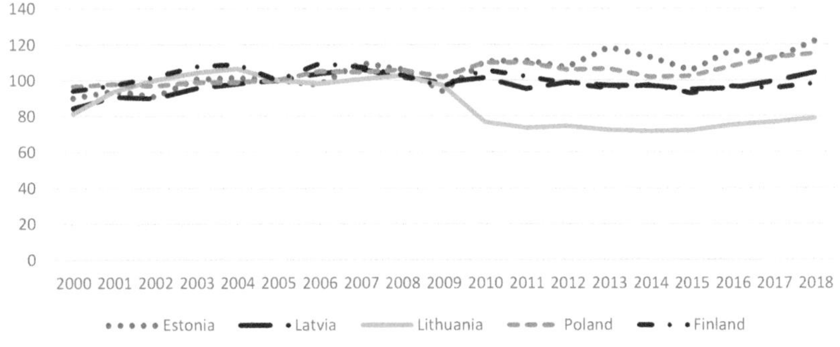

Fig. 9.3 Primary energy consumption (index: 2005 = 100) (*Source* The Author, based on Eurostat 2021)

It is interesting to analyse the gross available energy by product to see the differences in the relevance of natural gas in the energy portfolio in each of the five countries. Figure 9.4 illustrates the CCGT capacities available for electricity and heat production. Finland and Latvia are leading in this respect while Estonia has no CCGT capacity at all. Given the requirements of energy and climate policy targets it can be predicted with high probability that Poland is going to invest in gas-fired power plants to replace coal power plants in the next decade and beyond. Thus, there is enough justification for natural gas and therefore also LNG to remain part of energy portfolios. Although Estonia is seeking a different path to carbon neutrality than choosing a different fossil fuel to cover its power production needs, it still cannot be excluded that small capacity natural gas CHPPs might have their role, provided they find sufficient heat demand sources to justify the investment in the technology. Alternatively, natural gas may continue to have a certain role as a fuel of choice for boiler houses for district heating.

In terms of gross available energy, the total numbers for the Baltic States are similar (Estonia 6,587 toe, Latvia 4,831 toe and Lithuania 7,996 toe) while the significantly higher numbers for Finland (5–7 times higher) and Poland (up to 20 times higher) reflect the different scale of energy needs. The figures for natural gas follow the same layout. However, they also indicate the differences in the need to ensure natural gas imports in terms of volumes to be secured. Poland is well above

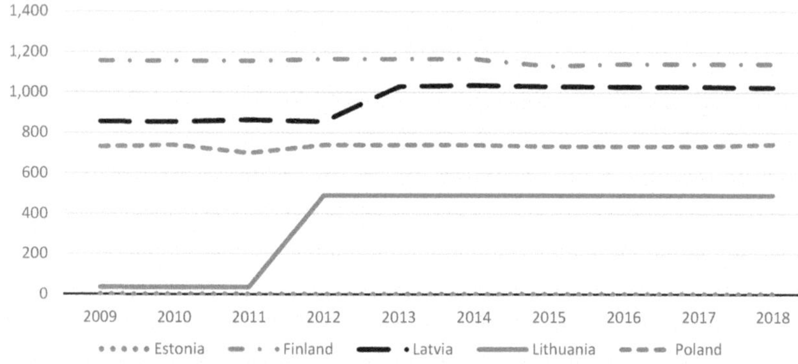

Fig. 9.4 Electricity production capacities using CCGT technology (MW) (*Source* The Author, based on Eurostat 2021)

of the volumes of natural gas required to cover the needs in Estonia, Latvia, Lithuania and Finland, which are technically a part of a single gas market.[2] Again, the GIPL interconnection would not only serve as a security backup for the supply of pipeline gas from European destinations via Poland to the Baltic States but has the potential to play a role from the market perspective.

There is, however, a trend in energy consumption, which cannot be ignored. This trend indicates large changes that energy sector is facing, and this trend has implications for the future role of natural gas in the region. Although renewables and biofuels have been gaining ground slowly in the Baltic States and have had only a slightly quicker pace in Poland and Finland, their share in gross available energy, especially in Latvia and Finland and to a lesser extent also in Lithuania and Estonia, has been increasing. It must be noted though that Finland and Latvia already are among the three EU nations with the highest overall share of renewable energy, and Latvia has the third highest share of renewable energy in electricity production in the EU (European Commission, 2020). The policies aimed at increasing the share of renewables in energy production and gross final energy consumption have had result, and a gradual fuel change away from fossil fuels is part of that. However, the use of natural gas in transport sector is a different story as it contributes to a fuel change from petroleum products to environmentally more friendly solutions and has the potential to serve as a transition fuel. A 2018 Nordic Energy Research study has identified ability to coupling of renewable power to other sectors such as heat and transport, and gas has significant potential for increased flexibility of energy system (Farid et al., 2018).

Regional Gas Market Context

The Klaipeda LNG terminal and the Balticconnector interconnection are operational and are used for supplying natural gas to customers in the Baltic States and Finland. This infrastructure represents an alternative route of supply allowing imports of natural gas differently than via pipelines from Russia. It must be noted though, that natural gas in the Finnish gas transmission system originates from Russia. As the Klaipeda LNG facility is not always utilised to its full technical capacity, a question

[2] Lithuania is not a part of the single gas market of the Baltic States and Finland from the legal and regulatory point of view.

remains whether developing own LNG infrastructure in Latvia is a necessary and viable solution. There is no simple answer, but the following sections provide a hint of an answer to this question.

Natural gas has had an important role in Latvia and Lithuania and will continue to have such a role although with slightly different emphasis. Prior to the construction of the Klaipeda LNG import terminal, pipeline gas from Russia used to be the sole source and route of supply to the Baltic States. While gas import dependence of Latvia, Lithuania and Poland has been fluctuating, the indicator for Estonia and Finland has remained at 100% over the course of 20 years.[3]

Single Gas Market of the Baltic States and Finland

Because of the small size of the individual gas markets in the Baltic States and because of the need to make the best out of the existing gas infrastructure in the region, the liberalisation of gas market brought about understanding in Estonia, Latvia and Lithuania that a regional gas market would serve the needs best. Initially, the idea was to establish a single gas market incorporating the three Baltic States, but the understanding that the Baltic market would be more liquid and interesting also for gas suppliers if Finland became a part of this single market area was soon reached. The pragmatism of this development was strengthened by the construction of the Balticconnector gas interconnection between Estonia and Finland (Baltic Connector Oy, 2020; Elering, 2020).

The gas TSOs of Estonia, Finland and Latvia signed an agreement (so called ITC agreement) about transmission system operators' compensation mechanism in 2019. The agreement came into force on the 1st of January 2020 (Conexus Baltic Grid, 2019), effectively marking the beginning of a single gas market area in these three countries. Although Lithuania had not formally become a part of this area by November 2020, Lithuania plays an important role in the regional gas supply as the only LNG import terminal of a regional significance for the Baltic States is situated in Klaipeda, Lithuania. The LNG terminal can supply up to approximately 80% of the cumulative demand in all three Baltic States. In 2019, Lithuania supplied 0.54 bcm of natural gas to Latvia, which is approximately 22% of the total gas supply of Latvia. Amber Grid,

[3] Natural gas import dependence illustrates the share of imported natural gas in natural gas consumption of a country.

Lithuania's gas TSO, has implemented transmission system development projects that have increased the capacity of gas transmission pipelines to transport (gasified) natural gas from the Klaipeda LNG terminal into the rest of Lithuania's gas transmission system and across the border into Latvia's gas transmission system.

Latvia's gas transmission system is operationally managed by Conexus Baltic Grid - Latvia's natural gas transmission system operator. It is well-developed and can comfortably accommodate capacities that ensure secure gas supplies to consumers in Estonia, Latvia and Lithuania. It provides gas transit services to Estonia or Finland, and gas storage at the Inčukalns UGS, which has 2.4 billion cubic metres storage capacity (Conexus Baltic Grid, 2019).[4] It serves as an important element in the Baltic system of security of gas supply.

The Inčukalns UGS After the Market Liberalisation

Natural gas lobby in Latvia initiated a debate, including discussions in the Latvian Parliament, just before the liberalisation of the Latvian gas market in April 2017 on the ability of the UGS to survive if the gas incumbent and actual monopolist JSC Latvijas gāze would decide to avoid using the UGS for storing gas there. As decisions about gas market liberalisation had already been made a year earlier, the purpose of such debate was to exercise pressure on the government and decision makers to finance a guaranteed volume of natural gas to be stored in the UGS (SKATIES, 2017). However, the data of Conexus Baltic Grid indicates that despite warnings and threats that Inčukalns UGS might experience shortage of gas for storage because of the market liberalisation, there has been a sufficient interest from companies to store gas in Inčukalns. There was an initial drop in the volume of stored gas right after the market liberalisation. The stored volume of the Inčukalns UGS reached 1.55 bcm in 2015, 1.25 bcm in 2016, 1.16 bcm in 2017 and 1.11 bcm in 2018 of the total storage capacity of 2.4 bcm (Conexus Baltic Grid, 2017, 2021). In 2019, however, the volume of stored gas (1.58 bcm) reached two thirds of the total capacity (Conexus Baltic Grid, 2019, 2021), which is a good result

[4] The Inčukalns UGS is a part of Conexus Baltic Grid, Latvia's gas transmission and storage operator. JSC Augstsprieguma tīkls, Latvia's electricity TSO, holds 68.46%, MM Infrastructure Investments Europe Limited 29.06% and other shareholders 2.48% of the shares of Conexus Baltic Grid.

considering the market is going through the early days of development and understanding what works and what needs to be adjusted.

The pattern of the use of the natural gas transmission and storage infrastructure has changed since the liberalisation of gas market in the Baltic States in general and in Latvia in particular, as it possesses the only gas storage facility of large scale in Inčukalns. Natural gas used to be mostly used during the heating season and the gas flows between Latvia and Russia had distinctly seasonal character with most of gas coming to the Inčukalns UGS during spring and summer months and flowing out of the UGS to the consumers in Latvia and North-West Russia during the heating season (Aboltins & Akule, 2014).[5] With the implementation of the EU Gas Directive 2009/73/EC unbundling requirements and the liberalisation of the gas market in Latvia in 2017, gas market stakeholders and participants have adjusted their patterns of gas consumption (European Union, 2009). Incoming and outgoing gas flows at the Inčukalns UGS have become more dynamic owing to a competitive interest from suppliers and traders to store gas for later use according to market situation.

The Beginning of the LNG Story in Latvia

When it comes to LNG specifically, making LNG as an alternative to pipeline gas from Russia was a matter of a debate already a decade ago. Latvia, along with Estonia and Lithuania, became increasingly aware that they are hostages to a situation, where they must rely on gas supplies from one source and in Latvia's case—via one route. Most importantly, they had to pay the price that is asked with no leverage whatsoever to negotiate for more lucrative conditions for the buyer.

The European Union was also aware of the Baltic States as an energy island within the EU that needs to develop their energy system away from dependence on too few suppliers and supply sources. A study on LNG infrastructure of regional importance for the DG Energy of the European Commission in 2012 identified several potential landing points for

[5] The gas flows crossing the Korneti exit point from Latvia to Russia have shrunk significantly since the 2015–2016 season when 0.26 bcm were transported to Russia, amounting to 0.1 bcm in the 2016–2017 season, 0.05 bcm in the 2017–2018 season, 0.07 bcm in the 2018–2019 season and 0.04 bcm in the 2019–2020 season (Conexus Baltic Grid, 2017, 2021).

incoming LNG deliveries in the Baltic States: three in Estonia, two in Latvia and one in Lithuania. The study concluded that project costs in all six location would generally require a sizeable investment, but noted that Paldiski in Estonia would make most sense when it comes to costs and benefits from the implementation of a project of a regional significance especially if the Balticconnector interconnection on the Estonian side would land near Paldiski (booz&co, 2012).

The Skulte LNG Project

No early discussion about LNG supplies to the Baltic States seriously considered the Skulte LNG import terminal project as a potential or viable project. Instead, Riga and Ventspils were the two destinations under consideration. The most likely reasons for considering Riga as the location for an LNG terminal are the fact that Riga is the capital city and most of natural gas consumption is concentrated in and around Riga because of district heating demand, which is covered by two large units. In turn, the most likely reason for considering Ventspils was its large maritime port. However, Ventspils is not connected to the national gas transmission system and it does not have a gas distribution system either. On the other hand, it could have one and Ventspils could be connected to the national transmission grid by transforming the existing oil product pipeline into a gas pipeline.[6] LatRosTrans, which is the operator of the pipeline, has been investigating a possibility to convert the crude oil pipeline into a natural gas pipeline and make it a part of the gas transmission system, albeit with no success so far (LatRosTrans, 2021).

The idea of creating an offshore LNG import and regasification terminal in the small port of Skulte on the East Coast of the Gulf of Riga and just 34 kilometres from the Inčukalns UGS, dates back to late 2013 and early 2014 (Skulte Port Authority, 2021). Then, a group of

[6] LatRosTrans has two parallel pipelines connecting Polotsk in Belarus and Ventspils in Latvia. One of the pipes used to be for petroleum products and another one for crude oil. The length of the petroleum products pipeline is 340 kilometres and the crude oil pipeline is 336 kilometres long. The pipelines can hold 242,819 m^3 of oil. The Polotsk-Ventspils crude oil pipeline has been emptied, cleaned and conserved. The petroleum products pipeline transports diesel fuel at a throughput capacity of up to eight million tonnes per year. LatRosTrans is owned by JSC Latvijas kuģniecība (Latvian Shipping Company) (66%) and JSC Transnefteproduct (34%) (LatRosTrans, 2021).

Latvian individuals and investors of Norwegian and US origin were interested in building of LNG terminal in Latvia. According to the initial idea, the terminal would be able to receive LNG carriers with a capacity from 40,000 cubic metres to 170,000 cubic metres.

The project would consist of two essential components: (1) an offshore regasification unit and (2) the pipeline. The terminal itself would be a floating regasification unit (FRU) without an LNG cold storage facility. A pipeline between the terminal and the Inčukalns UGS need to be constructed. The total length of the pipeline from the offshore terminal near Skulte to Inčukalns is estimated to be 39 kilometres with five kilometres of a subsea pipeline and 34 kilometres of an onshore pipeline. The LNG import capacity is estimated at three million tonnes per annum, which equals to 4.08 bcm of natural gas per year. The terminal indicates that the regasification capacity could reach 4.18 bcm annually (Skulte LNG Terminal, 2020a). Costs of building the import terminal are estimated approximately at USD 120 million.

The Skulte LNG terminal company (Skulte LNG) was established in 2016 (Skulte LNG Terminal 2020a). It has few employees, its registered capital is USD 50,820, and the ownership is split between two shareholders, namely National Gas Terminal Society (83.33%) and Pēteris Ragaušs (16.67%) (LURSOFT, 2021a), an American businessman of a Latvian origin with experience in managing positions in oil and gas industry (Skulte LNG Terminal, 2020b).[7] In addition, Arnfinn Unum, a Norwegian businessman, has been reported to be a co-owner and chairperson of the Supervisory Board of the Skulte LNG Terminal (Skulte LNG Terminal, 2020a; Unum, 2021). The turnover of Skulte LNG in 2019 was merely USD 2,904 (LURSOFT, 2021a).

Skulte LNG has been advocating a development of the LNG terminal project with different stakeholders since. The emphasis has been on achieving agreement with a state-owned energy company JSC Latvenergo, which is the largest natural gas consumer in Latvia. In addition, Skulte LNG has been lobbying its interests with the national gas TSO

[7] The National Gas Terminal Society (Nacionālā gāzes termināļa biedrība in Latvian), an NGO, was established in August 2013 with two defined goals: (1) facilitate construction and operation of gas terminal in Latvia and (2) facilitate the development of the market of energy carriers in Latvia. The annual report for the year 2019 indicates that it had just one unpaid employee. The society's balance sheet indicates an income of USD 67 and an expenditure of USD 52 in 2019 (LURSOFT, 2021b).

Conexus Baltic Grid about the guaranteed use of infrastructure for the gas imports to ensure the terminal and the pipeline connecting Skulte LNG terminal and the Inčukalns UGS are economically viable.

According to Skulte LNG, the success of the project is largely based on the assumption that Conexus will either buy the pipeline from Skulte LNG or build the pipeline itself, making it part of the Latvian gas transmission system. Costs of building the pipeline are estimated to be some USD 36 million. Approximately 0.8–0.9 bcm need to be regasified annually to cover the costs associated with building the FRU without a state subsidy. The aforementioned volume would ensure that the regasification tariff stays at USD 1.45/MWh. Skulte LNG presumes that approximately one third of the minimal annual capacity of the terminal (0.28 bcm) will be used by JSC Latvenergo. A business plan of the project stipulates that JSC Latvenergo would have to pay up to USD 3.63 million annually for using the services of the terminal. Last but not least, regasification service agreements would have to be concluded with the potential users of the Skulte LNG terminal for the FID to be reached (Skulte LNG Terminal, 2020b).

The developers of the project have been busy pursuing two main goals: (1) to identify a potential strategic investor and (2) to lobby for the status of an object of national interest. The second goal is needed to avoid the possibility that municipalities and residents affected by the project can formally challenge it and thus effectively derail it (SKATIES, 2019). Certain progress in building strategic partnerships was allegedly achieved at the end of 2019. Then, Korea's Kogas was identified as having interest in the project (Zalite & Neimane, 2019). However, the status of these negotiations was unknown to the general public by the end of 2020. Moreover, attempts to lobby the project as a PCI with the Latvian Government and the European Network of Transmission System Operators for Gas (ENTSO-G) persist.

As for the status of an object of national interest, lobbying efforts had not succeeded by the end of 2020. In other words, the project has not received any particularly favourable status by that time. According to the Spatial Development Planning Law, objects of national interests are territories and objects necessary to ensure essential public interests, protection and sustainable use of natural resources. A proposition about granting a project or an object this status is prepared by sectoral ministries and the status is officially established by the Cabinet of Ministers by adopting Latvian Government regulations about a particular object (The

Latvian Parliament, 2011). In this case, the relevant sectoral ministry would be the Ministry of Economics, which bears the responsibility for energy sector. This status can be useful because it provides a fast-track decision-making about issuing construction permits. It stems from the Construction Law that a construction permit can be issued if the construction intention conforms to the spatial plan, local plan (if such has been drawn up) and detailed plan (if such is necessary in accordance with laws and regulations) of a local government, except when a construction intention is related to an object of national interest (The Latvian Parliament, 2014). The law, however, stipulates that the proposal about granting the status of an object of national interest shall contain the justification for the choice of location and the results of the environmental impact assessment (The Latvian Parliament, 2011). The environmental impact assessment of the project has been ongoing since December 2018, and it is expected to have a critical role for the future of the project.

The Energy Demand in Latvia

Natural gas incumbent JSC Latvijas gāze forecasted in 2015 that natural gas consumption in Latvia will shrink by 50% by 2030 primarily due to two reasons: (1) an increase in energy efficiency and (2) a fuel switch. This is confirmed by energy demand models for 2030 and beyond (Allena-Ozolina et al., 2020).

Primary energy consumption in Latvia has slightly decreased between 2005 and 2015, whereas thereafter consumption has been gradually increasing (Fig. 9.5). A forecast until 2050 indicates that gas demand may vary depending on climate and energy policy instruments that will be chosen to align energy and climate policy with the EU and national climate targets.[8]

[8] The TIMES (MARKAL EFOM) model was used by the researchers of the Institute of Energy Systems and Environment of the Riga Technical University in a study in 2020. The model has three scenarios: (1) the reference scenario, (2) the baseline scenario and (3) the NECP2030 scenario. 2017 is the reference year. The reference scenario does not include the existing taxes, such as the CO_2 tax and natural resource tax. Compared to the baseline scenario, the reference scenario allows to assess an impact of the existing tax policy. The baseline scenario considers the development of the energy sector according to the business-as-usual principle. The NECP2030 scenario takes into consideration policy measures indicated in Annex 4 of the NECP2030 to factor stimuli for renewable energy technologies, energy efficiency, fuel change in energy and transport

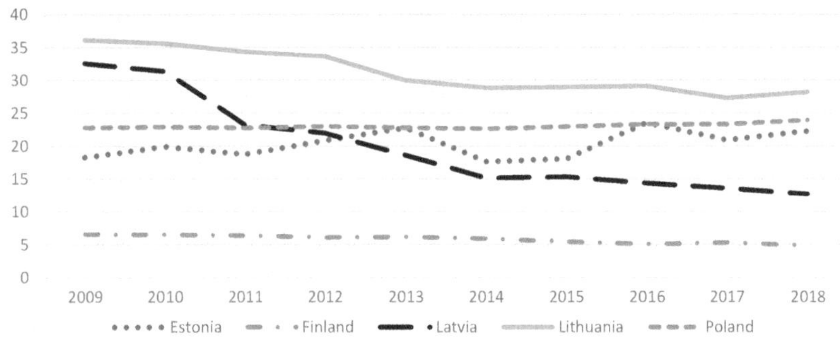

Fig. 9.5 Share of natural gas in final energy consumption of industry (%) (*Source* The Author, based on Eurostat 2021)

The results of the model show that consumption of natural gas increases in the reference scenario by 2030 as well as by 2050. A similar trend is projected in the base scenario, albeit the increase of natural gas consumption is smaller in 2030 than in the reference scenario and the level of consumption in 2050 is close to that in 2017. In the NECP scenario, natural gas consumption decreases only slightly by 2030.[9] It decreases significantly by 2050 dropping to 26% of all primary energy consumption while the share of wind and solar photovoltaic energy experiences its largest increase by 12 and 15% respectively (Allena-Ozolina et al., 2020).

Another model shows either a gradual or radical decrease of the role of natural gas over the next 20 years (Blumberga et al., 2020). Natural gas has been a key primary energy resource for district heating. Unlike in electricity production and supply, heating (including district heating) requires the heat to be produced close to the place of consumption. The role of natural gas in a number of models shrinks, and modelling results indicate that this is especially true for gas consumption outside the capital city Riga. It is likely that the main sources of natural gas consumption will remain with larger industrial gas users in Riga and its agglomeration, and in the regions where enterprises use natural gas in their industrial

sectors, as well as measures aimed to disincentivise investment in fossil energy technologies into the calculations of the TIMES model (Allena-Ozolina et al., 2020).

9 NECP stands for National Energy and Climate Plan of Latvia.

processes. Larger residential areas in Riga and other cities with the established gas distribution system are likely to experience a gradual phase-out of natural gas. However, gas prices and changes in factors influencing gas prices can have a significant impact on the technology transition for space heating purposes (Blumberga et al., 2020).

The share of natural gas used in industrial sector has been decreasing in Latvia steadily. The main drop was experienced when JSC Liepājas metalurgs, a steel producing company and one of the two largest gas consumers in Latvia, switched its production processes from using natural gas over to electricity. In the Baltic States, natural gas has maintained its proportion in final energy consumption with no radical changes. Beyond the Baltic States, there are prospects that the role of natural gas will be notably increasing in Poland due to a fuel change.

Latvia's National Energy and Climate Plan 2030 (NECP2030) projects shrinking of the share of natural gas in primary energy consumption towards the year 2030. In addition, final energy consumption and primary energy intensity in the baseline and target scenarios is projected to decrease approximately by a half between 2017 and 2030 (Government of the Republic of Latvia, 2019).

Key Factors Having Positive Effect on Gas Demand

A fuel change in heat and power production, the transport sector (municipal, commercial, private household), LNG for shipping (deployment of vessels and bunkering), and a deployment of alternative fuels on land and for maritime shipping (European Commission, 2014) are all factors that continue to influence future consumption of natural gas in Latvia and the Baltic States in general.

The requirements for the development of the EU core Trans-European Transport Network (TEN-T) transport infrastructure envisages availability of charging infrastructure for electric vehicles as well as CNG stations to facilitate a fuel change in the transportation sector from diesel and petrol to natural gas (blue gas) and biogas (biomethane or green gas). Fiscal policies are used to stimulate the production of biomethane, which is predominantly used in transport sector primarily to fuel public and commercial vehicles, but also support deployment of CNG-fuelled private passenger vehicles.

When forecasting the use of LNG in the future energy system, Conexus Baltic Grid has identified LNG as a replacement fuel in the transport sector, arguing that the use of gas as a fuel will speed up the progress towards the target of carbon neutrality in the transport. It also supports the idea of developing a network of gas filling stations that would make CNG, LNG as well as bio-CNG and bio-LNG available to fleets of commercial enterprises as well as private passenger vehicles (Conexus Baltic Grid, 2019), as the transport sector is one of the main sources of the greenhouse gas (GHG) emissions.

The development in Estonia's transport sector with the introduction and the rapid development of gas for transport infrastructure followed by an increase of the share of natural gas (mostly biomethane) in final energy consumption in transport are indicative of the changes that can be expected to take place in Latvia as well (Fig. 9.6). JSC Latvijas gāze, former gas monopoly and the dominant gas supplier, is developing new strategies to diversify its business to encompass CNG and establish itself as a leader in the transport sector.

On the energy efficiency side, households (individual houses and multi-apartment buildings) are a segment that has a significant potential to consume less natural gas through implementing energy efficiency measures, such as insulating houses and apartment buildings as well as pursuing a more Nordic approach to choosing electricity instead of natural gas as the main source of energy for cooking. Despite the good

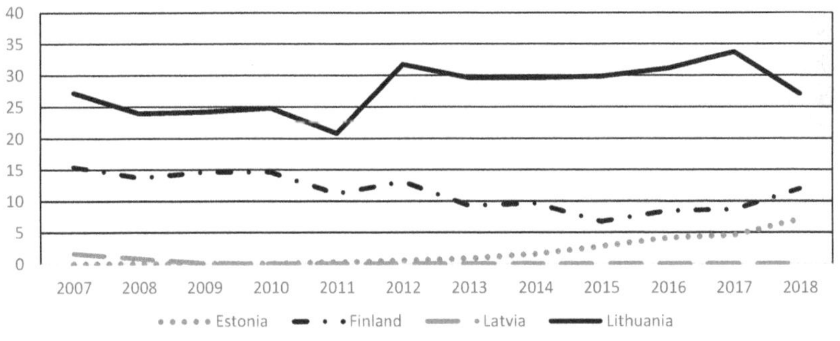

Fig. 9.6 Final energy consumption of natural gas in transport (thousand toe) (*Note* The data on Poland has been omitted to allow a meaningful comparison between the Baltic States and Finland. The figures for Poland stand at just under 500,000 toe, which is over 30 times more than in the Baltic States.) (*Source* The Author, based on Eurostat 2021)

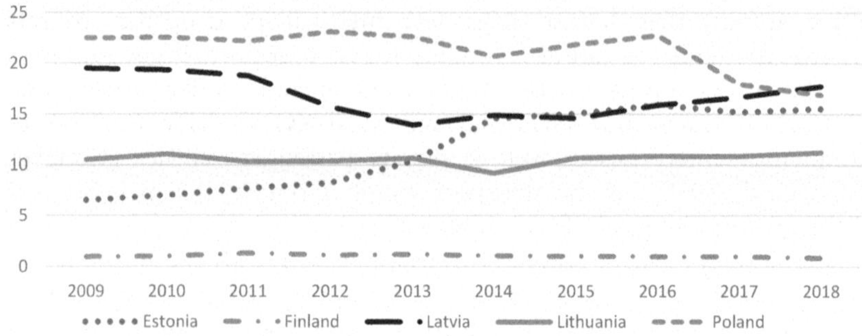

Fig. 9.7 Share of natural gas in final energy consumption: commercial and public services (%) (*Source* The Author, based on Eurostat 2021)

prospects for electricity in medium term and long term, natural gas has been a resource and technology of choice in households as the technology is well-known, mostly reliable, and natural gas is experiencing a prolonged period of low prices, which are the result of global hydrocarbon market development over the recent years. In addition, households do not worry about the broader context of using imported fossil fuel, since a tradition, a reliability and an affordable price are the key factors influencing their choices.

A more widespread use of heat pumps instead of natural gas boilers is also a future trend, even more so because natural gas supply has its limitations. In other words, if there is no connection to the gas distribution system, using natural gas requires additional infrastructure, which is costly and needs a regular maintenance unlike its rival electricity.

The share of natural gas in final energy consumption in commercial and public services has remained rather stable in the Baltic States since 2014. The increase in Latvia has been a bit faster than in Lithuania and Estonia where the indicator has largely maintained its level since the year 2014 (Fig. 9.7).

Global Gas Market Trends

Although there is no immediate link between the global gas market and Latvia, it is essential to provide the global context of natural gas and LNG business as it influences gas prices in Latvia. A major factor in favour of liquefied natural gas as energy choice is its potentially low price on the world market. Gas prices, including LNG prices, however, can be volatile with all the risks associated with the volatility.

Global market trends are set by changes in gas demand in prime markets (East Asia and South-East Asia), which correlates with meteorological conditions during the heating season. LNG production and supply has also changed. New production and export facilities have been built, especially in North America. The global LNG tanker fleet has grown to surpass 540 LNG vessels by end of 2019 with more than 40 more vessels in production in 2020 highlighting the expectations that LNG trade will continue to grow (International Gas Union, 2020).

With the warmer winters over the recent years, gas demand has declined for heating purposes although industrial use still remains in place and is subject only to the volatility on the global commodities markets. As the major urban areas in South-East Asia reduce their gas consumption and gas prices decrease, LNG increasingly finds its way to other destinations that are next in line as 'the next best buyer', and the European markets serve this role well. LNG supplies to Europe have soared over the past five years pushing down the price of pipeline gas, including the imports from Russia. A warm winter in Asia reduced price differentials between European and Asian spot natural gas prices, which led to increased volumes of the US LNG exports delivered to European destinations (U.S. Energy Information Administration, 2019).

The United States have invested heavily in building its gas export capacity and there are eight LNG export terminals and six of those are commercially operational and two are under construction (U.S. Energy Information Administration, 2020a). A fuel change in the light of new energy and climate policies in Europe and around the world are among the factors that have been interpreted as a clear signal to the industry that gas demand will grow for some time to come, while the last coal mines and coal-fired power plants retire.

However, the economic growth has been modest, and the COVID-19 pandemic has had a freezing impact on the world economy seeing energy consumption and demand shrink dramatically. This pushed down gas and LNG prices making it a buyers' market even more than it has been over the past four to five years (Reuters, 2020), but due to changes in global demand gas prices bounced back in 2021. Under these circumstances, LNG supplies from the United States have to compete on an open and transparent market with other LNG suppliers from different continents, be it LNG producers in Algeria, Australia, Norway, Qatar or

Russia. In addition, it should be kept in mind that Russia and Norway are by far the EU's largest suppliers of natural gas and the competition is fierce (Slav, 2020). Thus, the keywords for any LNG supplies to European destinations are competition and price.

It should be noted, however, that the US LNG export capacities have increased significantly since the first two trains of the LNG export terminal in Sabine Pass entered service in 2016. Five other LNG export terminals have gone online making the total number of available trains reach seventeen by mid-2020. Two more terminals, Golden Pass and Calcasieu, are under construction and are expected to enter service between 2023 and 2025 adding thirteen more trains (U.S. Energy Information Administration, 2020b). In this context, the Klaipeda LNG import terminal comes in handy for the Baltic States potentially allowing to make the best out of the competitive LNG spot prices by combining the possibilities provided by the Klaipeda LNG terminal in Lithuania and the Inčukalns underground gas storage in Latvia.

The result of availability of historically cheap natural gas has made gas-fuelled energy technologies more competitive: gas-fired CCGT CHPPs have managed to adjust their production to the market situation and have made it possible to operate with commercial success even in condensation mode even during summer months.

European Energy and Climate Policy Context

The EU energy and climate policy might bring changes in the EU as well as local regulatory framework making fossil fuels less competitive vis-à-vis non-fossil alternatives. This poses a question whether own LNG facility in Latvia would be able to survive purely on commercial terms or would the government intervention be necessary and if so, then what cost would be acceptable.

Implementation of the EU Gas Directive (European Union, 2009) brought about changes in the energy market and resulted in the unbundling of the national gas enterprise and gas market liberalisation in 2017. By then the natural gas industry had established itself as a key player in the energy sector through emphasising the importance of a continued and close co-operation with suppliers of natural gas as well as technologies and know-how to ensure operation, maintenance and further development of the Inčukalns UGS. Besides, with the support of the local gas industry, a lot of emphasis was put on renovating Riga

CHPP-2 by constructing two new CCGT turbine blocks replacing the older technologies, making heat and electricity production more efficient and adding significant extra capacity. These actions were justified, at least in public, on the assumption that gas consumption will remain the same over the next decade or so, and additional power production capacity will be needed to ensure secure supply of energy. In reality, things are set to develop in a slightly different direction: a fuel change and a reduction of energy consumption as the result of building renovation and other energy efficiency measures is going to contribute to a gradual phase-out of natural gas technologies used to produce space heating for residential, commercial and industrial buildings.

Over the 2010s, the European Union has pursued energy policy that focuses on reducing its dependence on fossil energy and imports of fossil primary energy resources in particular. Reduction of excess consumption of energy has become a key goal putting energy efficiency policies at the centre of attention of the EU member states. The 'energy efficiency first' principle is enshrined in the landmark EU Clean energy for all Europeans package resulting in a new energy efficiency target for the EU for 2030, a revised Renewable Energy Directive and Energy Performance in Buildings Directive (EC DG Energy, 2019). The revised Renewable Energy Directive sets a new binding renewable energy target for the EU for 2030 of at least 32% with a clause for a potential upwards revision by the year 2023 (European Union, 2018a). The buildings are the largest single source of energy consumption in the EU constituting approximately 40% of energy consumption and approximately 36% of GHG emissions. Therefore, Energy Performance in Buildings Directive is set to achieve ambitious goals of significantly improving energy performance of the current building stock, roughly one third of which is over 50 years old and decrease energy consumption and CO_2 emissions by as much as five percent (European Union, 2018b).

Latvia's building stock, both residential and industrial, that was constructed during the second half of the twentieth century cannot boast high energy efficiency levels. Residential multi-apartment buildings have particularly poor energy efficiency performance, providing space for significant energy efficiency improvements. Reducing the need for heating in the residential sector is inevitably going to result in a reduction of heat demand in the capital city Riga, which hosts over 50% of all residential buildings in Latvia, as well as in other large cities and towns. Most of the buildings have the potential to improve their energy efficiency by 50–70%, which means that the two large gas-fired CHPPs in Riga will be facing a challenging situation already in the near future. JSC Latvenergo, the state-owned energy producer and trader and operator of the CHPPs, will most likely have to consider phase-out of one or more CCGT units.

The European Energy Union, Clean energy for all Europeans and the European Green Deal have all made an enormous impact on energy and climate policies of the EU member states. Most notably, national energy and climate plans are compulsory and need to identify concrete policy measures and instruments to ensure prioritisation of climate policy goals and reaching of these goals during the nearest decade.

Latvia's National energy and climate plan 2030 (NECP2030), which is an integral part of the larger EU energy and climate policy picture, also contains several references to the role of gas in the '*Energy security, reducing energy dependency, full integration of energy markets and modernising of infrastructure*' section (Measure 6 of Annex 4 of the NECP2030) and more specifically—in the Measure 6.1 titled '*Ensuring energy security, reducing energy dependency and ensuring full energy market integration*' (Government of the Republic of Latvia, 2019). Although there is no explicit reference to LNG, it stems from the formulation of activities in the respective subsection that alternative suppliers need to be attracted to and involved in the gas market. Gas interconnection project between Latvia and Lithuania has to be finalised to ensure that this section of the Baltic gas transmission network has sufficient transmission capacity. It is quite clearly relevant to ensure physical gas flows between the Klaipeda LNG terminal in Lithuania and Latvia, Estonia and Finland.

Geopolitical Context

As the three Baltic States used to be 100% reliant on Russian gas supplies for many decades with political and economic influences stemming from this dependence, the intuitive prediction would be that geopolitics will always be in favour of energy infrastructure projects in the Baltic States that strengthen and ensure energy independence from the dominant neighbour.

Ownership unbundling in the energy sector has improved energy independence of the Baltic States in general and Latvia in particular, given the role that energy infrastructure objects, such as the Inčukalns UGS, have in secure supplies of energy in Latvia and the Baltic States altogether. The gas market liberalisation in Latvia was opposed by the gas lobby trying to postpone any changes in the *status quo* for as long as possible and making Latvia the last of the three Baltic States to liberalise its gas market and become less dependent on gas supplies from Russia.

Debates over the Nord Stream 2 pipeline project have been on the agenda of politicians, but not on the agenda of households, as the project has no direct influence on potential gas supplies associated with Russia. The project is perceived to be a key factor in the regional geopolitical dynamics and a major issue in relations between Russia and three other big players in international politics, namely the United States, Germany and the EU. The USA has historically been active introducing sanctions against businesses involved in the implementation of the Nord Stream 2 project, targeting the operators of the pipe-laying vessels and slowing down the work and postponing the schedule of accomplishing the project. The situation changed though in July 2021 with the USA and Germany reaching an agreement allowing completion of the project under a precondition that Russia is not going to use it as a weapon against Ukraine.

It is a well-known fact among Latvia's political leadership that energy relations play a major role in the German–Russian relations. The appointment of Gerhard Schröder, former Chancellor of Germany, as the top official in Russia's major energy company did not incur positive attitudes in the Baltic States, Latvia included, as this move potentially explained certain aspects of Germany not taking a more solid stance against Russia's near abroad policy doctrine of influence and intervention in its neighbours' affairs.

Germany is the largest gas consumer in the EU and its frustration around the Nord Stream and Nord Stream 2 projects can be understood. At the same time, those EU member states, which have had controversial experience with Russia in the past do not appreciate Germany's support to the project, including its reluctance to see the geopolitical influences of this pipeline project on Ukraine and beyond. A critical moment in Germany's relations with the Baltic States and East European states occurred when Germany expressed its opposition to the amendments of the EU Gas Directive in 2018 and 2019 that would complicate the implementation of the Nord Stream 2 project and would make it less profitable to operate because of limitations related to capacity booking.

In Latvia's energy relations with Russia, nevertheless, when it has come down to business, it has always been about the availability of leverage to negotiate prices for natural gas as natural gas supplies from Russia to Latvia have never been disrupted as the Latvian consumers were always paying the price that was asked and paying the price on time. The situation has fundamentally changed since the liberalisation of the Baltic gas market though, and Gazprom is competing for its market share in Latvia just as other competitors.

Apart from just doing business, LNG supplies to the Baltic States have the potential to facilitate development of closer economic ties with the United States, which has become a major international LNG trader over the recent years since it opened its energy market for exports to build on the momentum of high shale gas output. Although LNG imports from the USA can contribute significantly to improving gas supply options in European destinations, the share of the US LNG exports landing in Europe constituted only 6.6% of total LNG exports by mid-2018 (Aboltins, 2018), but they grew significantly afterwards, reaching over 38% of total exports in 2019 and pushing the cumulative share to over 26% during the period from 2016 until 2019 (U.S. Department of Energy, 2020; U.S. Energy Information Administration, 2019).

There can possibly be a role of LNG supplies to the three Baltic States in a broader context of the Central and Eastern Europe region, but their importance should not be overestimated and cannot be compared with the role of the Świnoujście LNG import terminal in Poland, which will be able to serve as an alternative route of supply of natural gas to the four Visegrad countries (so called V4) with pipelines connecting gas transmission systems of Poland with those of Czechia, Hungary and Slovakia(ENTSO-G, 2020; Ruszel, 2020).

Despite almost permanently tense political relations between the Baltic States and Russia, supplying natural gas from sources other than Russia is not necessarily a goal in itself. The goal is to ensure the best price from the supplier, be it from Norway, Qatar, Russia or the USA. If Russian pipeline gas or Russian LNG can offer a competitive price, it can compete with other suppliers on equal footing and based on the same market conditions and rules (Henderson & Mitrova, 2015).

Conclusions

Several conclusions can be drawn from the multiple contexts in which the future role of LNG has to be looked at. First and foremost, there is no need to supply LNG if there is no demand for natural gas. Thus, the factors affecting demand forecasts should not be overlooked. Consumption is set to decrease primarily as the result of a fuel change and energy efficiency measures. The rate at which the role of natural gas will shrink will depend on energy and climate policies and policy instruments implemented to ensure transition to climate neutrality with the first threshold of energy and climate targets to be reached by 2030 but looking forward to 2050.

The potential of LNG in Latvia is mainly associated with the use of natural gas generally and LNG specifically in transport sector as a replacement to diesel and petrol in road transport as well as shipping. Market deployment will depend on the choice of policy instruments to support deployment of gas as transport fuel. Lower excise tax for natural gas in Latvia as of the beginning of 2021 aims at facilitating the introduction of CNG-fuelled vehicles and production of biomethane, or so called green gas. The side effect of this policy is favourable conditions for natural gas, or so called blue gas. One of the main challenges will be the rate of the introduction of electric vehicles and potentially the hydrogen transport fleet as well.

As there is a plenty of space for improvement in energy efficiency in buildings it can be expected that active policy measures will be adopted to decrease energy consumption for heating. The main potential lies in the residential sector where *carrots and sticks* will be used actively to achieve rapid changes, but industrial consumers will base their energy efficiency measures on business decisions. This will be one of the two main reasons for shrinking gas demand. Natural gas consumption has been gradually declining since 2010 with forecasts of consumption dropping to as low as 0.75 bcm in Latvia by 2030 and even lower by 2050 owing primarily to energy efficiency measures reaching mass scale.

Energy efficiency and a fuel switch will influence developments in all three Baltic States, requiring the gas business to re-focus on those segments of economy where gas is seen as a contributor to mitigating climate change. This, once again, points towards broader use of gas in transport sector. The bet would rather be on the development of LNG for shipping and LNG for local and district heating serving as the main fuel in places with no gas distribution system or as a backup fuel in the areas with an access to natural gas distribution system. Further development of green gas production, including bio-LNG, might add to the list of factors in favour of new LNG infrastructure in the region.

Whether these projected changes will create positive balance for natural gas in primary energy consumption and, if so, will that be enough to justify introduction of new LNG import infrastructure of sizeable capacity, remains an open question. The potential of any new LNG import project rests on a mix of factors including business decisions locally, regionally and globally, as well as on energy and climate policy decisions, which may sway in favour of natural gas and LNG in short term and medium term but are likely to indicate a gradual phase-out of fossil fuels, including natural gas, in long run.

References

Aboltins, R. (2018). Prospects of the American shale gas and LNG export to the Baltic states. In A. Spruds & M. Andzans (Eds.), *Security of the Baltic sea region revisited amid the Baltic centenary*. The Rīga Conference Papers 2018. Latvian Institute of International Affairs. https://www.researchgate.net/publication/328017721_Security_of_the_Baltic_Sea_Region_Revisited_amid_the_Baltic_Centenary_The_Riga_Conference_Papers_2018. Accessed 31 October 2020.

Aboltins, R., & Akule, D. (2014). *Liberalization of the natural gas market in Latvia: Overview and challenges*. http://providus.lv/article_files/2866/original/gaze_EN_marts.pdf. Accessed 29 October 2020.

Allena-Ozolina, S., Pakere, I., Jaunzems, D., Blumberga, A., & Bazbauers G. (2020). *Integrated MARKAL-EFOM System (TIMES) model for energy sector modelling*. http://www.conference.rtu.lv/qazcdeTGBmjU/RTUCON2020_paper_99Ln97dW10Bi87.pdf. Accessed 25 February 2021.

Augstsprieguma tīkls. (2021). *JSC Augstsprieguma Tīkls*. https://ast.lv/en. Accessed 18 January 2021.

Baltic Connector Oy. (2020). *Baltic connector*. http://balticconnector.fi/en/. Accessed 30 October 2020.

Blumberga, A., Blumberga, D., Indzere, Z., Kalnbalkite, A., Kalnins, S. N., Ozarska, A., & Gravelsins, A. (2020). *Establishment of system dynamics model in the territorial context* (Part of the Research Project Assessment of Latvia's Renewable Energy Supply-Demand Economic Potential and Policy Recommendations Project No. VPP-EM-2018 / AER_1_0001).

booz&co. (2012). *Analysis of costs and benefits of regional liquefied natural gas solution in the East Baltic area, including proposal for location and technical options under the Baltic energy market interconnection plan*. https://ec.europa.eu/energy/sites/ener/files/documents/20121123_lng_baltic_area_report.pdf. Accessed 22 February 2021.

Conexus Baltic Grid. (2017). *Gas transmission and storage capacities (till April 2017)*. https://capacity-m3.conexus.lv/?lang=eng. Accessed 17 January 2021.

Conexus Baltic Grid. (2019). *Natural gas transmission system operator – Annual Assessment Report 2019*. https://conexus.lv/uploads/filedir/Zinojumi/tso_report_2019.pdf. Accessed 14 September 2020.

Conexus Baltic Grid. (2021). *Capacities actually used*. https://capacity.conexus.lv/?id=158&lang=eng. Accessed 17 January 2021.

EC DG Energy. (2019). *Clean energy for all Europeans*. Publications Office of the EU. https://op.europa.eu/en/publication-detail/-/publication/b4e46873-7528-11e9-9f05-01aa75ed71a1/language-en?WT.mc_id=Searchresult&WT.ria_c=null&WT.ria_f=3608&WT.ria_ev=search. Accessed 31 October 2020.

Elering. (2020). *Balticconnector*. https://elering.ee/en/balticconnector. Accessed 31 October 2020.

ENTSO-G. (2020). *ENTSO-G Ten-Year Network Development Plan*. https://www.entsog.eu/sites/default/files/2020-11/TYNDP_2020_TRANSMISSION_map_1.pdf. Accessed 25 February 2021.

European Commission. (2014, October 28). *Directive 2014/94/EU - Deployment of Alternative Fuels Infrastructure*. Official Journal of the European Union. L 307 (pp. 1–20). https://eur-lex.europa.eu/legal-content/EN/TXT/?uri=celex:32014L0094. Accessed 25 February 2021.

European Commission. (2020). *EU energy in figures—Publications office of the EU*. https://op.europa.eu/es/publication-detail/-/publication/87b16988-f740-11ea-991b-01aa75ed71a1. Accessed 25 February 2021.

European Union. (2009). *Directive 2009/73/EC of the European Parliament and of the council of 13 July 2009 concerning common rules for the internal market in natural gas and repealing directive 2003/55/EC*. Official Journal of the European Union. https://eur-lex.europa.eu/legal-content/EN/TXT/PDF/?uri=CELEX:32009L0073&from=EN. Accessed 2 November 2020.

European Union. (2018a). *Directive (EU) 2018/2001 of the European Parliament and of the council of 11 December 2018 on the promotion of the use of energy from renewable sources (recast)*. https://eur-lex.europa.eu/legal-content/EN/TXT/PDF/?uri=CELEX:32018L2001&from=EN. Accessed 31 October 2020.

European Union. (2018b). *Directive (EU) 2018/844 of the European Parliament and of the council of 30 May 2018 amending directive 2010/31/EU on the energy performance of buildings and directive 2012/27/EU on energy efficiency*. https://eur-lex.europa.eu/legal-content/EN/TXT/PDF/?uri=CELEX:32018L0844&from=EN. Accessed 31 October 2020.

Farid, K., Lund, P., Skytte, K., & Bergaentzlé, C. (2018). *Better policies accelerate clean energy transition focus on energy system flexibility*. https://www.nordicenergy.org/wp-content/uploads/2018/02/Flex4RESPolicyBrief_final_160218.pdf. Accessed 31 October 2020.

Government of the Republic of Latvia. (2019). *Latvia's National Energy and Climate Plan 2021–2030*. https://ec.europa.eu/energy/sites/ener/files/documents/lv_final_necp_main_en.pdf. Accessed 30 October 2020.

Henderson, J., & Mitrova, T. (2015). *The political and commercial dynamics of Russia's gas export strategy*. The Oxford Institute For Energy Studies (September): 89. https://www.oxfordenergy.org/wpcms/wp-content/uploads/2015/09/NG-102.pdf. Accessed 24 February 2021.

International Gas Union. (2020). *World LNG Report 2020*. https://www.igu.org/app/uploads-wp/2020/04/2020-World-LNG-Report.pdf. Accessed 28 February 2021.

LatRosTrans. (2021). *LatRosTrans – About LRT*. LatRosTrans. http://www.latrostrans.lv/en/about-lrt/about-latrostrans/. Accessed 10 January 2021.

Latvenergo. (2021). *Latvenergo—Generation*. https://latvenergo.lv/en/par-mums/razosana. Accessed 23 February 2021.

LURSOFT. (2021a). *JSC Skulte LNG terminal—Company data*. https://company.lursoft.lv/en/skulte-lng-terminal/40103976384. Accessed 16 January 2021.

LURSOFT. (2021b). *Nacionala gazes terminala biedriba*. https://company.lursoft.lv/en/nacionala-gazes-terminala-biedriba/40008213645. Accessed 5 November 2020.

Reuters. (2020). *Asian spot prices edge higher as supply tightens*. https://www.reuters.com/article/global-lng-idUSL4N2AZ2ZL. Accessed 31 October 2020.

Ruszel, M. (2020). The significance of the Baltic Sea region for natural gas supplies to the V4 countries. *Energy Policy, 146*, 111786.

SKATIES. (2017). *'Latvijas Gāze' Pārtrauks Izmantot Inčukalna Pazemes Krātuvi Un to Nāksies Slēgt, Draud Kalvītis*. https://skaties.lv/zinas/latvija/sabiedriba/latvijas-gaze-partrauks-izmantot-incukalna-pazemes-kratuvi-un-to-naksies-slegt-draud-kalvitis/. Accessed 5 November 2020.

SKATIES. (2019). *Skultes Gāzes Termināļa Attīstītāji Grib Nacionālo Interešu Objekta Statusu; Tad Pašvaldību Un Iedzīvotāju Iebildumi Būvniecību Neietekmēs*. Nekā personīga. https://skaties.lv/zinas/latvija/neka-personiga/skultes-gazes-terminala-attistitaji-grib-nacionalo-interesu-objekta-statusu-tad-pasvaldibu-un-iedzivotaju-iebildumi-buvniecibu-neietekmes/. Accessed 21 October 2020.

Skulte LNG Terminal. (2020a). *Skulte LNG—About the project*. https://www.skultelng.lv/en/the_project/. Accessed 3 November 2020.

Skulte LNG Terminal. (2020b). *Skulte LNG project overview* (Unpublished report).

Skulte Port Authority. (2021). *Skulte Port—Skulte Port Authority*. https://skulteport.lv/en/port. Accessed 16 January 2021.

Slav, I. (2020). *Why U.S. LNG can't win in Europe*. https://oilprice.com/Energy/Natural-Gas/Why-US-LNG-Cant-Win-In-Europe.html. Accessed 31 October 2020.

The Latvian Parliament. (2011). *Spatial development planning law*. https://likumi.lv/ta/en/en/id/238807-spatial-development-planning-law. Accessed 17 January 2021.

The Latvian Parliament. (2014). *Construction law*. https://likumi.lv/ta/en/en/id/258572-construction-law. Accessed 17 January 2021.

Unum, A. (2021). *Arnfinn Unum*. https://www.linkedin.com/in/arnfinn-unum-86271319/. Accessed 16 January 2021.

U.S. Department of Energy. (2020). *LNG monthly map shows countries of destination of exports of domestically-produced LNG*. https://www.energy.gov/fe/listings/lng-reports. Accessed 18 January 2021.

U.S. Energy Information Administration. (2019). *U.S. LNG exports to Europe increase amid declining demand and spot LNG prices in Asia*. https://www.eia.gov/todayinenergy/detail.php?id=40213. Accessed 18 January 2021.

U.S. Energy Information Administration. (2020a). *Short-term energy outlook—U.S. Energy Information Administration (EIA)*. https://www.eia.gov/outlooks/steo/. Accessed 31 October 2020.

U.S. Energy Information Administration. (2020b). *U.S. liquefied natural gas export capacity to more than double by the end of 2019—Today in energy—U.S. Energy Information Administration (EIA)*. https://www.eia.gov/todayinenergy/detail.php?id=37732. Accessed 31 October 2020.

Zalite, I., & Neimane, Z. (2019). *South Korean giant reportedly interested in Latvian gas project*. https://eng.lsm.lv/article/economy/economy/south-korean-giant-reportedly-interested-in-latvian-gas-project.a334579/. Accessed 17 October 2020.

CHAPTER 10

New Sources of Natural Gas for Finland: The Balticconnector Pipeline and LNG Imports

Laura Klemetti and Hanna Mäkinen

Introduction

The Finnish natural gas sector experienced notable changes at the beginning of the 2020s. The natural gas market was opened to competition by unbundling the transmission and sales of gas and by launching the Balticconnector pipeline between Finland and Estonia. Balticconnector also enabled the creation of integrated gas market for Finland and the Baltic States. Since the mid-1970s, Finland has been receiving piped natural gas from a single supplier, first from the Soviet Union and subsequently from Russia. Creating new gas supply routes has been visioned for years in Finland and at first, building a connecting pipeline to Sweden was under consideration. However, in the 2010s, creating a connection between

L. Klemetti · H. Mäkinen (✉)
Pan-European Institute, University of Turku, Turku, Finland
e-mail: hasoma@utu.fi

L. Klemetti
e-mail: Laura.Klemetti@utu.fi

K. Liuhto (ed.), *The Future of Energy Consumption, Security and Natural Gas*, https://doi.org/10.1007/978-3-030-80367-4_10

Finland and Estonia became established as the main development direction. The construction of Balticconnector begun in 2018 and the work was completed by the end of 2019 (Gasgrid, 2020c; Gasum, 2019b). Finland has also facilitated the construction of LNG import terminals to enable the delivery of gas outside the reach of the national gas transmission network. The LNG imports to Finland began in 2016, when the first import terminal in Pori was opened for commercial use (Gasum, 2016). Both LNG terminals and Balticconnector are seen as contributing to diversified gas supply in Finland.

This chapter examines the impact of new sources of natural gas on the Finnish energy sector and the diversification of gas supply, focusing on pipeline imports through Balticconnector and LNG imports. For Finland, Balticconnector brings promises of diversifying gas transfer routes and hence, enhancing energy security. However, when examining the potential sources of gas imported through Balticconnector, this study raises the question if the pipeline alone will bring true diversification for the sources of gas supply. The LNG imports to Finland, in turn, have remained small-scale, mainly due to the lack of a large-capacity import terminal. While the share of natural gas in the Finnish energy mix is rather small, the country's natural gas market also remains limited, creating challenges for the cost-effectiveness of gas infrastructure projects. Within this context, this chapter addresses the challenges related to LNG infrastructure development in Finland, as well as the more general question of the sustainability of natural gas use in the face of tightening climate goals.

This chapter proceeds as follows: first, the recent developments in the Finnish natural gas sector, including natural gas consumption and the market liberalisation are reviewed. The chapter then turns to examine the sources of natural gas supply to Finland and the significance of the Balticconnector pipeline in terms of their diversification. Next, the prospects and limitations of LNG use in Finland are analysed, paying particular attention to the LNG infrastructure development, as well as the environmental impact of gas use and its potential alternatives. The chapter ends with conclusions.

Recent Developments in the Finnish Natural Gas Sector

Natural Gas Consumption in Finland

According to Statistics Finland (2020a), total energy consumption in Finland in 2019 was 1.36 million terajoules (TJ). In 2019, wood fuels, oil and nuclear energy had the largest shares in Finland's total energy consumption—28, 23 and 18% respectively—and the share of natural gas was five percent. Compared with the previous year, total energy consumption fell by one percent, mainly due to the six percent fall in the consumption of fossil fuels and peat. The decrease in the consumption of fossil fuels and peat resulted, among others, from the reduced use of fossil fuels in separate production of electricity, tax increases for particularly coal and peat, and the considerable rise in the prices of emission rights (Koistinen, 2019; Statistics Finland, 2020a; Tax Administration, 2019). The consumption of natural gas decreased by four percent compared with the previous year, amounting to 73,000 TJ, or 2.1 bcm. During the past ten years, the natural gas consumption has approximately halved, as has also its share in total energy consumption (Fig. 10.1).

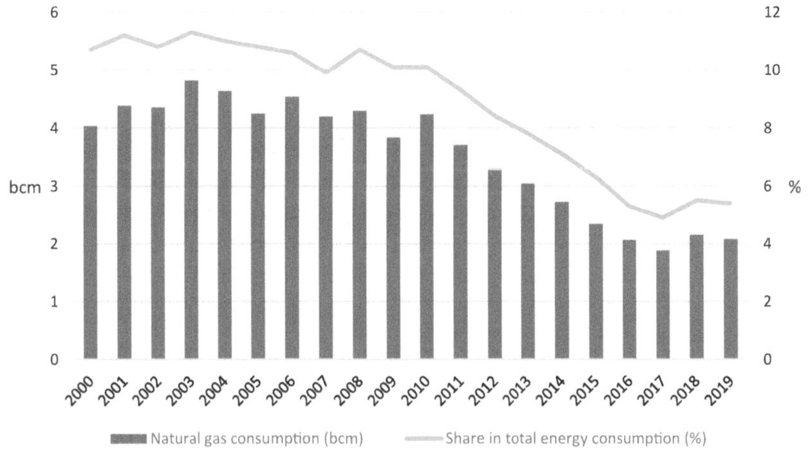

Fig. 10.1 The consumption of natural gas and its share in total energy consumption in Finland in 2000–2019 (*Source* The Authors, based on Statistics Finland [2020c])

In Finland, the main consumers of natural gas are industry and energy production and, unlike in Central and Eastern Europe, household consumption of gas is marginal. The share of industry in natural gas consumption is almost 60% and the share of heat and power production nearly 40% (Energy Authority, 2019), making the share of other uses of gas, such as direct gas heating of buildings and cooking in households and restaurants, insignificant. Chemical and forest industries are the main industrial users of natural gas. Natural gas is utilised as raw material in the production of hydrogen in oil refining and other chemical industry's processes. It is also an ideal fuel in industrial processes where, for instance, high temperatures and fast adjustability are needed. In energy production, natural gas is mainly used in combined heat and power production where both electricity and heat are produced in the same power plant and, to a lesser extent, in the production of district heating. One of the main benefits of the gas-based heat and power production is its fast adjustability for the changes in energy demand (Finnish Gas Association, 2020). The gas transmission network covers the southern and south-eastern parts of Finland, as well as the Pirkanmaa region around the City of Tampere (Gasgrid, 2020b). Natural gas is available for consumption in around 40 municipalities (Energy Authority, 2019).

The limited transmission network restricts the growth of the natural gas consumption. Although the CO_2 emissions of natural gas are lower than other fossil fuels, the consumption of gas in Finland has dropped remarkably during the past ten years (Statistics Finland, 2020c). Some reasons behind the downward trend in consumption have been the raising taxation of natural gas and the decreasing use of gas in electricity production (Energy Authority, 2019). In 2019, the share of natural gas in electricity production was six percent whereas nuclear power (35%), biomass (18%) and hydropower (19%) constituted the main energy sources in electricity production (Finnish Energy, 2020). In 2010, the share of natural gas in electricity production was more than twice higher, i.e. 14% (Statistics Finland, 2011).

Figure 10.2 shows the development of natural gas prices for non-household consumers in Finland from 2010 to 2020, with non-recoverable taxes included and all taxes excluded. According to Eurostat (2020a), in the second half of 2019, the share of non-recoverable taxes in the price of natural gas in Finland was the highest among the EU member states, i.e. 34%. Due to the high taxation, the price for natural gas for

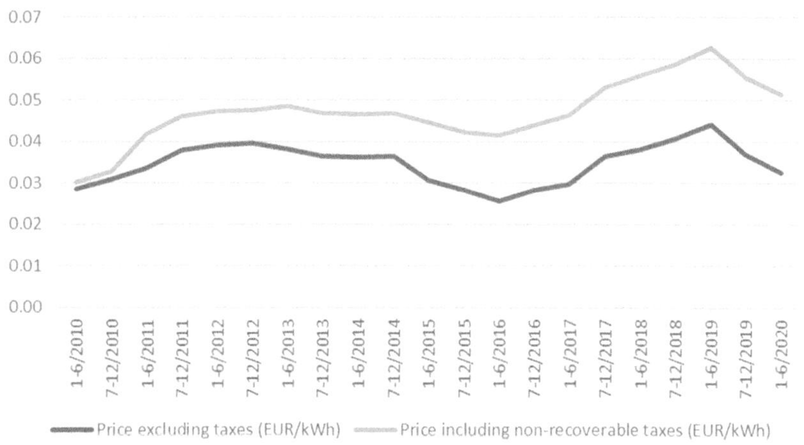

Fig. 10.2 Bi-annual natural gas prices for non-household consumers in Finland in 2010–2020 (EUR/kWh) (*Source* The Authors, based on Eurostat Data Browser [2020])

non-household consumers, excluding value added tax and other recoverable taxes and levies, was also the most expensive among the EU member states, EUR0.0555 per kilowatt hour (EUR/kWh) (Eurostat, 2020a). During the first half of 2020, the natural gas price in Finland has slightly dropped, to EUR0.0513/kWh, but the share of non-recoverable taxes has grown to 37%. Excluding all taxes and levies, the respective prices are EUR0.0369/kWh for the second half of 2019 and EUR0.0326/kWh for the first half of 2020 (Eurostat Data Browser, 2020). When looking at the report of the working group on energy taxation reform appointed by the Finnish Ministry of Finance, it seems that no tax reductions for natural gas are in sight. On the contrary, in the report published in September 2020, the working group proposes a moderate increase in the taxation of natural gas, along with other fossil fuels (Ministry of Finance, 2020).

Regarding the security of supply of natural gas, the gas supply from Russia to Finland has been steady during the past decades and no significant supply disruptions have occurred. Nevertheless, because Finland has no gas storage facilities, it has to prepare to replace natural gas by another energy production method or alternative fuel in case of a supply disruption. According to National Emergency Supply Agency (2019), if a disruption occurs in the single largest gas infrastructure—the second parallel gas import pipeline from Russia—Finland's total gas demand can be satisfied for a day of exceptionally high gas consumption with the capacity of the remaining infrastructure. However, a long-term disruption in the supply of pipeline gas from Russia would create a challenging situation for Finland. In that case, gas companies have to deliver either vapourised LNG or biogas to protected gas customers, that is households connected to the gas distribution network. Regarding all imported fuels (coal, natural gas and oil), Finland keeps reserves equivalent to five months of normal consumption. However, this does not include gas consumption in industry. Excluding households, other users of natural gas are primarily responsible for their own preparedness plans and the functioning of the potential reserve fuel systems (Energy Authority, 2019; National Emergency Supply Agency, 2019). The latest preventive action and emergency plan concerning the security of gas supply in Finland has been prepared before the commissioning of the Balticconnector pipeline and the integration of the gas markets of Estonia, Finland and Latvia. Hence, the need to reassess the risk scenarios concerning supply security and update the contingency plan is acknowledged in the document (National Emergency Supply Agency, 2019).

The Liberalisation of the Natural Gas Market

The Finnish natural gas market experienced notable changes at the beginning of 2020 when the import and wholesale of natural gas were opened to competition. Until January 2020, the Finnish gas company Gasum had a monopoly in the transmission and sale of natural gas in Finland (Gasum, 2019a).[1] Since the beginning of the year 2020, transmission and sale of natural gas were unbundled from each other and a new state-owned company, Gasgrid Finland, took over the responsibility of the TSO. In accordance with the new market model, Gasgrid Finland sells transmission capacity whereas shippers and traders sell gas energy in gas exchange or over the counter (OTC) (Gasgrid, 2020a). The construction of the Balticconnector natural gas pipeline between Finland and Estonia was an essential part of the market opening. The launch of the pipeline at the beginning of 2020 indicated the creation of common gas market for Finland and the Baltic States. As a part of the integrated gas market,

[1] Gasum has been fully state-owned since the State of Finland acquired the remaining 25% share of Gasum from Gazprom in December 2015 (Gasum, 2015b).

Finland, Estonia and Latvia agreed on the formation of a regional tariff zone, which included removing cross-border transmission tariffs between the countries and harmonising entry point tariffs on the zone's external borders (Gasgrid, 2020c).

Lithuania did not join the single market area due to disagreements over its exact design, in particular regarding the compensation mechanism between the TSOs. Lithuania's absence from the regional tariff zone can, for instance, complicate the functioning of virtual trading platform GET Baltic that is used to trade gas in the Baltic States (Jakštas, 2019), and from the beginning of 2020 also in Finland. Along with the opening of the Balticconnector, Finland gained connection to the Inčukalns UGS in Latvia and the Klaipeda LNG terminal in Lithuania. Furthermore, through GIPL Finland will gain connection to the Central European gas network and be able to further diversify the potential gas sources (Gasgrid, 2020a). Consequently, the Balticconnector pipeline is important in terms of Finnish energy security because it diversifies natural gas supply routes. Not being dependent on one single source of gas also provides an asset for Finland to negotiate for the gas price with the suppliers. Thus, the pipeline promotes competition in the gas market.

Creating a regional gas market for Finland and the Baltic States by constructing the interconnecting Balticconnector pipeline was one of the goals in the National Climate and Energy Strategy until 2030, prepared by the previous government in Finland in 2016. According to the strategy, the regional gas market facilitates gas use both as raw material and fuel in the period of transition towards a carbon neutral society (Ministry of Economic Affairs & Employment, 2017). At the time of writing this article, the Finnish Government has begun to prepare the new climate and energy strategy that is traditionally prepared by each government. The policy measures and the related scenarios outlined in the new strategy will pay particular attention to achieving the government programme's target of carbon neutrality by 2035 and the EU's energy and climate targets for 2030 (Ministry of Economic Affairs & Employment, 2020). The key targets of the EU's 2030 Climate and Energy Framework include cutting greenhouse gas emissions by at least 40% from 1990 levels, raising the share of renewable energy to at least 32% and improving energy efficiency by over 32% (European Commission, 2020f). In December 2020, the European Council decided to raise the target for the reduction of greenhouse gas emissions to at least

55% by 2030 (European Council, 2020). The more ambitious emission reduction target is intended to act as a stepping stone to reach carbon neutrality by 2050 (European Parliament, 2020b). Regarding the progress in the EU's energy and climate targets, the 2020 target of 20% emission reduction was reached ahead of schedule (European Parliament, 2020a). EU-wide assessment of National Energy and Climate Plans of the European Commission (EC) (2020c) indicates that if fully implemented, the member states' energy and climate plans will enable surpassing the renewable energy target, as well as the previous emission reduction target of 40% by 2030 but fall a little short of the energy efficiency target. However, in order to reach the emission reduction target of 55% by 2030—and carbon neutrality by 2050—the EU countries need to adopt new measures and accelerate the pace further.

Decreasing dependence on energy imports from outside the EU, diversifying energy sources and supplies and creating a single energy market are among the main goals of the EU's Energy Union strategy adopted in 2015 (European Commission, 2015a). Because being dependent on one single supplier, Finland was granted an exception from the EU's Natural Gas Directive (European Union, 2009) that establishes common rules for the internal market in natural gas, including the separation of gas distribution networks from production, supply and storage activities. In terms of energy security, the natural gas transit from Russia to the EU via Ukraine has been among the main concerns for the EU, particularly since the 2014 Ukrainian crisis (Europe Information, 2015). The creation of the regional gas market for Finland and the Baltic States is in line with the EU's goals of increasing security of supply of natural gas and forming a functional and interconnected internal gas market.

The Supply of Natural Gas to Finland

Overview on Pipeline and LNG Imports

Finland does not have any natural gas reserves of its own and, consequently, neither any natural gas production. Hence, all natural gas consumed in Finland is imported. From the mid-1970s until the opening of Balticconnector, all pipeline gas consumed in Finland was imported from Russia through a twin pipeline via the south-eastern border town of Imatra. Finland's total monthly natural gas imports by the country of origin since January 2016 (measured by the import value in euros) are illustrated in Fig. 10.3.

According to the Finnish Customs (2020), in January–October 2020, one third of the total pipeline gas imports have originated from Estonia through Balticconnector and two thirds from Russia, when measured by the import value in euros. Exact information on the original sources of the gas imported through Balticconnector is not available, but it is either from Russia or from the Klaipeda LNG terminal in Lithuania (Kyytsönen, 2020; Nuotio, 2020). In addition to pipeline gas, Finland has been importing LNG since July 2016. According to the Finnish Customs (2020), the first imports originated from Belgium but throughout the years, the largest LNG importers to Finland have been Russia and Norway, with roughly 40% share each when measured by the import value in euros. Other countries from which Finland has been importing LNG include Lithuania and the Netherlands. LNG imports from Russia began in June 2018 on small scale but have since grown in value. In fact, during the first ten months of 2020, over 80% of the total LNG imports have originated from Russia, more than one tenth from Lithuania and roughly seven percent from Norway, when measured by the import value

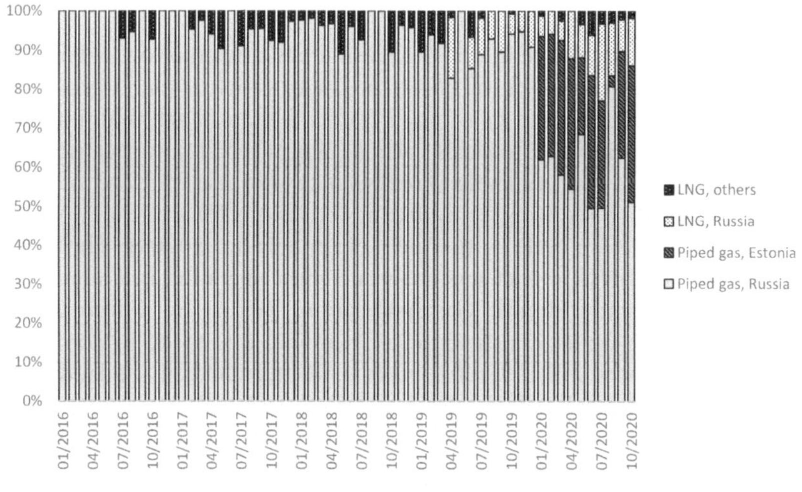

Fig. 10.3 Finland's total monthly natural gas imports by origin in January 2016–October 2020 (*Source* The Authors, based on Finnish Customs [2020])

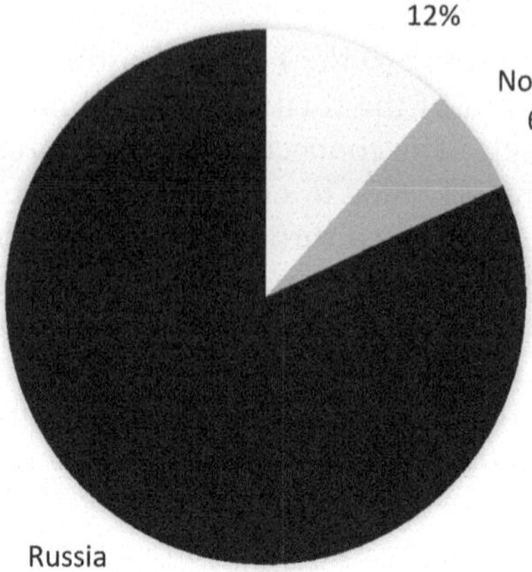

Fig. 10.4 LNG imports to Finland by origin in January–October 2020 (*Source* The Authors, based on Finnish Customs [2020])

in euros (Fig. 10.4). Regarding the total value of natural gas imports in 2020, almost 70% originated from Russia and a little over 30% from other countries (Finnish Customs, 2020). When considering the potential sources for gas flowing through Balticconnector, Finland's dependence on Russian natural gas is even higher.

Due to the market limitations, the natural gas consumption in Finland can mainly grow in the form of LNG, the use of which as fuel is growing, for instance, in marine and heavy road traffic. LNG can act as an interim solution in the transition towards carbon–neutral economy because it is the cleanest fossil fuel available. For instance, the use of LNG as ship fuel is estimated to reduce greenhouse gas emissions for a maximum 21% during the whole life cycle of the fuel (Liikennefakta, 2020a). There are two small-scale LNG import terminals currently operating in Finland, in Pori and in Tornio (Finnish Gas Association, 2020). In addition, one LNG terminal is under construction in Hamina, due to be in commercial use in October 2021. Unlike other LNG terminals in Finland, the Hamina LNG terminal will be connected to the Finnish gas transmission network and will thus be serving as a new entry point to the gas market of Finland and the Baltic States. The connection to the transmission network is expected to be completed in August 2021 (Hamina LNG, 2020b).

The benefits of LNG include that transforming natural gas into liquid phase allows maintaining the energy content of the gas while simultaneously reducing the gas volume by 600 times, and it can thus be transported by tankers and trucks over very long distances (IGU, 2020). Consequently, LNG is flexible fuel in the sense that its trade is not dependent on existing pipeline infrastructure. LNG trade has been growing on a global scale, and in 2019, the focus of LNG import growth has shifted from Asia to Europe. In 2019, LNG imports to Europe increased by almost 70%, totalling to 120 bcm. The main sources of LNG imports to Europe were Qatar, Russia, the USA, Nigeria and Algeria (BP, 2020). The utilisation of LNG also brings promises of diversifying Finland's energy mix and thus strengthening the energy security of the country. Nevertheless, due to the small capacity of the LNG import terminals in Finland, only pipeline gas has strategic significance for the country for now.

Balticconnector: Ending Isolation?

Balticconnector, a bi-directional gas pipeline between Finland and Estonia, entered into commercial use at the beginning of 2020. The pipeline is co-owned by two state-owned companies: Finnish Gasgrid and Estonian Elering. With a daily transmission capacity of 7.2 million cubic metres (annual capacity of 2.6 bcm), the Balticconnector pipeline has three sections: a 21-kilometre-long onshore pipeline in Finland, a 77-kilometre-long offshore part and a 54-kilometre-long onshore pipeline in Estonia. The stated aim of the project is to enable diversified gas supply, as well as to improve regional supply in general (Baltic Connector, 2019). On the Estonian side, the pipeline brings a new direction for possible gas supply. For Finland, it primarily opens the national market for competition. It also strengthens the security of supply in the country.

The Balticconnector pipeline would not have been commercially viable without considerable support from the EU (Baltic Connector, 2020b). In fact, the project was originally initiated by Gasum in 2008 but deemed to be financially unfeasible in 2015 (Gasum, 2015a). However, a state-owned company created for the implementation of the Finnish part of the project, Baltic Connector Oy, subsequently picked the project up and agreed on the joint construction of the pipeline with Estonian Elering in 2016 (Baltic Connector, 2020a). The CEF, a key EU financial instrument for infrastructure, provided 75% of Balticconnector's USD294 million, or

EUR250 million, budget (European Commission, 2020a). For the EU, Balticconnector has a status of a PCI (European Commission, 2020d).

The Russian-Ukrainian gas dispute of 2009 gave the EC an incentive to conduct a stress test on the EU gas supply. The study found that in addition to the EU's Eastern neighbours (in this context, the so-called Energy Community countries) the Eastern member states—along with Finland and the Baltic States—are the most vulnerable to disruptions in gas supply. The calculations indicate that both Finland and Estonia would have been faced with a 60% deficit of natural gas in the event of cessation of gas supply from Russia. The EC press release on the stress test states co-operation as the key to improving the resilience of gas-consuming countries within the EU and the neighbouring area (European Commission, 2014). Purely national projects would not be truly in the interest of any gas-consuming country. This is relevant for Balticconnector, which as a joint project between two member states has worked towards reducing vulnerability of both Finland and Estonia, as well as the Baltic Sea region in general.

In addition to improving regional resilience, Balticconnector is an important step towards enhancing Finland's energy security. The annual capacity of Balticconnector exceeds the yearly demand of natural gas in Finland that for the past few years has been around two billion cubic metres. Hence, in theory, Finland could cover its gas consumption with supplies through Balticconnector. Nevertheless, when considering the security of supply, the key benefit brought by the Balticconnector project seems to have been the diversification of transfer routes. Until the launch of Balticconnector, the only natural gas entry point was for the Russian imports in Imatra. In addition to traditional natural gas, Balticconnector can be used to transfer regasified LNG, as well as biogas. In the future, LNG terminals could be connected to the gas grid and thus serve as entry points. It is also possible to create entry points for biogas (Gasum, 2019b) although in its present state, biogas production is very small scale in Finland.

However, it is important to note that Balticconnector alone will not suffice to end the isolation of the Finnish gas grid. The fulfilment of this goal also depends on GIPL that will connect the Finnish-Baltic grid to Poland and the common EU gas network. When completed, GIPL will further improve the resilience of the gas pipeline network in the Baltic Sea region, bringing economic benefits and possibly leading to lower gas prices. GIPL is a bi-directional pipeline, with an annual capacity of

2.4 bcm from Poland to Lithuania and 1.9 bcm to the opposite direction (Amber Grid, 2020). With technical adjustments, GIPL also renders possible the delivery of gas to Belarus or Ukraine (Patricolo, 2020). However, since Belarus alone consumed more than 19 bcm natural gas in 2019 (BP, 2020), the capacity of GIPL is not sufficient to reduce the dependence of Belarus and Ukraine on Russian energy and thus influence the balance of energy market in a larger sense.

The GIPL project is implemented by two natural gas TSOs, Lithuanian Amber Grid and Polish Gaz-System. According to Amber Grid that is responsible for the project implementation in Lithuania, the construction of the 165-kilometre-long Lithuanian part of GIPL began in January 2020. By the end of the year 2020, 60% of the construction work has been completed, including filling the first 72 kilometres of the pipeline with gas and welding a 125-kilometre-long section of the pipeline. Amber Grid expects to complete the construction of the pipeline to the Lithuanian–Polish border in 2021 and open GIPL for commercial use in the beginning of 2022 (Amber Grid, 2020). However, while we could not find any information on the progress of the construction of the 343-kilometre-long Polish section of the pipeline, the timely completion of GIPL remains unclear.

Even combined, the gas market of the Baltic States and Finland is rather small, with an annual consumption of approximately six billion cubic metres of natural gas in 2019. Of the three Baltic States, Lithuania consumed the largest amount of natural gas, i.e. 2.4 bcm (Ministry of Energy of the Republic of Lithuania, 2020). Latvia consumed 1.4 bcm (Central Statistical Bureau of Latvia, 2020) and Estonia 0.5 bcm natural gas in 2019 (Elering, 2020). Finland and the Baltic States have shared the dilemma of being dependent on Russian gas and isolated from the EU grid. According to Eurostat (2020b), during the first half of 2020, Estonia and Latvia relied on Russia for 75–100% and Lithuania for 25–50% of their natural gas imports. In Finland, one third of pipeline gas imports originated from Estonia through Balticconnector and two thirds from Russia during the first ten months of 2020 (Finnish Customs, 2020). On the face of it, this clearly indicates a change compared to the situation preceding Balticconnector. However, as Estonia and Latvia rely almost completely on Russian pipeline gas, one has to bear in mind that in practise, there are only two possible sources for the gas flowing through Balticconnector, i.e. the Klaipeda LNG terminal in Lithuania and pipeline gas from Russia.

The Klaipeda LNG terminal, that has been in operation since 2014, aims to become a regional gas hub supplying natural gas not only to the Baltic States but also to Finland and Poland (Sytas, 2019). The terminal comprises an FSRU called 'Independence', owned by a Norwegian company Leigh Höegh LNG, a berth and an 18-kilometre-long pipeline connecting the LNG terminal to the Lithuanian gas grid. The terminal is operated by a Lithuanian oil and gas company Klaipėdos Nafta. The total capacity of the terminal tanks is 170,000 cubic metres and it can regasify up to 3.8 bcm per year (CEEnergynews, 2020; Klaipėdos Nafta, 2020). In 2019, Lithuania received 1.4 million tonnes of LNG in net imports, which equals to 1.9 bcm of natural gas. A little over 70% of LNG imports originated from Norway, more than 20% from Russia and five percent from the USA (GIIGNL, 2020).

The combined annual supply capacity of GIPL and the Klaipeda LNG terminal is around six billion cubic metres, which is roughly the same as the annual gas consumption in the Baltic States and Finland. However, in 2019, Lithuania delivered only 0.6 bcm of natural gas from the Klaipeda terminal to Estonia and Latvia (Ministry of Energy of the Republic of Lithuania, 2020). In 2020, the LNG imports from the USA have grown due to the favourable market situation. There has been an abundance of supplies from the USA while many European gas storage facilities have been full. Consequently, the users of the Klaipeda terminal have been able to purchase LNG imported from the USA for affordable prices (Woellwarth, 2020). Nevertheless, LNG input from overseas would need to radically increase in order to change the overall dominance of Russian gas in the gas market of the Baltic States and Finland. Furthermore, the completion of GIPL is important for source diversification in both Finland and the Baltic States.

Whereas Lithuania aims to strengthen the security of gas supply by importing LNG, Latvia has constructed a UGS facility that ensures the availability of natural gas when it is needed the most, that is during the heating season. The Latvian company JSC Conexus Baltic Grid that operates the gas infrastructure in Latvia also owns the Inčukalns UGS (Conexus Baltic Grid, 2020b).[2] The Inčukalns UGS is the only functioning gas storage within the reach of the gas market of the Baltic States and Finland and has a capacity of up to 3.2 bcm of active natural gas. The

[2] The largest shareholder (68.5%) of Conexus Baltic Grid is AS Augstsprieguma tikls AST, a power transmission company fully-owned by the Latvian State (AST, 2020).

storage is filled up with natural gas in the summer and it fully covers the demand for gas in Latvia during the heating season. Consequently, Latvia does not need to rely on pipeline imports from Russia in wintertime when the pipelines are very loaded. Along with the launch of Balticconnector, Finland also gained connection to the gas storage, which could also be used to store gas for Finnish needs (Conexus Baltic Grid, 2020b).

Balticconnector faced some difficulties in its first year of operation in 2020. The unexpected reconstruction work of Conexus Baltic Grid threatened to shut the pipeline down at a time when continued transport was critical for the operation of the pipeline. Conexus' repairs were connected to the Latvia-Lithuania Interconnection Improvement (LLSU) project, which is also the EU's PCI project. LLSU is further linked to the gas priority corridor of the BEMIP (Conexus Baltic Grid, 2020a). Estonian and Finnish energy companies, having received an advance notice one month beforehand, appealed jointly to the governments and national system operators to postpone the shutdown for one year. The complication came amidst the COVID19 crisis, during which the additional expenses would bare dire consequences for the market participants (Reiljan, 2020). Conexus justified the repairs stating that the improvements would increase supply volumes to Finland (Conexus Baltic Grid, 2020a). This example reveals the geopolitical nature and vulnerability of gas infrastructure: projects have commercial goals but are tied to the physical reality and involve actors on various levels. As gas sale contracts are made long term, sudden disruptions in the access to the pipeline itself create stress for the seller as well as raise questions of reliability of supply for the buyer. Energy infrastructure development supported by the EU aims at improving the function of the internal energy market. However, while the goal of creating a more secure energy market in the EU is common, the actors are bound to have conflicting interests.

The launch of Balticconnector has improved Finland's position on the natural gas market in many ways. However, some questions remain. The realisation of Balticconnector's function in securing the diversification of sources of supply is dependent on the pipeline grid upstream. When writing this article, the construction of GIPL was still in progress. What will be the consequences for Balticconnector and, more broadly, to Finland's energy security, if the operations of the connecting pipelines in the Baltic States or Poland are for some reason halted or delayed? Finally, it is relevant to consider the larger question of what is actually the significance of Balticconnector for the Finnish gas market. While the liberalisation of the gas market and the construction of Balticconnector have diversified the market for Finland, they have not removed all restrictions and issues related to pipeline gas. While it would be too early to judge how Balticconnector will influence diversification in the long term, for the time being it seems that the ultimate source of imported gas has not changed that much. This reflects the nature of pipeline gas as a relatively 'slow' commodity. In this context, it is worthwhile to ask, whether LNG could bring true diversification and flexibility for the natural gas and even the whole energy market in Finland?

LNG in Finland: Prospects and Limitations

LNG Infrastructure Development

The import and use of LNG in Finland have been modest to date. The existing LNG infrastructure is both new and small scale, and intended to serve mostly local industry needs near the LNG terminals. The first Finnish LNG import terminal in Pori, owned by Gasum, was commissioned in 2016. The terminal has a storage capacity of 30,000 cubic metres and it delivers LNG to industrial customers. The second terminal, the Manga LNG import terminal in Tornio, was constructed as a joint venture of the industrial companies Outokumpu and SSAB Europe and the Finnish energy companies EPV Energy and Gasum. At the time when the Manga terminal began its operations in 2019, it was the largest LNG terminal in the Nordic countries with a storage capacity of 50,000 cubic metres. The terminal is designed to deliver LNG to industrial customers, as well as to LNG-fuelled ships (Gasum, 2020b; Reuters, 2019). While it would be technically possible to feed regasified LNG to the Finnish gas grid, the two existing LNG import terminals in Finland are located outside of the reach of the national grid. A third Finnish LNG import terminal in Hamina (with the storage capacity of 30,000 cubic metres) is planned to commence commercial operations in 2021. The terminal is jointly-owned by Hamina Energy Ltd, Estonian company Alexela and the Finnish technology company Wärtsilä.[3] It will be the first LNG terminal

[3] Alexela Group is an Estonian holding company that operates in three areas: energy, metal industry and property development. Alexela's majority owner is Estonian businessman Heiti Hääl. Until 2014, 50% of the company's shares were owned by Kazakh businessman Igor Bidilo (ERR, 2014).

in Finland to be connected to the national gas grid. In addition, the terminal will be connected to the local gas network in Hamina (Hamina LNG, 2020a). The terminal's daily entry capacity to both networks will be 0.5 million cubic metres of gas in total (Ministry of Economic Affairs & Employment, 2019). All three LNG terminals have received investment support from the Finnish State (European Commission, 2015b, 2016; Ministry of Economic Affairs and Employment, 2014a).

The liberalisation of the Finnish gas market brought about the creation of market rules also for LNG. Consequently, there is an institutional readiness to develop LNG capacity further and to start new operations in the country. This also clears the path for new actors to operate in the field and helps to create a more versatile gas and energy market in Finland (Gasum, 2019b). As forthcoming terminals enhance the availability of LNG, new actors may start utilising it for instance in heat and power production, which would then further increase its demand. However, despite the positive developments, practical barriers remain, and due to the small size of the Finnish gas market, the challenge to ensure financial feasibility of LNG infrastructure projects is the main obstacle for further development. Some plans to build LNG infrastructure have already been abandoned as commercially unviable: for instance, the gas company AGA halted its plans to build an LNG terminal in Rauma (Pukkila, 2015), despite receiving a positive decision on state investment support (Ministry of Economic Affairs and Employment, 2014b). Gasum, in turn, gave up the implementation of the Finngulf LNG terminal project on the South Coast of Finland. Finngulf LNG project was part of the Finnish-Estonian plan to construct a joint LNG import terminal either in Inkoo, Finland or in Paldiski, Estonia, together with an interconnecting pipeline. The terminal would have been large scale, with annual capacity of 2.5 bcm (Enerdata, 2015; Ministry of Finance, 2014). The Finnish state-owned gas company Gasum plays a central role in the LNG infrastructure development in Finland. Gasum's operating area stretches to other Nordic countries as well and the company's strategic goal is to create a Nordic gas market and infrastructure (Gasum, 2020a). Tightening co-operation in the Nordic gas sector, as well as industry collaboration and creation of clusters may increase the profitability of LNG projects, reducing both costs and emissions for the industrial partners. Furthermore, state aid has been a precondition for carrying out LNG infrastructure projects in Finland.

While Finland lacks a large LNG terminal, following the creation of the gas market of the Baltic States and Finland it can benefit from the pre-existing infrastructure elsewhere, such as the LNG terminal in Klaipeda, Lithuania. The LNG import terminals on the shores of the Baltic Sea are listed in Table 10.1.

Table 10.1 LNG import terminals on the shores of the Baltic Sea

Status	*Location*	*Name*	*Nominal annual capacity*
Operational	Finland (Pori)	Pori LNG terminal	0.1 bcm
	Finland (Tornio)	Manga LNG terminal	0.4 bcm
	Lithuania (Klaipeda)	FSRU Independence	4.0 bcm
	Poland (Świnoujście)	Świnoujście LNG terminal	5.0 bcm (current), 7.5 bcm (by 2021)
	Russia (Kaliningrad)	FSRU Marshal Vasilevskiy	3.7 bcm
	Sweden (Lysekil)	Lysekil LNG terminal	0.3 bcm
	Sweden (Nynäshamn)	Nynäshamn LNG terminal	0.3 bcm
Under construction	Finland (Hamina)	Hamina LNG terminal	–
Planned	Estonia (Tallinn)	Muuga LNG terminal	0.5–4.0 bcm
	Estonia (Paldiski)	Paldiski LNG terminal	2.5 bcm
	Finland (Rauma)	Rauma LNG terminal	–
	Germany (Rostock)[a]	Rostock LNG terminal	–
	Latvia (Riga)	Kundzinsalas LNG terminal	–
	Latvia (Skulte)	Skulte LNG terminal	5.0 bcm
	Poland (Gdańsk)	Gdańsk LNG terminal (FSRU)	4.1–8.2 bcm
	Sweden (Gothenburg)	Gothenburg LNG terminal	0.5 bcm
	Sweden (Gävle)	Gävle LNG terminal	0.3 bcm

[a]There are also other LNG terminal projects planned in Germany (such as Brunsbüttel, Stade and Wilhelmshaven) but because they are not located on the shores of the Baltic Sea, they are not included in this table

Source The Authors, based on GIE (2019)

However, when assessing the importance of LNG imports for the security of supply, the original sources of the imports need to be taken into consideration. As regards the Klaipeda LNG terminal, the Russian company Novatek, which owns an LNG export terminal in the Russian Baltic Sea port of Vysotsk jointly with Gazprombank, aims to increase its LNG imports to the terminal (*Baltic Times*, 2020). Gazprom and RusGazDobycha also aim to construct an LNG production and export facility in the Russian Baltic Sea port of Ust-Luga (Argus, 2020). In the case of Finland, from the first Russian LNG imports in June 2018 until October 2020, nearly 60% of the total LNG imports in terms of import value have originated from Russia (Finnish Customs, 2020). Consequently, so far the role of LNG imports in the diversification of gas supply sources has been rather modest. On the other hand, the focus of the Finnish LNG strategy has been in creating terminal infrastructure that mainly serves local industry needs close to the terminals and LNG-fuelled vessels. A central function of constructing LNG terminals in Finland has been to allow the delivery of gas outside the reach of the gas transmission network, thus contributing to diversified gas supply together with Balticconnector.

Furthermore, the infrastructure intended for LNG imports have other functions as well. For example, the terminal in Tornio can also utilise liquefied biogas (LBG) of Finnish origins. According to industry sources, the use of domestic LBG could decrease the CO_2 emissions by as much as 85% (Tiihonen, 2019). Consequently, this would remarkably reduce not only the shipping costs and the transportation distance, but also the climate effects of gas use in Finland. The multi-purpose use of the terminals for various types of gas, co-operation with industry partners as well as relieved environmental effects brought by the use of LNG, are all inter-connected benefits that increase the cost-effectiveness of the gas infrastructure initiatives. The position on the energy market as well as the physical location of the terminals near the industry actors increase their viability in the new applications, such as hydrogen, that the transition to carbon neutral future will require (Simon, 2020).

Environmental Impacts of LNG Use and Future Alternatives

Concerning the environmental impacts of energy production, the general tone in which gas is discussed in the EU policy has been changing. The earlier view is well expressed for instance in the EC's Energy Roadmap

2050, which stated that the role of gas in energy production is relatively stable. According to the document, investments in gas infrastructure are facilitated by low risks and stable returns. Investment cost of building gas-fired power stations is relatively low and the risk of unfavourable energy price development is reduced by the fact that gas-fired generation often sets the wholesale price for electricity (European Commission, 2011). In the more recent EC document, A Clean Planet for all—A European strategic long-term vision for a prosperous, modern, competitive and climate neutral economy (European Commission, 2018, 8), the prospects for the future of natural gas are already less optimistic: "*Sustainable renewable heating will continue to play a major role and gas, including liquefied natural gas, mixed with hydrogen, or e-methane produced from renewable electricity and biogas mixtures could all play a key role in existing buildings as well as in many industrial applications.*" In other words, new buildings are visioned to contain heating technology beyond gas-based solutions. Furthermore, the document Clean Planet for all mentions LNG mixed with bio-methane as one short-term solution for fuelling long-distance transportation (European Commission, 2018). To conclude, natural gas remains a solution to meet both the energy needs of different sectors as well as the goals regarding the reduction of greenhouse gas emissions. Natural gas is to be utilised in combination with low-emission alternatives.

Already in 2011, the EU Energy Roadmap 2050 recognised natural gas as an interim solution while the energy production chain is reorganised. The document suggests that after the introduction of additional carbon-free options, the operational costs of gas-fired power stations may rise and the gas infrastructure may get less use. The large-scale application of CCS technology could reduce the emissions of gas and maintain its role in the power sector, but without CCS gas may stand to lose ground for greener options and remain a back-up technology (European Commission, 2011). The CCS technology development has not taken remarkable steps in recent years. However, in 2020 the Norwegian Government announced it would fund a large-scale CCS project called Longship with a total budget of close to three billion US dollars. The Finnish energy company Fortum is also partially involved in the project through its waste-to-energy plant in Klemetsrud, which could get funding jointly with the Longship project if additional funding will be granted by the EU or via investments from the private sector (Rokke, 2020). While the CCS project in Norway will have an essentially local application tied to capturing CO_2 emissions from a cement plant near Oslo, projects such as this could lead to further technological advancement and reduction of the emissions created both by CO_2-intensive industries and the heat and power production using fossil fuels.

In marine traffic, LNG has been introduced as an alternative to conventional marine petroleum fuels. LNG is indeed a relatively clean fuel: LNG produces practically no sulphur oxides, nitrogen oxides or particulate matter, in addition to which it has lower CO_2 emissions than traditional ship fuels. However, when full cycle emissions and the impact of methane slip (emission of unburnt methane) are considered, the advantages of LNG in terms of greenhouse gas emissions are less evident (Le Fevre, 2018). Maritime transport emits substantial amounts of CO_2. In the case of the EU, over three percent of all CO_2 emissions are from the shipping sector and they are expected to grow further in the future. Therefore, as a method of reducing emissions and reaching the targets, the industry has increased its use of LNG. Nevertheless, its use is still modest. In 2018, only three percent of the overall fuels used in the European Economic Area maritime transport were LNG, while heavy fuel oils, marine gas oil and diesel were widely used. LNG is mostly used by vessels that transport LNG and other gas products. Its use has been increasing as a result of stricter emission regulation (European Commission, 2020e).

As the Baltic Sea is an Emission Control Area (IMO, 2014), the use of LNG has special significance for the Finnish sea areas. In Finland, the share of water traffic in the total CO_2 emissions of the domestic traffic is four percent (Liikennefakta, 2020b). Alternative fuels and power sources are used by 15 vessels sailing under the Finnish flag, consisting of two percent of the Finnish merchant fleet. Five vessels are using LNG and two vessels bio-oil as fuel, whereas eight vessels are using either electricity or wind power (Liikennefakta, 2020a). Regarding LNG-fuelled vessels in Finland, the Viking Line's passenger ship Viking Grace, that started operating on Turku-Stockholm route in 2013, was the first LNG-powered large ferry both on the Baltic Sea and globally (Viking Line, 2020). The second passenger ship to adopt LNG as fuel was the Estonian shipping company Tallink Silja's LNG-powered fast ferry called Megastar, currently operating under Estonian flag on Helsinki-Tallinn route. Both Viking Grace and Tallink Megastar were built in the Meyer Turku Shipyard in Finland (Finnish Shipowners Association, 2020; AS TallinkGrupp, 2020). The Finnish shipping company ESL Shipping has two LNG-fuelled bulk carriers that commenced operations in 2018 (ESL

Shipping, 2018). Finland also has an icebreaker with a dual-fuel engine and a patrol vessel that operates on LNG (Arctia, 2020; *Navigator Magazine*, 2014). In Finland, LNG is currently available for ships to bunker in two LNG import terminals, in Pori and in Tornio (Finnish Gas Association, 2020). LNG is also distributed to ports by trucks (Liikennefakta, 2020a). LNG-fuelled ships have been mostly bunkered truck-to-ship but bunkering ships are also entering the market, thus alleviating fuel availability issues. Currently, two LNG bunker ships operate on the Baltic Sea (Liikennefakta, 2020a).

LNG was, for some time, the fuel of the future. However, the acceleration of climate concerns calls for new solutions especially for the sectors that are not easily transformed into the utilisation of electricity. One potential solution is to use renewable hydrogen that can be produced through electrolysis from water using renewable electricity. As flexible fuel, it is in many ways similar to LNG. Alternatively, fossil-based hydrogen can be made more sustainable by applying carbon capture technologies (European Commission, 2020b). The EC officials have urged the gas industry to accelerate the transition to hydrogen. While the existing gas infrastructure can be utilised, the introduction of hydrogen requires changes: any new reconstruction plans should include hydrogen-relevant technology, in addition to which the current pipeline infrastructure needs to be retrofitted for the transition to be possible (Simon, 2020). The gas industry faces an interesting challenge: the fuels can be seen as rivals but on the other hand, the development of hydrogen capacity creates continuity for the gas infrastructure in the face of the inevitable change towards zero-net emissions. Regarding the production chain of hydrogen in the EU, one option is to seek co-operation with neighbouring countries: an initiative by Hydrogen Europe to increase electrolyser production in Europe includes close co-operation with North African countries and Ukraine (van Wijk & Chatzimarkakis, 2020). The environmental sustainability of hydrogen and other renewables depends on the arrangements in the logistics chain. If the transportation of hydrogen is fuelled by renewable or zero-emission source of energy, then the new solutions can be seen to be applicable for Finland as well.

Besides hydrogen, the use of natural gas and LNG can open doors to the use of biogas and its derivative, LBG. However, the biogas industry in Finland is equally small scale as the LNG industry. According to Statistics Finland (2020b), approximately 0.9 TWh of biogas was produced in 2019, equalling to 0.2% of the total energy consumption in Finland. The potential of the biogas production is estimated to be 15 to 20 times the amount of the current production (Lampila, 2018). The benefits of LBG include that it is completely renewable energy source and has the similar characteristics to LNG. The same infrastructure can be used for both and they can even be mixed. However, large-scale production of biogas would necessitate gathering masses of organic waste to one spot. One further obstacle to the use of LBG is its price. Currently, LBG is over one third more expensive than natural gas. However, the relative attractiveness of LBG may in the future rise due to increasing emissions trading costs of competing fuel sources (Sallinen, 2020). In general, particularly the farming industry has been recognised to have potential in biogas production, which would improve the recycling of nutrients and enhance the energy independence of farms. So far, only a few new plants have been constructed on Finnish farms, mainly due to the high cost of investment (Ministry of Agriculture & Forestry, 2020; Natural Resources Institute Finland, 2020). The fact that biogas and LBG can utilise gas infrastructure is quite promising. However, it seems unlikely that LBG production will reach a scale similar to that of the current LNG exporters. Actors in the field will continue to protect their economic interests, while enjoying the benefits of the image of natural gas and LNG as the lesser of many fossil fuel evils.

Conclusions

The share of natural gas in the Finnish total energy consumption is rather small—only five percent. Furthermore, the consumption of natural gas in Finland has decreased by half during the past decade, amounting to 2.1 bcm in 2019. The downward trend in consumption is mainly related to the high taxation of natural gas in Finland compared to other energy sources. Natural gas as fuel and raw material is significant in particular for the chemical and forest industries as well as for combined heat and power production, whereas its use in households is marginal. The gas transmission network covers only southern Finland and in addition to that, the two LNG terminals located on the coast of the Gulf of Bothnia can supply gas locally to industrial users, as well as to ships. Consequently, the market for natural gas in Finland is rather small.

In general, the production, transmission and use of natural gas are characterised by the interdependence of countries. In the EU, this interdependence can lead to positive consequences for the member states' energy security as the community facilitates energy co-operation and the integration of energy infrastructure reduces risks to individual countries. This also allows the EU to strengthen its bargaining position as a buyer of energy. Due to the small size of the national gas market, gas infrastructure projects in Finland have struggled with commercial viability, despite the financial backing from the Finnish State and the EU. This concerns particularly the expensive LNG infrastructure development. Co-operation across industries and national borders is a precondition for making these projects profitable, as well as for working towards the general aim of improving Finland's energy security.

The Balticconnector pipeline as a joint project between Finland and Estonia, as well as the integration of the gas markets of Finland and the Baltic States are steps towards the creation of the EU-wide internal gas market and integrated gas transmission network, which improves the resilience of gas-consuming member states. Balticconnector has been promoted as contributing to energy security in the region by enabling a diversified gas supply. However, the pipeline alone does not bring true diversification for the sources of gas supply because also the Baltic States lack alternative gas suppliers to Russia. In practice, natural gas of Russian origin will likely continue to dominate the Finnish gas market in the near future. Enhancing the security and diversification of gas supply in Finland and the Baltic States necessitates the completion of GIPL. The interconnection between the Finnish-Baltic and the Central European gas networks will enable Finland to benefit from existing and forthcoming gas infrastructure projects in other EU countries as well.

Finnish energy policies are formed in the framework of the EU's energy policies. The Programme of the Finnish Government in office has an ambitious target of achieving carbon neutrality by 2035. The EU's energy and climate targets for 2030, in turn, aim to significant reduction of greenhouse gas emissions and increase in the use of renewable energy sources. Furthermore, the EU aims to reach carbon neutrality by 2050. Consequently, the general tone in which natural gas is discussed is shifting from labelling it as the most climate-friendly fossil fuel to seeing it as an interim solution in the transition towards carbon–neutral future. Overall, it seems that the diversity of energy sources and technologies is growing, which necessitates individual countries, such as Finland, to keep up with the development. Particularly in the transition phase, this includes balancing between reaching the climate targets and developing financially and technologically feasible forms of energy production. On the other hand, the diversity of alternative energy sources can enhance the energy security of countries such as Finland, lacking conventional energy resources. Consequently, the climate goals create future challenges for the whole natural gas sector. They also raise the question whether investments in pipeline and LNG infrastructure are actually viable in the long term or would it be more sensible to develop solutions related to renewable fuels directly. On the other hand, the benefit of the natural gas infrastructure is that it can be utilised also in the transmission and use of biogas and retrofitted to the use of hydrogen. LNG, in turn, may have potential in some applications, for instance as marine fuel, for some time still.

References

Amber Grid. (2020). *Gas Interconnection Poland–Lithuania (GIPL)*. https://www.ambergrid.lt/en/projects/gas-interconnection-poland-lithuania-gipl. Accessed 30 October 2020.

Arctia. (2020). *Jäänmurtajat IB Polaris*. https://www.arctia.fi/yritys/kalusto/ib-polaris.html. Accessed 30 October 2020.

Argus. (2020, June 9). *Gazprom signs Ust-Luga project agreements*. https://www.argusmedia.com/en/news/2112743-gazprom-signs-ustluga-project-agreements. Accessed 12 January 2021.

AS TallinkGrupp. (2020). *Helsinki-Tallinn: Megastar*. https://www.tallinksilja.com/tallink-shuttle-megastar-helsinki-tallinn-helsinki. Accessed 30 October 2020.

AST. (2020). *In brief*. https://ast.lv/en/content/brief. Accessed 4 January 2020.

Baltic Connector. (2019). *Finland and Estonia celebrated the commissioning of the Balticconnector gas pipeline*. http://balticconnector.fi/en/finland-and-estonia-celebrated-the-commissioning-of-the-balticconnector-gas-pipeline/. Accessed 30 October 2020.

Baltic Connector. (2020a). *The company*. http://balticconnector.fi/en/company/. Accessed 31 October 2020.

Baltic Connector. (2020b). *The project*. http://balticconnector.fi/en/the-project/. Accessed 31 October 2020.

Baltic Times. (2020, February 4). *Russian gas imports via Klaipeda named as risk to Lithuania's energy independence*. https://www.baltictimes.com/russian_gas_imports_via_klaipeda_named_as_risk_to_lithuania_s_energy_independence/. Accessed 1 November 2020.

BP. (2020). *Statistical review of world energy 2020*. https://www.bp.com/en/global/corporate/energy-economics/statistical-review-of-world-energy/downloads.html. Accessed 30 October 2020.

CEEnergynews. (2020, April 24). *The allocation of LNG terminal capacity begins in Klaipėda*. https://ceenergynews.com/oil-gas/the-allocation-of-lng-terminal-capacity-begins-in-klaipeda/. Accessed 31 October 2020.

Central Statistical Bureau of Latvia. (2020). *EN020m. Imports and consumption of natural gas*. https://data.csb.gov.lv/pxweb/en/vide/vide__energetika__isterm/EN020m.px/. Accessed 1 November 2020.

Conexus Baltic Grid. (2020a, March 20). *In order to increase supply volumes to Finland, Conexus plans to repair the transmission system*. Press release. https://www.conexus.lv/press-releases/lai-palielinatu-piegades-apjomus-somijai-conexus-plano-parvades-sistemas-remontdarbus. Accessed 31 October 2020.

Conexus Baltic Grid. (2020b). *Inčukalns UGS*. https://www.conexus.lv/incukalns-ugs-459. Accessed 31 October 2020.

Elering. (2020, February 13). *Consumption of natural gas decreased by 8 per cent last year*. https://elering.ee/en/consumption-natural-gas-decreased-8-cent-last-year. Accessed 1 November 2020.

Enerdata. (2015, October 6). *Gasum cancels regional LNG terminal and Finland-Estonia gas pipeline*. https://www.enerdata.net/publications/daily-energy-news/gasum-cancels-regional-lng-terminal-and-finland-estonia-gas-pipeline.html. Accessed 30 October 2020.

Energy Authority. (2019). *Kaasun toimitusvarmuus vuonna 2019*. https://energiavirasto.fi/documents/11120570/12722768/Raportti-kaasun-toimitusvarmuus-2019.pdf. Accessed 30 October 2020.

ERR. (2014, November 5). *Hääl to buy remaining 50% of Alexela for €35 million*. https://news.err.ee/114144/haal-to-buy-remaining-50-of-alexela-for-35-million. Accessed 1 February 2021.

ESL Shipping. (2018). *ESL Shipping and Nauticor sign long-term LNG supply contract for the world's greenest bulk carriers Haaga and Viikki*. https://www.eslshipping.com/en/news/esl-shipping-and-nauticor-sign-long-term-lng-supply-contract-for-the-worlds-greenest-bulk-carriers-haaga-and-viikki. Accessed 30 October 2020.

European Commission. (2011). *Communication from the Commission to the European Parliament, the Council, the European Economic and Social Committee and the Committee of the Regions. Energy Roadmap 2050*. COM/2011/0885 final. https://eur-lex.europa.eu/legal-content/EN/ALL/?uri=CELEX%3A52011DC0885.Accessed 30 October 2020.

European Commission. (2014, October 16). *Gas stress test: Cooperation is key to cope with supply interruption*. Press release. https://ec.europa.eu/commission/presscorner/detail/en/IP_14_1162. Accessed 30 October 2020.

European Commission. (2015a, February 25). *Energy Union Factsheet*. Memo. https://ec.europa.eu/commission/presscorner/detail/en/MEMO_15_4485. Accessed 30 October 2020.

European Commission. (2015b, September 22). *State aid: Commission approves aid for Finland's first LNG terminal*. Press release. https://ec.europa.eu/commission/presscorner/detail/en/IP_15_5689. Accessed 30 October 2020.

European Commission. (2016, March 18). *State aid: Commission approves aid for Finnish LNG terminal at Hamina*. Press release. https://ec.europa.eu/commission/presscorner/detail/en/IP_16_923. Accessed 30 October 2020.

European Commission. (2018). *Communication from the Commission to the European Parliament, the European Council, the Council, the European Economic and Social Committee, the Committee of the Regions and the European Investment Bank. A Clean Planet for all—A European strategic long-term vision for a prosperous, modern, competitive and climate neutral economy*. COM/2018/773 final. https://eur-lex.europa.eu/legal-content/EN/TXT/?uri=CELEX:52018DC0773. Accessed 30 October 2020.

European Commission. (2020a, January 8). *Balticconnector gas pipeline up and running since 1 January 2020*. https://ec.europa.eu/info/news/balticconnector-gas-pipeline-ready-use-1-january-2020-2020-jan-08_en. Accessed 31 October 2020.

European Commission. (2020b). *Communication from the Commission to the European Parliament, the Council, the European Economic and Social Committee and the Committee of the Regions. A hydrogen strategy for a climate-neutral Europe*. COM/2020/301 final. https://eur-lex.europa.eu/legal-content/EN/TXT/?qid=1594897267722&uri=CELEX%3A52020DC0301. Accessed 30 October 2020.

European Commission. (2020c). *Communication from the Commission to the European Parliament, the Council, the European Economic and Social Committee and the Committee of the Regions. An EU-wide assessment of National Energy and Climate Plans Driving forward the green transition and promoting economic recovery through integrated energy and climate planning*. COM/2020/564 final. https://eur-lex.europa.eu/legal-content/EN/TXT/?qid=1600339004657&uri=COM:2020:564:FIN. Accessed 14 January 2021.

European Commission. (2020d). *PCI examples and their benefits*. https://ec.europa.eu/energy/topics/infrastructure/projects-common-interest/PCI-examples-and-their-benefits_en. Accessed 31 October 2020.

European Commission. (2020e). *2019 annual report on CO_2emissions from maritime transport*. https://ec.europa.eu/clima/sites/clima/files/transport/shipping/docs/swd_2020_82_en.pdf. Accessed 30 October 2020.

European Commission. (2020f). *2030 climate & energy framework*. https://ec.europa.eu/clima/policies/strategies/2030_en. Accessed 30 October 2020.

European Council. (2020, December 10–11). *European Council conclusions*. https://www.consilium.europa.eu/en/press/press-releases/2020/12/11/

european-council-conclusions-10-11-december-2020/. Accessed 14 January 2021.
European Parliament. (2020a, July 27). *EU progress towards its climate change goals (infographic)*. https://www.europarl.europa.eu/news/en/headlines/society/20180706STO07407/eu-progress-towards-its-climate-change-goals-infographic. Accessed 14 January 2021.
European Parliament. (2020b, October 8). *What is carbon neutrality and how can it be achieved by 2050?* https://www.europarl.europa.eu/news/en/headlines/priorities/climate-change/20190926STO62270/what-is-carbon-neutrality-and-how-can-it-be-achieved-by-2050. Accessed 14 January 2021.
European Union. (2009). *Directive 2009/73/EC of the European Parliament and of the Council of 13 July 2009 concerning common rules for the internal market in natural gas and repealing Directive 2003/55/EC*. https://eur-lex.europa.eu/legal-content/EN/ALL/?uri=CELEX%3A32009L0073. Accessed 30 October 2020.
Europe Information. (2015, April 8). *Mikä energiaunioni? Uutinen*. https://eurooppatiedotus.fi/2015/04/08/mika-energiaunioni/. Accessed 30 October 2020.
Eurostat. (2020a). *Natural gas price statistics*. https://ec.europa.eu/eurostat/statistics-explained/index.php?title=Natural_gas_price_statistics. Accessed 30 October 2020.
Eurostat. (2020b). *EU imports of energy products—Recent developments*. https://ec.europa.eu/eurostat/statistics-explained/index.php/EU_imports_of_energy_products_-_recent_developments. Accessed 30 October 2020.
Eurostat Data Browser. (2020). *Gas prices for non-household consumers—Bi-annual data (from 2007 onwards)*. https://ec.europa.eu/eurostat/databrowser/view/nrg_pc_203/default/table?lang=en. Accessed 30 October 2020.
Finnish Customs. (2020). *ULJAS Foreign Trade Statistics Database*. https://uljas.tulli.fi/v3rti/. Accessed 12 January 2021.
Finnish Energy. (2020, January 22). *Energiavuosi 2019. Sähkö. 3 January 2020*. https://energia.fi/files/4428/Energiavuosi_2019_Sahko_paivitys_20200122.pdf. Accessed 5 January 2021.
Finnish Gas Association. (2020). *Kaasu Suomessa*. https://www.kaasuyhdistys.fi/kaasu-suomessa. Accessed 30 October 2020.
Finnish Shipowners Association. (2020). *Environmental innovations*. https://shipowners.fi/en/responsibility/environment-and-climate/environmental-innovations/. Accessed 30 October 2020.
Gasgrid. (2020a). *Gas market*. https://gasgrid.fi/en/gas-market/. Accessed 31 October 2020.
Gasgrid. (2020b). *Gas network*. https://gasgrid.fi/en/gas-network/. Accessed 30 October 2020.

Gasgrid. (2020c, June 17). *This is how the gas market opened in Finland*. Gasgrid Finland Oy. https://gasgrid.fi/en/2020/06/30/this-is-how-the-gas-market-opened-in-finland/. Accessed 31 October 2020.

Gasum. (2015a). *Finngulf terminal and Balticconnector pipeline not commercially viable*. https://www.gasum.com/en/About-gasum/for-the-media/News/2015/Finngulf-terminal-and-Balticconnector-pipeline-not-commercially-viable/. Accessed 30 October 2020.

Gasum. (2015b). *Gasum now 100% in Finnish ownership*. https://www.gasum.com/en/About-gasum/for-the-media/News/2015/Gasum-now-100-in-Finnish-ownership/. Accessed 4 January 2021.

Gasum. (2016). *Finland's first LNG import terminal opened—Provides access to LNG deliveries also outside the gas pipeline network*. https://www.gasum.com/en/About-gasum/for-the-media/News/2016/Finlands-first-LNG-import-terminal-opened-provides-access-to-LNG-deliveries-also-outside-the-gas-pipeline-network/. Accessed 4 January 2021.

Gasum. (2019a). *Kaasumarkkina avautuu—Viisi faktaa*. https://www.gasum.com/ajassa/energia--teollisuus/2019/kaasumarkkina-avautuu--viisi-faktaa/. Accessed 30 October 2020.

Gasum. (2019b). *Suomen maakaasumarkkina avautuu kilpailulle—uusi malli tehtiin yhdessä*. https://www.gasum.com/ajassa/energia--teollisuus/2019/suomen-maakaasumarkkina-avautuu-kilpailulle/. Accessed 30 October 2020.

Gasum. (2020a). *Taloudellinen katsaus 2019*. https://www.gasum.com/globalassets/pdffiles/vuosiraportointi/q4/gasum_financial_review_2019_fi_low_24_page-view.pdf. Accessed 4 January 2021.

Gasum. (2020b). *Terminals & liquefaction plant*. https://www.gasum.com/en/our-operations/lng-supply-chain/terminals--liquefaction-plants/. Accessed 31 October 2020.

GIE. (2019). *LNG map 2019*. https://www.gie.eu/download/maps/2019/GIE_LNG_2019_A0_1189x841_FULL_Final3.pdf. Accessed 12 January 2021.

GIIGNL. (2020). *The LNG industry. GIIGNL Annual Report 2020*. https://giignl.org/sites/default/files/PUBLIC_AREA/Publications/giignl_-_2020_annual_report_-_04082020.pdf. Accessed 5 January 2021.

Hamina LNG. (2020a). https://www.haminalng.fi/. Accessed 30 October 2020.

Hamina LNG. (2020b). *Schedule of commercial commissioning and transmission system connection of LNG terminal*. Release 30.9.2020. https://www.haminalng.fi/wp-content/uploads/2020/09/HLNG-Release_28_9_2020.pdf. Accessed 8 December 2020.

IGU. (2020). *Natural gas advantage facts & figures*. https://igu.org/facts-figures/. Accessed 30 October 2020.

IMO. (2014, December 23). *Ships face lower sulphur fuel requirements in emission control areas from 1 January 2015*. https://www.imo.org/en/MediaCentre/PressBriefings/Pages/44-ECA-sulphur.aspx. Accessed 31 October 2020.

Jakštas, T. (2019). *Creation of regional gas market in the Baltic States and Finland: Challenges and opportunities* (BSR Policy Briefing. 8/2019). https://www.centrumbalticum.org/files/4383/BSR_Policy_Briefing_8_2 019.pdf. Accessed 13 January 2021.

Klaipėdos Nafta. (2020). *Klaipėda LNG terminal*. https://www.kn.lt/en/our-activities/lng-terminals/klaipeda-lng-terminal/559. Accessed 31 October 2020.

Koistinen, A. (2019, July 21). *Saastuttaminen on nyt kalliimpaa kuin kertaakaan 11 vuoteen—hiilivoima ajautui pulaan Keski-Euroopassa, kiitos kuuluu päästökaupalle*. Yle. https://yle.fi/uutiset/3-10886059. Accessed 30 October 2020.

Kyytsönen, J. (2020, April 1). Kaasun hinta alentunut Viron-putken käyttöönoton jälkeen—kolmannes Suomen kaasusta tulee etelästä. *Maaseudun tulevaisuus*. https://www.maaseuduntulevaisuus.fi/talous/artikkeli-1.103 6686. Accessed 30 October 2020.

Lampila, J. (2018, November 12). *Biokaasun tuotanto Suomessa etenee vaikeuksista huolimatta*. Kestävä Energiatalous. https://www.energiatalous.fi/?p= 2234. Accessed 5 January 2021.

Le Fevre, C. N. (2018). *A review of demand prospects for LNG as a marine transport fuel* (OIES Paper: NG 133). The Oxford Institute of Energy Studies. https://doi.org/10.26889/9781784671143. Accessed 1 November 2020.

Liikennefakta. (2020a). *Meriliikenteen kasvihuonekaasupäästöjen vähentäminen*. https://www.liikennefakta.fi/fi/ymparisto/meriliikenteen-kasvihuonekaasu paastojen-vahentaminen. Accessed 30 October 2020.

Liikennefakta. (2020b). *Liikenteen kasvihuonekaasupäästöt ja energiankulutus*. https://www.liikennefakta.fi/fi/ymparisto/liikenteen-kasvihuonekaasu paastot-ja-energiankulutus. Accessed 30 October 2020.

Ministry of Agriculture and Forestry. (2020). *Maatalous uusiutuvan energian tuottajana ja käyttäjänä*. https://mmm.fi/ruoka-ja-maatalous/bio kaasu. Accessed 30 October 2020.

Ministry of Economic Affairs and Employment. (2014a). Päätös investointituen myöntämisestä LNG-terminaalin investointihankkeeseen. Päätös 18.9.2014. TEM/642/05.02.05/2014.

Ministry of Economic Affairs and Employment. (2014b). Päätös investointituen myöntämisestä LNG-terminaalin investointihankkeeseen. Päätös 18.9.2014. TEM/2488/05.02.05/2013.

Ministry of Economic Affairs and Employment. (2017). *Valtioneuvoston selonteko kansallisesta energia- ja ilmastostrategiasta vuoteen 2030*. Työ- ja elinkeinoministeriön julkaisuja 4/2017. http://urn.fi/URN:ISBN:978-952-327-190-6. Accessed 30 October 2020.

Ministry of Economic Affairs and Employment. (2019). *Finland's Integrated Energy and Climate Plan.* Publications of the Ministry of Economic Affairs and Employment 2019:66. http://urn.fi/URN:ISBN:978-952-327-478-5. Accessed 30 October 2020.

Ministry of Economic Affairs and Employment. (2020). *Ilmasto- ja energiastrategia.* https://tem.fi/ilmasto-ja-energiastrategia. Accessed 30 October 2020.

Ministry of Energy of the Republic of Lithuania. (2020, January 14). *In 2019, Lithuania transported the highest ever recorded amount of gas to the Baltic States.* https://enmin.lrv.lt/en/news/in-2019-lithuania-transported-the-highest-ever-recorded-amount-of-gas-to-the-baltic-states. Accessed 1 November 2020.

Ministry of Finance. (2014). *Suomi ja Viro sopivat yhteisestä LNG-etenemissuunnitelmasta.* Valtioneuvoston viestintäosasto. Tiedote 511/2014. https://vm.fi/-/10184/suomi-ja-viro-sopivat-yhteisesta-lng-etenemissuunnitelmasta. Accessed 30 October 2020.

Ministry of Finance. (2020). *Energiaverotuksen uudistamista selvittävän työryhmän loppuraportin ehdotukset ja niiden vaikutukset.* Muistio VN/11347/2019 VM148:00/2019. https://vm.fi/hanke?tunnus=VM148:00/2019. Accessed 30 October 2020.

National Emergency Supply Agency. (2019). *Suunnitelmat maakaasun toimitusvarmuuden riskien ennaltaehkäisemisestä ja toimista toimitushäiriötilanteissa (hätäsuunnitelma).* https://cdn.huoltovarmuuskeskus.fi/app/uploads/2019/10/31111328/Finland-gas-preventive-action-plan-and-emergency-plan.pdf. Accessed 13 January 2021.

Natural Resources Institute Finland. (2020, August 14). *Nurmi, lanta ja energia onko biokaasusta tulevaisuuden maaseudun energiaksi?* https://www.luke.fi/nurmi-lanta-ja-energia-onko-biokaasusta-tulevaisuuden-maaseudun-energiaksi/. Accessed 30 October 2020.

Navigator Magazine. (2014, May 12). STX Finland luovutti ulkovartiolaivan Rajavartiolaitokselle. https://navigatormagazine.fi/uutiset/meriteollisuus/stx-finland-luovutti-ulkovartiolaivan-rajavartiolaitokselle/. Accessed 6 April 2021.

Nuotio, T. (2020, January 7). Maakaasun käyttö on vähentynyt teollisuudessa lähes puolella, mutta sitä ei nähdä katoavana energianlähteenä—Baltian putki haastaa Venäjän tuonnin. *Kainuun Sanomat.* https://www.kainuunsanomat.fi/artikkeli/maakaasun-kaytto-on-vahentynyt-teollisuudessa-lahes-puolella-mutta-sita-ei-nahda-katoavana-energianlahteena-baltian-putki-haastaa-venajan-tuonnin-175714725/. Accessed 30 October 2020.

Patricolo, C. (2020, May 7). *The construction of the GIPL gas pipeline proceeds as scheduled*. CEEnergynews. https://ceenergynews.com/oil-gas/the-construction-of-the-gipl-gas-pipeline-proceeds-as-scheduled/. Accessed 30 October 2020.

Pukkila, T. (2015, August 21). *SK: AGA hyllytti Rauman LNG-terminaalin*. Yle. https://yle.fi/uutiset/3-8243455. Accessed 30 October 2020.

Reiljan, K. (2020, April 6). An unexpected shutdown of Balticconnector is to result in millions in losses. *The Baltic Times*. https://www.baltictimes.com/an_unexpected_shutdown_of_balticconnector_is_to_result_in_millions_in_losses/. Accessed 31 October 2020.

Reuters. (2019, June 11). *Finland opens largest Nordic LNG terminal after delay*. https://www.reuters.com/article/finland-lng/finland-opens-largest-nordic-lng-terminal-after-delay-idUSL8N23I2UC. Accessed 31 October 2020.

Rokke, N. (2020, September 21). Norway to build $3 billion 'longship' carbon dioxide capture project. *Forbes*. https://www.forbes.com/sites/nilsrokke/2020/09/21/norways-18-billion-ccs-proposal-is-great-news-for-the-climate/?sh=6a713f09179e#238af076179e. Accessed 30 October 2020.

Sallinen, P. (2020, March 20). *Nesteytettyä biokaasua Raumalle*. Energiauutiset. https://vanhalehti.energiauutiset.fi/etusivu/nesteytettya-biokaasua-raumalle.html. Accessed 6 April 2021.

Simon, F. (2020, May 18). *Gas industry urged to 'accelerate' transition to hydrogen*. EurActiv. https://www.euractiv.com/section/energy-environment/news/gas-industry-urged-to-accelerate-transition-to-hydrogen/. Accessed 30 October 2020.

Statistics Finland. (2011, October 6). *Appendix figure 1. Electricity production by energy sources 2010*. https://www.stat.fi/til/salatuo/2010/salatuo_2010_2011-10-06_kuv_001_en.html. Accessed 15 January 2021.

Statistics Finland. (2020a). *Consumption of fossil fuels decreased by 6 per cent in 2019*. https://www.stat.fi/til/ehk/2019/04/ehk_2019_04_2020-04-17_tie_001_en.html. Accessed 30 October 2020.

Statistics Finland. (2020b). *Energy supply and consumption. Production and consumption of biogas by plant type, 2017–2019*. Modified 21 December 2020. https://pxnet2.stat.fi/PXWeb/pxweb/en/StatFin/. Accessed 12 January 2021.

Statistics Finland. (2020c). *Energy supply and consumption. Total energy consumption by energy source (all categories), 1970–2019*. Modified 21 December 2020. https://pxnet2.stat.fi/PXWeb/pxweb/en/StatFin/. Accessed 12 January 2021.

Sytas, A. (2019, January 21). *Lithuania LNG port aims to be Baltic hub, double flows*. Reuters. https://www.reuters.com/article/lithuania-lng-idUSL8N1ZL2C9. Accessed 30 October 2020.

Tax Administration. (2019, January 11). *Energiaverotukseen muutoksia 1.1.2019 ja 1.4.2019*. Uutinen. https://www.vero.fi/tietoa-verohallinnosta/uutishuone/uutiset/uutiset/2019/energiaverotukseen-muutoksia-2019/. Accessed 30 October 2020.

Tiihonen, J. (2019, June 11). *Tornioon avattu LNG-terminaali on Pohjoismaiden suurin—Kasvihuonepäästöt vähentyvät viidenneksellä*. Yle. https://yle.fi/uutiset/3-10826144. Accessed 30 October 2020.

van Wijk, A., & Chatzimarkakis, J. (2020, April 15). *Green hydrogen for a European green deal. A 2x40 GW initiative*. Hydrogen Europe. http://www.hydrogeneurope.eu/wp-content/uploads/2021/04/Hydrogen-Europe_2x40-GW-Green-H2-Initative-Paper.pdf. Accessed 6 April 2021.

Viking Line. (2020). *LNG—Nesteytetty maakaasu*. https://www.vikingline.com/fi/ymparisto/lng/. Accessed 30 October 2020.

Woellwarth, L. (2020, May 26). *Lithuanian LNG terminal proving to be a player in the global market*. LNG Industry. https://www.lngindustry.com/liquid-natural-gas/26052020/lithuanian-lng-terminal-proving-to-be-a-player-in-the-global-market/. Accessed 30 October 2020.

CHAPTER 11

How Much Gas Is Enough?: Energy Security and Natural Gas Infrastructure in the Baltic Sea Region

Anna Mikulska

Introduction

The story about the natural gas market in the Baltic Sea region is of dependence, diversity, and change. Much of this is about the role of Russia, until recently the dominant and, for some countries, exclusive supplier of natural gas. Almost a non-issue before the fall of the Iron Curtain, strong natural gas dependence on Russia has become a pressing matter, especially for countries previously associated with the Soviet Union. In the Baltic Sea region, Estonia, Latvia, Lithuania, and Poland–no more under Russia's direct political and economic influence–have become the target of geopolitical pressure and a source of economic rent that Russia could and has derived from its dominant or monopolist position on the Baltic Sea region's gas market. As a pushback and in the effort to boost their energy security, these countries have undertaken two

A. Mikulska (✉)
Baker Institute for Public Policy, Rice University, Houston, TX, USA
e-mail: anna.b.mikulska@rice.edu

K. Liuhto (ed.), *The Future of Energy Consumption, Security and Natural Gas*, https://doi.org/10.1007/978-3-030-80367-4_11

interrelated initiatives: (1) build-up of new gas infrastructure to diversify supplies and (2) development of the market's interconnectivity to ensure region's integration. Other countries in the Baltic Sea region, including Denmark, Finland, Norway, and Sweden, have also become involved in these initiatives.

This chapter argues that actions towards diversification and integration of the Baltic Sea region are two sides of the same coin and only if both of them are balanced they can further the goals of regional energy security. As such, the chapter starts with a definition of the Baltic Sea region and its countries as well as the idea of energy security as it applies to the region's natural gas markets. It then provides a quick survey of those markets as well, major existing infrastructure and projects that are currently undergoing and are conducive to both, diversifying and integrating the market. An empirical section follows where we suggest a measure of security of supply that captures 'the credible threat' idea, according to which already the ability to access supply has substantial energy security benefits. We look at different scenarios of Baltic Sea region diversification and how it affects security of supply. In conclusion, we point to the results of our analysis underscoring the need for more gas infrastructure in the region. This at times may seem redundant but is necessary under 'the credible threat' assumption. How much more infrastructure will be needed will depend not only on its capacity, however, but also on the level of market integration and co-operation to which the countries in the region are willing and able to commit.

Defining the Terms

The Baltic Sea Region

For the purposes of this chapter, the Baltic Sea region is defined as including whole territories of: the three Baltic States, namely Estonia, Latvia, Lithuania, as well as Denmark, Finland, Germany, Norway, Poland, and Sweden. This is a variation of a middle-of-the-road approach that includes Baltic Sea's all littoral states (Klemeshev et al., 2017) with the modification that excludes Russia from the analysis. This is mandated by the scope of the analysis, as the energy security agenda in the region is built–in majority of cases–directly in opposition to Russia's influence as a historically dominant supplier to the region. To some degree and for reasons this chapter explores later, Germany is also considered an outlier.

Energy Security

One of the basic ways to define energy security is via the four 'As' approach as: available, affordable, accessible, and acceptable access to energy supply. The more suppliers and supply diversification, the more secure the environment is in terms of ability to deliver the needed amount of gas, at any given time, at the lowest possible price and under as advantageous as possible contractual obligations. Lack of supply diversification can lead to potential disruptions in supply, as well as high prices. Though the traditional approach had been recently challenged to include issues, such as climate change and local pollution (Cherp & Jewell, 2014), this chapter stays with the traditional approach as it provides quantitative information, which can be used as baseline to build upon by adding new factors.

Post-Soviet countries are of particular interest as they have been exposed to many of the downsides of energy dependence given Russia's dominant position in the region, allowing it to extract both geopolitical and economic benefits. Recent growth in LNG trade and a larger, liquid global natural gas market have, however, awarded new opportunities for diversification of gas supply to the countries in the Baltic Sea region and, in doing so, boosting their energy security. This critically hinges on the ability of the region to build up new natural gas infrastructure that will both make direct deliveries of LNG possible and distribute them in an effective manner to balance demand in the region. As such the supply becomes available and accessible but does it become affordable? After all, new supply comes from sources that are characterised by higher production and/or transportation cost than Russian gas, e.g. much of the LNG from the USA, Qatar, or Norway.

There are three caveats, however, that modify typical economic calculus when it comes to applying it to natural gas supplies in the Baltic Sea region. First, while Russia could outcompete much of the alternative supply on production and transportation cost, it will not do so until an alternative is present, i.e. until there is sufficient infrastructure to bring non-Russian gas when needed. In this sense, the existence of supply diversifying infrastructure creates the so-called 'credible threat' that induces market participants to compete on price and/or contract conditions. In case of the Baltic Sea region, if countries can secure competing gas supplies at any point in time, even if Russia is the only supplier at the moment, it cannot dominate and dictate conditions when it comes to contracts and price. Rather, it needs to adjust those to its competitors with market pricing becoming a ceiling to what Russian suppliers can charge its customers.

Second, some countries may be willing to pay a so-called security premium to diversify their gas, making higher prices acceptable due to energy security considerations. Third, where pricing of Russian gas has been high based on Russia's dominant position (e.g. Poland and Lithuania), non-Russian, market-priced gas does not necessarily have to result in 'a sticker shock' and as such will be both economically and politically palatable (Mikulska, 2018b).

The Role of Natural Gas in the Baltic Sea Region and Its Countries

As any natural gas pipeline map of Europe will attest (ENTSOG, 2019), the Baltic Sea region has been significantly poorer in natural gas pipeline infrastructure than Western Europe. The notable exception is Germany where natural gas pipeline network is much more expansive and interconnected with other market participants. The reasons explaining the scarcity of gas infrastructure in the Baltic Sea region vary depending on the country group. Countries from the sphere of previous Soviet influence (Estonia, Latvia, Lithuania, and Poland) have historically relied on a limited set of one-directional (East to West) pipelines that would pipe exclusively Russian gas into their economies and further into Western Europe. Lack of sizeable pipeline network in the Nordic countries of Denmark, Finland, Norway, and Sweden, stems from limited use of gas within these countries as they reach for energy alternatives, such as hydropower, biomass, and nuclear energy. And this is despite Denmark's and Norway's status of net gas exporters.

As per Fig. 11.1, since 2000, the average consumption of natural gas in the region (excluding Russia, Norway, and Denmark–the region's net-gas exporters) has increased slightly–by around 7.6 bcm.[1]

[1] Denmark has recently been struggling with its status as net gas exporter after its largest natural gas field, Tyra, was shut down for re-development in September of 2019. It was first estimated that the Tyra will be back online in 2022 but the COVID-19 pandemic has slowed down the progress and it is now assumed the field will not be back until mid-2023. In the interim, Denmark has been importing large amounts of gas from

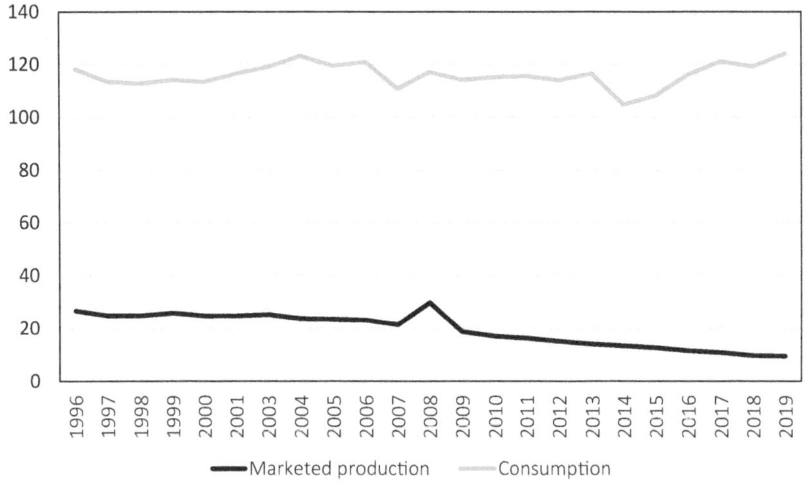

Fig. 11.1 Natural gas balance in the Baltic Sea region's net gas importing countries (bcm) (*Source* The Author, based on Cedigaz, 2020c)

However, the picture is much more nuanced. We see Germany and Poland–the region's largest gas consumers (Russia is excluded)–increasing their consumption of natural gas after 2014 (Fig. 11.2).

Meanwhile, consumption in other net importers of gas in the Baltic Sea region has not gone beyond 2003 levels or decreased (Fig. 11.3).[2]

When it comes to sources, natural gas piped from Russia has been dominating the region's imports. However, the dominance has diminished over the last decade, particularly in the former Soviet bloc countries and most significantly where LNG infrastructure has increased, i.e. in Lithuania and Poland (Table 11.1).

To shed more light on these developments, we will now explore in more detail the region's countries, their natural gas markets, and infrastructure.

Germany, which–given that the latter is not significant gas producer and imports most of its gas from Russia, Norway, and the Netherlands (Katona, 2020).

[2] We use 2003 as a benchmark here as the 2002 data was missing for Estonia, Latvia, and Lithuania.

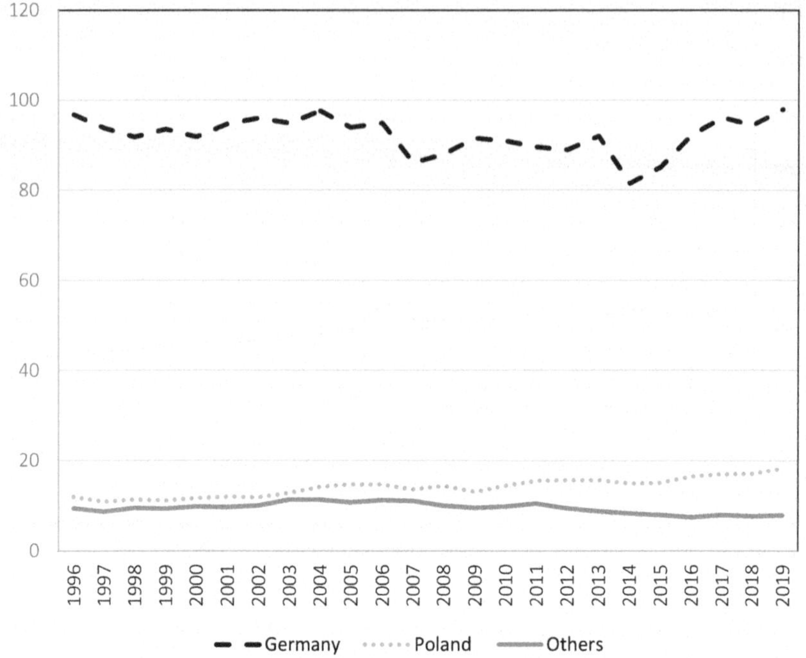

Fig. 11.2 Natural gas consumption in Poland, Germany and other net gas importing countries in the Baltic Sea region (bcm) (*Source* The Author, based on Cedigaz, 2020c)

The Baltic States: Estonia, Latvia, and Lithuania

Until recently, Lithuania was completely dependent on Russia for delivery of natural gas. The country has no domestically available gas supplies and, until 2014, the only way to bring in gas was through the Russian gas-transporting pipelines inherited from the Soviet era. As reported by Hinchey (2018), the dependence resulted in Gazprom–Russian state-controlled natural gas supplier and only piped gas exporter–charging the country prices much higher than prices it charged Germany or Italy. In addition, the actual level of pricing was likely influenced by geopolitical considerations. For example, in 2011 Gazprom awarded Estonia and Latvia with a 15% discount but did not extend it to Lithuania, which at the time signalled its readiness to liberalise its gas market in line with

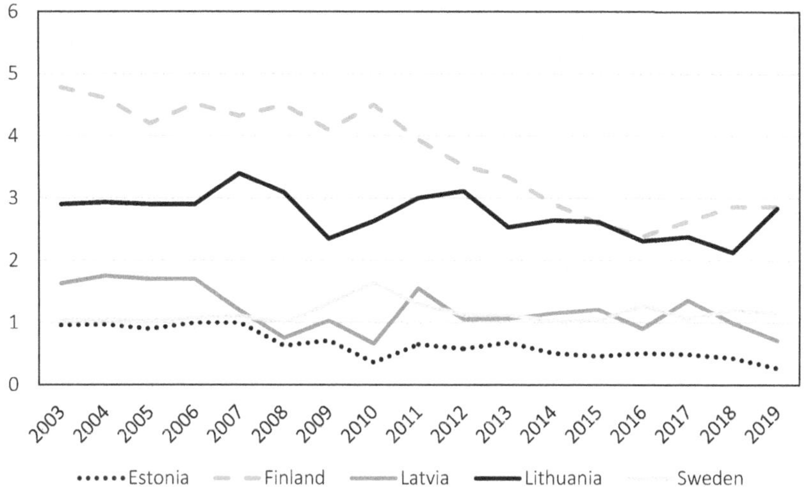

Fig. 11.3 Natural gas consumption in selected Baltic Sea region countries (bcm) (*Source* The Author, based on Cedigaz, 2020c)

Table 11.1 Share of Russian gas in imports by country (%)

	2010	*2019*
Denmark	0.0	0.0
Germany	36.2	48.8
Estonia	100.0	99.0
Latvia	100.0	100.0
Lithuania	100.0	43.3
Poland	89.5	54.3
Finland	100.0	97.0
Sweden	0.0	0.0

Source The Author, based on Eurostat (2021)

the EU Third Energy Package (Hinchey, 2018). This has hardly been an exception as more instances of gas and oil-related geopolitical meddling related to Russia's dominant position, including in the Baltic Sea region have been documented (Collins, 2017).

Unwilling to suffer the consequences of continuing the Russian monopoly, Lithuania decided to extend its gas import options by introducing LNG. In 2014, the country began operating 'Independence', an

FSRU in Klaipeda with a maximum annual capacity of four billion cubic metres. Originally leased until 2024 from Höegh LNG, a Norwegian shipping company, the FSRU will be bought by Lithuania at the end of the leasing term. The EU and the Lithuanian Parliament approved the move towards the end of 2018 (The Baltic Course, 2018), even as the terminal operated below its full capacity in the years preceding the decision (13.0% in 2015, 35.0% in 2016, 30.0% in 2017) (KN, 2019). The decision was rather a recognition that access to LNG introduces competition, effectively lowered Russian gas prices, and improved security of supply (Hinchey, 2018). Despite a decline in utilisation rate in 2018 (20.5%), it has since significantly picked up (44.6% in 2019 and 49.0% in 2020) (KN, 2021), a level consistent with the utilisation rate of LNG terminals elsewhere in the EU, which bodes well for Lithuanian plans to buy the terminal by 2024 and use it until 2044.

Lithuania's success with LNG imports has not been lost on Latvia and Estonia, with both countries aiming at building LNG terminals of their own. Latvia is currently planning for a Skulte LNG terminal, a floating unit which could leverage the country's existing Inčukalns underground gas storage with an active capacity of 2.3 bcm, expandable up to 3.2 bcm. The country advertises the project as significantly cheaper to build and maintain given the lack of need to (1) build storage facilities (which amounts to 70–80% of the cost) and (2) maintain cold storage once the terminal is finished (Conexus, 2021). According to information provided by the project website, this puts the costs of maintenance at 1/8 of the FSRU in Klaipeda (Skulte LNG Terminal, 2021). Estonia's plans for direct LNG access include two potential terminals, Paldiski and Tallinn, each up to 3 bcm/year of capacity and comparable to the Klaipeda terminal in Estonia in terms of construction and cold storage maintenance needs. Estonia is an important link connecting the region with Finland. The country is also weary of Russian influence as it can attest first-hand to the threat of Russian meddling. In 1993, Russia cut supply of gas in response to Estonia's new law that would require non-citizens (mostly Russians) to apply for residency or leave the country (Bohlen, 1993).

Of the prospective LNG terminals in Estonia and Latvia, the Paldiski terminal seems to be closest to beginning constructions as all formalities are now fulfilled and the workers only await politicians' green light (Saarmann, 2020). Still, any of the proposed terminals has yet to secure European funding, which could become increasingly difficult as the EU moves away from funding fossil fuel projects, including within the Project of Common Interest initiative (Elliott, 2020).

The Baltic States together with Finland and Poland have also been involved in the construction of interconnector projects, Balticconnector and GIPL. Given their collective nature, we will describe those projects in more detail in the next section.

Poland

In contrast to the Baltic States, Poland has never relied completely on Russian gas. It has had access to domestic natural resources and, more recently, to the EU imports. Nevertheless, the majority of Poland's imports have come from Gazprom. And with no other source to fill the gap, Gazprom has had strong bargaining position, resulting in rather high gas prices and, similarly to the Baltic States, the potential for Russia's geopolitical meddling (Mikulska, 2018b). This led Poland not only towards pursuing the goal of diversification of gas supply but also to the declaration that it would completely stop importing Russian gas after the long-term contract with Gazprom expires in December of 2022. To achieve these objectives, Poland built an LNG terminal in Świnoujście that began operations in 2016 and is currently in the process of expanding its capacity from 5.0 bcm to 7.5 bcm, which is enough to cover over a third of Poland's current gas demand. If needed, the terminal could be expanded to ten billion cubic metres (Czyżewski, 2020). Furthermore, a floating terminal is being planned in Gdańsk with a capacity of 4.5 bcm or more. The project is currently in the design stage with a projected completion date in 2026/2027 (Klein, 2021). Poland is also heavily engaged in the Baltic Pipe project. Work on the Polish portion of the pipeline began in October 2020 and the pipeline is supposed to be completed in October of 2022. Given the global COVID-19 pandemic, this deadline could become difficult to make despite official assurances of timelines of the project so far (Ciężadło, 2021). Once completed, Baltic Pipe will be able to bring up to ten billion cubic metres of natural gas from Norway and, once the Tyra natural gas field is back online, from Denmark. Some of the gas imported via Baltic Pipe, Poland is planning to sell further into the Baltic Sea region via interconnector with Lithuania (GIPL) that is currently being built and beyond the region via interconnectors with Slovakia and Ukraine.

Germany

Germany is the EU's largest natural gas consumer and–because it does not own substantial domestic natural gas resources–is also the EU's largest gas importer. In 2019, Germany consumed 98.0 bcm, produced 5.7 bcm, imported 134.1 bcm, and exported (or rather re-exported) 41.8 bcm of natural gas (Cedigaz, 2020a). The majority of Germany's imported gas came from Russia (56.3 bcm), followed by Norway (31.3 bcm), and the Netherlands (24.1 bcm). The rest (mostly re-exports) was delivered from a mix of other European countries (Austria, Belgium, Czechia, Denmark, France, and Hungary). Germany imports all its gas via pipelines and there is no existing LNG facility there, with some being planned but yet to be built. There are two potential locations for LNG import terminal, including Stade, which at 12 bcm is the largest LNG import terminal option under consideration and Brunsbüttel where final investment decision has yet to be reached (Elliott, 2021). That being said, Brunsbüttel has already hosted ship-to-ship operations and has refuelled ships via trucks (LNG Prime, 2021).

The most interesting natural gas project in Germany is actually not about LNG but about pipeline from Russia. The Nord Stream 2 project consists of two parallel pipelines with a maximum capacity of 55 bcm/annum to accompany the already functioning twin pipelines of Nord Stream (also 55 bcm/annum). For Germany, some of this capacity could replace imports from the Netherlands, given that production there is destined to decrease dramatically after the Groningen field shuts down by mid-2022 (Moestue, 2021). But Nord Stream 2 is mostly focused on replacing the Russian supply to Europe (as a whole), which currently transits via Ukraine.[3]

A very limited LNG development and serious pipeline build-up to deliver Russian gas comes at the time when Germany is likely to need much more natural gas as it phase-outs its nuclear and coal generation by the end of 2022 and 2038, respectively (Deutsche Welle, 2019, 2020). The issue has become a concern among some of the Baltic Sea region countries, in particular Poland and the Baltic States, all of which–as described earlier–experienced geopolitical meddling and/or high pricing related to Russia's dominant position in their natural gas markets. The result is a strong disagreement between these countries and Germany

[3] See Box 11.1 for more details about the difficult history of Nord Stream 2.

when it comes to the value, purpose, and consequences of Nord Stream 2. This disagreement, combined with the German commitment to Russian imports and the close relations between Germany's gas utilities and Gazprom, makes Germany very much an outlier in the Baltic Sea region, where energy security is in principle defined in opposition to, rather than in tandem with, Russian gas.

Box 11.1. Nord Stream 2 Opposition and US Sanctions

The Nord Stream 2 pipeline has been one of the most contested natural gas projects in Europe. It has been vehemently opposed by countries in Central and Eastern Europe (especially Poland and Ukraine but also the Baltic States) as well as the USA, which see the investment as a way for Russia to continue to dominate the region, subjugate Ukraine, and potentially increase its influence over Western Europe, in particular Germany. In contrast, Russia as well as Germany argue that the investment is very much a market-based undertaking that is geared towards providing greater energy security for Europe, which they see as undermined currently by unreliable Ukrainian transit (for a detailed analysis of the pipeline's history, see Mikulska, 2018a).

In an effort to stop the pipeline from being completed, the USA has issued set of sanctions, including in 2019 sanctions on pipeline laying vessels that caused the Swiss-based company Allseas to back out from the projects and stalled the progress of construction for almost a year. In response, Russia has prepared its own vessels–the Academic Czerskiy and Fortuna–to take over the task, with the latter beginning to lay pipeline towards the end of 2020 and consequently sanctioned by the outgoing Trump administration (Collins & Mikulska, 2021). The sanctioned have been upheld in February 2021 by the Biden administration, which to the dismay of many in Central and Eastern Europe, however, has restrained itself from sanctioning any other entities involved in Nord Stream 2. Such sanctions are still possible given that the US Congress expanded potential for sanctions on Nord Stream 2 on the 1st of January 2021 as per the 2021 US National Defence Authorization Act

(NDAA). The Biden administration is currently in the process of identifying any entities involved in sanctioned activities and potentially imposing new sanctions in their report that by law it is required to submit every 90 days. Even up to 120 European companies could be affected and reportedly 18 companies have already dropped from the project (Gardner, 2021). It is unclear, however how much of an appetite for Nord Stream 2 sanctions that would impact many of companies located in US allied countries but also many which do business in the USA. In addition, with the report scheduled for May 2021, one could not eliminate the possibility that the pipeline would be built by that time as only about 150 kms remain to be completed.

This outlier attitude is grounded not only in the long history of Russian gas imports but, generally, in Germany's position as well-established and large natural gas demand centre. As mentioned earlier, the country's gas pipeline network is relatively well-developed but also well-integrated as part of the Western European so it can quite smoothly balance its market through arranging gas flows from other Western European countries. As previously pointed out, the lack of existing LNG infrastructure, the rather limited plans for any LNG infrastructure build-up, and the plans to expand transit from Russia involve a risk of limited diversification of supply in the future. Until now, Germany has avoided the dependence trap experienced by other gas-importing countries in the region through sustained interconnectedness. This strategy has proven effective even at the time when nearly the entire supply of German gas is imported, and Russian gas constitutes its main supply source (Table 11.1). It is also not without significance that, as Russia's largest European customer, Germany has over the years enjoyed a strong bargaining position, leading to lower natural gas prices charged by Gazprom compared to other countries in the region (Hinchey, 2018).

The Nordics: Between Small Importers and Net-Exporting Countries

Among the Nordic countries, Finland and Sweden are gas importers. Historically, Finland has relied completely on Russian natural gas supplies. However, this has changed in recent years as two LNG terminals began their operations: in 2016 in the port of Pori and in 2017 Manga LNG terminal in the City of Tornio (fully operational in mid-2019). Another LNG terminal in the port of Hamina has been authorised in August 2020 and its commercial commissioning is projected to take place in October 2021. The terminals have small storage capacity but–given Finland's small natural gas usage–are anticipated to provide enough of the liquid fuel to satisfy Finnish LNG demand. The terminals in Hamina and Pori are on the smaller side with storage capacity of about 30,000 cubic metres each. The Manga LNG terminal is slightly larger, at 50,000 cubic metres. Hence, 2016 and 2017 marked the onset of a broken Russian monopoly, though at a relatively small scale. A larger breakthrough happened in 2020 when Balticconnector began operations, which resulted in about 35% cut in Russian gas supplies to Finland in the first months of 2020, with most of the Balticconnector gas coming from the Klaipeda LNG terminal (Energy News Monitor, 2021). It remains unclear if the trend will continue or expand going forward given that 2020 has been marked by unusual LNG supply glut and record low spot LNG prices. Higher LNG prices may prove it difficult for the fuel to compete with Russia's gas in the future. But given new points of access to alternative supply as well as Finland's rather small total gas demand, persisting dependence on Russian gas becomes less likely, even if Russian gas continues to constitute a majority of supply.

Sweden uses natural gas in a very limited fashion, with gas constituting only three percent of its primary energy demand. The Swedish gas network is very small with only 30 out of 290 Swedish municipalities able to access natural gas directly. Sweden buys its gas from Denmark (piped gas and biogas) (Klackenberg, 2019) and, more recently, from Norway (LNG) (Eurostat, 2021). There has been a steady increase in LNG and biogas use in recent years. Both of which are often combined and used in the transportation sector (Klackenberg, 2019), which is supported by the urban (500 km of pipeline) and vehicle (40 km of pipeline) gas networks in the Stockholm area. In addition, Sweden has a set of small local gas networks, which are mainly used to supply biogas from production plants for transport purposes (CEEP, 2019). Neither the urban and vehicle gas networks nor the local gas network are connected with Sweden's main gas transmission network in the west of the country, however. Most recently, the Swedish Government has also denied a permit for the planned LNG terminal at the port of Gothenburg to be connected to the transmission network, a move which provoked speculations that the plans for the terminal had been cancelled (350.org, 2019). In 2019, Sweden has withdrawn the terminal from the Project of Common Interest list. However, there has been persistent news about LNG terminal construction in that port throughout 2020, though with a specific focus on bunkering rather than serving the needs of Swedish consumers. Gas bunkering is also planned for the port of Oxelsund to include LNG and green methane, with the latter planned to serve the needs of Sweden's steel production and to potentially be redistributed to other parts of the country via rail and/or tracks (Ship & Bunker, 2020).

On the 1st of April 2019, Sweden and Denmark created Joint Balancing Zone between their gas markets. The common setup aims to help security of supply by enabling the rise in pipeline pressure in Sweden, thus facilitating efficient and closer cross-border co-operation (Swedegas, 2019).

Though Denmark's long-term (by 2050) goal is to phase out all North Sea oil and gas production, in the short term the production is supposed to rise after redevelopment of Tyra, the country's largest natural gas field, is completed. As it currently stands, the return to operation will be delayed until 2022 due to the COVID-19 pandemic. Hence, for the 2020–2022 period we should expect continuing low production levels consistent with those observed in recent years (Katona, 2020). Production decreased from 5.0 bcm in 2017, to 4.2 bcm in 2018, to 3.2 bcm in 2019 (Cedigaz, 2020a). Once Tyra is operational again, however, the trend is more than likely to reverse as the final investment decision for the field's redevelopment should allow Tyra to produce for another 25 years (Elliott & Hunter, 2020).

Norway is the one country in the Baltic Sea region that is going to be a major natural gas supplier well into the future. The country has been producing hydrocarbons since the 1970s and, at least when it comes to gas, its resources are far from being depleted. As reported by Norwegian Petroleum (2021), 2/3 of the country's expected resources are yet to be produced and production is expected to stay at a current, or higher level, for the next 15–20 years. Also, Hall (2018) underscores Norway's potential to continue its gas production into the 2030s if current levels of activity are sustained and recovery rates continue to improve. Per Cedigaz (2020a), in 2019 Norway marketed production was 115 bcm, somewhat lower from the year before (122bcm) or the country's all-time high in 2017 (125 bcm). This puts Norway in the eighth spot among the world's top natural gas producers and able to sustain approximately three percent of global demand. More significant is the fact that the country exports the vast majority of its production (113 bcm in 2019). This makes Norway third-largest gas exporter globally and second-largest gas supplier to the EU. Approximately 95% of Norwegian gas is exported via pipelines. The remaining five percent of gas exports are in the form of LNG, which is produced from offshore subsea development in the South Barents Sea, Snøhvit. The gas produced there from 20 wells is piped for liquefaction to the Hammerfest LNG, Europe's largest and the world's northernmost natural gas liquefaction facility. Norway is also a place with robust development of small-scale LNG, used mostly as bunkering fuel for ships and trucks.

Norway's most important customers for natural gas are Germany, Belgium, the UK, and France but the list is growing, also thanks to the country's LNG production allows.[4] While LNG from Norway has found its destination in other countries of the Baltic Sea region, it is a pipeline development that can impact the energy security of the region the most. The Baltic Pipe project, which we will describe in the next section, is currently well underway and promises access to ten billion cubic metres of gas from Norway into Denmark and Poland and from there to the neighbouring markets, including those in the Baltic Sea region.

Whole Versus Sum of Its Parts

As indicated above, natural gas markets within the Baltic Sea region are extremely diverse when it comes to volumes and share of gas in energy mix. So why are we talking about the Baltic Sea region as an area for developing security of gas supply? Why are we not focusing at each country separately and developing a country-level strategy that would be best for that entity's energy security?

It is because–as it often happens–the whole is greater than the sum of its parts. A well-designed co-operation and co-ordination on part of all those countries can render the entire region more secure in terms of energy supply and decrease the influence of Russia. Successful co-operation and use of each country's comparative advantage can also

[4] In the meantime, however, the Hammerfest facility has been experiencing some setback as the September 2020 fire shutdown the LNG terminal's operations for what is estimated to be even an entire year (Maritime Executive, 2020).

significantly reduce costs of infrastructure as fewer barriers to trade can facilitate economies of scale.

Diversification of Supply

In recent years, most countries in the Baltic Sea region have undertaken infrastructure build up to diversify their supply of natural gas. Currently, two major facilities importing non-Russian gas are functioning in the region: the Lithuanian LNG terminal in Klaipeda, which began operating in 2014 and Poland's LNG terminal in Świnoujście that accepted first LNG cargo in 2016.

The annual capacity of the Lithuanian terminal is four billion cubic metres, which is beyond what are Lithuanian natural gas needs (Table 11.3). Unfortunately, lack of sufficient interconnection to sell imported LNG to its neighbours, as well as Russian competitive push that resulted in lower prices offered by Gazprom to Lithuania, the capacity of the terminal has not been fully used, although the utilisation rate has grown recently and in 2019 and 2020 has been close (46.6% and 49.0%, respectively) to the EU's average LNG utilisation rate of 50% (European Commission 2020a). Interestingly, a fifth of the LNG that Lithuania imported in 2019 has come from Russia's LNG development in the Arctic, Yamal LNG (GIIGNL, 2020). This is, however, much different than pipeline-based monopoly that Gazprom had over the country's gas supply not so long ago. Novatek, the Russian LNG producer, is a private company and–more importantly–one that has to compete on a market level with other LNG producers and pipeline gas.[5] As a matter of fact, to the extent a competitive marketplace exists, buying natural gas from Gazprom is also not problematic as the price is set by the market and the ability to supply gas does not bestow geopolitical benefits on Russia. The LNG facility in Lithuania also offers substantial benefits in the context of the entire Baltic Sea region and co-operation between the countries. Since its maximum capacity is larger than Lithuania's demand it can provide a point of significant, additional supply for Estonia, Latvia, and Finland (an example of such potential we have already seen in 2020 when Balticconnectorbegan its operations).

[5] Since admittedly in Russia private ownership can be questioned as a factor guaranteeing complete independence from the Russian State, in particular when it comes to crucial economic and geopolitically-useful resources, such as gas.

In contrast, the five-billion-cubic-metre capacity of Poland's LNG terminal in Świnoujście, even at maximum of its current capacity could at most cover a third of Poland's total gas imports and a quarter of the country's total demand.[6] The Polish LNG terminal has recently boasted some of highest utilisation rates in Europe (CEEP, 2019). Starting with 33 and 30% in 2016 and 2017 respectively, in 2018 the utilisation reached 55%, and in 2019 went even higher to 70% (Sikora & Sikora, 2019). Building on the success of the terminal in Świnoujście, Poland has currently moved to expand the capacity of the terminal to a total of 7.5 bcm by 2023. And there is a potential to expand this capacity even further (to 10 bcm/annum) if needed. Poland is currently looking into building a second LNG terminal–this time an FSRU with 4.5 bcm/year maximum capacity–in Gdańsk.[7]

As mentioned earlier, Estonia and Latvia have been considering building their own LNG import terminals as well. Finland is currently operating two small-scale (around 30,000 cubic metres of storage capacity) LNG terminals and is building another one (of only slightly larger storage capacity at 50,000 cubic metres) in the port of Hamina. All the Finnish LNG terminals are focused more on small-scale LNG use to satisfy local and transportation demand rather than regional security of gas supply. Similarly, the LNG terminals planned in Sweden and Germany focus on LNG bunkering for ships and vehicles rather than broader, regional energy demand.

Baltic Pipe is a major infrastructure project in the region that will result in pipeline delivery of non-Russian gas. The pipeline will include 230–280 kms of new pipelines (for the total of 900 km of new and old pipelines) and bring annually up to ten billion cubic metres of natural gas from Norway to Poland via Denmark and Sweden and approximately three billion cubic metres to Denmark and Sweden from Poland (Gaz-System, 2020). It is projected to start operations by the fall of 2022 but some

[6] Poland produces domestically enough gas to satisfy about one quarter of its total demand.

[7] Currently, the port in Gdańsk is undergoing a serious infrastructure upgrade, which will be conducive to the building of an FSRU. However, the details about when the investment would take place are yet to be established. At this time, a letter of intent was signed between Port of Gdańsk, Gaz-System (Poland's state gas system operator) and the Maritime office in Gdynia with Gaz-System emerging in a leading role, including the specific details where and when the investment will take place (Lee, 2021).

delay could be expected given issues related to heavy rains in Denmark and the COVID-19 pandemic (Biznes Alert, 2020).

But to take full advantage of the new, non-Russian supply of natural gas, the countries in the Baltic Sea region must be well interconnected, i.e. able to move with relative ease natural gas supplies at times when demand either unexpectedly rises (i.e. due to unusually cold/hot weather) or when usual source of demand is not able to deliver gas (be it due to technical disruption or geopolitics).

Integration of the Baltic Sea Region Market

New gas import infrastructure, even the largest or most advanced, cannot rise to its true regional potential unless countries can move gas between each other whenever necessity arises. This makes pipeline interconnectors and common gas markets across the region an important element of the regional security of supply. This includes especially two projects: (1) already functioning Balticconnector and (2) GIPL.

Balticconnectoris a gas pipeline that connects Estonia and Finland with maximum capacity to transfer up to 2.6 bcm of gas a year in either direction. It was commissioned in December 2019 and began operation in the beginning of 2020. The pipeline is shorter and less expensive than GIPL at 146 kms and EUR 250 million versus 500 kms and EUR 558 million, respectively. Not only is the pipeline able to supply a significant part of the Finnish demand it also provides Finland with access to the Latvian gas storage and to re-gasified LNG from Lithuanian FSRU in Klaipeda. That being said, currently the pipeline's functioning is impaired. Due to delays in upgrading the compressor stations, Balticconnector has been limited for now to approximately one billion cubic metre of annual capacity.

GIPL is a pipeline designed to facilitate interconnections and allow the flow of natural gas in both directions (Argus, 2021). The pipeline that extends over 500 kms (357 kms in Poland and 165 kms in Lithuania) will effectively diminish Russian dominance not only over Lithuania but also over Latvia and Estonia and will allow for better balancing of gas supplies in the region. GIPL is slated to be commissioned in 2022 with construction completed by end of 2021. The total cost of the investment amounts to approximately EUR 558 million, EUR 276 million of which is supported by the EU via the CEF (European Commission, 2020b).

More integrated markets can complement the new physical connections between the Baltic Sea region countries. These include initiatives such as the 2016 Latvia-Lithuania-Estonia-Finland proposal to establish a unified Baltic gas market. In early 2017, major Baltic gas operators agreed to implement an Implicit Capacity Allocation model beginning in summer 2017 designed to improve gas trading between the three Baltic States and Finland. On the 14th of February 2019, Latvia, Estonian, and Finnish TSOs made an important step towards a regional gas market by signing an official agreement that removed tariffs and transmission cost compensation between those countries. Lithuania did not sign the agreement but negotiations are ongoing and the merger is still expected to proceed in several stages (ICIS, 2019).The market has been already much more flexible and registered successes due as the common trading platform in 2020 registered total traded volumes at all-time highs and a robust short-term market. This allowed the Baltic States and Finland to capture the extremely low spot prices caused by an oversupply of LNG (and gas in general) at the time (Get Baltic, 2020).

Measuring Security of Gas Supply

But how do we know if the supply of natural gas to the region is secure and whether any of the new infrastructure described above contributes to an increase in the security of gas supply? Several measures have been used to assess security of supply. Some suggest import dependence is a relevant starting point. But relying on imports does not necessarily mean a supply is not secure, particularly if the supply is abundant elsewhere and many competitors can access the market. As such, the measure does not capture diversification of supply as an important element of the security of supply equation. Meanwhile, diversification has become easier than ever before as global trade in LNG has grown and new gas producers have built up their supplies and are ramping up their export capacity, including but not limited to the USA, Qatar, Australia, and Russia.

Another measure used to capture energy security, one that includes diversification, is Herfindahl–Hirschman Index (Constantini et al., 2007), which is calculated as the sum of the squares of individual exporters market share. While more accurate than import dependence, this measure does not capture 'the credible threat' mechanism, which–as we argued earlier–is a crucial element in the energy security equation for ensuring available, accessible, affordable, and acceptable supply of natural gas.

To include 'the credible threat' into the energy security equation, we will refer to the Agency for the Cooperation of Energy Regulators

(ACER), which points to the Residual Supply Index (RSI) as an important factor for measuring security of gas supply. Per ACER, for the supply of natural gas to be considered secure a country has to have an access to at least three different suppliers and the RSI needs to exceed 110%, i.e. at any given time a country must be able to ramp up gas supply in excess of 110% of its demand, excluding its largest supplier (Box 11.2 explains the methodology in detail).

Box 11.2. Conceptualising and Operationalising the Variables

In addition to capturing 'the credible threat' idea, the Residual Supply Index is more refined as it captures bargaining power of suppliers, which is independent of the volumes that the supplier transfers. If a country cannot substitute for a potential lack of imports from a supplier, the bargaining power of that supplier increases. In this sense, the supplier does not even have to supply majority of natural gas. If supply from other sources is rigid, i.e. cannot be ramped up to provide additional volumes when needed, then even small supplier with spare capacity can exercise considerable market power that can result in higher prices and/or ability to exert geopolitical influence. In this case, technological or other failure in the supply infrastructure (e.g. the Baumgarten incident) can have serious, detrimental effects to countries' natural gas access.

However, ensuring each country's energy security can be a daunting task, given that not all countries have access, ability, and/or resources to build additional import infrastructure that provides enough diversification in gas supply. Thus, ACER also recommends assessing RSI at the regional level. Regional approach allows countries in the region to combine their market power and use each of the countries' comparative advantage so each sources of gas available to each country is maximised. The proposal, however, assumes that a region is well interconnected. This recommendation is consistent with and adds weight to the idea behind the integration of the Baltic Sea region where newly constructed and planned natural gas import infrastructure can provide flexible source of gas supply throughout the region if market's interconnectedness exists.

Given the above, it is important to calculate RSI for the Baltic Sea region to estimate what level of diversification understood in the context of 'credible threat' and not necessarily actual supply is needed for interconnectedness to become a real force in the region.

Per ACER, we use the following equation: ***RSI= (Total supply−Largest supplier)/Total demand.***

The variable 'Total supply' is operationalised as country's total gas consumption plus any unused capacity of gas-importing infrastructure (which is 'the credible threat'). Unused capacity includes the capacity of currently existing natural gas infrastructure that can bring non-Russian gas supplies to the region, i.e. unused capacity in LNG terminals in Lithuania (unused LNG Lithuania) and Poland (unused LNG Poland). To determine those unused volumes, we use actual utilisation rates of both terminals in 2019: 70% rate for LNG terminal in Świnoujście and 43% for the Independence terminal in Lithuania. Given small-scale LNG focus of the LNG terminals operating in Finland, we do not include them into the analysis. 'Total demand' is operationalised as sum of country-level consumption.

Security of Natural Gas Supply and Choice of Countries

The issue of supply security relates directly to the lack of domestic supply sources to cover domestic demand. As such, the analysis can only apply to countries which are considered net-importers of natural gas in the region, which includes Norway and Russia as well as Denmark.

The Special Case of Germany

As mentioned earlier in the country profile section, Germany is rather an outlier within the region given the country's large consumption and imports of natural gas as well as due to its relatively well-developed pipeline network, interconnections with other countries, especially in Western Europe, and large storage capacity. In addition, Germany's long-standing and very close relations with Russia when it comes to natural gas supply put it more often than not in opposite corner when it comes to what constitutes the security of gas supply. Germany is certainly here in Russia's corner, arguing that Russia is the regions and Europe's in general cheapest and most dependable gas supplier. In contrast, all other gas-importing countries in the region, see enhancement of energy security and security of gas supply in diversifying away from Russia. The dispute over Nord Stream 2 is probably best illustration of that difference with Germany firmly pushing for the pipeline's completion despite strong opposition from many countries in Central and Eastern Europe. For all those reasons, we think it would be a mistake to incorporate Germany into the calculations of energy security within the region.

As per Table 11.2, in 2019 countries in the Baltic Sea region received gas from a total of 13 exporting countries, with five from the region itself (Norway, Denmark, Sweden, Germany, and Lithuania) and four being major gas exporters (Russia, the Netherlands, Norway, and the USA).[8] Exports from Austria, Belgium, Czechia, France, Hungary, Germany, and Lithuania have been generally re-exported volumes of previously imported gas.

Based on these numbers, a major takeaway is that ACER's formal requirement of at least three suppliers to ensure energy security has been met for the region, but not for each of the countries separately. Estonia and Latvia had only one supplier (Russia) in 2019.[9] And Russia remains the largest exporter to the region for a total of 73.13 bcm (47% of the region's imports), of which only 0.27 bcm in the form of LNG, coming from Novatek, a Russian independent producer.[10]

For the purpose of calculating the RSI for the region, we operationalise the variable 'Largest supplier' as Russian pipeline imports, with Gazprom as the sole Russian company allowed export of natural gas via pipelines.

It is important to point out that by calculating regional RSI, we can only assess the level of 'diversification of supply' but need to make an

[8] Six if Russia is included as a part of the region.

[9] This has changed somewhat in 2020 as Balticconnector began its operations but complete data for 2020 has yet to become available. In addition, 2020 has been, in all likelihood, an outlier given the global COVID-19 pandemic as well as the LNG glut we have observed that year, which makes the data potentially less generalisable across time.

[10] In this context, it is also important to underscore that the actual number of suppliers is much larger than the number of countries from which gas supply comes. In case of Russia, Gazprom and Novatek are separate suppliers, which are being governed by different factors. And this is especially applicable to US LNG where multiple companies export their product.

Table 11.2 Trade indicators for net gas importing countries in the Baltic Sea region in 2019 (bcm)

Importer	*Exporter*	*Pipeline*	*LNG*	*Largest supplier*
Estonia	Russia	0.27	0.00	Russia
Finland	Lithuania	0.00	0.01	Russia
	Norway	0.00	0.05	
	Russia	2.67	0.12	
	Sweden	0.00	0.01	
Germany[a]	Austria	1.30	0.00	Russia
	Belgium	12.10	0.00	
	Czechia	0.30	0.00	
	Denmark	0.90	0.00	
	France	6.00	0.00	
	Hungary	1.80	0.00	
	Netherlands	24.10	0.00	
	Norway	31.30	0.00	
	Russia	56.30	0.00	
Latvia	Russia	0.71	0.00	Russia
Lithuania	Norway	0.00	1.49	Norway
	Russia	1.19	0.09	
	United States	0.00	0.09	
Poland	Czechia	0.46	0.00	Russia
	Germany	2.00	0.00	
	Norway	0.00	0.23	
	Russia	10.11	0.00	
	United States	0.00	0.87	
Sweden	Belgium	0.00	0.03	Denmark
	Denmark	0.85	0.00	
	Germany	0.06	0.00	
	Lithuania	0.00	0.01	
	Netherlands	0.00	0.04	
	Norway	0.00	0.11	
	Russia	0.00	0.06	
Total		154.33	3.21	

[a]Germany excluded from RSI calculations based on exclusions specified in Box 11.2
Source The Author, based on Cedigaz (2020c)

assumption of 'perfect interconnectedness', meaning that the countries in the Baltic Sea region can move natural gas across the market in an unobstructed manner. This is, of course, a simplification one that is focused on estimating the minimum requirements of diversification of supply that need to be met for interconnectedness to work. The next step, which this study encourages, would be to combine the two factors to see what levels of diversification require what level of interconnectedness for energy security to be achieved.

Box 11.3 provides formula and calculations for RSI for the net-importing countries in the Baltic Sea region (excluding Germany and under assumption of perfectly interconnected markets). Data for the calculations is provided in Table 11.3.

Box 11.3. RSI Formula for the Net-Importers of Natural Gas in the Baltic Sea Region*

Total supply 1 = Consumption + (unused LNG Poland) + (unused LNG Lithuania).

unused LNG Poland = total capacity−utilisation rate of 70% = 5.00 bcm−3.50 bcm = 1.50 bcm.

unused LNG Lithuania = total capacity−utilisation rate of 43% = 4.00 bcm−2.28 bcm = 1.72 bcm.

Total supply 1 = 0.27 + 2.86 + 0.71 + 2.84 + 18.23 + 1.15 + 1.50 + 1.72 = 29.28.

Thus,

Table 11.3 Country-level indicators in 2019

Country	*Reserve (bcm)*	*Gross production (bcm)*	*Marketed production (bcm)*	*Total exports (bcm)*	*Total imports (bcm)*	*Consumption (bcm)*
Denmark[a]	66.00	3.17	3.10	2.05	1.91	2.96
Estonia	0.00	0.00	0.00	0.00	0.27	0.27
Finland	0.00	0.00	0.00	0.00	2.86	2.86
Germany[a]	24.80	6.60	5.70	41.83	134.10	97.97
Latvia	0.00	0.00	0.00	0.00	0.71	0.71
Lithuania	0.00	0.00	0.00	0.02	2.86	2.84
Norway[a]	2,165.00	148.15	115.25	112.79	0.00	2.46
Poland	85.38	5.33	3.73	1.30	15.80	18.23
Sweden	0.00	0.00	0.00	0.10	1.16	1.15

[a]Countries excluded from RSI calculations based as explanation in Box 11.2
Source The Author, based on Cedigaz (2020a)

RSI = (Total supply–Largest supplier)/Total demand.
RSI 1 = (29.28–4.24)/26.06 = 0.58.
RSI 1 (%) = 58%
*Excludes Germany per discussion in Box 11.2.

The RSI for the region (58%) is far below the ACER's mark of 110% required to reach supply security, indicating that even under ideally interconnected market and with current LNG infrastructure the region would not achieve energy security in 2019. The infrastructure is important as it diversifies the suppliers, but it is not sufficient to ensure the diversification level in terms of potential for volume replacement.

To further refine our analysis, we investigate a second counterfactual scenario, which assumes that not only existing but also major planned supply diversification infrastructure projects operated in 2019. This includes the expansion of the Świnoujście terminal (2.5 bcm), the new Gdańsk LNG terminal (4.5 bcm), Baltic Pipe (10 bcm), as well as the proposed LNG import terminals in Latvia (4 bcm) and Estonia (3 bcm + 3 bcm). The results of this analysis are presented in Box 11.4.

Box 11.4

Total supply 2 = Total supply 1 + total capacity of all prospective infrastructure.

Total supply 2 = 29.28 + 26.50 = 55.78.
RSI 2 = (55.78–14.24)/26.06 = 1.59.
RSI 2 (%) = 159%

The obtained RSI of 159% indicates that under the aforementioned conditions, the region would achieve security of gas supply in 2019 (RSI > 110%) if all currently planned infrastructure were operational. The fates of some of the proposed infrastructure is, however, not yet set. While expansion of the Świnoujście terminal and the Baltic Pipe project are well on their way, this cannot be said for all the planned LNG terminals in Poland, Latvia, and Estonia. In particular, it is difficult to imagine that both Latvia and Estonia actually built both terminals given the existence of currently underutilised terminal in Lithuania, as well as small (and potentially decreasing) gas consumption in the Baltic States (smaller than those terminals' nameplate capacity). If none of those terminals actually end up being built (or is/are built later into the future), the RSI index falls just below the required 110 to 106%.

One more wrinkle to add to this scenario is the assumption that in 2019 Poland can deliver on its promise of not buying Russian gas and Świnoujście expansion and Baltic Pipe are completed. Russia would remain the largest supplier to the region, but with Germany excluded, Russia would no longer supply the majority of the region's imported gas.

Instead, this would be more evenly divided between Norway (pipe and LNG), and other LNG suppliers. A more realistic estimate of the projected RSI is presented in 'Total supply 3' (Box 11.5), where we included only the projects currently in advanced stages and closer to their realisation (the expansion of Świnoujście at 2.5 bcm and Baltic Pipe at 10 bcm) and where we assume Poland does not import Russian gas. We then reduce the total value of Russian imports delivered to the region by imports that were in 2019 delivered to Poland (14.24 bcm–10.11 bcm).

Box 11.5

Total supply 3 = Total supply 1 + (Świnoujście LNG expansion + Baltic Pipe).

Total supply 3 = 29.28 + 12.50 = 41.78.

RSI 3 = (41.78–4.13)/26.06 = 1.44.

RSI 3 (%) = 144%

In this case, the RSI jumps to 144%, a value much higher than the 110% required for security of supply. Additional scenarios could be drawn to explore the impact of different natural gas import strategies. What if, for example, Lithuania decides to bring in more Russian gas based on its lower price?

To achieve an even more complete picture, one could also add storage that allows for temporal arbitrage. These will be crucial for boosting energy security in the region, as perfect interconnectedness is an extremely difficult if not impossible task. As Table 11.4 indicates, there is some movement to increase the storage capacity of some of the net-importing countries in the region, most notably in Poland and Latvia, both of which can be very important for expanding benefits of the LNG and new pipeline capacity that enters the region.

Policy Implications and Conclusions

The analysis here is admittedly a simplification of the actual state of gas market affairs in the region. But as such, it provides an excellent tool for adding layers of complexity. It is simple enough to be used and understood by non-experts but flexible and customisable enough to incorporate, envision, and assess many sophisticated scenarios, depending on what the question at stake. The analysis provided in this work constitutes a valuable step towards the creation of a customisable framework to address energy security, integrating both actual and potentially available supply, therefore fostering the concept of 'credible threat' and all its implications. The model can be easily built upon and improved to include additional intricacies of the markets. The findings from our analysis particularly underscore the importance and the expanded role played by infrastructures, as their diversification power extends far beyond what is actually needed. Our work allows us to draw important conclusions on whether diversification is needed, and, if so, what capacity is required and what acceptable investment costs can be made towards infrastructure in the light of actual utilisation rates.

For the Baltic Sea region, our findings underscore that energy security demands gas import infrastructure capacity of which exceeds the real-time demand. This is a necessary condition to effectively prevent market dominance by any single supplier. However, this condition is not sufficient. The diversity of supply and market integration are in fact two sides of the same coin: energy security cannot be achieved when either of them is failing. Market integration via increase in gas interconnections and common markets are crucial. While this work assumes perfect interconnectedness of the market, in reality this is not the case. As such a balance between the level of market integration and access to supply needs to be achieved for any given entity to reach security of supply. This balance will be different for different regions and countries, depending on their specific circumstances.

Table 11.4 Underground storage capacity (UGS) in the Baltic Sea region's net gas-importing countries as of November 2020

Country	*Name of UGS facility*	*Status*	*Working gas capacity (bcm)*
Germany	Hähnlein	In operation	0.080
	Stockstadt 1	In operation	0.045
	Kiel-Rönne	In operation	0.063
	Wolfersberg	In operation	0.365
	Bernburg	In operation	0.971
	Bierwang	In operation	1.000
	Huntorf	In operation	0.308
	EpeUniper	In operation	1.916
	Bad Lauchstädt Reservoir	In operation	0.440
	Krummhörn	In operation	0.154
	Frankenthal	In operation	0.090
	Bad Lauchstädt caverns	In operation	0.720
	Nüttermoor	In operation	1.311
	Inzenham-West - Horizon 17 + 23	In operation	0.425
	Empelde	In operation	0.378
	Schmidhausen	In operation	0.154
	Xanten	In operation	0.178
	Bremen-LesumWesernetz	In operation	0.068
	Epeinnogy, H Gas	In operation	0.405
	Sandhausen	In operation	0.030
	Stockstadt 2	In operation	0.090
	Breitbrunn/Eggstätt	In operation	0.992
	Rehden	In operation	3.900

Country	*Name of UGS facility*	*Status*	*Working gas capacity (bcm)*
	Etzel EGL 1 and 2	In operation	1.182
	Harsefeld	In operation	0.110
	Eschenfelden	In operation	0.072
	Alimenhausen	In operation	0.062
	Fronhofen-Illmensee	In operation	0.010
	Stassfurt	In operation	0.664
	Uelsen	In operation	0.860
	Bremen-LesumStorergy	In operation	0.147
	Reckrod	In operation	0.110
	Kraak	In operation	0.257
	Peckensen	In operation	0.349
	Epe NUON	In operation	0.300
	EpeTrianel	In operation	0.192
	Rüdersdorf	In operation	0.100
	Epe ENECO	In operation	0.094
	Epeinnogy, L Gas	In operation	0.176
	Etzel EKB	In operation	0.913
	Etzel ESE	In operation	1.914
	Etzel FSG Crystal	In operation	0.390
	Katharina	In operation	0.301
	Epe KGE	In operation	0.188
	Jemgum-EWE	In operation	0.366
	Epeinnogy, NL	In operation	0.300

(continued)

Table 11.4 (continued)

Country	*Name of UGS facility*	*Status*	*Working gas capacity (bcm)*
	Jemgum-astora	In operation	0.760
	Frankenthal expansion	Cancelled	*
	Behringen	Cancelled	1.000
	Bierwang expansion	Cancelled	*
	Fronhofen-Illmensee expansion	Cancelled	0.035
	Lehrte expansion	Cancelled	0.039
	EpeGelsenwasser	Cancelled	0.180
	Jemgum-EON	Cancelled	2.000
	Neuenhuntorf	Cancelled	0.017
	Ohrensen	Cancelled	0.440
	Bernburg expansion (phase 2)	Cancelled	0.080
	Xanten expansion	Cancelled	0.125
	Burggraf-Bernsdorf	Closed	0.003
	Reitbrook	Closed	0.350
	Kirchheilingen	Closed	0.190
	Buchholz	Closed	0.175
	Kalle	Closed	0.220
	Berlin - Grünewald	Closed	0.143
	Lehrte	Closed	0.035
	Dötlingen	Closed	1.065

Country	*Name of UGS facility*	*Status*	*Working gas capacity (bcm)*
	Epe ZES	On hold	0.177
	Moekow	On hold	2.000
	Harsefeld (expansion)	On hold	0.120
	Peckensen expansion (phase 2 exp)	On hold	0.480
	EpeUniper expansion (1 cavern)	Planned	0.050
	Etzel-STORAG (24 caverns)	Planned	2.020
	Bad Lauchstädt caverns (1 cavern)	Under construction	0.071
	Jemgumastora (8 caverns)	Under construction	0.450
	Katharina (6 caverns)	Under construction	0.313
Latvia	Inčukalns	In operation	2.320
	Inčukalns (modernisation)	In operation	*
	Inčukalns (expansion)	On hold	0.480
	Inčukalns (enhancement)	Under construction	0.000
Lithuania	Genciu/Kretinga	Cancelled	0.500
	Syderiai	On hold	0.500
Poland	Brzeźnica (GSF Sanok)	In operation	0.065
	Swarzów (GSF Sanok)	In operation	0.090
	Strachocina (GSF Sanok)	In operation	0.150
	Husów (GSF Sanok)	In operation	0.350
	Wierzchowice	In operation	0.575
	Mogilno (GSF Kawerna)	In operation	0.585
	Bonikowo	In operation	0.200
	Daszewo	In operation	0.060

(continued)

Table 11.4 (continued)

Country	*Name of UGS facility*	*Status*	*Working gas capacity (bcm)*
	Strachocina (GSF Sanok) expansion 1	In operation	0.210
	Wierzchowice expansion phase I	In operation	0.625
	Kosakowo (GSF Kawerna)	In operation	0.239
	Husów (GSF Sanok) expansion	In operation	0.150
	Brzeźnica (GSF Sanok) expansion	In operation	0.035
	Strachocina (GSF Sanok) expansion 2	On hold	*
	Damaslawek	Planned	0.800
	Kosakowo (GSF Kawerna) Expansion	Planned	0.050
	Mogilno (GSF Kawerna) expansion	Planned	0.215
	Wierzchowice expansion phase II	Potential	1.700
	Wierzchowice expansion phase II	Under construction	0.100
	Kosakowo (GSF Kawerna) development	Under construction	0.011
Sweden	Skallen	In operation	0.009

Notes (1) operating storage is shaded in grey, (2) Estonia and Finland do not possess any gas storage infrastructure and, hence they are excluded from this table, and (3) * means that no information was available

Source The Author, based on Cedigaz (2020b)

These will include additional tools to prop the market, with storage becoming an important element of the equation. Policy support for security driven-redundancy of infrastructure will also be valuable. While of little impact under ideal market conditions, these mechanisms can make a significant difference under the conditions of imperfect market integration and/or under imperfect co-operation.

In this context, it should be noted that not all redundancy will create sizable energy security benefits. For example, the proposals for Latvian or Estonian LNG terminals may not be needed as the existing LNG terminal in Lithuania could potentially serve the needs of all Baltic States. And high storage capacity in Latvia can be a better choice for infrastructure investment. Thus, co-operation can reduce costs and bring in sizable benefits for all parties. Evidently, the extent of such co-operation will depend on the level of trust between countries and whether any agreement can be reached on the division of cost. This has, unfortunately, not always been the case, including between the Baltic States where stakes of co-operation are high, but disagreements persist over each country's role and their own goals, including in the energy security arena. The less trust, the more need for redundancy of infrastructure, leading to a higher individual cost for providing energy security within the region and for each country.

Our analysis also provides insightful information on how to assess the benefits of funding gas infrastructure. The results obtained indicate that funding of gas infrastructure should not be assessed solely based on its contribution to either market integration or diversification. Instead, both must be considered in tandem in the view of existing market conditions. For example, while an LNG terminal in Estonia would be potentially better suited to the goals of market security, it may not make sense given the already existing LNG terminal in Lithuania. Thus, the funding could be reallocated to a better use, including building more interconnections between the countries or supporting Estonia's purchases of LNG delivered to Klaipeda. One encouraging sign that this all-encompassing thinking approach is gaining traction is that the EU appears to heed this recommendation and funds most of the projects mentioned here within its PCI programme. For example, although it did not designate the Lithuanian LNG terminal as a PCI, the EU has recognised its importance for enhancing competition.[11] The EU also approved Lithuania's

[11] It has not been seen as instrumental for increasing diversification and energy security of the entire region, however as other chapters of this book reveal the Lithuanians

requirement that heat and electricity generators use certain quantity of gas sourced from LNG (European Commission, 2018). That being said, current policies of decarbonisation and voices against funding of any fossil fuel infrastructure from EU funds could negatively impact regions ambitions to become independent of the Russian gas supply.

Another limiting factor is the current lack of success of the EU in furthering liberalisation that goes beyond unbundling in CEE, including in the Baltic Sea region. While CEE countries have moved towards implementing the package (by transposing it into national laws and deregulating their markets to some degree), they remain substantially less liberalised than their Western counterparts. For example, Poland's market is highly centralised around state-based companies, i.e. PGNiG and Gaz-System. The current setup makes it almost impossible for other players to access the market, as PGNiG is responsible for all LNG supplied into the LNG terminal in Świnoujście. The EU's Third Energy Package pushed the process of gas market liberalisation in Europe, but it was not able to eliminate this visible divide. Slow speed of liberalisation is often defended within the CEE on the grounds of energy security in the face of dominant natural gas supplier, such as Russia. The concerns about energy security have been also coupled with a culture of broad government administration and a relatively strong tradition of state-owned enterprises protecting and dominating vulnerable markets.

Thus, many CEE countries have favoured diversification over liberalisation efforts where initiatives such as LNG terminals, pipelines, and interconnections have been spearheaded by the governments and implemented by state-run enterprises that enjoy monopoly or close-to-monopoly position over the country's domestic market. Meanwhile, liberalising access to countries' natural gas infrastructure could benefit efforts to enhance market integration. By providing more open access to the region's gas market the Baltic Sea region countries could encourage not only competition but also investment in new interconnections and/or infrastructure (Collins & Mikulska, 2018). Of course, the liberalisation should not be 'a

constructed the Klaipeda LNG terminal by themselves, though a report ordered by the European Commission recommended that the best location for a common LNG terminal of three Baltic States would have been in Estonia. A unilateral construction of own LNG terminal by the Lithuanians may have been a reason why countries do not see eye to eye when it comes to creating a common gas market with Lithuania lagging others and remaining outside the structure.

carte blanche' but should be aided by conscious policy efforts to prevent any large gas supplier from monopolising the market.

An interesting point can be also made about Poland's policy of diversification that includes the possibility of completely weaning itself of Russian gas once its long-term contract with Gazprom expires in 2022. On the face of it, the declaration does not make economic sense: if Poland establishes a more competitive natural gas market, why would it not take advantage of the ability to negotiate better pricing with Russia? But, as pointed out earlier, economic calculus does not always convey the elements of security of supply. The calculations presented earlier indicate that if Poland wants to achieve security supply and contribute to the security within the Baltic Sea region, its move away from Russian gas can actually help.[12]

Such a move would not only help the country's geopolitical position vis-à-vis Russia, especially if associated with commissioning of expansive new gas infrastructure to bring non-Russian gas. It would also improve Poland's position in the region vis-à-vis Germany. Both countries are admittedly vying for influence in CEE and having access to abundant supply of natural gas and ability to distribute surplus gas within the region can bring additional influence. Given Germany's affinity for Russian gas, Poland may become a crucial element of balancing the region's dependence. If gas that Poland imports can also serve other areas of CEE, including countries in the Baltic Sea region as well as Ukraine, Czechia, or Slovakia, Poland can become an important player in ensuring security of their supply and gain geopolitical benefits.

References

350.org. (2019). *Sweden rejects major gas terminal on climate grounds*. https://350.org/press-release/sweden-rejects-major-gas-terminal-on-climate-grounds/. Accessed 10 February 2021.

Argus. (2020). *German LNG demand for transport more than doubles*. https://www.argusmedia.com/en/news/2166616-german-lng-demand-for-transport-more-than-doubles. Accessed 10 February 2021.

[12] It may be worth to note that Poland's stipulation of 'no Russian gas' likely refers to no long-term contracting of Russian gas, while Poland would/could still take advantage of low prices of Russian gas on spot markets.

Argus. (2021). *Clarity on Polish-Lithuanian gas link expected mid-2021.* https://www.argusmedia.com/en/news/2182073-clarity-on-polishlithuanian-gas-link-expected-mid2021. Accessed 10 February 2021.

Biznes Alert. (2020). *Polish Briefing: Baltic Pipe delay in Denmark and nuclear energy ahead of Three Seas summit*. https://biznesalert.com/baltic-pipe-delay-nuclear-energy-three-seas-summit/. Accessed 14 February 2021.

Bohlen, C. (1993, June 26). Russia cuts gas supply to Estonia in a protest. *The New York Times*. https://www.nytimes.com/1993/06/26/world/russia-cuts-gas-supply-to-estonia-in-a-protest.html. Accessed 10 February 2021.

Cedigaz. (2020a). *Country indicators*. https://www.cedigaz.org/. Accessed 10 February 2021.

Cedigaz. (2020b). *Infrastructure*. https://www.cedigaz.org/. Accessed 10 February 2021.

Cedigaz. (2020c). *Trade*. https://www.cedigaz.org/. Accessed 10 February 2021.

CEEP. (2019). *LNG proves to be a reliable solution for Poland and CEE region's energy security*. Central Europe Energy Partners. https://www.ceep.be/lng-proves-to-be-a-reliable-solution-for-poland-and-cee-regions-energy-security/. Accessed 10 February 2021.

Cherp, A., & Jewell, J. (2014). The concept of energy security: Beyond the four as. *Energy Policy, 75*, 415–421.

Ciężadło, A. (2021). *Czyobostrzeniazatrzymająbudowę Baltic Pipe? Tawerna Skipperow*. https://www.tawernaskipperow.pl/czytelnia/wiesci-z-oceanow/czy-obostrzenia-zatrzymaja-budowe-baltic-pipe%253F/8221. Accessed 10 February 2021.

Collins, G. (2017). *Russia's use of the "Energy Weapon" in Europe*. The Baker Institute. https://www.bakerinstitute.org/research/russias-use-energy-weapon-europe/. Accessed 10 February 2021.

Collins, G., & Mikulska, A. (2018). *Gas geoeconomics in Europe. Using strategic investment to promote market liberalization, counterbalance Russian revanchism, and enhance European energy security*. Baker Institute for Public Policy. https://www.bakerinstitute.org/media/files/files/74c5d977/ces-pub-gasgeoeconeurope-060318.pdf. Accessed 10 March 2021.

Collins, G., & Mikulska, A. (2021). *Gas geoeconomics: A strategy to harden European partners against Russian energy coercion. Recommendations for the new administration*. Baker Institute for Public Policy. https://www.bakerinstitute.org/media/files/files/0fb54354/bi-brief-0211221-ces-geoeconomics.pdf. Accessed 14 March 2021.

Conexus. (2021). *Inčukalns USG*. http://www.conexus.lv/incukalns-ugs-459. Accessed 10 February 2021.

Constantini, V., Gracceva, F., Markandya, A., & Vicini, G. (2007). Security of energy supply: Comparing scenarios from a European perspective. *Energy Policy, 35*(1), 210–226.

Czyżewski, D. (2020). *Nadzwyczajnewykorzystanieterminala LNG w ŚwinoujściunatleEuropy.* https://www.energetyka24.com/atom/terminal-lng-w-swinoujsciu-z-najwiekszym-wykorzystaniem-w-europie-komentarz. Accessed 10 February 2021.

Deutsche Welle. (2019). *Germany shuts down atomic plant as nuclear phase-out enters final stretch.* https://www.dw.com/en/germany-shuts-down-atomic-plant-as-nuclear-phase-out-enters-final-stretch/a-51845616. Accessed 10 February 2021.

Deutsche Welle. (2020). *Germany approves coal closeout by 2038.* https://www.dw.com/en/germany-approves-coal-phaseout-by-2038/a-54040605. Accessed March 14 2021.

Elliott, S. (2020). *EU proposes to stop funding natural gas infrastructure, shift focus to hydrogen.* SPGlobal. https://www.spglobal.com/marketintelligence/en/news-insights/latest-news-headlines/eu-proposes-to-stop-funding-natural-gas-infrastructure-shift-focus-to-hydrogen-61769734. Accessed 10 February 2021.

Elliott, S. (2021). *Belgium's Fluxys to join HEH's Stade LNG import terminal project in Germany.* SPGlobal. https://www.spglobal.com/platts/en/market-insights/latest-news/coal/030321-belgiums-fluxys-to-join-hehs-stade-lng-import-terminal-project-in-germany. Accessed 14 March 2021.

Elliott, S., & Hunter, N. (2020). *Denmark's Tyra gas field restart pushed back to June 2023: Total.* SPGlobal. https://www.spglobal.com/platts/en/market-insights/latest-news/natural-gas/110620-denmarks-tyra-gas-field-restart-pushed-back-to-june-2023-total. Accessed 10 February 2021.

Energy News Monitor. (2021). Observer Research Foundation. 17(31). https://www.orfonline.org/research/energy-news-monitor-31/. Accessed 14 March 2021.

ENTSOG. (2019). *Transmission capacity and development maps.* https://www.entsog.eu/maps#transmission-capacity-map-2019. Accessed 20 February 2021.

European Commission. (2018). *State aid: Commission approves support for Klaipeda LNG terminal in Lithuania.* https://ec.europa.eu/commission/presscorner/detail/en/IP_18_6266. Accessed 10 February 2021.

European Commission. (2020a). *Quarterly Report on European Markets with special focus on the role of hydrogen in the future EU energy mix.* Market Observatory for Energy. DG Energy. 13(2). https://ec.europa.eu/energy/sites/ener/files/documents/quarterly_report_on_european_gas_markets_q2_2020.pdf. Accessed 10 February 2021.

European Commission. (2020b). *Gas Interconnector Poland-Lithuania: Works in progress*. https://ec.europa.eu/inea/en/news-events/newsroom/gas-interconnector-poland-lithuania-works-progress. Accessed March 12 2021.

Eurostat. (2021). *Data browser*. Energy Import Dependency. http://appsso.eurostat.ec.europa.eu/nui/show.do?dataset=nrg_ind_id&lang=en. Accessed 2 February 2021.

Gardner, T. (2021, February 24). Exclusive: Baker Hughes, AXA Group, 16 others quit Nord Stream 2 pipeline—U.S. *Reuters*. https://www.reuters.com/article/us-usa-nord-stream-2-companies-exclusive/exclusive-baker-hughes-axa-group-16-others-quit-nord-stream-2-pipeline-u-s-idUSKBN2AO285. Accessed 15 March 2021.

Gaz-System. (2020). *Baltic Pipe Project: Offshore gas pipeline—Implementation stage*. https://www.baltic-pipe.eu/wp-content/uploads/2020/08/BalticPipe-Project-Implementation-Stage.pdf. Accessed 10 February 2021.

Get Baltic. (2020). *Natural gas exchange trading report*. https://www.getbaltic.com/wp-content/uploads/2021/01/Baltic-Finnish-Gas-Exchange-Trading-Report-for-the-December-2020.pdf. Accessed 10 February 2021.

GIIGNL. (2020). *Annual Report 2020 Edition*. https://giignl.org/sites/default/files/PUBLIC_AREA/Publications/giignl_-_2020_annual_report_-_04082020.pdf. Accessed 10 February 2021.

Hall, M. (2018). Norwegian gas exports: Assessment of resources and supply to 2035. *The Oxford Institute for Energy Studies*. https://doi.org/10.26889/9781784671037. Accessed March 14 2021.

Hinchey, N. (2018). The impact of securing alternative energy sources on Russian-European natural gas pricing. *The Energy Journal, 39*(2), 87–102.

ICIS. (2019). *Finland, Estonia and Latvia to be single gas transport zone from 2020*. https://www.icis.com/explore/resources/news/2019/02/14/10319058/finland-estonia-and-latvia-to-be-single-gas-transport-zone-from-2020/. Accessed 10 February 2021.

JegeleviciusL. (2017). *Uniper Divests Gas Grid Stake in Latvia*. Natural Gas World News. https://www.naturalgasworld.com/uniper-divests-gas-grid-stake-to-latvia-57742. Accessed 10 February 2021.

Katona, V. (2020). *Why is Denmark ditching natural gas? Oil price*. https://oilprice.com/Energy/Natural-Gas/Why-Is-Denmark-Ditching-Natural-Gas.html. Accessed 10 February 2021.

Klackenberg, L. (2019). Biomethane in Sweden—Market overview and policies. *Energiegas Sverige*. https://www.energigas.se/library/2907/biomethane-in-sweden-191107-cw.pdf. Accessed 10 February 2021.

Klein, J. (2021). *Pływający terminal gazowy w ZatoceGdańskiejgotowybędzie za 5–6 lat*. https://dziennikbaltycki.pl/plywajacy-terminal-gazowy-w-zatoce-gdanskiej-gotowy-bedzie-za-56-lat/ar/c3-15384272. Accessed 10 February 2021.

Klemeshev, A. P., Korneevets, V. S., Palmowski, T., Studzieniecki, T., & Fedorov, G. M. (2017). Approaches to the definition of the Baltic Sea Region. *Baltic Region, 9*(4), 4–20.

KN. (2019). *Presentation*. https://ec.europa.eu/energy/sites/ener/files/documents/molis_arunas_-_klaipedos_nafta.pdf. Accessed 10 February 2021.

KN. (2021). *Unaudited Financial Results of KN Group for 2020*. https://ml-eu.globenewswire.com/Resource/Download/2119af76-7732-4f15-a4f0-00379a80fd33. Accessed 10 February 2021.

Lee, H. L. (2021). *Key stages of Gdansk port's $1.6bn infrastructure upgrade will complete in 2021 Seatrade and Maritime News*. https://www.seatrade-maritime.com/ports-logistics/key-stages-gdansk-ports-16bn-infrastructure-upgrade-will-complete-2021. Accessed 10 February 2021.

LNG Prime. (2021). *Brunsbüttel hosts first LNG bunkering op for Greenferry I*. https://lngprime.com/europe/brunsbuttel-hosts-first-lng-bunkering-op-for-greenferry-i/13854/. Accessed 14 March 2021.

Maritime Executive. (2020). *Equinor expects Hammerfest LNG plant fire repairs to take up to a year*. https://www.maritime-executive.com/chapter/equinor-expects-hammerfest-lng-plant-fire-repairs-to-take-up-to-a-year. Accessed 10 February 2021.

Mikulska, A. (2018a). Nord stream: Between monopoly and diversification. *SprawyMiędzynarodowe, 71*(4), 45–75.

Mikulska, A. (2018b). Try harder, Gazprom. Why Poland could choose LNG. *Forbes*. https://www.forbes.com/sites/thebakersinstitute/2018/12/21/try-harder-gazprom-why-poland-could-choose-lng/?sh=7323b3ef1153. Accessed 16 February 2021.

Moestue, H. (2021). *Dutch Groningen Gas output may halve to 3.9 bcm from October*. https://www.montelnews.com/en/story/dutch-groningen-gas-output-may-halve-to-3-9bcm-from-october/1194555. Accessed 10 February 2021.

Norwegian Petroleum. (2021). *Exports of oil and gas*. https://www.norskpetroleum.no/en/production-and-exports/exports-of-oil-and-gas/. Accessed 10 February 2021.

Saarmann, T. (2020). *Estonia. Paldiski—An industrial town for nearly 300 years*. https://estonia.ee/paldiski-the-baltic-sea-regions-important-industrial-centre-of-the-future/. Accessed 10 February 2021.

Ship & Bunker. (2020). *Sweden: Gas bunkering planned for Oxelsund*. https://shipandbunker.com/news/emea/169987-sweden-gas-bunkering-planned-for-oxelosund. Accessed 10 February 2021.

Sikora, A., & Sikora, M. (2019). *Polskie LNG—podsumowanie 2019 roku*. https://www.cire.pl/item,191423,13,0,0,0,0,0,polskie-lng---podsumowanie-2019-roku.html. Accessed 10 February 2021.

Skulte LNG Terminal. (2021). *The project*. https://www.skultelng.lv/en/the_project. Accessed 10 February 2021.

Swedegas. (2019). *Joint gas market in Sweden and Denmark from April 1*. https://news.cision.com/swedegas/r/joint-gas-market-in-sweden-and-denmark-from-april-1,c2777492. Accessed 10 February 2021.

The Baltic Course. (2018). *Lithuanian parliament green-lights purchase of Klaipeda LNG terminal's FSRU*. http://www.baltic-course.com/eng/good_for_business/?doc=145982. Accessed 10 February 2021.

CHAPTER 12

Epilogue

Kari Liuhto

As the editor of this book, I have taken it upon myself to pick out some of the observations found in the articles. I want to emphasise, however, that the research results highlighted in this chapter do not necessarily represent the views of all the contributors of this book. Secondly, it is good to underline that all the significant observations of the book cannot be presented here. Thirdly, the collection of observations presented in the epilogue is in an extremely condensed form without source references, which is why the reader should read those chapters which discuss the said matters more broadly and in more detail.

Natural gas production and consumption: the Baltic Sea presents a selection of countries that are very interesting as to the production and consumption of natural gas. First of all, the easternmost country in the Baltic Sea region, Russia, is the world's second largest producer of natural gas after the United States. This naturally means that Russia is the largest gas producer in Europe. Secondly, Europe's second largest natural gas producer, Norway, is also found within the Baltic Sea region. Thirdly, the EU's only net exporter of natural gas, Denmark, is situated in the region.

K. Liuhto (✉)
University of Turku, Turku, Finland
e-mail: Kari.Liuhto@utu.fi

K. Liuhto (ed.), *The Future of Energy Consumption, Security and Natural Gas*, https://doi.org/10.1007/978-3-030-80367-4_12

Fourthly, the EU's largest natural gas consumer, Germany, is among the coastal states of the Baltic Sea. Germany consumes nearly 100 billion cubic metres of natural gas each year, i.e. a quarter of all natural gas consumed in the EU. Although Germany does produce natural gas, its own gas production covers only five percent of its consumption. Poland, on the other hand, is able to cover one-fifth of its gas consumption with its own production. The Baltic States, Finland and Sweden are the only countries in the Baltic Sea region, which do not produce natural gas. On the other hand, neither do they consume much of it. In 2019, the five countries listed above consumed only a total of seven billion cubic metres of natural gas.

In this millennium, the consumption of natural gas has increased by approximately ten percent in the Baltic Sea region, excluding natural gas exporters Denmark, Norway and Russia. When Germany shuts down its nuclear power plants in 2022, its natural gas consumption will increase further. If Germany choses to use only natural gas to fill the energy gap left by closing the nuclear power plants, it should consume nearly 20 billion cubic metres more than it does today. Among the Baltic Sea region countries, Germany is an exception, because most of the other countries in the region will continue to decrease their natural gas consumption.

Examining the future development of the region's natural gas production, we see that Russian natural gas production is prognosed to increase by 10–25 percent in the next 15 years. While Russia increases its gas production, the situation is reversed in the other natural gas producing countries of the region. Their gas production has already started to decline. The decrease in Norway's natural gas production has a significant impact not only on the Baltic Sea region, but also the entire European Union.

The significance of natural gas: currently, 23 percent of the EU's primary energy consumption is satisfied with natural gas. In the ten coastal states of the Baltic Sea region, the share of natural gas of the primary energy consumption is 20 percent, i.e. slightly smaller than the EU average. However, there are considerable differences between the Baltic Sea countries. Natural gas is most important to Russia, where more than half of its primary energy consumption is met with natural gas. Sweden represents the other extreme; only a couple of percent of the country's total consumption is satisfied with gas. In addition to Sweden, the share of natural gas of the country's primary energy consumption is under ten percent also in Estonia, Finland and Norway, of which the last-mentioned focuses on exporting the natural gas it produces. In other words, Norway does not use large amounts of natural gas, the country exports its gas. Norway primarily uses hydroelectric power to cover its domestic energy needs. In Denmark and Poland, slightly less than one-fifth of the primary energy consumption consists of natural gas, whereas in Germany the share of gas is one-fourth. Of the Baltic Sea countries, which import natural gas, Latvia and Lithuania are the ones most dependent on it. Natural gas covers more than 30 percent of the primary energy consumption of these two Baltic States.

Natural gas infrastructure: numerous natural gas pipelines have been built from both Norway and Russia to the European Union. Several underwater natural gas pipelines go from the Norwegian gas fields to Germany, the Netherlands and Great Britain. Correspondingly, gas pipelines from Russia to the European Union go through Belarus, Ukraine and under the Baltic Sea and the Black Sea.

Even before December 2019, when the United States imposed sanctions on Nord Stream 2, this pipeline has attracted a lot of media attention. Nord Stream 2 has eclipsed Balticconnector between Estonia and Finland, which started operation at the same time as the United States imposed its first sanctions on Nord Stream 2. The completion of Balticconnector connected the EU's two northern energy islands, the Baltic States and Finland. However, connecting these two islands isolated from the EU pipeline network does not solve the whole problem. Terminating their isolation requires the interconnection of Polish and Lithuanian gas networks, i.e. building the GIPL gas pipeline. Only when GIPL is completed are the Baltic States and Finland connected to the pan-European natural gas network. Fortunately, more than 60 percent of the GIPL pipeline is built when this is being written. The pipeline is expected to start its operations in 2022. In addition to the pipeline between Lithuania and Poland, a new gas pipeline, Baltic Pipe, is being built from Norway to Poland; it will be completed in the next few years.

In addition to the above gas pipelines, we must remember that several Baltic Sea region countries have underground gas storages, which enhance the security of energy supply of the entire Baltic Sea region. Besides gas storages, LNG import terminals have been built. In the past decade, Finland and Sweden have built on their shores a handful of small-scale LNG receiving ports, whereas Lithuania, Poland and Russia (the Kaliningrad region) have established LNG import terminals that are significant to their energy supply. Apart from these LNG import ports, the region's natural gas exporters Norway and Russia also have LNG sending ports. Although Denmark is a net exporter of natural gas, it focuses on deliveries through pipelines.

Despite the global LNG boom, of the Baltic Sea countries importing natural gas, Estonia, Latvia and Germany have not yet built any LNG import terminals on their soil. Germany does plan to build a few LNG ports of import, but the total capacity of these ports will be marginal considering Germany's total natural gas imports. In practice this means that Germany's dependence on pipeline gas supply continues in the future. It is also possible that none of the German LNG ports currently being planned become reality if Nord Stream 2 starts operating and annually more than 50 billion cubic metres of affordable Russian natural gas starts flowing into Germany and elsewhere in the European Union and even Great Britain. If Nord Stream 2 can stop the German LNG plans, the EU's Green Deal may do the same to Estonian and Latvian LNG terminal plans.

One of the central findings of this book is that the security of energy supply of the Baltic Sea region requires that the Baltic Sea countries build more natural gas import infrastructure than they need for their daily use. Furthermore, the gas import sources must be sufficiently well diversified so that no single supplier's share is so large that the importing countries are not able to replace it with other suppliers or with other alternative sources of energy.

LNG imports: seven countries in the Baltic Sea region import natural gas, and five of them, namely Estonia, Finland, Sweden, Lithuania and Poland, imported LNG. In other words, of the region's countries dependent on the gas imports, Germany and Latvia did not import any LNG.[1]

Even if Estonia, Finland and Sweden do import liquefied natural gas, LNG does not have a strategic role in their energy supply, because LNG forms less than ten percent of the natural gas imports of Estonia and Finland. Although LNG forms nearly 30 percent of Sweden's natural gas imports, LNG is not a strategic fuel for Sweden, because natural gas covers only a couple of percent of Sweden's primary energy consumption.

Lithuania and Poland have a different situation. LNG forms nearly 60 percent of Lithuanian natural gas imports, and over 30 percent of the

[1] To be precise, also Latvia imported a small amount of LNG in 2019, but the share of LNG was only 0.2 percent of its total imports of natural gas.

country's energy consumption relies on natural gas. Although the share of LNG is only 20 percent of Poland's natural gas imports, it is good to note that, by volume, Poland's LNG imports are the largest in the Baltic Sea region. In fact, Poland imported in 2019 more than twice as much as Lithuania, which is the second largest LNG importer in the Baltic Sea region.

In proportion to the overall import of natural gas, the Baltic Sea region's overall LNG imports are less than the average of the European Union. In 2020, a quarter of the EU's overall natural gas import consisted of LNG. In the EU countries of the Baltic Sea region, the average was 15 percent. The average would drop to below five percent if it was weighted by the amount of consumption, because Germany, the region's largest natural gas importer, does not import any LNG.

In 2019, two-thirds of Poland's LNG came from Qatar. The US share was approximately a quarter. In turn, Norway was Lithuania's largest LNG supplier with a share of over 70 percent. Lithuania's second largest LNG supplier Russia covered one-fifth. The US share was five percent. Sweden's largest LNG supplier was Norway, and Russia was Finland's leading supplier with an 80-percent share. The significant share of Russia in the LNG imports of many Baltic Sea region countries underlines the fact that LNG imports do not automatically lessen the dependence on natural gas imports from Russia. Here, it is good to remember that in 2020, Russia was the EU's third largest LNG supplier after the United States and Qatar. Russia's position is unlikely to weaken in Europe because Russia has extremely ambitious plans to increase its LNG exports. Namely, by 2035, Russia intends to be at least the second largest LNG exporter in the world. At the moment, Russia is on the fourth place after Qatar, Australia and the United States in the globe.

The Baltic Sea region's dependence on Russian energy imports: nearly half of the EU's gas imports came from Russia in 2020. Due to both geographic and historic reasons, the EU countries in the Baltic Sea region are on the average more dependent on natural gas import from Russia than is the rest of the EU. In the Baltic Sea region, only Denmark, Lithuania, Norway and Sweden have lower dependence on natural gas imports from Russia than the EU average.

If Nord Stream 2 is completed, Germany's dependence on Russian natural gas increases further from the current level of over 50 percent. Dependence of Lithuania and Poland on Russia has decreased thanks to their LNG terminals. Once the expansion of Świnoujście is completed, and the Gdańsk LNG terminal and Baltic Pipe are operational, Poland could in theory terminate all its natural gas imports from Russia. On the other hand, Estonia, Finland and Latvia continue to remain highly dependent on Russia natural gas, unless at least one more large-scale LNG import terminal is built in the Baltic States or Finland.

The decision to locate a new large-scale terminal in Latvia is supported by the country's large underground natural gas storage in Inčukalns. On the other hand, locating the terminal in Estonia is supported by earlier EU expert assessments that Paldiski in Estonia would be the best location for the common LNG terminal of the three Baltic States. Correspondingly, locating the terminal in southern Finland is justified, because it would increase the security of energy supply of the north-eastern corner of the European Union. From Finland, natural gas could be delivered through Balticconnector to Estonia and to the rest of the Baltic States. However, the EU's Green Deal may prevent or considerably reduce European Union's financing of new LNG terminal plans and therefore the Green Deal may mean a black future for these LNG terminal plans.

Although dependence of the Baltic States and Finland on Russia remains high also in the future, we must remember that the Inčukalns natural gas storage in Latvia is able to meet the natural gas needs of all Baltic States and Finland for an entire winter season. It is also good to remember that the nominal capacity of Lithuania's LNG terminal corresponds to more than a half of the total annual gas consumption of the Baltic States and Finland. It means that, in an emergency situation, Lithuania's LNG terminal is able to meet the winter-time gas needs of all the Baltic States and Finland. Thirdly, the security of energy supply of the Baltic States and Finland improves considerably when the GIPL gas pipeline between Poland and Lithuania is completed, finally ending the isolation of the Baltic States and Finland from the EU gas pipe network.

Even though connecting the gas networks of the Baltic Sea region countries enhances the region's security of energy supply, dependence on Russian gas supplies does not decrease until gas import sources are diversified as well. However, it is futile to expect a significant geographic diversification of natural gas imports in the near future, because the EU's largest natural gas producer the Netherlands is forced to stop regular production in the European Union's largest natural gas field in Groningen due to tremors, further decreasing the EU's indigenous gas production. Both closing the gas field in Groningen and Germany's nuclear power plants in 2022 are likely to increase further the already excessive share of Russia in the EU's natural gas imports.

Although this book focuses on natural gas, we must not forget that along with natural gas, Russia is also a strategic supplier of other energy forms to the European Union. Russia's share of the Union's coal imports is approximately 40 percent, of crude oil imports 30 percent and of uranium imports 20 percent. Lessening the EU's dependence on Russian energy will only be successful if the Union increases its LNG imports considerably and succeeds in implementing the ambitious Green Deal. In 2020, the EU's LNG imports, excluding Russia, was around less than 70 bcm, i.e. approximately 17 percent of the EU's overall gas consumption. The non-Russian LNG supplies should exceed 100 bcm, thus covering at least a quarter of the EU's gas demand.

It is necessary to decrease the dependence on Russian energy because Russia is ever further from the democratic principles and has started to practice aggressive foreign policy (the Russo-Georgian War in 2008 and the Ukraine War in 2014 onwards). Hopefully, Russia's operation mode changes before Russia drifts too far from the point, in which restoring the co-operation between Russia and the West is still possible. However, it is possible that Russia's distancing from the West continues until Russia realises that the West offers it a more stable and more reliable foundation for co-operation and future development than China.

The role of Norway: in 2020, with a share of 24 percent, Norway was the second most important natural gas supplier to the EU after Russia. Most of Norwegian gas deliveries are transported through pipelines to the UK, Germany, the Netherlands to be further distributed through a pipeline network to other EU countries. LNG exports cover only a few percent of Norway's total gas exports to the European Union, and this is not going to change in the future.

Norway's natural gas deliveries are not shadowed by a risk of geopolitical game as it is the case with Russia. Although there is no geopolitical risk in Norway's energy deliveries, the risk linked with Norway is in its limited natural gas reserves. Norway's proved natural gas reserves are less than five percent of those in Russia. Although theoretically, Norway will be able to maintain the current volume of natural gas production until the 2050s, it is more than likely that Norway's natural gas production will decrease significantly already within the next decade.

While Norway is concerned about the decrease in the EU's gas consumption, i.e. the disappearance of its main client due to the Green

Deal, the fears in the EU are that Norway's natural gas deliveries decline too rapidly. In my opinion, both fears will turn out to be unjustified. I believe that the European Union will consume enough natural gas to meet Norway's export needs for several decades to come, and when Norway's gas deliveries begin to end, the European Union is ready to move to the era of renewable energy and hydrogen.

The role of the United States: in 2020, the United States was the EU's largest LNG supplier. The United States delivered to the European Union 19 billion cubic metres of natural gas, covering some six percent of the EU's total natural gas imports. Although the EU brings much more natural gas from Russia and Norway than from the Unites States, there is no reason to underestimate the US role because its production and export potential is enormous. Moreover, one should carefully follow the LNG export terminal development in the East Coast of Canada. North American natural gas is a welcome addition to the European Union because it pushes down the price of Russian natural gas while enhancing the EU's security of energy supply. American LNG is an important addition also to the Baltic Sea region countries even though the US share of the natural gas imports of Baltic Sea countries is still at this point marginal.

It is possible that the golden era of North American LNG in Europe and the Baltic Sea region is still to come if the Americans and Canadians manage to lower their LNG production costs and compete with Russian pipe gas. To be sure, the future role of North American LNG is overshadowed by the EU's Green Deal. In this context, we must not forget the environmental policy decisions of individual EU countries. Take the Irish Government, for example, which recently decided not to grant building permits to two LNG import terminals for reasons of environmental protection. Ireland's decision demonstrated that it considers North American gas fracking environmentally harmful and did not want to support production methods that destroy the environment because most likely the Irish LNG terminals would have obtained most of their LNG from the United States. On the other hand, the LNG imports of Ireland's neighbour Great Britain show that geographic location would not have automatically made Ireland too dependent on American liquefied natural gas. Here, it is good to remember that the share of the United States was 15 percent of British LNG imports in 2019.

Because US gas fracking is considered generally harmful to the environment and US Nord Stream 2 sanctions show that, like Russia, also the

United States plays geopolitics with natural gas, it is more than understandable that the writers of this book have strongly differing views on the future role of American LNG in Europe and the Baltic Sea region. However, the writers may agree that the US LNG exports to the European Union are more about protecting European NATO countries from Russian energy leverage than mere business because LNG formed less than one percent of the total US commodity exports to the European Union in 2019.

Poland's role as a gas hub: the expansion of Poland's LNG terminal in Świnoujście, building the LNG terminal in Gdańsk and Baltic Pipe will diversify Poland's natural gas imports. It is very likely that, once these projects are completed, Russia no longer is Poland's largest supplier of natural gas. In order to avoid the Poland gas hub hype, we must remember that with the 50-percent capacity utilisation, Poland's two LNG terminals will increase Poland's LNG imports to approximately six billion cubic metres and the annual capacity of Baltic Pipe will be about ten billion cubic metres. Combining this with the fact that Poland consumes approximately 20 billion cubic metres and produces four billion cubic metres of the gas it consumes, we see that the aforementioned infrastructure projects are sufficient only to cover Poland's own needs if it intends to abandon Russian natural gas altogether. In other words, Poland's Świnoujście and Gdańsk LNG terminals and Baltic Pipe are not enough to make Poland a regional gas hub if it intends to completely stop importing Russian natural gas. However, it is hard to see that the Polish Government would completely abandon the Russian gas imports because it would be economically irrational and unjustified even from the point of view of Poland's security of energy supply once the aforementioned LNG import terminals and Baltic Pipe are operational.

The transit roles of Ukraine and Belarus: before the completion of Nord Stream and TurkStream, Russian natural gas was delivered to Western Europe solely through Ukraine and Belarus. Before the first Nord Stream started to operate approximately ten years ago, 80 percent of Russian natural gas was transported through Ukraine to the EU and the remainder went via Belarus. This all changed radically when the first pipeline pair of Nord Stream became operational. The change in Russian gas export logistics is shown by the fact that in 2020, only 30 percent of Russian pipe gas reached the European Union through Ukraine. With 40 percent, the first Nord Stream pipe became the main transport channel of Russian gas to the European Union in 2020.

When Nord Stream 2 pipeline is completed, the geopolitical position of Ukraine and Belarus will change further because then, Russia needs these countries to a very limited extent for natural gas transit, unless there is a significant increase in the EU's gas imports from Russia. Since there is not yet enough evidence of the latter, it is possible that the significance of Ukraine and Belarus as transit countries lessens radically, possibly resulting in Russia's hardening foreign policy towards Ukraine and Belarus once Nord Stream 2 has been completed. In fact, the geopolitical position of Belarus weakened already after the completion of the FSRU in the Kaliningrad region in January 2019, as Russia may already at this point stop natural gas transit through Belarus and Poland to Germany without relevant impediment to the energy supply of the Kaliningrad region.

It is not easy to forecast the future consumption of natural gas in the European Union, but several experts estimate that the Union's natural gas consumption will remain fairly even until 2030. After that, natural gas consumption begins to decrease. What the EU's natural gas consumption will be in 2050 depends largely on how common the other gaseous fuels, such as biogas, biomethane and hydrogen, will become. I believe that the Baltic Sea region, perhaps excluding Russia, will not essentially differ from the general development in the European Union.

Although the EU's Green Deal and the hydrogen revolution linked with it make predicting the future exceptionally difficult, it is clear that we all should be interested in future energy solutions at least for three reasons: (1) thanks to the Green Deal, the change in the structure of the EU's energy consumption will be revolutionary in the next few decades, (2) in the Baltic Sea region we find Europe's two largest natural gas exporters, Norway and Russia, and the EU's largest energy consumer, Germany, and finally (3) we should all be concerned about the future because we will have to spend the rest of our lives there, as an American industrialist Charles F. Kettering humorously uttered already nearly a century ago.

Index

K. Liuhto (ed.), *The Future of Energy Consumption, Security and Natural Gas*, https://doi.org/10.1007/978-3-030-80367-4

The manufacturer's authorised representative in the EU is Springer Nature Customer Service Centre GmbH, Europaplatz 3, 69115 Heidelberg, Germany. If you have any concerns regarding our products, please contact ProductSafety@springernature.com

Printed and bound by CPI Group (UK) Ltd, Croydon, CR0 4YY

30/09/2026

02225700-0014